Spanker

Radicalism, Racism, and Party Realignment

Map of the Border States.

RADICALISM, RACISM, AND PARTY REALIGNMENT

The Border States during Reconstruction

Edited by
RICHARD O. CURRY

THE JOHNS HOPKINS PRESS
Baltimore and London

The Johns Hopkins Press, Baltimore, Maryland 21218
The Johns Hopkins Press Ltd., London

Library of Congress Catalog Card Number 72–90743 DEC 17 '71

Standard Book Number 8018–1072–8

In Memory of Patricia Leist Curry

Acknowledgments

In preparing this book we have amassed numerous obligations. Professor Alexander wishes to express his appreciation to the University of Alabama Research Committee and to Professor Delmer D. Odell for their assistance in preparing his chapter on Tennessee. Dr. Hancock wants to thank Otterbein College for granting him a sabbatical leave and the American Philosophical Society for awarding him a grant-in-aid to complete his work on "Reconstruction in Delaware." Professor Gillette also wants to acknowledge the financial assistance received from the American Philosophical Society, which came at a critical stage of his research. Dr. Parrish is indebted to the American Association for State and Local History, which financed part of his research, and to the staffs of the State Historical Society of Missouri, the Missouri Historical Society, the Library of Congress, and the Reeves Library of Westminster College for facilitating his work. Professor Webb takes this opportunity to acknowledge the help of Dr. Thomas D. Clark, Professor Emeritus of the University of Kentucky, and Dr. Jacqueline Bull of the Special Collections Division of the Margaret I. King Library, University of Kentucky.

All of us owe a debt of gratitude to Professor David Donald who first called this collection to the attention of The Johns Hopkins Press, and later provided much needed advice and criticism.

In addition, I would like to express my own appreciation to the American Philosophical Society, the American Association for State and Local History, and the University of Connecticut Research Foundation for providing financial assistance at various stages of the work. My personal sense of obligation expressed a few years ago to Dr. Robert F. Munn, Director of Libraries at West Virginia University, and to Dr. F. Gerald Ham, State Archivist at the Wisconsin Historical Society, for their assistance on an earlier project carries over to this book. I also wish to thank Professor Vincent A. Carrafiello of the University of Connecticut and my former colleague Thomas More Brown of Upsala College, for their perceptive comments on the Introduction and on my own essay in this collection.

I owe my greatest debts to Patricia Montenegro Curry, my charming and perceptive wife, and to Michael, Kim, Rebecca, and Jonathan, our irrepressible children, who provided numerous diversions along the way.

RICHARD O. CURRY
Mansfield Depot, Connecticut

Contributors

THOMAS B. ALEXANDER is professor of American history at the University of Missouri, Columbia. He is the author of *Political Reconstruction in Tennessee* (Nashville, 1950, 1968); *Thomas A. R. Nelson of East Tennessee* (Nashville, 1956); and *Sectional Stress and Party Strength: A Study of Roll-Call Voting Patterns in the United States House of Representatives, 1836–1860* (Nashville, 1967).

JACQUELINE BALK is a doctoral candidate at the Pennsylvania State University. She is writing her dissertation on "The Liberal Republican Movement of 1872." She was awarded a Smithsonian Fellowship in 1967–68.

RICHARD O. CURRY is associate professor of American history at the University of Connecticut, Storrs. He is the author of *A House Divided: A Study of Statehood Politics and the Copperhead Movement in West Virginia* (Pittsburgh, 1964), and editor of *The Abolitionists: Reformers or Fanatics?* (New York, 1965).

WILLIAM GILLETTE is associate professor of American history at Douglass College of Rutgers University. He is the author of *The Right to Vote: Politics and the Passage of the Fifteenth Amendment* (Baltimore, 1965).

HAROLD B. HANCOCK is professor of history and chairman of the department at Otterbein College, Westerville, Ohio. He is the author of *The Delaware Loyalists* (Wilmington, 1941), and *Delaware During the Civil War* (Wilmington, 1961).

ARI HOOGENBOOM is professor of American history and chairman of the department at the Brooklyn College Campus of the City University of New York. He is the author of *Outlawing the Spoils: A History of the Civil Service Reform Movement, 1865–1883* (Urbana, Ill., 1961); co-author of *The Enterprising Colonials: Society on the Eve of the Revolution* (Chicago, 1965); co-editor of the *The Gilded Age* (Englewood Cliffs, N.J., 1967); ed., *Spoilsmen and Reformers* (booklet; Chicago, 1964); and contributor to Jacques Goimard, ed., *Le Sud au temps de Scarlett* (Paris, 1966).

W. AUGUSTUS LOW is professor of American history at the University of Maryland, Baltimore. His publications include *The Negro in North Carolina: A Demographic and Social Study* (Washington, 1949).

ix

WILLIAM E. PARRISH is professor of American history and chairman of the department at Westminster College, Fulton, Missouri. He is the author of *David Rice Atchison, Border Politician* (Columbia, Mo., 1961); *Turbulent Partnership: Missouri for the Union, 1861–1865* (Columbia, Mo., 1963); and *Missouri Under Radical Rule, 1865–1870* (Columbia, Mo., 1965).

CHARLES L. WAGANDT of Baltimore is the author of *The Mighty Revolution: Negro Emancipation in Maryland, 1862–1864* (Baltimore, 1964).

ROSS A. WEBB is professor of American history and Dean of Winthrop College, Rock Hill, South Carolina. He is the author of a forthcoming biography of Benjamin H. Bristow which is scheduled for publication in 1969 by the University of Kentucky Press.

Contents

Introduction

Richard O. Curry

In recent years an impressive body of historical literature has appeared to challenge or broaden older perspectives on the Reconstruction era. Traditional economic interpretations have been refuted, the role of Southern Negroes in postbellum politics is being re-evaluated, and historical perennials such as the motives of the "Radicals," the position of the Supreme Court on Reconstruction issues, and the significance of Andrew Johnson's collision with Congress continue to stimulate scholarly controversy. Opportunities for meaningful research on these and other aspects of presidential and congressional Reconstruction abound. Revisionist studies must be extended, however, far beyond the customary framework which focuses attention upon the Presidency, Congress, and the South. Present conceptions of the Reconstruction process must be broadened to include intensive studies of *internal politics* in both northern and border states.[1]

Congressional Reconstruction was the culmination of nearly two years of conflict during which a triumphant but war-weary North struggled to define the precise meaning of its victory. The Union had been preserved, but the status of the South and the future of the Republican party were open questions. Slavery was dead, but the Negro's fate was tenuous. The crucial battlegrounds in the epic struggle of 1865–67, which was to determine the future course of American history, were not located in Washington or the South, but in New England, the middle west, the border states, and the Middle Atlantic states. The fact that nineteenth-century politics on the national level was primarily a reflection of conflicts and cleavages within the states themselves would seem to be self-evident. The present state of Reconstruction historiography suggests that it is not.

Passing beyond the geographical and institutional limitations in present approaches to Reconstruction, it is necessary to investigate in greater depth the continuities that exist between antebellum, Civil War, and Reconstruction politics. Andrew Johnson may have been a

[1] This introduction is based primarily, though not entirely, on the material contained in this collection. Some independent judgments have been made which may or may not coincide with the views of other contributors.

"War Democrat" who eschewed partisanship for the duration, but in 1866 he led a conservative revival intent on re-creating as close an approximation to the old Federal Union of 1860 as was humanly possible. True, the National Union party failed to materialize, but in 1866, a slightly altered version of the wartime Democratic slogan "The Union As It Was, The Constitution As It Is, and the Negroes Where They Are" was no idle threat, but a viable political program designed to return the Democratic party to its traditional position of national dominance. A comprehensive treatment of Reconstruction politics must first come to terms with the nature of Civil War party struggles in the North.

In 1861 Unionists of all parties in all loyal sections of the country co-operated fairly well against their common foe to achieve a common objective: the restoration of the Union. In 1862, when the war for union was transformed into a crusade to subjugate the South and destroy slavery, unity was shattered beyond repair. Republicans equated opposition to the war policies of the Lincoln Administration with treason, or a desire for "peace at any price," while most Democrats associated the ideological commitments and the tactics of the "Black Republicans" with fanaticism, the end result of which would be disunion or the establishment of an authoritarian national state. Such wartime polemics clearly attest to the presence of outraged partisanship and war hysteria in the North, but they also serve to obscure the fact that both Republicans and the vast majority of Northern Democrats adhered to the concept of union while disagreeing violently over the nature of that union.

Democrats bitterly attacked such Republican measures as confiscation acts, suspension of the writ of *habeas corpus,* the Emancipation Proclamation, and the conscription of blacks into the Union Army. They demanded the preservation of the old Federal Union with slavery intact and the traditional rights of the states unimpaired. Racism and ideological rigidity—blind adherence to any form of social, political, and economic change—characterized their stand. John J. Davis, father of John W. Davis, accurately summarized the political philosophy of conservative Union Democrats when he wrote:

I look upon secession and abolition as twin brothers—I am no extremist—I condemn, abhor and detest the abolitionists and all their unconstitutional schemes. . . . I do not want the South subjugated, but I do want those citizens in rebellion subjected—I mean subjected to the laws and made obedient to them. The doctrine of "States' rights" as expounded by William L. Yancey and Jeff Davis is a heresy, fatal to the existence of any government constructed upon such a theory—On the other hand the idea of "Centralization," or conferring upon the Federal Government unlimited power over the states

is a heresy I do not countenance—Both dogmas are contrary to the spirit
and letter of the Constitution. The present Congress in session at
Washington is as much in rebellion against the government as far as words
and legislation can constitute rebellion, as are the armed legions of Jeff
Davis.[2]

Viewed in this way, both the Confederates, who wanted to destroy the
Union, and the Republicans, who wanted to preserve but transform
it, were revolutionary groups, while Democrats were traditionalists
who wanted to restore "the Union as it was" in 1860.

At present, a comprehensive synthesis of Reconstruction—an enor-
mous undertaking—is beyond the grasp of historians. In this group of
essays—an attempt at collective historical analysis—we hope to take
a step toward broadening the context of Reconstruction historiography
by closely focusing attention upon developments in the border states:
Delaware, Maryland, West Virginia, Kentucky, Missouri, and Tennessee. Tennessee is not ordinarily categorized as a border state, but
her re-admission into the Union in 1866 created a political situation
that conforms to border state patterns.

In the years immediately preceding the Civil War, political leaders
from this area had occupied the middle ground between pro-slavery
extremism and militant antislavery radicalism. When all attempts to
preserve the Union failed, the border slaveholding states were confronted with the grim choice either of fighting a war for Union or
Southern independence. With the exception of Tennessee, the border
states repudiated secession and remained loyal. The decision was an
agonizing one, for the failure of compromise solutions produced
extreme political fragmentation. Not only did border state Unionists
divide into radical and conservative camps, but the presence of a
sizable Confederate minority in this area, combined with its strategic
importance, transformed the borderland into "dark and bloody"
ground which experienced the savagery that accompanies all guerrilla
warfare.

Little wonder that border state politics during Reconstruction—
unlike the antebellum period—were not characterized by moderation.
The fact that Missouri, Kentucky, Delaware, Maryland, and West
Virginia remained loyal to the Union, and the fact that Tennessee
was re-admitted in 1866, meant that these states could not be subjected to congressional Reconstruction; but the issues Congress

[2] John J. Davis to Anna Kennedy, June 1, 1862, as quoted in Richard O. Curry,
"The Union As It Was: A Critique of Recent Interpretations of the 'Copperheads,'" *Civil War History* 13 (March, 1967): 32. Only those quotes not taken from
essays in this book are footnoted in the introduction.

attempted to resolve by military intervention in the South constituted the basis of intra-state, party power struggles throughout the borderland. Certainly, the patterns of conflict varied from state to state. Missouri and West Virginia were controlled by Republican régimes (1865–70). In Tennessee the Republicans were defeated in 1869. Kentucky, Maryland, and Delaware were dominated by the Democrats throughout the Reconstruction period. Nonetheless, loyalties were sharply divided in all these states, and conflict between Radical Unionists, Conservative Unionists and ex-Confederates over such issues as suffrage for freedmen, loyalty oaths, amnesty, party leadership, patronage, and socio-economic programs was inevitable.

Under the congressional plan of Reconstruction, Republican rule lasted longest in the states of South Carolina, Mississippi, Louisiana, and Florida—states where the percentage of freedmen in the total population was the largest. Southern whites were not disfranchised in significant numbers. Republican régimes managed to stay in power until 1870 in Missouri, West Virginia, and Tennessee solely by resorting to wholesale proscription of ex-Confederates. In these states ex-Rebels were systematically deprived of virtually all civil rights. "Iron-clad" test oaths were required of voters, lawyers, suitors, jurors, and, in Missouri's case, priests and ministers as well. In *Cummings* v. *Missouri* (4 Wallace 267), the Supreme Court banned loyalty oaths for clergymen, and in *Ex parte Garland* (4 Wallace 333), the Court ruled that federal test oaths for lawyers were unconstitutional. But the Court went no further, leaving state proscriptive programs virtually intact. As the *New York Times* editorialized on January 11, 1870, the border states had not only served as "the main campaigning grounds in war," but "in peace, the political cauldron has in them seethed with greatest fury."

If Republican ascendancy in the border states was a short-lived phenomenon, questions pertaining to motives, aims, objectives, and ultimate significance have long been debated by historians. In Missouri, as William E. Parrish points out, the social and economic program enacted by the Republicans was a progressive one which included the establishment of a public school system for both whites and blacks, the creation of state immigration and agricultural boards, and the passage of an eight-hour work law, as well as general incorporation and general banking laws. Missouri Radicals submitted a Negro suffrage amendment to the electorate in 1868, but it was defeated.

In Tennessee and West Virginia, Republican régimes failed to distinguish themselves either in the social or economic sphere. Holding the line against Rebel encroachment was their main and immediate concern. In Tennessee, the Brownlow régime did push a Negro suffrage law through the legislature in 1867, but Thomas B. Alexander observes that black suffrage in the "volunteer" state stemmed primarily from political expediency—an attempt by a Negrophobic, "Radical" minority to maintain power. As Jacqueline Balk and Ari Hoogenboom phrase it, "Negro suffrage was a weapon, not a cause."

In West Virginia, black suffrage was not a major political issue. The state contained a small Negro population, about 18,000 in 1860, in contrast to 283,000 in Tennessee and 118,000 in Missouri. Potential Negro voting strength in West Virginia did not exceed 3,600, as compared to 23,000 in Missouri and 64,000 in Tennessee. West Virginia's Republicans feared that if the Democrats regained power on local or national levels, the mountain state's separation from the Old Dominion would be nullified. By 1869 many Republican leaders in West Virginia and Missouri had concluded, albeit for different reasons, that legislative proscription had outlived its usefulness.

In West Virginia, "bitter end" Republicans reluctantly co-operated with Liberals in 1869–70 by voting to repeal test oaths for lawyers, plaintiffs, teachers, and jurors, but Radicals obstinately refused to consider the possibility of re-enfranchising ex-Confederates.. They believed that the removal of all restrictions could lead only to defeat at the hands of unrepentant Rebels. Liberal leaders, fully aware that re-enfranchisement could reduce the Republican party to political impotence almost overnight, were willing to run the risk, being convinced that the "Chinese shoe" could not indefinitely be kept upon the foot of the Democrats.

Granville D. Hall, editor of the Wheeling *Intelligencer,* the state's most influential Republican newspaper, candidly summarized the Liberal position in a letter to Charles Sumner. "Our only hope," Hall began, "of perpetuating Republican ascendancy in this State is by a magnanimous policy which shall bring a portion of the ex-Rebels into cooperation with us. . . . A very large number were old line whigs before the war. They do not like the Democracy. . . . But if we wait for the Democrats to enfranchise them, they will of course fall into that party." In West Virginia Liberal Republican expressions of good will toward ex-Confederates can be explained only as a calculated, if unsuccessful attempt by "Liberals" to avoid disaster for the Republican party.

Liberal Republicanism in Missouri was a far more complicated matter. In 1869 Liberals took the position that proscriptive legislation was no longer necessary to maintain Republican ascendancy. A united Republican party, Liberals argued, with its strength augmented by

Negro and immigrant voters, could easily defeat the Democrats. Missouri Radicals refused to consider re-enfranchisement in 1869, but in 1870, after the Fifteenth Amendment was ratified, party stalwarts agreed to submit three constitutional amendments to the electorate, which would bring the "era of the oath" to an end. It now appeared that the threatened schism in Republican ranks could be avoided. Later events decreed otherwise. While the Republican Convention of 1870 agreed to submit the proposed amendments to the voters, it refused to endorse them officially. This triggered the Liberal revolt. All subsequent attempts at accommodation proved futile. The Liberal minority proceeded to nominate its own candidates and adopted a platform markedly different from that endorsed by the stalwarts—so different, in fact, that one may question whether the failure of the Republican party to support three proposed constitutional amendments was anything more than a surface manifestation of deeper cleavages.

The stalwarts issued a vague statement on re-enfranchisement, warmly endorsed the Grant administration, and stood pat on their record of social and economic achievement since the war. Liberals, however, not only endorsed the proposed amendments but called for a low tariff, civil service reform, low taxes, and an end "to the alienation of government land to private corporations." Such a platform suggests that Missouri's Liberal minority, now that the issues of war and secession were receding, found themselves at odds with the mercantilistic philosophy of the dominant wing of the Republican party. The Liberal platform was clearly more attuned to Jacksonian than to national Republican principles.

In one sense Liberal Republicanism in Missouri is comparable to the abortive National Union movement of 1866. At that time conservatives from both the Republican and Democratic parties, though sharing a common ideological outlook on many issues, found it impossible to combine forces. Problems of patronage, leadership, and party identification, together with personal hatred caused by the scars of war and previous political affiliations, proved to be insuperable barriers. Almost the same dilemma confronted Missouri's Liberal Republicans.

In 1870 William E. Switzler, one of Missouri's Democratic chieftains, stated it this way: "This [Liberal Republican] bolt is planned on the verdant expectation that the Democratic party will join it and make it the majority! Or as a recent telegram from [Carl Schurz] expresses it, that the Republican bolters will furnish the candidates and the Democratic party the voters! But the Democrats feel no such dissatisfaction with their party as leads many Republicans to seek new political connections."[3]

After the election of 1872, many disheartened Liberals returned to the Republican fold. Of more significance, many eventually joined the Democratic party, finding the *laissez faire* principles of the Democrats more compatible with their own political convictions than the interventionist programs of the national GOP. The lack of precise figures makes it impossible to judge the full impact of such party realignment in the 1870s. Parrish suggests that "probably not more than 20,000" Missouri Liberals transferred their allegiance to the Democrats, but emphasizes that "we delve into murky waters" if we attempt to make a more precise estimate.[4] Yet, it is clear that after the failure of Liberal Republicanism to secure a permanent power base, a significant shift in party loyalties favorable to the Democrats did occur.

A similar situation existed in Tennessee. Alexander's analysis indicates that Liberal Republicans believed that universal amnesty would lead to a realignment of political parties. In the "volunteer" state, as in Missouri and West Virginia, the Democrats operated from a position of strength and co-operated with "let up" Republicans only as long as it suited their own partisan purposes to do so.

In attempting to place Liberal Republicanism in the border states in national perspective, it is well to keep in mind Henry Watterson's observation that "coherence was a missing ingredient" at the national Liberal Republican Convention of 1872. The presence of a diverse group, including civil service reformers, disappointed factional leaders, disaffected Democrats, and both high and low tariff advocates, did not augur well for the creation of a viable national party. As Balk and Hoogenboom aptly observe, "the Liberal Republican movement was preordained for defeat." Even so, the history of border state Liberalism, especially the Missouri experience, suggests that historians have yet to fully appreciate the continuing influence of Jacksonian and other antebellum ideals of government and society in leading many Republicans to seek "new political connections." By 1870 the issues of slavery, secession, and war, which once served as a forceful rallying cry and a binding political force, were no longer strong enough to hold all disparate elements of the Republican coalition together. Eventually many border state Liberals who feared irredentist Democracy, returned to the Republican party, but in Missouri, a

[3] William E. Parrish, *Missouri Under Radical Rule, 1865–1870* (Columbia, Missouri, 1965), p. 312.
[4] Parrish's formal analysis of Missouri politics in this book ends with the election of 1870. The quotation is taken from Parrish's letter to R. O. Curry, June 20, 1968.

large number of them found their way into the ranks of the Democrats. The extent to which Liberals in other border states and other sections of the country were influenced by the "Jacksonian persuasion"—whether they ultimately retained their affiliations with the Republican party or repudiated them—remains an intriguing question.[5]

As noted previously Kentucky, Maryland, and Delaware were Democratic strongholds throughout the Reconstruction period. During the war, Unionists in these states divided into radical and conservative factions. But in 1865 Conservative Unionists controlled the government, and all rights of citizenship were soon restored to ex-Confederates. In Kentucky and Maryland, as Ross A. Webb and Charles Wagandt point out, infuriated but impotent Republicans demanded congressional intervention. Such a response from Washington, considering the fact that both states had remained loyal to the Union, was virtually inconceivable. It is instructive to note, however, that in Kentucky the rapid re-enfranchisement of ex-Confederates and relatively weak Republican opposition did not produce political harmony. Factionalism within the ranks of the Democratic party was so rampant that one may conclude that a three-party system existed in this state until 1867.

At the end of the war, most Kentucky Democrats—Unionists and ex-Confederates—rallied once again to the standards of antebellum Democratic stalwarts. Many Union Democratic leaders, who had not occupied positions of political prominence before the war, bitterly resented losing coveted positions in the Democratic hierarchy to ex-Confederates. Consequently, some Union Democrats bolted the party in 1866 and formed a brief but untenable alliance with the Radicals. The following year dissident Union Democrats organized the Conservative Union party, hoping to attract support from both moderate Republicans and ex-Confederates of Whig antecedents. It was a futile effort. The Democrats emerged victorious from the elections of 1867, and most Conservative Union bolters returned to the Democratic fold. Thereafter, factionalism no longer presented a major threat to party unity, although a few dissidents, including Henry Watterson, editor of the Louisville *Courier-Journal,* did join Liberal Republican ranks in Cincinnati in 1872.

According to Webb, and Balk and Hoogenboom, Watterson's defection, unlike that of many displaced Union Democratic leaders,

[5] Patrick W. Riddleberger's essays, "The Break in Radical Ranks: Liberals vs. Stalwarts in the Election of 1872," *Journal of Negro History* 44 (April, 1959): 136–57, and "The Radicals' Abandonment of the Negro During Reconstruction," *ibid.* 45 (April, 1960): 88–102, provide a highly suggestive beginning in this direction.

resulted from disillusionment with the failure of the Kentucky Democrats to adopt a "new departure" philosophy, which called for
acceptance of the Fourteenth and Fifteenth Amendments and the
passage of progressive economic legislation that would encourage
Northern capital to develop mining, industrial, and railroad enterprises in the bluegrass state. As Webb phrases it, "Watterson may
have been sympathetic to, and possibly even derived his ideas from
the Republicans," but after the war he chose to remain a Democrat,
hoping to effect dramatic changes from within the party. He rightly
believed that the Republican party in Kentucky was destined to
retain its minority status for years to come. After participating in the
Liberal Republican debacle of 1872, Watterson returned to the
Democratic fold.

Maryland's political experience prior to 1870 was so similar to that
of Kentucky's, that the incidents of political turmoil in this state
need not detain us here. In 1865-66 Conservative Unionists combined
forces with ex-Confederates to defeat the Republicans. But in 1867 a
revitalized Democratic party, dominated by former Confederates and
aided by antiquated electoral procedures, swept into power, edging
most of their Conservative Union allies out of office.

Historians have correctly observed that "some" social progress was
made in the border states during the Reconstruction era. As W. A.
Low and others emphasize, the Freedmen's Bureau and various church-
related and secular freedmen's aid societies successfully pioneered in
the field of Negro education throughout the region. Numerous freedmen, despite hazards to life and limb, demonstrated remarkable courage in resisting the frenzied opposition of Negrophobic whites. With
the passage of time border state legislatures concerned themselves with
improving the quality of education for blacks as well as whites—along
segregated lines, of course. But limited progress in the field of Negro
education, during Reconstruction and after, cannot obscure the overwhelming evidence of the psychopathology which characterized the
outlook of significant numbers of white Americans on any question
pertaining to race.

In the borderland the influence of racism was pervasive and took
many forms: physical violence and terrorism, including instances of
mass murder; the reduction of blacks to economic peonage; destruction of property, especially the burning of Freedmen's Bureau schools
and Negro churches; the passage and enforcement of Jim Crow legislation; and electoral and judicial fraud and intimidation.

"With political victories under their belts," William Gillette writes,
"border conservatives felt free enough and secure enough to blaze a

trail backward. In doing so, they were to show the way for Southerners to follow." Tennessee not only gave birth to the Ku-Klux Klan but introduced the poll tax in 1870. Tennessee and West Virginia "pioneered" in the enactment of segregation laws, while Delaware's voter registration law of 1873 ingeniously deprived Negroes of their franchise without violating the letter of federal enforcement statutes.

Overt violence, while common to all border states, was most pronounced in Tennessee, Kentucky, and Missouri. The congressional elections of 1874 provide a case in point. The most publicized incident of violence occurred in Gibson County where sixteen blacks were seized by a band of one hundred night riders, taken to a river bank and shot. Five of the victims died. A federal grand jury indicted fifty-three men for this crime, but no convictions were obtained. Eye-witnesses, fearful for their own lives, refused to testify. Such results were typical. Gillette calculates that under the Force Acts, passed by Congress to uphold the Fifteenth Amendment, federal attorneys secured only 66 convictions in a total of 1,142 cases tried in the borderland between 1870–80, a record far worse than in the Deep South.

It is also important to observe that "the first great migration of Negroes" to Northern cities began during the Reconstruction period. W. A. Low estimates that at least 40,000 blacks left the states of Kentucky and Missouri between 1865–70 in the wake of violence and terrorism. The magnitude of violence is suggested by General O. O. Howard's report of 1867, which states that during a fifteen-month period, beginning in October, 1866, Kentucky Negroes were victims of at least 20 murders, 18 shootings, 11 rapes, and 270 other cases of maltreatment. Low's analysis suggests that these figures are far too conservative.

The complexities involved in interpreting Reconstruction politics in the border states, or even in the South, are also highlighted by Gillette's analysis of the failure of federal enforcement legislation to protect Negro voting rights after the ratification of the Fifteenth Amendment. As stated earlier, Gillette describes the effects of fraud and intimidation in preventing enforcement officials from carrying out their duties, and attorneys from securing convictions. He also treats the failure of enforcement legislation from other vantage points, including the attitudes of federal enforcement officials in Washington, the framing of enforcement laws by Congress, and their narrow interpretation by the Supreme Court.

At no time did Congress appropriate sufficient funds to enable enforcement officials to properly carry out their duties. Nor were federal troops utilized in numbers sufficient to cope with the imposing problems faced. Only 185 federal troops were stationed in the entire state of Tennessee during the crucial elections of 1874. Their number was reduced to fifty after 1876. As Gillette phrases it, "Negro voters and federal marshals were, in effect, like soldiers going into battle only to find that their comrades on the battlefield had vanished." Furthermore, Gillette not only suggests that enforcement legislation contained serious statutory defects but stresses that enforcement acts, "given the prevailing values of the nineteenth century" in regard to federal-state relationships, exceeded the constitutional boundaries that the federal judiciary was willing to uphold.

In 1876, in the case of *United States* v. *Reese,* which originated in Lexington, Kentucky, the Supreme Court rejected the federal government's contention that "Congress could ban and rectify any racial discrimination in any election—local, state or federal—by the force of the Fifteenth Amendment alone." Chief Justice Morrison Waite, who spoke for the majority, argued that the Fifteenth Amendment "did not confer the right to vote on anyone," and was not intended to cover every instance where a qualified voter was refused the ballot, but "only when the wrongful refusal at . . . an election is because of race." Waite observed that the language of the Enforcement Act of May 31, 1870, "was broad enough to cover every conceivable instance in which Negroes, for whatever reason, were denied the franchise." In the Court's view, the Enforcement Act could lead only to "an undermining of state control over suffrage regulation by Congress." Waite held that Congress had "merely the negative or latent power to confer suffrage outright and regulate it accordingly." "Waite found, in effect, that the fourth and fifth sections of the Enforcement Act of May 31, 1870 were null and void." The effects of this decision were devastating, "making future enforcement vastly more difficult, if not, in some cases, clearly impossible."

Gillette has concluded in his previously published study of the issue that Republican leaders did not expect to utilize the Fifteenth Amendment to perpetuate an effective two-party system in the border states and in the South. The Fifteenth Amendment, considering the political and judicial attitudes of the period, was clearly inadequate as a means of accomplishing this purpose. In his view, "The primary object of the Amendment" was to guarantee Negro suffrage in the North.[6]

[6] William Gillette, *The Right to Vote: Politics and the Passage of the Fifteenth Amendment* (Baltimore, 1965), p. 165.

John and LaWanda Cox, in a recent article, have vigorously disputed this position, arguing that "Republican party leadership played a crucial role in committing this nation to equal suffrage for Negroes not because of political expediency but *despite* political risk." The Coxes contend that "Race prejudice was so strong in the North that Republican sponsorship of Negro suffrage meant flirtation with political disaster."[7]

It is beyond the scope of this book to attempt to resolve the issues posed by Gillette and the Coxes on Republican motivation. As far as the borderland is concerned, it is clear that while some Republican leaders acted from ideological conviction in supporting the Fifteenth Amendment, political necessity, aggravated by the hatreds engendered by guerrilla warfare, were also major motivating factors. In many instances motives were mixed and cannot be neatly attributed either to idealism or political expediency. United States Senator Charles Drake, one of Missouri's foremost Radicals, was at once an ideologue, a political opportunist, and a man whose political behavior was influenced by an undisguised and undiminished hatred of Rebels.

It is also important to observe that if the Republicans courted political disaster by endorsing Negro suffrage, the Coxes do not explain why the Democrats, whose "exploitation of prejudice . . . was blatant and unashamed," failed to recoup their fortunes nationally.[8] One possible explanation is the fact that race was not the only issue confronting potential "white backlash" voters in the Republican party. The questions of loyalty and amnesty—indeed, the specter of a Southern participation in national politics that would turn Union victory into a mockery—loomed large during the early Reconstruction years. The results of state and national elections between 1866 and 1872 suggest that the fear of a "Confederate revival" in the borderland and the South led many conservative Nothern Republicans to swallow their racial prejudice and VOTE FOR THE PARTY THAT SAVED THE UNION. If this is true, Democratic victories in the borderland, based as they were on reactionary redemption policies, would partially account for Republican success in marginal Northern states.

Whether this observation is valid is an open question, but the essays in this volume do call into doubt the relevance of the Coxes' conclusion that "Any hope . . . of gaining substantial strength in the loyal border states [from Negro suffrage] was lacking in realism."[9] The fact

[7] LaWanda and John H. Cox, "Negro Suffrage and Republican Politics: The Problem of Motivation in Reconstruction Historiography," *The Journal of Southern History* 33 (August, 1967): 317, 319.

[8] *Ibid.*

[9] *Ibid.*, p. 327.

was that the ratification of the Fifteenth Amendment did offer hope, however illusory it proved to be, to border state Republicans who had not been able to overcome the combined strength of Conservative Unionists and ex-Confederates.

Delaware had been controlled by the Democrats without difficulty since 1865. Then, as a result of Negro enfranchisement, the Republicans managed to win the presidential and congressional elections of 1872. Harold B. Hancock conclusively proves that Delaware Republicans, supported by 4,500 eligible Negro voters, looked forward to becoming the dominant political force in the state for years to come. Only in 1873, when the state legislature enacted a registration law which barred Negroes from the polls, did it become clear that the Republicans were to be denied political supremacy.

In Tennessee, where the Republicans were defeated in 1869 and 1870 by a coalition of Conservative Unionists and ex-Confederates, the Republican party staged a dramatic comeback in 1872. Factionalism weakened the Democratic party after its victory in 1870. These divisions, combined with a heavy Negro vote, enabled the Republicans to emerge victorious in the congressional elections. The Democrats, however, retained control of most state offices. By 1874 the Democrats had resolved their internal differences and inaugurated a massive campaign of physical intimidation to neutralize Negro voting strength. It was not the lack of potential black electoral power which undermined the Republican party in the border states, but the success of the Democrats in utilizing force and fraud to seize the offices of government. The inadequacies of the Fifteenth Amendment were not nearly as important in accounting for the Democratic sweep in the border states as the failure of the Grant Administration to provide the necessary protection for Negro voters. The devastating blow by the Supreme Court, which declared portions of the Force Acts unconstitutional, was yet to come.

More important in the long run was the fact that despite the determined use of redemption policies, the margins of Democratic victories in presidential and congressional elections during the late 1870s and throughout the 1880s were razor thin.[10] This book does not deal in depth with border state politics during the last years of the nineteenth century. A few of the essays do raise important questions about the nature of social and political change which had occurred in this

[10] In Maryland, freedmen voted in substantial numbers from 1870 onward. Reactionary racial policies were not as systematically utilized in this state as they were in other border states during the 1870s and 1880s. The Republicans, despite the support of Negro voters, simply were in no position to challenge Democratic supremacy until the 1890s.

region by that time. If the border states were the first to adopt reactionary racial policies, they were also the first to modify them. During the 1890s, while blacks in the Deep South were experiencing some of their darkest hours, border state freedmen were beginning to overcome entrenched resistance to black suffrage on the part of the Democrats.[11] Increased participation by black voters in the electoral process is a major factor in accounting for the victory of the Republican party in a number of elections in the border states from the mid-1890s onward.[12] Why the border Democrats began, during this period, to resume the middle ground they had occupied during the antebellum period is a question that cannot be answered satisfactorily in this book, which focuses attention on developments during the 1860s and 1870s. But it is a crucial one. If taken seriously, we can look forward to future studies which will provide insight into one important aspect of social, intellectual, and political change in late nineteenth-century America—that transitional era in which the dilemmas of our own age began to emerge.[13]

[11] This generalization does not apply to Maryland. At the turn of the century, when Democratic supremacy was threatened by the GOP, Maryland Democrats began, for the first time, to employ violence and intimidation against Negro voters in an *unsuccessful* attempt to maintain power.

[12] Ross A. Webb points out that in Kentucky Republican success in the gubernatorial election of 1895 and the presidential election of 1896 was attributable, in part, to the fact that many Democrats voted for Populist candidates.

[13] John A. Fenton's *Politics in the Border States* (New Orleans, 1957) is an able study of modern political patterns.

Radicalism, Racism, and Party Realignment

CHAPTER ONE

Reconstruction Politics in Missouri, 1865-1870

William E. Parrish

On January 2, 1865, Governor Thomas C. Fletcher stood before the Twenty-third General Assembly of Missouri to deliver his inaugural address. Jubilant members of his recently triumphant Radical Union party thronged the chamber. Missouri seemed to stand on the brink of a grand new era, and the Governor challenged those who would lead it in ringing tones: "Being victorious everywhere, let magnanimity now distinguish our action; and, having nothing more to ask for party, let us, forgetful of past differences, seek only to promote the general good of the people of the whole commonwealth."[1]

Had the Radical majority paid more heed to his message they might have built a strong, progressive, long-lasting party. Radicalism was the dominant note as Missouri emerged from four long, vexatious years of civil strife. Dismayed by the seeming overcaution and ineptness of the conservative groups that had long dominated the state's politics and economics, a strong majority of the voters had cast their lot with the Radical Union party in the election of 1864. This new political force included an amazing potpourri of the discontented: the Germans, who first began coming to Missouri in large numbers during the 1850s, with their strong antislavery bent and forward-looking social outlook; the small farmers and the poor whites of the Ozark area, who had no interest in slavery but who saw their region continually torn by guerrilla warfare because of it; the St. Louis merchants and would-be capitalists, who feared that the presence of slavery would stifle the state's potential for economic growth after the war; and a few ardent abolitionists, who sincerely desired the betterment of the Negro's lot. A group of opportunists, few of them had enjoyed any measure of prestige or political power before the war. Once they gained the halls of government they determined to hold their new power by any and every means at their disposal. Rather than follow the broad path of conciliation outlined by their new governor, they were extremely vindictive to their political enemies, real

[1] Grace G. Avery and Floyd C. Shoemaker, eds., *The Messages and Proclamations of the Governors of the State of Missouri* (University of Missouri Press, Columbia, Mo., 1924), 4:54.

and imagined. This overshadowed their positive program and ultimately split and destroyed their party.

The ranks of Missouri's Unionists had begun to show the strain of the emancipation issue during the second year of the war. The politically dominant Conservatives considered the demise of slavery unthinkable and clung to their hopes that the future would be as ordered as the past. The voters shattered this delusion somewhat in the election of 1862 by electing a majority to the legislature pledged to some form of emancipation. The General Assembly deadlocked over a specific plan, however, whereupon conservative Governor Hamilton R. Gamble called the old convention of 1861 into session for the fifth time. After heated debate, this group passed an ordinance providing for the extinction of slavery by July 4, 1870.[2]

The more forward-looking Unionists deplored such a long delay and called a protest convention to be held in Jefferson City in September, 1863. There some 700 delegates from approximately three-fourths of Missouri's counties launched the Radical Union party. Denouncing conservative rule as a roadblock to progress, they particularly deplored that group's intransigence on the emancipation issue and the seeming inability of the Provisional Government to control guerrilla warfare.

The Radicals' first opportunity to test their growing political power came with the election of Supreme Court justices in the fall of 1863. This campaign initiated tactics that were to become increasingly familiar. At every rally Radical speakers branded their Conservative opponents as "copperheads" who sought to undermine the Union. The Radicals displayed an unrelenting vindictiveness toward anyone who challenged their political platform. On a more positive level they appealed to the business interests to support them as the party of progress, promising to promote immigration and commercial investment. They urged the laboring man to join them in the battle of democracy versus aristocracy by warning that conservative circles looked upon him merely as "poor white trash." The military received impassioned pleas to vote as they shot—that is, to support the "loyal men" working to secure protection at home for all "true Unionists."

As the political group in power the Conservatives had control of most of the state offices and the accompanying patronage. They appealed to the basicly conservative natures of Missourians by attacking

---

[2] William E. Parrish, *Turbulent Partnership: Missouri and the Union, 1861–1865* (University of Missouri Press, Columbia, Mo., 1963), pp. 135–48. This convention had been elected in 1861 to decide the secession issue. It established the provisional government in July, 1861, and then served as a quasi-legislative arm for the next two years. This was its final session.

their Radical opponents as political opportunists more hungry for office than concerned with working for the welfare of the state. They pointed to the Radicals' incendiary statements and pictured them as desperate men ready to undertake revolution, if necessary, to accomplish their ends. Thus, both sides conducted highly charged emotional campaigns which failed to really grapple with major issues.

The judicial election was a cliff-hanger with the final outcome in doubt for some weeks. Bitter controversy centered on the soldier vote with the Conservatives contending that some returns were fraudulent, while the Radicals charged that many legal ballots went uncounted. The final official returns showed a Conservative victory by some 2,500 votes. An analysis of this initial test of Radical strength indicates that the party polled its heaviest vote in the southwest (wracked by guerrilla warfare), in the extreme northern tiers of counties with their relatively low Negro population and rather high incidence of people of Northern backgrounds (this area, too, had seen its share of guerrillas), and in St. Louis and its immediate vicinity (which contributed a large

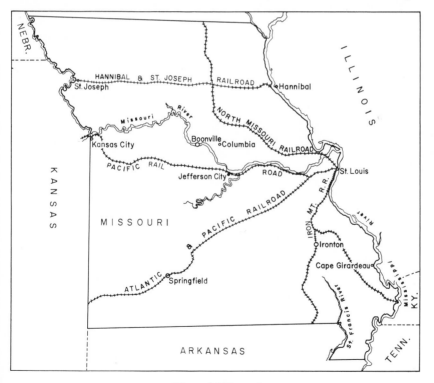

Map of Missouri.

German bloc). The Conservatives dominated the central and south-eastern regions along the rivers, where large landowners were concerned with the security of their slaves and other tangible property.[3]

The Radicals soon offset this defeat with the election of B. Gratz Brown to the United States Senate. Apparently part of a behind-the-scenes arrangement in the legislature which returned moderately conservative John B. Henderson to the other seat, this, nevertheless, proved a signal victory. Brown's election had been thwarted the previous winter by a three-way split among conservatives, moderates, and immediate emancipationists. Now enough moderates shifted to send him to Washington.[4]

By February, 1864, the Radicals had mustered enough strength in the General Assembly to place a referendum on the fall ballot calling for a new state convention to consider emancipation, limits on suffrage, and a general revision of Missouri's constitution. Confidently expecting voter approval, they provided for the election of convention members at the same time so that body could meet in January, 1865.[5]

Division threatened Missouri's Radicals as they faced the question of a presidential ticket in 1864. Many of them believed Lincoln too conservative for the postwar era. They distrusted his recently announced reconstruction program and condemned him for not going beyond the Emancipation Proclamation to free all the slaves. Although some, led by Brown, courted General John C. Fremont at Cleveland, most party leaders realized they had little choice but to support the President if they wished to have a future. With the Conservative Unionists organizing Lincoln clubs throughout the state and nominating delegates for the Union (Republican) convention in Baltimore, Radicalism might be left out in the cold if it failed to contend for regular party recognition. Consequently the Radical state convention sent an uncommitted delegation to Baltimore. Seated over their Conservative rivals, after certain political manipulations, they thereby received the

---

[3] St. Louis *Missouri Democrat, passim,* Sept.–Nov., 1863; St. Louis *Missouri Republican, passim,* Sept.–Nov., 1863; Ida M. Nowells, "A Study of the Radical Party Movement in Missouri, 1860–1870" (M.A. thesis, University of Missouri, 1939), p. 35.

[4] *Missouri Republican,* Nov. 18 and 20, 1863. An ardent antislavery man of long standing, Brown had been active in the Radical movement from its outset. As editor of the *Missouri Democrat* in the 1850s he had built a considerable reputation for Liberalism. A prewar Democrat from Pike County, Henderson belonged to that small conservative minority who early realized that Missourians must accept the eradication of slavery. Sensing the trend of the times he had begun to move cautiously toward the Radical camp in the summer of 1863 to protect his political future.

[5] *Laws of the State of Missouri, 22nd General Assembly, Adjourned Session, 1863–1864* (Jefferson City, Mo., 1864), pp. 24–26.

national party's official stamp of acceptance. The withdrawal of Fremont from the presidential race later that fall made full unity of the Missouri Radicals possible.

The national convention's rejection of the Missouri Conservatives placed that group in an untenable position politically. Some of them supported the Lincoln ticket but refrained from any action on the state level. The rest drifted into the ranks of the Democratic party, which had been resuscitated in June.[6]

The state-wide election contest in 1864 thus revolved around the Radical and the Democratic tickets. Mounting their campaign along much the same lines as that of the previous year, the Radicals nominated Fletcher for governor, while judiciously distributing the other places on their ticket among various rival groups. A railroad entrepreneur before the war, Fletcher had been active in the formation of Missouri's fledgling Republican party in 1860. For two years he had been removed from the tumultuous Missouri political scene as a brigade commander with Sherman's Army of the Tennessee which made him an ideal compromise candidate. Fletcher would enhance his military record further by playing a prominent role in repulsing Sterling Price's raiders on the eve of the election. General Thomas L. Price headed the Democratic ticket. A wealthy merchant and landowner, he had earned his commission with state troops during the Mexican War. He had a long record of party service including brief terms in both the Missouri General Assembly and Congress, but generally proved a colorless campaigner.

The invasion of Missouri by General Sterling Price (no relation to the Democratic candidate) in late September disrupted the electoral campaign. With Confederate raiders roaming the state little opportunity existed for an extensive canvass. By the time Price retreated into Arkansas only a few days remained before the election. Missouri's voters went to the polls and clearly indicated their desire for a change. They made Fletcher governor by a 40,000 majority and indicated their approval of Lincoln by about the same margin. The Radicals secured large majorities in both houses of the new General Assembly. They swept every congressional race except one. The electorate also strongly endorsed a new state convention and gave the Radicals a comfortable working control of its membership.

[6] *Missouri Democrat*, April 13 and May 30, 1864; Columbia *Missouri Statesman*, May 27, 1864; *Missouri Republican*, June 6 and 17, 1864; Charles D. Drake, "Autobiography," (manuscript, State Historical Society of Missouri, Columbia, Mo.), pp. 951–52; William F. Zornow, "The Missouri Radicals and the Election of 1864," *Missouri Historical Review* 45 (July, 1951): 368–69; James S. Rollins Papers (State Historical Society of Missouri), Peter L. Foy to Rollins, Feb. 7, 1865.

A comparison of the election map of 1864 with that of the previous year gives an even clearer picture of the Radical triumph. The Democrats secured majorities in only fifteen counties: a bloc along the Missouri River on the western border of the state, the area of "Little Dixie" in central Missouri, and four scattered counties in the southeast. With a single exception, these counties remained consistently Conservative, or Democratic, throughout the postwar era. Their stand can generally be attributed to either a relatively large Negro population or a high per capita value of real and personal property, or in some cases to both.[7]

Several factors account for the Radical victory. The decision of the Baltimore convention linked the Radicals with the Lincoln administration, thereby strengthening their appeal to the uncommitted portion of the electorate. The relentless military campaigns of Grant and Sherman, which seemed to point to the collapse of the Confederacy, bolstered the administration ticket in Missouri, as elsewhere. The Price raid, coming after a prolonged renewal of guerrilla warfare, pointed up the Conservatives' seeming incapacity and gave emphasis to the Radicals' promises that they could restore a semblance of order to the state. The death of Governor Gamble early in 1864 had removed the Conservatives' strongest political figure, and they had no one who could adequately fill the void. The test oath of 1861, enacted by the Provisional Government, disfranchised many Missourians who would probably have voted the Democratic ticket. Other Conservative adherents had left the state. Nearly 52,000 fewer Missourians went to the polls in 1864 than in the previous presidential election. Underlying all this was the apparent feeling of many Missourians that new times demanded new leadership. As they faced a future fraught with many problems, social and economic, Missourians decisively handed the Radicals the reins of power.

In many respects, the Missouri state convention, which convened on January 7, 1865, was a study in microcosm of what followed over the next five years. If anything besides Radicalism characterized most of the sixty-six delegates it was a general lack of political experience. Only a handful had seen previous legislative service, with but three having served in the convention of 1861–63. Not quite half had their origins in the free states and abroad. Nine were native Missourians, with most of the remaining members coming from other border states. Only thirteen lawyers could be found in the delegate ranks; fourteen

[7] Floyd C. Shoemaker, *Missouri and Missourians: Land of Contrasts and People of Achievements* (Chicago, 1943), 1:934–37; Nowells, "Study of the Radical Party Movement," pp. 35–36, 93–95. A dozen other counties that were consistently in the Conservative or Democratic column during the Reconstruction period broke over in this election for reasons that are difficult to discern.

followed agricultural pursuits; twelve were merchants; fourteen practiced medicine. They were a relatively young group with one-third of their membership under forty years of age and only fifteen above the age of fifty-one.[8]

In examining the roster of his fellow delegates, Charles D. Drake viewed them "almost without exception . . . [as] sensible, upright, and worthy men," but he hastened to add that "only a very small number of them had ever had experience in lawmaking." Drake had emerged over the past two years as one of the party's ablest leaders and certainly its foremost orator. A St. Louis attorney, successively a Whig, an ardent Know-Nothing, and a Democrat, he had served several terms in the General Assembly in the 1850s. As late as July, 1861, he spoke out strongly against antislavery agitation. The turmoil of the following winter brought a complete metamorphosis in his political thinking, however, and he began to look upon slavery as the root of all the state's difficulties. Thereafter he became a fervent advocate of emancipation.

Immediately upon his election to the convention, Drake began to scrutinize every part of the existing state constitution to see what changes might be needed. He also studied the policies of other states that Missouri might profitably borrow. By mid-December, 1864, Drake's ideas for a new constitution began to take shape. He denied any ulterior motive in this, believing simply that every conscientious delegate had the responsibility of thus preparing himself. At least, so he reported in his highly egotistical autobiography.

Whatever the reason for his labors, Drake dominated the convention proceedings from the outset. A skilled demagogue and opportunist, he nevertheless possessed considerable progressive vision. He worked actively at his job within the convention as well as in preparation for it. Having secured a sizable following in rural Missouri through his speaking efforts on behalf of the party, Drake could count on the support of that region's Radical delegates in nearly every crucial vote. Although occasionally forced to trim his sails to suit their temperament, the basic document which emerged from the convention was aptly called "Drake's Constitution."[9]

[8] *Journal of the Missouri State Convention Held at St. Louis, 1865* (St. Louis, 1865), pp. 3–4. Hereafter cited as *Convention Journal.*

[9] Drake, "Autobiography," pp. 1054–56; Allen Johnson and Dumas Malone, eds., *Dictionary of American Biography* (New York, 1930), 5:425–26; David D. March, "The Life and Times of Charles Daniel Drake" (Ph.D. diss., University of Missouri, 1949), pp. 349–50. Drake served the convention as vice-president, chairman of the committee on the legislative department, chairman of the revising and enrolling committee, a member of the special committees on emancipation and elective franchise, and a member of the committee on boundaries. Yet, most of his work was accomplished on the convention floor and in the committee of the whole.

With an overwhelming Radical majority the convention experienced no difficulty in effecting a working organization. A Drake resolution establishing eleven standing committees passed without dissent. Each committee was charged with carefully examining those parts of the constitution referred to them for any necessary amendments.

Having organized, the convention quickly moved to accomplish emancipation. Given the chaotic situation within the state, the existence of the federal Confiscation Act, and the active recruitment of Negro troops since the previous summer, there were few Negroes who still remained with their masters under the old arrangement. But for this group the convention, with only four dissenting votes, cut the final cord on January 11. In their zeal for a general end to slavery, the delegates also adopted a resolution urging Missouri's senators and representatives to push the emancipation amendment then before Congress. When the Thirteenth Amendment was sent to the states for ratification the following month, the General Assembly promptly approved it, thereby giving Missouri's firm assent to nationwide emancipation.[10]

The convention remained in session for an additional three months, becoming a storm center of controversy both within and without. It passed its major crisis in early February when Drake carried the day for a completely new constitution. Considerable feeling had been building up that with emancipation completed the convention should deal quickly with disfranchisement and then adjourn, leaving to the General Assembly the solution of other problems facing the state.

Drake, however, saw the convention as the ideal opportunity for a thorough revamping of the state's code; he had no desire to let the chance pass through the Radicals' fingers. Many joined Drake in a basic distrust of the General Assembly; they feared the day when conservative forces might regain control of the legislature. Much ground might then be lost in advancing the social and economic development of both races in Missouri, if constitutional guarantees were not provided. Drake bolstered his followers with continual assurances that the popular vote in 1864 had given them a mandate declaring: "We intend to erect a wall and a barrier in the shape of a constitution that shall be as high as the eternal heavens, deep down as the very center of the earth, so that they [the Democrats in the legislature] shall neither climb over it nor dig under it, and as thick

[10] *Convention Journal*, pp. 5, 16–17, 25–27, 30; Shoemaker, *Missouri and Missourians*, 1:578, 941.

as the whole territory of Missouri so that they shall never batter it down nor pierce through it."[11]

Overcoming the use of delaying tactics and chronic absenteeism by his opponents Drake pushed ahead with his project. The question of suffrage qualifications probably absorbed the greatest amount of time and energy. Drake proposed an article which went to extreme lengths in providing for "Rebel" disfranchisement. It required a would-be voter to swear under oath that he never committed any one of eighty-six different acts of supposed disloyalty against the state or the Union. All candidates for public office, jurors, lawyers, corporation officials and trustees, ministers, and teachers would also have to take this test oath. The General Assembly by an absolute majority in each house might revoke this requirement for voting after January 1, 1871; it would have to wait an additional four years, however, to rescind the oath in the other instances.

The Conservatives and some Germans and moderates objected to such stringent restrictions. Many Missourians had taken stands and made statements early in the war that they soon regretted. A number of those who had supported Missouri's original secessionist state government in the initial enthusiasm of asserting states' rights took advantage of the Provisional Government's offer of amnesty at the end of 1861. Drake's critics argued that to make the test oath retroactive beyond that date would be a breach of faith. This Drake denied. The earlier action had assured the repentants security "in their persons, in their property, in their lives"—nothing more. Loss of suffrage in no way interfered with any of these, in Drake's opinion.

In the end he prevailed, with the backing of the more ardent extremists from the strife-torn western and northern borders. These men introduced atrocity stories of guerrilla cruelty to support their demands for even sterner measures. To insure the oath's enforcement, the convention gave the General Assembly the duty of establishing machinery for a systematic biennial registration of all voters. Most Radicals believed that persons guilty of treason and disloyalty would readily commit perjury. Thus they saw a registration system as a means of uncovering those who would take an oath under false pretenses. As the final judges of loyalty, the registering officers could

---

[11] *Missouri Democrat,* Jan. 20, Feb. 17, and March 1, 1865; *Missouri Republican,* Feb. 3 and 6, 1865; Drake, "Autobiography," 1061a–1065; *Convention Journal,* pp. 89–90. The major restrictions on the legislative power are found in the *Constitution of the State of Missouri, 1865,* Art. 4, Secs. 23–25, 27; Art. 8, Secs. 4 and 5; Art. 12, Secs. 2 and 3.

pass on the validity of each oath, thereby determining whether each prospective voter fulfilled the constitutional requirement.[12]

Two other aspects of the suffrage question stirred considerable debate. The first concerned the possible enfranchisement of the new freedmen. The discussion of emancipation naturally gave rise to the question of the Negro's fundamental civil rights. Fearful that the Negro might be set free and forgotten, Drake sought to amend the emancipation ordinance:

> That no person can, on account of color, be disqualified as a witness, or be disabled to contract, or be prevented from acquiring, holding, or transmitting property; or be liable to any other punishment, for any offense, than that imposed on others for a like offense; or be restricted in the exercise of religious worship, or be hindered in receiving an education; or be subjected in law to any other restraints, or disqualifications, in regard to any personal rights, than such as are laid upon others under like circumstances.

A wide range of differences quickly became evident. Not wishing to disrupt the all-important emancipation process, the convention tabled Drake's amendment for the time being.

With the Negro freed, Drake, as chairman of the committee on the legislative department, presented the identical proposals as Section III of the Declaration of Rights. He worked hard to overcome opposition in the form of weakening amendments and ultimately secured his version virtually intact.

Most Missourians questioned the wisdom of enfranchising the Negro at this time. While not opposing Negro suffrage per se, Drake feared that to include it in the constitution would lead to rejection of that document by the voters. Inasmuch as few Negroes had had an opportunity for any education that would enable them to make wise choices, Drake believed it best to withhold suffrage for the time being as an inducement to the Negroes "to elevate themselves in the scale of humanity." Hopefully, free-state immigration into Missouri would help mitigate existing prejudices against the race.[13]

The convention also faced the question of suffrage for aliens who had declared their intentions of becoming citizens. Here the Germans reacted strongly, arguing that a liberal suffrage policy would attract more immigrants. Although Drake opposed noncitizen voting, he could give no compelling reasons for his views, except that it might

[12] *Convention Journal*, pp. 35, 40, 49, 211; *Missouri Democrat*, Jan. 27, Feb. 8, and April 3, 1865; *Missouri Republican*, Jan. 30 and Feb. 3, 1865; Drake, "Autobiography," p. 1076; *Missouri Constitution, 1865*, Art. 2, Secs. 3–5.
[13] *Convention Journal*, pp. 25–26; *Missouri Democrat*, Jan. 20, Feb. 6 and 8, 1865; *Missouri Constitution, 1865*, Art. 2, Sec. 18; Art. 4, Secs. 3 and 5; Art. 5, Sec. 2.

alienate the ratifying electorate. Retorted one German delegate, "Who would defeat it because of this amendement? The Know-Nothings?" Replied Drake, "I thought that party was dead and buried." "You are living proof that it is not," the German shouted. In the end, the constitution granted the vote to any alien who had declared his intention of seeking citizenship one year before exercising the suffrage.[14]

Drake further incurred the enmity of the Germans by proposing that counties with more than one representative or senator in the General Assembly elect their legislators through single-member districts. This would considerably reduce the German influence in St. Louis County, the principal area affected. The Germans could wield power if all the St. Louis legislators were elected at large. The district plan would confine their strength to the one or two areas where they made up the bulk of the population. Drake denied a German charge that he hoped hereby to supplant B. Gratz Brown in the Senate. He insisted that he advocated this arrangement only because he believed it more democratic. This time Drake prevailed.

He failed to have his way, however, when he urged the rural delegates to consider a drastic reapportionment of the General Assembly. Drake contended that the existing constitution made possible the selection of a majority of the House by only one-fifth of the total vote cast. He proposed as a corrective the establishment of one-hundred House districts based on population, without regard to county equality. This was asking too much of his rural supporters. They retained the old system although the convention did change the divisor by which the ratio for additional seats was determined from 140 to 200.[15]

Over-all, Drake and his colleagues produced a generally progressive document for the mid-nineteenth century. They laid down broad guidelines for the General Assembly to follow in the promotion of industrial growth and corporate development, in the general development of Missouri's resources, and in the establishment of a broad-based public education system for both races with an equitable method of financing. They sought to make both state and local government more responsible to the people through a broadened referendum power and by shortening the terms of elected officials. They curbed a number of abuses that had crept into the governmental set up in the prewar years. Had its more negative portions not created the enmity they did, the constitution might have survived longer than ten years. When in 1875, after most of the objectionable features had already

[14] *Missouri Republican,* March 29, 1865; *Convention Journal,* pp. 201–2.
[15] *Missouri Republican,* Feb. 20 and 22, 1865; *Missouri Democrat,* February 13, 1865; *Missouri Constitution, 1865,* Art. 4, Sec. 2.

been eliminated, Missouri's voters were asked to decide on a new convention, they answered affirmatively by a mere 283-vote majority, an indication that many had learned to live quite well under what remained of the 1865 document.

In addition to the new constitution, the 1865 convention produced three ordinances. The first, as cited, dealt with emancipation; the second, with Missouri's complicated prewar involvement in railroad construction; the third, known as the "Ousting Ordinance," declared some 800 offices vacant on May 1, 1865, and handed the Governor the power to fill them by appointment until the next election. Begun as a Radical attempt to purge the judiciary "from the Supreme Bench down" of "hostile" conservative elements, this last measure had ultimately been extended to include all county courts, county recorders, and circuit attorneys. By it the Radicals gained control over those branches of state and local government which they had not secured in the last election.[16]

The convention completed its work on April 10, after three months of almost continuous sessions. A hard-fought ratification campaign followed. The Radicals set June 6 as the day of decision, in the hope that a brief, hard-hitting effort would sell the document. Drake attempted to stack the cards in its favor by providing that the test oath determine the eligible electorate and by giving Missouri's soldiers in the field the opportunity to participate. Without these provisos, the constitution could not have carried.

Drake led in the fight for ratification, leaving no doubt that he considered support of the constitution a matter of party loyalty. Not all Radicals agreed. Most prominent in the ranks of the opposition was Governor Fletcher who believed the document too proscriptive in its limitations on the franchise. Other sections, he wrote, "though suited perhaps to our present condition, will soon be wholly inapplicable to the condition of a progressive people." It would have been better to let the legislature decide many of its provisions, so that they could "be more easily altered or repealed as experience may show to be our best interest." The Governor also hinted, in rather broad terms, his disappointment at the failure to provide for Negro suffrage.

[16] *Convention Journal*, pp. 22, 25–28, 101, 109, 155–59, 278–79. With 842 offices to fill, Governor Fletcher was content to retain in office those men whose loyalty could be proven, especially if they had been elected on the Radical ticket the previous November. In other instances he acted on the recommendations of county Radical committees. Howard L. Conard, ed., *Encyclopedia of the History of Missouri* (New York, 1901), 5:169. The complete list of new officeholders can be found in the Jefferson City *Missouri State Times*, May 20, 1865.

Although Governor Fletcher gave no indication that he planned an active role against the constitution, the German and Conservative press rallied to his support. The Governor declined to be drawn into a fight, however, and the constitution's opponents had to look elsewhere for active leadership. They found it in Dr. Moses Linton of St. Louis, a convention member whose caustic pen was used with telling effect against Drake, and in Edward Bates, Lincoln's staunchly conservative attorney general, who wrote a series of effective letters with the theme: "The Convention was revolutionary, in its origins, in its character and in its acts."

Both of Missouri's senators and all of her Radical congressmen ultimately endorsed the constitution, although in most cases their action lacked the enthusiasm for which Drake might have hoped. That individual wrote and spoke ceaselessly for the cause as the contest went down to the wire.[17]

The results of the referendum remained in doubt for three weeks after the polls closed. Defeat seemed certain, as St. Louis carried a majority of 5,926 votes against the constitution out of 16,570 votes cast. Southeastern Missouri and the Missouri River counties, dominated by a Conservative-German coalition, also brought in a strong negative vote. The *Missouri Democrat*, chief Radical organ in St. Louis, raised an immediate cry of fraud and published letters from the interior charging many had practiced "pious perjury" in taking the test oath despite "past sins."

But the ratification forces slowly gained ground as the results trickled in from the border areas. The Radical strongholds of northern and southwestern Missouri produced huge majorities for the constitution. These regions, which had suffered most heavily from guerrilla warfare, accepted Drake's proscriptions readily. Furthermore, they hoped to benefit from immigration and increased capital investment, which adoption of the constitution would seemingly encourage.

Now complaints of violence and intimidation came from the Conservatives who charged the Radicals with keeping many of their number from the polls. Undoubtedly there were varying degrees of enforcement of the test oath as a criterion for voter eligibility. In all probability, its rigid enforcement in highly partisan Radical areas was equalized by a laxity elsewhere.

[17] *Missouri Constitution, 1865*, Art. 13, Sec. 6; *Convention Journal*, p. 283; *Missouri Democrat*, April 10, 24, 26, 28, May 1, 3, June 2, 1865; *Missouri Republican*, May 3, 1865; Drake, "Autobiography," pp. 1078, 1095½–96, 1115–18; Howard K. Beale, ed., *The Diary of Edward Bates, 1859–1866* (U.S. Printing Office, Wash., D.C., 1933). *The Annual Report of the American Historical Society for the Year 1930* (Washington, 1933), 4:470–85, 571–612.

The final official count revealed a bare majority of 1,862 votes for ratification, out of a total of 85,478 votes cast. The soldier vote which produced a majority of 2,827 proved crucial as the civilian population rejected the constitution by the scant margin of 965. With the results known, the Radicals quickly closed ranks, and Governor Fletcher issued a proclamation stating that the constitution would be in force as of July 4, 1865.[18]

Controversy did not end with the acceptance of the constitution. Many contended that the document had been ratified by a minority interest using irregular methods. In the months that followed, numerous proposals were heard recommending a new convention or the submission of amendments to rid the constitution of its more objectionable features. None of these petitions bore full fruit until the election of 1870.

During the winter of 1865–66 the Missouri courts became the storm center of controversies over the validity of the test oath, particularly as it affected lawyers and preachers. Under the constitution the members of the various professions had sixty days from the date of the Governor's proclamation to subscribe their loyalty. In early August several leading St. Louis attorneys met and declared the requirement ex post facto in nature. Most of them indicated that they would not take the oath, and the September 2 deadline passed with many non-Radical lawyers failing to comply.

Enforcement of the oath varied, with the state providing no general agency to police the problem. Several judges in rural Missouri refused to require the oath in their courts. One jurist contended that President Johnson's amnesty policy superseded any contrary provisions of the state constitution. In St. Louis, however, nonconforming attorneys found themselves barred from the courts. Two test cases resulted, involving Samuel T. Glover and Alexander J. P. Garesche. When the Missouri high tribunal upheld the oath, Garesche filed a bill of exceptions to carry his case to the United States Supreme Court.[19]

[18] *Missouri Democrat,* June 9 and 16, July 3, 1865; *Missouri Republican,* June 13, 1865; James O. Broadhead Papers (Missouri Historical Society, St. Louis), James Brown to Broadhead, June 23, 1865; Robert C. Fulkerson to Broadhead, June 26, 1865; Avery and Shoemaker, *Messages and Proclamation,* 4:262–64. Eighteen thousand fewer voters went to the polls than in the election the previous November. No doubt this is partly due to the more stringent test oath. On the other hand, fourteen counties, mostly along the southern border of the state where population was small and scattered, reported no returns whatever.

[19] St. Louis *Dispatch,* Aug. 9 and Sept. 21, 1865; *Missouri Democrat,* Sept. 1, 13, 15, 22, Oct. 2, 20, Nov. 8, 1865; *Missouri Statesman,* Oct. 6, 1865; Charles P. Johnson, *Personal Recollections of Some of Missouri's Eminent Statesmen and Lawyers* (Columbia, Mo., 1903), pp. 25–30.

Meanwhile another case involving Father John A. Cummings, a young Roman Catholic priest of Louisiana, Missouri, was proceeding in the same direction. One of numerous clergy who refused to take the oath because of conscience, Father Cummings was arrested for preaching illegally, refused to make bond, and so had his case become an overnight sensation as he languished in the Pike County jail.

By a chance encounter with Frank Blair aboard a Mississippi River steamer, Father Cummings managed to enlist Frank's brother, Montgomery, as chief defense counsel before the United States Supreme Court, with Reverdy Johnson and David Dudley Field assisting. That tribunal heard arguments in the case of *Cummings* v. *Missouri* in mid-March, 1866, with George P. Strong, prominent St. Louis attorney and convention member, and Senator John B. Henderson representing the state. Cummings' lawyers contended that the oath constituted both ex post facto legislation and a bill of attainder, while the state's attorneys argued that the oath intended no punishment per se for past offenses, but merely sought to prescribe qualifications for certain professions. The punishment came, quite constitutionally, only if the individual refused to take the oath.

The Supreme Court handed down its decision on January 14, 1867. By a 5-to-4 majority, it upheld the contentions of Cummings' lawyers and reversed the judgment of the Missouri high tribunal. Also affected was the case of *ex parte Garland,* involving the constitutionality of a national statute requiring an iron-clad oath for attorneys practicing before the Supreme Court. Consequently not only was a free pulpit restored in Missouri, but Garesche, Glover, and other attorneys found themselves welcomed once more to the bar of the St. Louis courts after an absence of a year and a half.[20]

Charles D. Drake might rave about the necessity for continued resistance to prevent disloyal lawyers from practicing, but few heeded his words. "The war is now over," declared the *Missouri Democrat,* "and whether such restrictions were or were not legal and necessary during its continuance, the demand for them no longer exists, and the decision as confined to its legitimate scope and effect, will do but little practical harm."[21]

The Cummings case in no way affected the test oath for voting. This was being challenged in yet another case instigated by Frank Blair in the late fall of 1865. Blair had tried to vote in a local St. Louis election with his own oath, which simply declared his allegiance to the state

[20] Harold C. Bradley, "In Defense of John Cummings," *Missouri Historical Review,* 57 (Oct., 1962): 1–15; *Missouri Democrat,* Jan. 23, 1867.
[21] *Ibid.,* Jan. 16 and Feb. 18, 1867.

and nation. When the election officials refused his ballot and demanded that he take the test oath, Blair stated his ineligibility to do so on the ground that he had taken up arms against pro-Confederate Governor Claiborne Jackson in 1861. Still barred from the polls, Blair brought suit against the election officials, asking $10,000 damages. With his staunch Union record, Blair felt certain that he could win and thereby overthrow the test oath for voting. The case followed a tortuous path through the state and federal courts over the next four years.[22]

Frank Blair had long since become the spearhead of the Conservative opposition to Radical rule in Missouri. He had returned to the state early in October, 1865, to try to weld a united front between the supporters of President Johnson's reconstruction program and those who opposed the vindictive features of the new state constitution. He and other Conservative Unionists issued a call for a mass convention on October 26 at Verandah Hall in St. Louis. In the interim he toured rural Missouri to arouse the opposition to its duty.

Nearly 1,000 enthusiastic delegates attended the three-day Verandah Hall convention to hear Blair and other Conservative leaders from all corners of the state in their now-quite-familiar denunciations of Charles D. Drake, the Fletcher administration, and the constitution. At its final session the group adopted a wide range of resolutions and appointed two committees: one to visit Washington and present the convention's proceedings to President Johnson, the other "to organize the people of the State in opposition to the new Constitution." After their return home, many of the delegates called county meetings to ratify the St. Louis proceedings and thereby keep the fires alive for the 1866 electoral campaign. In making their plans the Conservatives deliberately avoided the Democratic label, because of past connotations attached to it, while welcoming all members of that party.[23]

The Radicals, through their control of the General Assembly, sought to forestall the opponents by passing a comprehensive registry bill. Largely the work of Drake, this provided for a highly partisan setup whose officials had almost unlimited power in determining the loyalty of any individual wishing to register.[24]

---

[22] Gist Blair Papers (Library of Congress), Frank Blair to Montgomery Blair, Nov. 4, 1865; *Missouri Republican,* Nov. 8 and 10, 1865; *Missouri Democrat,* Jan. 5, 1866.

[23] Gist Blair Family Papers, Thomas T. Gantt to Montgomery Blair, Oct. 6, 1865; Frank Blair to Francis P. Blair, Nov. 2, 1865; *Missouri Statesman, passim,* Oct.–Nov., 1865.

[24] Drake, "Autobiography," p. 1209; *Laws of the State of Missouri, 23rd General Assembly, Adjourned Session, 1865–1866* (Jefferson City, Mo., 1866), pp. 117–24.

As President Johnson and the Radicals in Congress locked horns in the spring of 1866, national issues came increasingly to the fore in Missouri politics. Missouri's Radical leaders had had high hopes when Johnson succeeded the martyred Lincoln that he would lend his prestige to their program and manipulate the federal patronage to their advantage. By mid-winter they saw their dreams turning to nightmares as Frank Blair and other Conservatives moved into the President's inner circle. The Radicals of Putnam County bluntly proclaimed: "Andrew Johnson, having abandoned the party which elected him, and the principles upon which he was elected, we unhesitatingly denounce him as a traitor, to said party, and to the great principles of our government."[25]

As the state and national struggles merged, matters of patronage became increasingly important. The Radicals had been trying for nearly a year to make inroads into the postal and revenue services, but with little success. At best, their senators, Brown and Henderson, could block new Johnson appointees by withholding their endorsements. But, as the President refused to yield to them, an impasse developed until Congress adjourned that summer. Johnson then proceeded with interim appointments which hopefully would be ratified by a more conservative Congress after the November elections.[26]

Both parties had their 1866 campaigns under way by mid-May. The Radicals imported Governor William M. Stone of Iowa to stump the state on their behalf. Conservative speakers dogged his steps. Radical strategy deliberately cultivated the veterans' vote. Soldiers' leagues and soldiers' associations sprang up in county after county. Although not officially connected with the Radical party organization, their instigators were usually active party members. Ostensibly these associations served a twofold purpose: to secure the ex-soldiery its full share of postwar benefits and to make certain that the general citizenry fully appreciated their military services. They also vowed to stand between their country and the disloyal classes if this became necessary. These veterans' organizations proved an excellent means of re-enlisting the rank-and-file Germans in the Radical cause. The Germans had formed the hard core of Missouri's volunteers

[25] Andrew Johnson Papers (Library of Congress), Henry T. Blow to Johnson, Oct. 26, 1865, and March 19, 1866; Chillicothe *Spectator,* April 12, 1866.
[26] Johnson Papers, Blow to Johnson, Aug. 10, 1865; James S. Rollins to Johnson, Sept. 2, 1865; Frank Blair to Francis P. Blair, May 2, 1866; O. D. Filley to Montgomery Blair, July 30, 1866; Samuel T. Glover to Johnson, Aug. 1, 1866; George Knapp to Montgomery Blair, Aug. 3, 1866.

in the Union military cause. Now they fell in line behind their old leaders to enlist in a new campaign.[27]

As the summer wore on, scattered violence broke out over the state. In part this grew out of earlier difficulties stemming from the extreme zeal of certain Radicals in taking political and economic reprisals against returning ex-Confederates. Increasingly, it took on heavier political overtones as Radical officials began the process of registration. Governor Fletcher ultimately felt the necessity of calling up militia in certain areas to keep order. Made up primarily of Radicals, and armed by the state, they frequently performed their duties in such a highly partisan manner that they stirred up as much unrest as they quelled.

Conservative leaders denounced the Governor's moves and petitioned President Johnson for federal troops to help keep the peace. General Sherman, from his St. Louis headquarters, tried to work out an equitable solution between the two sides but with only partial success. Eventually, against his wishes, a few troops were dispatched from Fort Leavenworth to certain areas of western Missouri to hold down violence.[28]

Little uniformity existed in the registration process. The extent to which local registering officials scrutinized the test oaths depended upon the sentiments of the county. In the more ardent Radical areas they readily listened to informers and sometimes found it necessary to rely on armed guards. Where Conservative strength predominated some later cried that they had been intimidated to enroll many persons known to them to be ineligible.[29]

A serious outbreak of cholera in St. Louis slowed down the campaign during August, but as fall weather dissipated the sickness both sides drew up their "big guns." The Conservatives brought President Johnson to St. Louis on his "swing around the circle," while the Radicals countered with Ben Butler the following month. Each party had its key speakers stumping the rural areas during October.[30]

The Radicals triumphed decisively in the November balloting. "There is no use mincing matters," declared one Conservative editor.

[27] *Missouri Democrat*, *passim*, June–Aug., 1866. The Conservatives also tried to woo the veterans' vote, although without much success. *Missouri Republican*, Aug. 8 and 11, 1866, Feb. 6, 1867.

[28] Johnson Papers, *passim*, July–Aug., 1866; Records of the Department of the Missouri (National Archives), Letters Sent, Volume 532, Letters Received, Registers 525 and 526; Gist Blair Family Papers, Winfield S. Hancock to Frank Blair, Nov. 2, 1866.

[29] Records of the Department of the Missouri, Letters Received, Register 526; *Missouri Statesman*, Feb. 15, 1867.

[30] Drake, "Autobiography," p. 1196; *Missouri Democrat*, Sept. 10 and Oct. 15, 1866.

"The registry act has laid us out cold. We went in lemons and came out squeezed." The Radicals would control both houses of the new legislature by overwhelming majorities—Senate: 28 to 8; House: 103 to 36. Eight of the nine congressional districts sent Radicals to Washington. This became possible in the Ninth, however, only because the Radical Secretary of State threw out all the ballots of one Conservative county on the ground that he knew it could have no more than a few hundred "loyal men" in spite of its 1,895 registered voters.[31]

Some two weeks after the election twenty-nine prominent Radicals from all parts of the state gathered at the Planters House in St. Louis. The group included Governor Fletcher, Charles D. Drake, and Missouri's Radical congressmen and senators. Retiring Senator B. Gratz Brown had instigated the meeting in the hope that the high-riding Radicals might now be ready to show their magnanimity and move toward universal franchise. He proposed amendments to the state constitution, enfranchising both the Negroes and those whites currently barred from the ballot. He would also remove the test oath restrictions on the professions (the United States Supreme Court had yet to make its final decision).

This move caught Drake and the more ardent Radicals completely off guard. Ten of them walked out, but Drake remained to listen and argue. He was willing to accept Negro suffrage, but considered the rest of Brown's program "an abandonment of all that the Radicals of the State had gained after an unequalled struggle, and a proffer of pusillanimous and unmashed surrender of the party, its principles, and its achievements to our adversaries."

Brown prevailed at this meeting, however, for the group finally adopted his resolutions by a vote of sixteen to three. They were presented to the General Assembly, but as that body largely reflected the more ardent partisanship of the Drake wing, it agreed to submit an amendment for Negro suffrage to the electorate in 1868, then turned its back on the other proposals. It further showed its true bent by electing Drake overwhelmingly to a full six-year term in the United States Senate, succeeding Brown.[32]

[31] Richmond *Conservator*, Nov. 10, 1866; *Missouri Democrat*, Dec. 7 and 12, 1866; *Missouri Statesman*, Jan. 4, 1867. In throwing out the vote of Callaway County, Secretary of State Francis Rodman relied on the testimony of the supervisor of registration there that he had been pressured into enrolling many whom he knew to be disloyal. The House of Representatives rejected a contest brought by the unsuccessful Conservative candidate. *Ibid.*, Feb. 15, 1867, and July 24, 1868.
[32] Drake, "Autobiography," pp. 1216–25; *Missouri Democrat*, Jan. 17, 1867; *Missouri Statesman*, March 15, 1867. Brown had announced on June 27, 1866, that he would not seek re-election because of ill health.

For all their extreme vindictiveness against their political enemies, the Radicals did a great deal to move Missouri forward in the post-war era. Although some would have been content to free the Negro and then let him shift for himself, the great bulk of the party's leadership, spurred on by Drake, realized that they must provide for the basic rights of the new freedmen. This they did through the new constitution as already mentioned.[33]

The educated Negroes of Missouri and many white Radicals, particularly those among the German element, regretted the convention's failure to enfranchise the freedmen. They organized the Missouri Equal Rights League in October, 1865, and brought in John M. Langston, prominent mulatto attorney from Oberlin, Ohio, for a state-wide speaking tour early the following year. After a year and a half of agitation, the group's efforts bore fruit early in 1867, as seen above, when the new Radical General Assembly voted to submit a Negro suffrage amendment to the voters in 1868.[34]

As a part of their progressive program to build a better Missouri, the Radicals did a great deal to promote public education for both races. A system of free public schools fit perfectly into their image of their party as the protector of the Union and the champion of equal opportunity. Although legally established two decades before the war, public education lacked widespread support in Missouri. The constitution of 1820 expressly forbade any education for the Negro although some of it was carried on through their churches. The war years brought almost total neglect to the state's schools outside the St. Louis area.

The state convention established the framework for the new educational system that arose out of the ashes of the war. Considering "a general diffusion of knowledge and intelligence [as] being essential to the preservation of the rights and liberties of the people," it charged the General Assembly with maintaining free public schools for all youths between the ages of five and twenty-one, with separate establishments for Negroes if it deemed this desirable. All eligible

[33] Although granted basic rights by the state convention, many of Missouri's Negroes found themselves the victims of harassment that winter and spring (1864–65). A good summary is found in *The War of the Rebellion: Official Records of the Union and Confederate Armies* (Washington, 1896), ser. I, vol. 48, Part 1, p. 1257. Once the war ended, their lot improved considerably with the help of the Freedmen's Bureau, Radical officials, and a concerned citizenry. For a summary see William E. Parrish, *Missouri Under Radical Rule, 1865–1870* (Columbia, Mo., 1965), pp. 108–38.

[34] *Missouri Democrat*, Oct. 4, 16, Nov. 29, 1865; Jan. 12, 1866; *Missouri Statesman*, March 15, 1867.

pupils might be required to accumulate a minimum attendance of sixteen months at some time before the age of eighteen.

The General Assembly consequently passed several laws early in 1866, providing a thorough and detailed public school system for both races. It also established the most adequate basis for state and local tax support seen up to that time. Local boards could build schools and tax their districts to cover the costs without having to submit the levy to the voters for approval. This greatly facilitated badly needed school construction, especially in areas that might have proved recalcitrant because of dominant conservative influence.

The legislature required each township or city board of education to establish and maintain one or more separate schools for Negro children within their respective jurisdictions where the number of such youngsters exceeded twenty. These must be kept open for a winter term equivalent to that for white schools. Should there be less than twenty black children, their portion of any tax levy might be appropriated for their education as the board saw fit. Subsequent laws improved on this situation, and considerable progress was made toward fulfilling the expectations of the lawmakers at the local level.[35]

To provide an adequate staff of teachers, the Radical superintendent of public schools, T. A. Parker, a young energetic administrator, toured the state, holding clinics and institutes. He reorganized the Missouri State Teachers Association and through it pushed for the organization of state normal schools. Two such were established at Kirksville and Warrensburg in 1870, the closing year of his term of office. In that same year the General Assembly granted state aid to Lincoln Institute at Jefferson City, established in 1866 through funds raised by Missouri's Negro regiments, with the proviso that it become a normal school for the training of black teachers.[36]

The Radicals, during their five years of rule in Missouri, also laid a firm foundation for the future economic growth of the state. Prewar Missouri had been dominated by agricultural and trading interests deeply imbued with a conservative philosophy stressing the sanctity of property rights and the soundness of the dollar through rigid

[35] Shoemaker, *Missouri and Missourians*, 1:806–7; Robert I. Brigham, "The Education of the Negro in Missouri" (Ph.D. diss., University of Missouri, 1946), pp. 60–77; *Missouri Constitution, 1865*, Art. 9; *Laws of Missouri, 1865–1866*, pp. 171–77, 183–84, 189–94.
[36] *Report of the Superintendent of Public Schools of the State of Missouri to the General Assembly, 1867* (Jefferson City, Mo., 1868), pp. 20–21; *Missouri Democrat*, June 22, 1866; *Laws of the State of Missouri, 25th General Assembly, Adjourned Session, 1870* (Jefferson City, Mo., 1870), pp. 134–37.

banking controls. In the postwar era, the Radicals sought to broaden the tax base by subjecting to taxation all property, real and personal, not held by public schools or government corporations. Their willingness to empower local school boards to tax without special elections for school construction purposes has been noted. In accordance with the new constitution, the General Assembly, on March 19, 1866, passed a comprehensive general incorporation law that did away with the prewar practice of granting individual charters through the legislature and thereby greatly facilitated corporate growth and manufacturing development. A general banking law quickly followed.

By 1870 Missouri had 11,871 manufacturing establishments with a work force of 65,354 persons—a threefold increase in ten years. Capital investment had quadrupled to $80,257,244, with a total production of $206,213,429—five times that of 1860. Approximately 75 per cent of investment and total production centered in St. Louis County where a wide variety of manufactories existed. At least nineteen industries in the St. Louis area claimed a capital investment in excess of $1,000,000 each. The river city had nearly doubled its population during the 1860s and now stood fourth in the nation, with 310,825 residents.[37]

An active labor movement secured a number of gains, especially in the building trades, as the St. Louis area experienced a tremendous construction boom. Senator Brown and other Radical leaders encouraged labor to push for an eight-hour day, one of the major goals of the newly organized National Labor Union. The result was a somewhat emasculated bill passed by the General Assembly in 1867. It declared eight hours to be the standard unit of a day's work, but provided that if labor and management so contracted, longer hours might prevail. The new legislation would not affect agricultural workers or those employed by the month. Weak as these provisions made it, the Missouri bill still represented one of the few eight-hour laws secured by labor at this time.[38]

Radical leaders co-operated closely with St. Louis merchants and shippers to try to secure federal aid for the improvement of Missouri's

---

[37] Shoemaker, *Missouri and Missourians*, 1: 796–98; *Missouri Constitution, 1865*, Art. 8, Sec. 4; *Laws of Missouri, 1865–1866*, pp. 20–70; *A Compendium of the Ninth Census (June 1, 1870)* (Washington, 1872), pp. 796–97, 830–31; *The Statistics of the Wealth and Industry of the United States*, vol. 3 of the Ninth Census (Washington, 1872), pp. 686–90.

[38] *Missouri Democrat*, Nov. 6, 1865; St. Louis *Industrial Advocate*, *passim*, Aug., 1866–Feb., 1867; *Laws of the State of Missouri, 24th General Assembly, Regular Session, 1867* (Jefferson City, Mo., 1867), p. 132.

waterways, so vital to the state's commerce. Even more important, they pushed the finishing of Missouri's basic rail network. In spite of large-scale federal, state, and local assistance in the 1850s only one railroad (the Hannibal and St. Joseph) had been completed by the eve of the Civil War. New doses of state aid in 1864 helped bring the Pacific Railroad into Kansas City by September, 1865, and allowed the North Missouri Railroad to resume construction toward the Iowa border.

Then the convention moved to tighten the drawstrings on state and local credit, hoping this action would force private capital to take up the slack. It forbade the General Assembly to use the state's credit to aid "any person, association, or corporation," nor could the state become a stockholder or association unless for the purpose of securing loans already extended. Local governmental units must receive a two-thirds approval by their voters before they could grant aid to private corporations.

Although the constitution also prohibited the release of the state's lien upon any railroad, the General Assembly in 1868 conveniently ignored this stipulation without serious challenge. After numerous difficulties, both Governor Fletcher and the legislature decided that the only way to secure completion of Missouri's debt-ridden railroads was to release them from past obligations to the state, so that the money thus saved in scheduled payments could be plowed into construction. In doing so, however, they established a specific schedule for the final construction of each line. All deadlines were met, with Missouri's trackage reaching 1,540 miles by the end of 1870.[39]

The Radicals created a state board of immigration early in 1865 to attract potential residents from the East and Europe. Working in co-operation with Missouri's railroads and other interested parties, this agency could accept a great deal of credit for the 45.6 per cent boost in population which Missouri enjoyed during the decade (a gain even more remarkable considering the loss of population during the war). Many of the new immigrants settled in rural Missouri. Land sales boomed, and the state's agricultural production made strong gains. Missouri ranked seventh among the states in the value

[39] Wyatt W. Belcher, *The Economic Rivalry between St. Louis and Chicago, 1850–1880* (New York, 1947), pp. 170–76, 193–96; John W. Million, *State Aid to Railways in Missouri* (Chicago, 1896), pp. 44–139, 145–90, 227–28, 232–43; Edwin L. Lopata, *Local Aid to Railroads in Missouri* (New York, 1937), pp. 43–59; *Missouri Constitution, 1865,* Art. 11, Secs. 13–15. The total railroad debt of Missouri stood at $31,735,840 in bonds and interest due on Jan. 1, 1868. The total amount realized in the disposition of the roads was $6,131,496, which left $25,604,344 for the taxpayers of Missouri to retire.

of its agricultural products in 1870, with a figure of $103,035,759. The Radicals established a state board of agriculture which promoted the advantages of new machinery and techniques, while Norman J. Colman made known the blessings of scientific agriculture through his St. Louis-based *Rural World*.[40]

The Radicals reached the zenith of their political power in Missouri in the election of 1868. They faced a revived Democratic party that year; but, with the help of the registry act, they had little difficulty in crushing it. They elected Joseph W. McClurg[41] governor and carried the entire state ticket by an approximate 20,000-vote margin. General Grant received the state's electoral votes by a similar majority. Twenty-five Radicals and nine Democrats would constitute the new Senate, with the new House containing ninety-two Radicals, thirty-five Democrats, and two Independents.

At first glance it appeared that the Democrats had picked up three congressional seats to go with the one they already had. But the *Missouri Democrat* immediately charged fraud in the Sixth and Ninth districts and called on the Radicals' "hatchet-man," Secretary of State Francis Rodman, to throw out the vote of certain counties as he had done in 1866. The Secretary obliged by refusing to open and certify the ballots of eight counties on the ground of illegal registration. Then he issued certificates of election for Congress on the basis of the remaining "official" vote. This insured Radicals of election in the disputed districts and made the Missouri congressional delegation one of eight Radicals and two Democrats. The General Assembly certified the votes as Rodman presented them and ordered new elections for local offices and the legistature in the counties in question.[42]

Only one disappointment marred the results for the Radical leaders: the decisive defeat of the Negro suffrage amendment. A strong defection of Radical voters, combined with almost solid opposition by the Democrats, produced a negative result of 74,053 to 55,236. St. Louis County, with a large black population, rejected it

[40] Norman L. Crockett, "A Study of Confusion: Missouri's Immigration Program, 1865–1916," *Missouri Historical Review* 57 (April, 1963): 250–55; *Ninth Census Compendium*, pp. 688–90; Shoemaker, *Missouri and Missourians*, 2:446–51.

[41] A colonel in the state militia during the war, McClurg had also served in the wartime state convention. Although trained in the law, he had spent most of his life as a merchant and trader in southwestern Missouri. For the preceding six years he had been in Congress. One Democratic paper characterized McClurg as "the embodiment of all that is narrow, bigoted, revengeful, and ignorant in the Radical party." *Dispatch*, quoted in Thomas S. Barclay, "The Liberal Republican Movement in Missouri," *Missouri Historical Review* 20 (Jan., 1926): 320n.

[42] *Missouri Statesman*, Nov. 13, 20, Dec. 25, 1868; Feb. 12, 1869. Again contests were filed with the House of Representatives, to no avail.

by better than two to one. Although supported actively by Drake, Fletcher, and every other Radical leader of consequence, prejudice among the party's rank-and-file overcame all moral and political arguments in its favor. Many Missourians feared an inundation of Negro immigration if their state proved more liberal than her northern neighbors. Consequently enfranchisement of Missouri's blacks had to await the ratification of the Fifteenth Amendment in 1870.

Radical leadership sought to place responsibility for the amendment's defeat squarely on the shoulders of the Democrats. William M. Grosvenor, the editor of the *Missouri Democrat,* expressed the opinion that most Radicals would support the removal of all restrictions if the Democrats would go along with impartial suffrage. It quickly became evident that he did not speak for the party hierarchy when Drake wrote from Washington that restoration of the franchise to "rebels" could come only after Negro suffrage.[43]

Missouri Radicals found a new leader in the election of 1868, one who adroitly played upon a growing popularity to reach the United States Senate. Carl Schurz had arrived in St. Louis on April 16, 1867, to become co-owner of the *Westliche Post,* one of the largest German-language papers in the country and an ardent Radical journal. He brought with him a rich background of political experience. A German *émigré* of 1852, Schurz was a forceful personality with considerable ambition. He had moved rapidly to the fore of the German community in Wisconsin and had played an active role in the Republican party from its beginnings. During the war he performed notably in rallying the Germans to the Union cause. He wrote and lectured continually, possessing an equal facility in English or German. A thorough Radical in his outlook, he became a popular figure on the lecture circuit.

Schurz settled in Missouri at an opportune moment politically. While Charles D. Drake seemed solidly entrenched in power, his success simply increased his tendencies toward arrogance and inflexibility. After March, 1867, he spent much of his time in Washington, where he entered actively into the Radical quarrels with the Johnson administration over reconstruction policy. He soon lost touch with changing Missouri currents.

[43] *Missouri Democrat,* Nov. 17, Dec. 14 and 25, 1868. Grosvenor had become editor of the *Democrat* during the 1866 election campaign, after a stint as editor of the *New Haven Morning Journal and Courier.* He and his paper had become increasingly identified with the more liberal wing of the party over the preceding two years.

B. Gratz Brown, the unacknowledged leader of the more liberal element, had gone into temporary retirement, nursing ill health and a feeling of political frustration. Following the election triumph of 1866 he had tried to move Radicalism down a more enlightened path through the Planters House proposals only to see them stifled by the Drake-dominated legislature. Senator John B. Henderson, who might have filled the void left by Brown's retirement, followed a more independent course in Washington than most Radicals liked. He eventually killed himself politically by voting against the President's impeachment conviction. Governor Fletcher, avowedly a liberal, remains something of an enigma. A popular speaker and an able executive, he seemed to find politics an increasingly frustrating profession which he would just as soon do without.

Thus Carl Schurz found a Radical party full of inner tensions, for all its appearance of surface calm. It needed a leader who could appeal to all its factions. As a newcomer, the German editor did not bear the scars of previous party battles, so that he might readily serve as reconciler. While staunchly Radical on national issues, he saw the need to give the Missouri party a more positive emphasis.

Beyond all this, Schurz had certain overriding political ambitions. When, against the advice of all of the state's party leaders. Henderson "betrayed" Missouri Radicalism by voting to sustain Andrew Johnson at his trial, Schurz began to eye the Senator's seat, due to be filled by the legislature that winter. The fiery German became quite active in the 1868 campaign on both the national and state levels. He chaired the Missouri delegation to the Republican national convention and delivered the keynote address there. After campaigning tirelessly throughout the Midwest he deliberately set aside the final six weeks for a speaking tour of Missouri on behalf of state and national candidates. While Drake "waved the bloody shirt" in his usual ardent fashion, Schurz took a somewhat calmer view, talking of the necessity for congressional reconstruction in order to assure a "New South." He stressed the harmony of progress rather than the specter of the past.

Schurz made a sufficiently favorable impression with rural Radicals to catapult into Henderson's seat. In doing so, he met heated opposition from Drake who personally appeared before the Radical caucus to champion his own hand-picked candidate and try to stave off what he believed was a threat to his political power. This action gave the skillful Schurz an excellent opportunity to paint Drake as a would-be party dictator and hold him up to ridicule in debate. Drake never fully recovered, and Missouri Radicalism had a new leader.[44]

Some moderates thought that Schurz's election might pave the way for the General Assembly to submit dual amendments to the people, enfranchising the Negro and the "rebel element" at the same time. These hopes were quickly dashed. The majority of the Radicals in the legislature showed little inclination to tackle the suffrage question in any form during the 1869 session. The election of 1870 was still far off, and many of them wished to see the trend of certain national events before committing themselves. Meanwhile debate continued with some suggestion of a general convention to completely over-haul the constitution.[45]

Few had changed their minds when the General Assembly recon-vened in January, 1870. Governor McClurg tried to find middle ground by suggesting the resubmission of the Negro suffrage amend-ment and thorough discussion of the wisdom of ending rebel dis-franchisement. In the latter, stress should be placed on the constitu-tional provision allowing the General Assembly to remove restrictions by a simple majority vote after January 1, 1871. To thus skirt this issue might better preserve Radical harmony.

The more liberal element showed no willingness to compromise on this seemingly moderate position. As another impasse appeared im-minent, Missourians' attentions were caught by two outside events. The United States Supreme Court handed down its decision in *Blair* v. *Ridgely, et al.* at the end of January. This case, in which Frank Blair challenged the validity of the test oath for voters, had been dragging through the judicial mill for the past four years. Now, in a rare occurrence, the high tribunal divided evenly, four to four, thereby refusing to overthrow the decision of the Supreme Court of Missouri against Blair. Democrats saw their high hopes for a greater voice in 1870 vanish. To most Radicals the result justified their postwar policy, but the liberals now deemed it all the more impera-tive that the restrictions be ended by the group that had imposed them.

A few days later, the Fifteenth Amendment completed the ratifica-tion process to become part of the federal Constitution. Thereby the

[44] Johnson and Malone, eds., *Dictionary of American Biography,* 16:466–68; March, "Charles Daniel Drake," p. 426; Barclay, "The Liberal Republican Move-ment," p. 303n; Joseph Schafer, ed., *The Intimate Letters of Carl Schurz, 1841–1869* (Madison, 1928), pp. 441–44, 460–68; *Missouri Democrat,* May 13, Sept. 16, Oct. 5, 12, 26, 1868; Jan. 8–18, 1869; William K. Patrick Papers (Missouri Historical Society), Samuel S. Burdett to Patrick, Jan. 19, 1869.
[45] *Missouri Democrat,* Jan. 28–Feb. 15, 1869.

Negro gained a national franchise. Feeling sure that this new bloc of votes would be theirs, many Radicals, including Drake, mellowed toward a direct submission of the disfranchisement question.

By the end of February, the liberals had pushed their program through the legislature with little difficulty. Those who still did not like it generally chose to keep silent once the caucus had made the decision to go ahead. Three amendments would be submitted to the voters: one would modify the test oath to a simple declaration of support for state and national constitutions; the second would eliminate it completely for jurors; the third would repeal the oath as a requirement for officeholding and for corporate or educational activity and remove all racial barriers to political office.[46]

Grosvenor assured the readers of the *Missouri Democrat* that these proposals would in no way endanger the Radical party's hold upon the state. If the amendments passed, the disfranchised could not vote in a state-wide election until 1872. By then augmentations from Negro voters and continued immigration would boost the Radical strength to some 141,000. The Democrats could not muster more than 83,700 votes, exclusive of the disfranchised. These, the liberal editor estimated at 25,000, undoubtedly a conservative count. Grosvenor argued that not all of the disfranchised would vote the Democratic ticket. New issues would arise as old animosities died out. With the proper platform the Radical party might have just as good a chance of drawing their votes as the Democrats.

Not wishing to take chances in the meantime, Grosvenor supported the decision of the Radicals in the legislature to continue the registry system as a means of holding Democratic prospects for 1870 to a minimum. In the light of this action, the opposition party determined on the "possum policy," which some of its leaders had been urging since the first of the year. In an official communiqué to local party functionaries the Democratic state central committee outlined the problems facing the party and their possible solutions. Acknowledging the hopelessness of electing a state ticket, it announced that no state convention would be called. Democratic efforts should be concentrated instead on electing local and congressional candidates, with particular emphasis on legislative nominees who would indicate their readiness to vote for the removal of all restrictions, should that issue be carried over into the new Assembly. As Radical quarrels increased, the wisdom of this program of "masterful inactivity" seemed to be

---

[46] Avery and Shoemaker, *Messages and Proclamation*, 4:408–9; *Missouri Democrat*, Jan. 12, Feb. 2, 7, 26, 1870; *Missouri Statesman*, Feb. 4, 1870; *Laws of Missouri, 1870*, pp. 502–4.

borne out. The absence of a state Democratic ticket left the Radicals with no one to fight but themselves. A split in their ranks would leave the Democrats in a particularly enviable bargaining position in local contests.[47]

Over the spring and summer the regular and liberal wings of the party in power had been uncovering more and more differences. Although agreed on the wisdom of submitting the amendments, they parted company on officially endorsing them. With many of the rank and file, especially in the border regions, strongly opposed to the relaxation of restrictions, the regulars thought it the better part of wisdom to let every man vote at the dictates of his own conscience without concern for an official policy. The liberals argued that this type of evasion would fool no one and reap a bad harvest in the future.

Further dispute came over the apportionment of seats at the state convention, particularly when the central committee gave Negro delegates, most of whom could be expected to support the regulars, an undue proportion of seats. Grosvenor thrust the tariff issue into the fray. Many liberals, including Schurz, were committed to the revenue principle, while the regulars favored protection for a variety of reasons. Prohibition entered the picture to some extent. Governor McClurg refused to serve liquor at receptions in the governor's mansion, giving rise to a fear by the Germans that he might attempt to rigidly control the liquor traffic.

Indeed McClurg became increasingly a storm center. The liberals thought him too much of a party hack because of his long association with the Drake regulars and deplored his antipathy toward the amendments. They began to look for an alternate candidate. Ultimately they rallied behind B. Gratz Brown who emerged from political retirement with a Memorial Day speech at Jefferson City calling for reconciliation and an end to the spirit of animosity.[48]

By the time the Radical state convention met at Jefferson City on September 1 the atmosphere had become electrified with charge and countercharge. Moderates hoped for conciliation through some backstage meetings of responsible leaders, yet no one could be sure what would happen. Although attempts were made to achieve a middle ground, compromise proved impossible with regard to either platform or gubernatorial candidate. The climax came when Carl Schurz,

---

[47] *Missouri Democrat*, Feb. 17 and March 25, 1870; *Missouri Statesman*, Aug. 19, 1870.
[48] *Missouri Democrat*, June 1, 2, 11, 27, Aug. 3, 4, 5, 1870; *Missouri State Times*, June 3, 17, 24, 1870.

as chairman of the resolutions committee, brought in a platform endorsing the amendments. A strong minority, backed by the regulars on the committee, dissented. It concurred in the propriety of submitting the proposals, but would leave each Radical free to vote as he chose. On all other planks the two elements had managed to reach agreement. After agreed upon debate, the convention adopted the minority report by almost a 100-vote margin.

The moment had arrived! All eyes turned to the Liberal leaders. As if by signal, General John McNeil shouted: "I desire to say to the friends of the majority report . . . and to the friends of enfranchisement to the white man, that they will withdraw from this convention to the Senate chamber." Approximately eighty delegates from thirty-five counties followed as he turned and strode from the Hall of Representatives.

Resolving themselves into another convention, the Liberals were augmented by a number of bogus delegations that had not been a part of the regular proceedings. The combined forces elected McNeil temporary chairman and then adjourned until afternoon. The Regulars followed suit.

Attempts by St. Louis moderates to effect a reconciliation during the interim proved futile. That afternoon both groups quickly nominated candidates (the Regulars a slate headed by McClurg, the Liberals one led by Brown) and adopted their respective platforms. That of the Regulars included a vague plank on re-enfranchisement; pledged continuation of present programs, which the Radicals claimed had brought Missouri unprecedented growth and prosperity during the past five years; and warmly endorsed President Grant's administration. The Liberal platform, drawn up by Grosvenor, included all of that editor's cherished ideas: re-enfranchisement, a revenue tariff, civil service reform, tax reduction, and opposition to the alienation of government land to private corporations. Deliberately omitted was any reference to the Grant administration, with which Schurz, Grosvenor, and others were becoming increasingly disenchanted.[49]

So the various elements of the Radical Union party in Missouri came to a formal parting of the ways. Theirs had been a marriage of convenience and never very harmonious. They had bickered among themselves, since the constitutional convention of 1865, about the dimensions of the new order they wished to impose upon Missouri and how it should be done. Unable to find a leader strong enough to

[49] *Missouri Democrat,* Sept. 1–6, 1870; *Missouri Republican,* Sept. 1–6, 1870; Springfield *Missouri Weekly Patriot,* Sept. 8, 1870.

cope with the magic of Charles D. Drake, the Liberals reconciled themselves with the role of vocal minority within the party. Their affinity to Governor Fletcher brought them a fair share of spoils. Drake's refusal to modernize his image and his personal panic and ineptness before Schurz's challenge in 1869 opened the door to the Liberals' hopes for a more progressive party policy under their direction. With the disintegration of Drake's power, however, compromise became increasingly difficult as both wings feared that any concession might result in a diminution of their own political influence. Their inability to find middle ground destroyed the Radical Union party.

With the election only two months away, both groups had to work rapidly. The Liberals, as might be expected, took the offensive. Schurz and other leaders issued a ringing manifesto explaining why they had broken with the regular party. A thorough canvass of the state followed, with enthusiastic crowds flocking to every rally.

The Radicals had trouble getting started. As the full implication of their plight dawned upon them, they began to fumble for the right formula. They had a good record of economic and social progress, yet somehow they could not come to grips with its presentation to the people. Into this climate of uncertainty stepped Charles D. Drake. He returned from Washington in mid-September determined to rescue his party from its lethargy. Stumping the state with his old vituperativeness, he charged the Liberals with selling their souls to the "Rebels" in return for support at future elections.[50]

Although both sides accused each other of plotting with the Democrats, there does not seem to have been any direct collusion by that group with either of the rival elements. The opposition party took no official stand, but various Democratic leaders endorsed the Brown ticket from mid- through late September. These men, together with the rank and file of their party, came quickly to realize that the principles of the Liberals coincided with those for which they had been struggling over the past few years. Furthermore, no amount of shifting by the Radicals could overcome the deep-seated hatreds they had aroused among Democrats during that time.

With the Liberals obviously in the minority, it would take Democratic votes to put their ticket and platform across. The opposition leaders made it clear, however, that any such aid derived from the

---

[50] *Missouri Democrat, passim,* Sept.–Oct., 1870; Frederic Bancroft, ed., *The Writings of Carl Schurz* (New York, 1913), 1:510–18; 2:37–43. For some strange reason, Governor McClurg did not actively campaign. *Missouri State Times,* Oct. 7 and 14, 1870.

expediency of the moment. "The Democratic party does not think at all of abdicating," wrote one editor. "It hopes, on the contrary, to welcome the Liberals into its own camp in 1872." Liberals and Democrats worked out coalitions at the local level where it seemed feasible to do so, but no attempt was made to establish a state-wide pattern. Neither group hesitated to enter into competition with the other, as well as with the Radicals, when it thought it had a chance to elect its own candidate. This particularly held true in legislative contests where the Democrats recognized their real opportunity to seize power for the future.[51]

The Radicals did not completely write off hope for Democratic support. As Democratic endorsements of Brown mounted, the Mc-Clurg men fully realized the danger. Hoping to stem the tide they began reversing themselves in several important ways. Governor McClurg wrote the superintendents of registration and the Radical state chairman urging a liberal interpretation of the registry law. Any man presenting himself as qualified should be enrolled, unless the registrar had direct and open evidence to the contrary.

The registration process got under way in September, with Democrats soon expressing general amazement at the liberal policy of most of the registrars. The release of the final registration figures clearly indicated that proscription had been much less rigorous than on previous occasions. Officially, 199,297 voters had registered as compared with 154,080 in 1868. The newly enfranchised Negroes accounted for 18,000 to 20,000 of this increase. The continuing flow of immigrants also contributed. A notable difference in the figures appeared in Democratic counties where the registrars had been unduly severe in previous contests. The three counties of Boone, Callaway, and Audrain in the heart of "Little Dixie" showed a striking increase of 4,000 registrants over 1868.

On the other hand, many who had voted in 1868 apparently failed to register. The *Missouri Democrat* complained constantly during the closing weeks of the campaign of seeming indifference by much of the potential electorate, especially in the St. Louis area. Final figures for St. Louis County showed 30,671 registered voters on the books, with 2,395 of these Negro and 1,500 new registrants. Analyzing these, the *Democrat* calculated a loss of almost 3,000 voters from 1868.[52]

[51] *Missouri Democrat*, Sept. 14 and Oct. 4, 1870; *Missouri Republican* and *Missouri Statesman, passim*, Sept.–Oct., 1870. The Democrats agreed to support Liberal candidates for Congress in the Second, Fourth, Seventh, and Eighth districts, while the Liberals backed the Democratic nominee in the Sixth district.

[52] *Missouri Republican*, Sept. 24, 1870; *Missouri Statesman*, Sept. 30, 1870; *Missouri Democrat*, Oct. 17, 27, 30, Nov. 8, 1870.

Aware that Democratic support probably hinged on their accept-ance of the amendments, Governor McClurg and other Radical leaders announced that they personally favored re-enfranchisement, although they could not commit their party. The week preceding the election, the secretary of the Radical state central committee sent a confidential circular to county committees and "all true Republicans" requesting them to subjugate all other interests to McClurg's re-election. This included support of local Democratic candidates where that party would agree to swing behind the Governor. The final returns indicate that this policy, even if tried, met with little suc-cess.[53]

With the fight going against them, the Radicals resorted to a broad use of federal and state patronage to keep would-be defectors in line. Drake warned President Grant that the bolt in Missouri marked the beginning of a general rebellion against the administration. To put down this threat, Grant gave the Senator free rein with Missouri patronage. Heads soon began to roll! Simultaneously Governor Mc-Clurg launched a purge of state employees. All state, district, and county officials received notice at the beginning of the campaign that they should contribute the equivalent of 5 per cent of their annual salaries to the party's war chest. Failure to respond promptly might force one to seek new employment.

It is doubtful that this policy won the Radicals many votes, for most Missourians naturally resented this further evidence of politi-cal proscription. The Liberals denounced it vehemently and asserted that it pointed up the need for civil service reform as advocated in their platform.[54]

Both the Radicals and the Liberals went after the votes of the newly enfranchised Negroes. In this, the former were far more success-ful. Their chief spokesman here was J. Milton Turner, long active in the movement for Negro education and suffrage in Missouri. Turner opposed the re-enfranchisement of the "Rebel" whites, which earned him the enmity of the Liberals and led to some questioning by his Negro followers. He had played a major role in the councils of the Radical central committee during the pre-convention planning and later assured McClurg that he could deliver the Negro vote al-most intact. This proved no idle boast. Although the Liberals coun-tered with their own Negro orators, Turner effectively reminded Missouri's black voters that such political, economic, and social gains

[53] *Ibid.*, Sept. 8, Oct. 31, Nov. 5 and 7, 1870; *Missouri Statesman,* Nov. 4, 1870; *Missouri State Times,* Nov. 11, 1870.

[54] *Missouri Democrat,* Sept. 22, 27, Oct. 10, 23, 28, Nov. 4, 1870; St. Joseph *Morn-ing Herald,* Sept. 20, 1870.

as they enjoyed had come to them through the state and national Republican parties. Frederick Douglass, replying to a Negro inquiry from Missouri, emphatically agreed: "In that party the colored voter is a power. There is no safety outside the ship." Most Missouri Negroes heeded this warning.[55]

Election day passed peacefully with better than 160,000 voters going to the polls. This represented an increase of 30,000 over 1868. The electorate ratified all of the amendments by overwhelming majorities. The entire Liberal ticket swept to a smashing victory. B. Gratz Brown outdistanced McClurg by 40,000 votes. With a 13,000-vote margin in St. Louis, he also ran a strong race in the rural areas, carrying 78 counties to McClurg's 36. The latter's vote came largely from the border areas, which remained steadfast to the Radical cause.

The Democrats also scored a significant triumph. They captured four of the five congressional races for which they contended. In three of these their nominee outpolled the total vote cast for both of his rivals. The Radicals and the Liberals split evenly in the four districts where the Democrats did not have a candidate, while a Radical incumbent carried the remaining district over his two opponents.

The greatest Democratic interest centered in the legislative contests, where they carried 77 of the 138 seats in the lower house. In many counties the Liberals had failed to nominate an independent ticket and had thrown their strength to the Democratic slate. Of the remaining seats, the Radicals secured twenty-seven and the Liberals twenty-one, while thirteen went to fusion candidates who could generally be counted on to support any progressive policy agreeable to the others.

Six Democrats and six Liberals were elected to the Senate with the fusionists capturing three seats and two going to the Radicals. Holdover senators numbered ten Radicals and seven Democrats. The Democrats thus possessed an absolute majority in the House and could control the Senate through coalition with the Liberals and fusionists. They also fared well in local contests. Acknowledged Democrats secured nearly three-fourths of the county offices, which augured well for the political rebuilding of the party.[56]

[55] *Missouri Democrat,* July 26, Sept. 7, 10, 29, Oct. 14, 1870; *Missouri State Times,* Sept. 30 and Oct. 14, 1870; Washington, D.C., *New National Era,* Sept. 22, 1870. As a reward for his services, J. Milton Turner received appointment as Minister Resident and Consul General to Liberia, thereby becoming the first Negro to enter the diplomatic corps. See Irving Dilliard, "James Milton Turner: A Little Known Benefactor to His People," *Journal of Negro History* 19 (Oct., 1934): 381.

[56] *Missouri Democrat,* Nov. 12 and Dec. 14, 1870; *Missouri Weekly Patriot,* Nov. 17, 1870; *Missouri Statesman,* Dec. 16 and 23, 1870.

Apparently Schurz and other Liberals hoped to create a new party of principle in the aftermath of their success. But if so, events in Missouri soon diminished that possibility. The Democrats looked upon the election as the rebirth of their own party and took most of the credit for Brown's triumph. Now that the disfranchised could vote once more they anticipated a great swelling of their ranks and saw no need for a new order unless it was of Democratic origin.

Their leaders lost no time in formulating a program for the coming session of the legislature, where they would dominate proceedings for the first time in ten years. Two issues stood foremost in party thinking: a new constitutional convention to revise the hated document of 1865 and the complete repeal, or at least drastic alteration, of the equally despised registry system. Hopefully, Brown and the Liberals would lend their support to both these projects.[57]

Before the legislature convened another task was tossed to it, much to the glee of the Democrats. This was the selection of a new United States senator. In the wake of the Radical defeat, the vanquished had begun to scramble for federal office. Leading the pack was Charles D. Drake, who secured the position of Chief Justice of the Court of Claims at the hand of President Grant.

It quickly became evident that Frank Blair considered himself the natural choice to succeed Drake, and few Democrats could quarrel with him in the light of his party leadership during the lean years. To many, Blair symbolized the resistance to Radical domination they had waged for the past half decade. His nomination by the Democrats forged a tenuous alliance of the Liberals and the Radicals behind the candidacy of John B. Henderson, but all to no avail as Blair swept the joint session without difficulty.[58]

Turning from this success the Democrats, with Governor Brown's help, pushed through a drastic modification of the registry system. Although most of them had called for total repeal during the campaign, the Governor persuaded them that some nominal registration procedure should be retained. As for constitutional revision, the Liberals and the Radicals united sufficiently in the Senate to block the call for a convention. The constitution of 1865 would remain the basic law of Missouri for another four years. When revision came in 1875, its predominant note was the restriction of state and local governmental units in the areas of finance and taxation, a reflection

[57] *Ibid.*, Dec. 2, 1870; Barclay, "The Liberal Republican Movement in Missouri," *Missouri Historical Review* 21 (Oct., 1926): 100.

[58] Rollins Papers, Frank Blair to Rollins, Dec. 14, 1870; Carl Schurz Papers (Library of Congress), Grosvenor to Schurz, Feb. 16, 1871.

of conservative discontent with some of the excesses of the preceding ten years [59]

Missouri politics in the last half of the 1860s had been marked by a turbulence not soon forgotten. Riding the whirlwind of discontent arising out of the war years the Radicals had swept everything before them in 1864. Concerned lest Missouri lose her rightful place in the new order emerging around her, they sought to reconstruct her along progressive lines. Their fear that the representatives of the conservative forces of the past might undo their handiwork led them to excessive measures for suppressing the opposition. They thereby aroused enmities that died hard. Even as their counterparts farther south, they forged within the opposition an *esprit de corps* based on a martyr complex which produced sufficient unity at election time to keep the Democrats in power in Missouri for the next thirty-five years.

Those Radical leaders who did not obtain federal patronage or manage to hold on to local power simply faded into obscurity. Many left the state seeking greener political pastures elsewhere. During their long exile from the state offices, Republican strength remained concentrated in the southwestern and northern border regions and in the German-dominated counties which returned to the fold after 1872. On the border particularly the memories of war-torn Missouri lived long.

[59] Avery and Shoemaker, *Messages and Proclamation,* 5:20–21, 131–32; *Laws of the State of Missouri, 26th General Assembly, Regular Session, 1871* (Jefferson City, Mo., 1871), pp. 67–73; *Senate Journal, 26th General Assembly, Regular Session* (Jefferson City, Mo., 1871), pp. 347–48, 358, 469–70, 499–502. Although the Liberal Republican–Democratic coalition continued in effect in 1872, it was on Democratic terms, and a Democratic governor was elected. This election showed in concrete terms the effect of the removal of voter restrictions. Based on the gubernatorial vote, 111,287 more ballots were cast in 1872 than two years earlier. Many counties nearly doubled their voting strength. After 1872 the Liberal movement completely collapsed, with its members seeking the particular party that best suited their individual needs. Shoemaker, *Missouri and Missourians,* 2:18–22.

CHAPTER TWO

Political Reconstruction in Tennessee, 1865-1870

Thomas B. Alexander

Political reconstruction in Tennessee involved principally two rival groups. One was the ever diminishing element among the white voters of the state that formed the Radical Republican party between 1865 and 1870. The other was a political coalition of former Confederates and Conservative Unionists. The disunion issue in 1861 initially separated Confederates from Unionists; but the Unionists subsequently disagreed among themselves about emancipation, truce or compromise with Confederates, and treatment of defeated foes. Furthermore, the original division on disunion was very substantially dictated by sectionalism within the state, distribution of the slave population, and party affiliation. Most of the political leaders during the immediate postwar years were well known throughout the state before 1861. Any coherent account of Tennessee reconstruction, therefore, must begin with long-standing elements and include the wartime impacts that so pervasively affected state-level politics of the postwar years.[1]

Tennessee extends from the crests of the Appalachian Mountains to the flood plain of the Mississippi River and comprises three geographic sections that were so clearly recognized as to be represented by three stars in the state flag. East Tennessee includes the valley system and the flanking highlands on east and west. Westward of the Cumberland Plateau lies Middle Tennessee, an extended basin surrounded by a highland rim of hills, sometimes referred to as the West Piedmont. West Tennessee consists of a slope westward from the highland rim to the Mississippi lowlands.

[1] This essay is in substantial measure an abridgment of my *Political Reconstruction in Tennessee* (Nashville: Vanderbilt University Press, 1950), now out of print. I am indebted to the Vanderbilt University Press for permission to make unrestricted use in this essay of all material in the book. There is a 1968 reprint publication of this book by Russell & Russell. I am making no effort to show by quotation marks when I am using sentences taken directly from the text of the book, and I am not citing the book hereinafter as a specific source. Source references are herein kept to a minimum because of the full source citations originally made available in the notes for the book. The organization, emphases, and interpretive elements in this essay are the result of a careful restudy of the whole topic in light of publications subsequent to 1950.

East Tennessee is separated from the rest of the state so decisively by the Cumberland Plateau, through which not even a feasible railroad route was surveyed before the end of the nineteenth century, that several separate statehood movements had flared there before 1860. Furthermore, this eastern section lacked a satisfactory river outlet for a staple crop or other bulky commodities. The Tennessee River was navigable within East Tennessee and was plied by steamboats, but the shoals, sucks, and rapids in the river downstream from the Chattanooga area rendered it almost useless for outside contacts. Middle Tennessee, in contrast, had commerical egress through the Cumberland River and to some extent through the Tennessee River, and West Tennessee was flanked by the northward flowing Tennessee on the east and the Mississippi on the west. Interest in railroad development appeared in East Tennessee very early, and governmental assistance to railroad building soon became an article of faith in that area. When during the 1850s rail connections were finally opened southward to the Western and Atlantic Railroad and northeastward to the Virginia and Tennessee Railroad, East Tennesseans felt released from imprisonment and attached extraordinary significance to their hard-won rail outlets.

Signally uneven distribution of slave population affected attitudes of white Tennesseans on Civil War and Reconstruction issues.[2] Negro slaves were more than one-fourth of Tennessee's 1860 total population and were so located as to reinforce geographic sectionalism. Few landowners in mountain, plateau, or very hilly areas had use for slaves, and farmers in East Tennessee's rich valley land had only limited incentive to employ slaves, because of the transportation bottlenecks for staple crops. As a result, in none of the thirty counties of East Tennessee did slaves constitute more than 15 per cent of the population. Twenty of these counties had 10 per cent or less, and eight had 5 per cent or less. In sharp contrast to the limited slaveholding of East Tennessee, the majority of Middle Tennessee counties and almost three-fourths of those in West Tennessee had greater than 15 per cent slave population. One-third of these Tennessee counties outside the Eastern section reported between 16 and 30 per cent slaves, and another third above 30 per cent. One Middle Tennessee county and two in West Tennessee had a majority slave population. It is evident that any issue critically involving either the institution of slavery or anticipated problems of a racial nature would evoke dif-

[2] Population figures are from *Eighth Census of the United States* (Washington, 1864).

ferent responses from Tennesseans on opposite sides of the Cumberland Plateau.

Tennesseans confronting the problems of restoring state government in 1865 were deeply conditioned by a stoutly maintained two-party system that originated a full generation earlier. The Jeffersonian Democratic Republican party was dominant in Tennessee from its admission to the Union in 1796 until 1824. In the division of that party into factions, Andrew Jackson's Tennessee supporters were able to hold their state firmly in line until he was in the White House for a second term. Determined opposition within Tennessee, however, then developed into a strong Whig contingent that opposed Jackson's choice for the succession, Martin Van Buren. Party rivalry within Tennessee was intense from 1835 until the outbreak of the Civil War, in both state and national contests. The governorship fell first to one then to the other party, and neither party was able to win more than 53 per cent of the popular vote in a presidential election after 1840, when the Whigs made their best showing by capturing almost 56 per cent.[3]

Throughout this period most of the voters were firmly aligned with the Democratic or the Whig party. Each party had strength in every portion of the state. So consistent was this political alignment that the political geography of Tennessee could be described as traditional by 1860. The basis of this antebellum party division was evidently a mixture of economic, regional, and personal leadership influences, with probably only slight weight to be assigned to the alleged issues in the several elections. The significance of this division for an understanding of Reconstruction politics in Tennessee is simply that partisan rivalry had before 1860 hardened into a fierce antagonism between political faiths. When the Civil War came, party leaders had for a generation been exhorting their followers to be faithful to party and insisting that little goodness or even sincerity resided in the opposition.

Most of the key political figures of Tennessee's political reconstruction episode established vivid public images long before the Civil War.[4] Among those whose names and personalities were household political commodities in 1860 were Andrew Johnson, the best-known Democrat in the state, and William G. Brownlow, who had founded his newspaper

[3] Election returns are from *The Tribune Almanac, . . . 1838 to 1868* (New York, 1868), and from W. Dean Burnham, *Presidential Ballots, 1836–1892* (Baltimore, 1955).

[4] A good source for the public careers of prominent Tennessee political leaders in the decade before the Civil War is Mary Emily Robertson Campbell, *The Attitude of Tennesseans Toward the Union, 1847–1861* (New York, 1961).

the *Whig* in Elizabethton, moved it to Jonesboro and then to Knoxville, and gained renown for an unrestrained partisan acrimony that had more than once involved him in personal violence. Horace Maynard, three-term Whig congressman from the Knoxville district, was a familiar figure in East Tennessee. A native of Massachusetts and graduate of Amherst, he had migrated to Tennessee in 1838. He was acknowledged to have superior learning and natural ability but was usually viewed as a cold and suspicious man.

William B. Campbell, former governor and Whig congressman, could claim status as elder statesman of his party in Middle Tennessee. Three-term Whig Congressman Emerson Etheridge was perhaps the most prominent West Tennessee officeholder of his party. Other former governors or congressmen were still active in all sections of the state, including Neill S. Brown, whose younger brother would become the "restoration" governor after Reconstruction. When the process of political reorganization after the war began, the voters were contemplating generally familiar names and reputations among the candidates for major offices.

Political party rivalry was translated during the 1860–61 crisis into antagonism on the issue of disunion. Tennessee Whigs interpreted their oft-claimed "Conservative principles" as dictating a cautious and compromising Unionism and blamed the Democratic party for the dangerous level of secession fever in the South. The state Whigs fervently supported their own John Bell as the nation's best hope and were as ardently opposed by Tennessee Democrats backing John C. Breckinridge or Stephen A. Douglas. After Abraham Lincoln's election, almost all Tennessee Whigs and a large portion of the Democrats favored a policy of watchful waiting; but when the Fort Sumter episode and Lincoln's call for troops forced the issue, Middle and West Tennesseans succumbed to disunion fervor, with Democrats in the lead and prominent Whigs reluctant, when not in actual opposition.

East Tennessee remained predominately Unionist, and Whig leaders there spoke of Unionism as the natural course of Whigs and welcomed Democratic Unionists as converts to their side. The greatest acquisition of all was Senator Andrew Johnson, who joined Union Whigs in stumping East Tennessee against disunion and subsequently refused to vacate his Senate seat, denouncing instead the "rebels" and "traitors" and thundering to applauding galleries: "I would have them arrested; and, if convicted, within the meaning and scope of the Constitution, by the Eternal God I would execute them. Sir, trea-

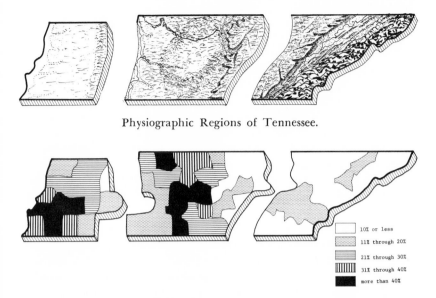

Physiographic Regions of Tennessee.

10% or less
11% through 20%
21% through 30%
31% through 40%
more than 40%

Percentage of Slaves in the Total Population of Tennessee in 1860.

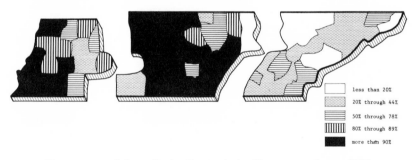

less than 20%
20% through 44%
50% through 78%
80% through 89%
more than 90%

Percentage of Secessionist Strength in Tennessee, June, 1861.

son must be punished. Its enormity and the extent and depth of the offense must be made known."[5]

East Tennessee leaders met in convention and formally submitted a separate-statehood petition that was ignored by the Confederate state legislature. When hostilities began in earnest, many East Tennessee Unionists and some from other parts of the state went into the military service of the United States. Brownlow was imprisoned by Confederate authorities for a time and upon his release went North, where he treated numerous enthusiastic audiences to pyrotechnic dis-

[5] *Congressional Globe,* 36th Cong., 2d sess., 1354.

plays of denunciatory rhetoric and published a lurid volume on his persecution by the "rebels."[6] He succeeded in making himself something of a personification of the martyrdom of southern Unionism.

During the course of the war Confederate sympathizers and Unionists alike experienced occupation by hostile military forces, under which the foundation was laid for much postwar bitterness. In addition, numerous Tennessee Unionists were so dismayed when the war objectives of the United States were expanded to include freedom for the slaves that some even concluded that Confederate success was the preferred choice of evils.[7]

Attempts to restore civil government in Tennessee under federal authority began in the spring of 1862, when Confederate forces evacuated most of Middle and West Tennessee. President Lincoln sent Andrew Johnson back to his home state as a military governor to arrange for restoration of loyal civil government. Johnson's first step toward resurrecting civil government was abortive because the voters of the Nashville area voted for an openly anti-Unionist candidate for the judgeship in contest. Even during 1863 it was not feasible to restore civil elections, although a conservative Whig Unionist element, perturbed by Lincoln's emancipation policy, conducted a token election in Bedford and Shelby counties. Emerson Etheridge of West Tennessee was the leader of this activity, which was an effort to select William B. Campbell for the governorship and have him replace Johnson.

As late as the spring of 1864, county elections ordered by Johnson were unsuccessful because he had required of all voters an oath so strongly Republican in tone as to require opposition to all armistices or negotiations with "rebels" in arms. The apparent repudiation of emancipation by the Northern Democrats in 1864 offered some distraught Tennessee Unionists hope for a conclusion to the war on the original set of objectives, usually expressed by conservative men in terms of "the Union as it was and the Constitution as it is." The presidential election in the fall of 1864 ran afoul of this same oath, however, so that Tennessee Unionists could not vote unless they swore to oppose the platform position of the Northern Democrats. Those Unionists who favored George B. McClellan in the hope that his election would be followed by an early compromise peace with slavery

---

[6] *Sketches of the Rise, Progress, and Decline of Secession; with a Narrative of Personal Adventures among the Rebels* (Philadelphia, 1862). The standard biography of Brownlow is E. Merton Coulter, *William G. Brownlow: Fighting Parson of the Southern Highlands* (Chapel Hill, N.C., 1937).

[7] A case study of one of this class is Thomas B. Alexander, *Thomas A. R. Nelson of East Tennessee* (Nashville, 1956), see especially pp. 97–103.

undisturbed were therefore forced to boycott the election in frustration.[8] The re-election of Lincoln ended that hope and left a significant number of Tennessee Unionists in a limbo between pro-Confederates and unconditional Unionists.

The Tennessee electoral vote of 1864 was not accepted by Congress, which viewed the state as yet unreconstructed, but the election had been a success in the eyes of those unconditional Unionists who supported Lincoln's war objectives. The state executive committee of the political party organization that had conducted the Lincoln campaign now issued a call for a convention to meet in Nashville on December 19, 1864. County meetings were recommended for the selection of delegates. The published notices stated, however: "if you cannot meet in your counties, come upon your own personal responsibility. It is the assembling of Union men for the restoration of their own commonwealth to life and a career of success."[9] The campaign of Confederate General John B. Hood, which ended in his disastrous repulse from Nashville, together with wintry weather that blocked travel between East and Middle Tennessee, necessitated a postponement. Finally, on January 9, 1865, more than five hundred men assembled in Nashville in response to these calls. Some had been selected by local meetings, others were self-appointed, many had not been in the counties they represented for months. This convention launched the restoration of civil government in Tennessee.

A majority of the men in the assemblage at Nashville had not previously held a state political position and would not later occupy one. Ninety-nine were commissioned officers, and Tennessee federal soldiers present were a majority of the convention. Antebellum Whigs outnumbered Democrats eight to one. A core of about fifty men were reasonably prominent in state politics, although no former governor or United States senator was present and only two former congressmen were there. Among these better-known men were several opponents of the Lincoln emancipation policy as well as many who were in full accord with Lincoln. Half of the most experienced men were from East Tennessee, almost half were from Middle Tennessee, while only four were from West Tennessee. A considerable number of the delegates, even some who had no former political experience, would occupy positions of prominence under the restored government. The most serious deficiency of the group in seeking to speak for Tennessee Unionism was the absence of many of the outstanding McClellan

[8] Clifton R. Hall, *Andrew Johnson: Military Governor of Tennessee* (Princeton, 1916).

[9] Joint Select Committee on Reconstruction, 39th Cong., 1st sess., *Report*, 5.

supporters. Having been effectively disfranchised the previous fall by
the oath instituted by the same organization that called the 1865
convention, a large number of sincere Unionists would take no part
in the Nashville proceedings.

This January convention in Nashville took steps that were to be
the subject of controversy throughout the Reconstruction period in
the state. The group initiated constitutional amendments, established
voting requirements, and ordered an election for state government
officials. For the most part, nominations for the legislature were made
by delegates to this convention assembled in county or district caucus
meetings. Some of the members present thought that they were
attending only a party nominating convention and would not participate in any of the other functions that the convention assumed as its
responsibility. Even the original chairman of the business committee,
Judge Daniel C. Trewhitt, asked to be relieved when he found that
more was contemplated than nominations for office. Others present
considered that at the very least they were justified in acting as a
state legislature for the sole purpose of issuing the normally required
legislative call for the election of a constitutional convention. The
dominant voice in the convention came to be for more drastic action,
however, action that could only be justified on the assumption that
the convention was itself a state constitutional convention. This extreme position was defended on the grounds of unprecedented circumstances and the fact that all decisions were to be submitted to the
voters for ratification. In point of fact, since this convention defined
the electorate, the concept of ultimate ratification by the people was
considerably damaged.[10]

Andrew Johnson, manifestly eager to see his state restored swiftly,
apparently favored the convention's acting as a constitutional convention. After a tense but indecisive struggle concerning proper functions of the convention, Johnson broke the deadlock by addressing
the group. Brownlow and many of the East Tennessee delegation had
evidently expected the convention to nominate a slate of one hundred
men to be supported as a state constitutional convention in a subsequent election on the general ticket plan, under which each voter
casts a ballot for a candidate for every seat. But Brownlow accepted
the plan of direct submission of amendments on the grounds of the
popular ratification to follow. Johnson did not want the convention
to go as far as it actually did, however, and was disappointed that his
advice against amending the qualifications for voters was ignored. He

[10] Accounts of the convention proceedings were carried in the Nashville *Dispatch*,
Nashville *Times and True Union*, and Nashville *Union*, Jan. 10–15, 1865.

probably feared another abortive election if vindictive disfranchisement characterized the movement.

The formal proposals of the convention did not come until January 14, after the departure of a large number of delegates who had become discouraged by the delays or disenchanted by the tenor of debate. By action of the convention a plebiscite was called for on Washington's Birthday on a state constitutional amendment prohibiting slavery. Submitted to the voters with this amendment was a schedule that designated those who might vote in the referendum, nullified the disunion action of Tennessee, repudiated all state actions under the Confederate constitution, and made specific provisions for subsequent political action. Johnson's appointments to state offices were ratified, election of a governor and legislature was set for March 4, and East Tennessee was granted a few additional seats in the legislature. The most significant political provision, which was to have important consequences, authorized the first legislature elected under the revised constitution to establish qualifications for voters.[11] Johnson, in his capacity as military governor, issued a proclamation authorizing the elections.

The privilege of voting in the referendum and elections was limited to white, known unconditional Union men and to those taking the oath that had been required for the presidential elections of the preceding November. The oath referred to was not an oath regarding past loyalty, rather it required only a pledge of future loyalty to the United States and, in addition, the sworn statement: "I will cordially oppose all armistices or negotiations with rebels in arms." Actually, almost every white man in Tennessee could have qualified had he been willing to acknowledge the hopelessness of the Confederate cause two months before Lee's surrender and to agree to unconditional surrender of the Confederate forces in the field. Probably some Tennesseans still held a desperate hope for Confederate success, but this perhaps was not the real issue. The fate of Confederate soldiers and the terms granted to the defeated people might well depend on whether the surrenders were unconditional or the result of negotiations before arms were laid down. Many prominent Tennessee leaders had advised against taking this oath a few months earlier, during the presidential campaign. Undoubtedly this advice still carried weight with many potential voters, keeping them from the polls in February and March.

---

[11] The text is published in Joint Select Committee on Reconstruction, 39th Cong., 1st sess., *Report*, 6–7.

The most important reason for failure to qualify and vote in the elections directed by the convention, aside from inconvenience or indifference, was unwillingness to support a policy of punishment for Confederates or to place in control of the state government a group of Unionists, running without opposition, whose chief spokesman sought revenge rather than accommodation after hostilities should end. The full impact of influences militating against voting cannot be recognized without taking into account that the whole movement for these elections was characterized by the attitudes of its sole nominee for the governor's chair, Brownlow. Editors supporting Brownlow made it abundantly clear that his policies would be vindictive. Typical of these comments was one by the Nashville *Union* editor (February 9, 1865): "We can rest assured that *leaders* of the rebellion will be punished if they venture on Tennessee soil again. Union men will be fully protected. *All* who have outlawed themselves by joining in the conspiracy will get what they deserve under him." Brownlow's own paper, re-established in Knoxville under the title *Whig and Rebel Ventilator*, carried many incendiary editorials. During the meeting of the January convention there appeared an editorial in typical *Whig* style (January 11, 1865):

. . . peace loving, constitutional, conservative, fence-riding, half-Union, half-rebel, half horse and half alligator men, of East Tennessee, complain at the severity of the articles written by the editor of this paper, and ascribe to their influence the murder of many of the rebels who have been welcomed with bloody hands to hospitable graves, since the Federal occupation of this end of the State. If we have been instrumental by our speeches or editorials, in bringing to a violent death any one or more of the God-forsaken and hell deserving persecutors of Union families in East Tennessee, we thank God most devoutly—shall take encouragement from the past and do more of the same sort of work!

Voluntary boycott of the elections was justified in the views of many Unionists and former Confederates on the grounds that a preferred optional course was open. Nashville newspapers carried numerous excerpts from national papers thought to be spokesmen for the Lincoln administration, all pointing to a peace in which punishment was not contemplated and political arrangements were to be restored to their antebellum condition swiftly, without disfranchising Confederates. The Washington *Chronicle* was widely thought to be a Lincoln organ and was quoted in the Nashville *Press* on January 17, 1865, just after the convention had adjourned, to the effect that Confederates "will have lost, and lost forever, the institution of slavery . . . but they will have lost nothing else. Their religious, their political and civil rights will remain to them. They will be equal in everything of those who defeated their attempt to break up the Union." Similar editorial comments from the New York *Times,* the New York *Herald Tribune,* and numerous other Northern sources appeared almost daily in the Nashville press.

East Tennessee had no conservative daily newspaper, and West Tennessee was still too disrupted for any substantial communication. But political leaders in all portions of the state were undoubtedly thoroughly aware of a more lenient attitude in places of power. Although Lincoln's "with malice toward none; with charity for all" was not delivered until the day of the second election, March 4, this attitude was manifest much earlier. Division of sentiment on the question of treatment of former Confederates, then, exerted a decisive influence in determining who would participate in these elections intended to restore civil government in the state. Those who abstained from participation could look to notable Union leaders in all parts of the state who shared an unsympathetic attitude toward Brownlow's posture—men like Thomas A. R. Nelson and John Baxter in East Tennessee, William B. Campbell in Middle Tennessee, and Emerson Etheridge in West Tennessee.

Brownlow, aware of the danger to his movement from conservative Unionists, editorially divided politics in Tennessee into three parts: "the Radical Union party, which had voted for Lincoln and Johnson and controlled the January convention"; "Rebels"; and the "Conservative-Constitutional-Peace party" that would coalesce with returning Confederates.[12] This editorial urged unswerving Union men to guard against the third party more than against rebels. By speeches and editorials the proponents of the convention's program pleaded for a large turnout, mentioning such hoped-for vote totals as sixty thousand or even one hundred thousand. The total popular vote in the state in the presidential election of 1860 had not reached one hundred and fifty thousand.

Brownlow's opponents, hoping that this entire effort would be just one more of the abortive attempts to restore civil government, begun as early as 1862, sought to keep the vote small by ignoring the election. Newspapers in opposition published nothing about the elections except paid, official notices. In the referendum of February 22 only 25,293 votes were cast for the constitutional amendment and schedule to 48 against. This small vote nevertheless represented more than the minimum of 10 per cent required by the Lincoln proclamation of 1863, and Johnson promptly proclaimed the amendment operative

[12] Knoxville *Whig,* Feb. 1, 1865.

and authorized organization of civil government. On March 4, therefore, the state elections were held—with polls opened in three-fifths of the East Tennessee counties, two-thirds of the Middle Tennessee counties, and Shelby County (where Memphis was located) alone in West Tennessee. The total vote was slightly more than 23,000.[13]

The status of freedmen was not a significant source of contention in Tennessee in the spring of 1865. That slavery was finished was too clear to contest, and little issue was made among whites of the civil or political rights to be accorded Negroes. Only an occasional mention of political rights for loyal men of whatever color was found in the Tennessee press. On the contrary, even the unconditional Unionists seemed to go out of their way to affirm their opposition to enlarging freedmen's rights. During the January convention sessions several strong racist statements were made. Roderick R. Butler of East Tennessee, soon to be a Republican congressman, drew applause from the delegates with his affirmation that he would never consent to the Negro's being equal with the white man. Butler later proposed, then withdrew, a section for the constitutional amendment to be submitted to referendum that would have forever excluded all Negroes, Indians, and "persons of mixed blood" from voting, holding office, or being competent witnesses against a white man.[14]

In a major address before the convention Harvey M. Watterson of Middle Tennessee disposed of the Negro consideration in the following words:

> This brings me to the everlasting *nigger*—that dark fountain from which has flowed all our woes. . . . I have always thought if the people of Tennessee, Kentucky, Maryland, Virginia, and Missouri were paid a fair price for their slave property, and the colored population removed beyond their limits, it would be a good operation for the *whites*. . . . Will the people of Tennessee permit the valueless negro to stand between them and the reestablishment of civil government. I cannot, I do not believe it. . . . I would not give one year of virtuous civil rule for all the *darkies* in America![15]

Judge James O. Shackelford of Middle Tennessee, in an appeal to the citizens of his judicial circuit to support the January convention plan by voting, felt called upon to affirm:

> You are told by the enemies of the Government the Federal authorities . . . will make the negro your equal, giving him social and political rights. Those who make such statements know them to be false, or are so profoundly ignorant that they are unworthy to be freemen. . . .

---

[13] Returns are in Tennessee *House Journal,* Brownlow Assembly, 1st sess., 16.
[14] Nashville *Press,* Jan. 13 and 14, 1865.
[15] Nashville *Dispatch,* Jan. 14, 1865.

He is inferior to the white man, and will be controlled and governed by him, subject to such laws as may be proposed for his government. . . . The God of nature has placed His fiat upon it, and no power on earth can make him the equal of the Anglo-Saxon; but as christian men we can elevate them in the scale of human beings. . . . They are human beings, with immortal souls, and as such, it is our duty as the superior race, to control, govern and elevate them from the degraded situation in which they are.[16]

It might have been possible for the Conservatives to have seized the reins in early 1865 had appropriate leadership and organization emerged somewhat sooner than actually occurred. The January convention converted itself so swiftly into an action group that the Conservatives were caught off guard. Military Governor Johnson had the power to make the January convention decisions effective and the power to accept the results of the meagerly supported elections in February and March. Boycotting these elections left the Conservatives almost entirely on the outside for the moment. A different course of events that would have established Conservatives as the controlling element or at least a partnership element in state government probably would have made little difference in the ultimate outcome of Reconstruction in Tennessee. Had the Conservatives won greater power, the legislature would have rejected the proposed Fourteenth Amendment, and the result would undoubtedly have been inclusion of Tennessee under the military Reconstruction measures of March, 1867. Conservatives might have had a more difficult time gaining control had this course eventuated. Radical authority was probably briefer for having seized control early enough to shield Tennessee from congressional Reconstruction.

The success of Radical Unionists in taking control of the state government in the process of restoring civil administration was a keen disappointment to the Conservatives. Radicalism and Conservatism were already in use as political terms of distinction, despite the fact that they did not yet define wholly identifiable opposing groups. There came to be a Radical and a Conservative view on each major question which confronted the political leaders or voters, and many of the leaders were inconsistent. The process of separation into definite parties was not sudden. Brownlow and the followers who finally constituted the core of his Radical party were a residual group after several losses of support. The process may be traced in a general way from the first election on the question of disunion, that of February, 1861, in which a large majority of Tennessee voters were Unionist. The calling of troops by Lincoln reduced that Unionist majority to

16 Nashville *Union*, Feb. 11, 1865.

a substantial minority in the election of June, 1861. Among the Unionist voters there were many who accepted the separation verdict and actively or passively supported the Confederacy. During the war others from the remaining Union group defected because of the emancipation policy of Lincoln, and in the 1864 presidential election, so many Tennessee Unionists seemed intent on supporting McClellan that the special clause against armistices or "negotiations with rebels in arms" was added to the test oath to assure a Lincoln victory in the state. With the war almost at an end, treatment of former Confederates and the actual manner of concluding hostilities were issues that caused the McClellan supporters and some of the other residual Unionists to sheer off.

During the Radical régime in Tennessee, additional steps unacceptable to the Conservatives continued to reduce Brownlow's support until Negro enfranchisement was the only way he could keep his faction in power, and this step in turn cost him further white support. The Radical party in Tennessee soon, therefore, mustered only a few thousand white voters, disproportionately East Tennesseans, and it lost control of the state government as early as 1869.

The legislature that convened on April 3, 1865, was known as the Brownlow Assembly. Almost half of the members had been delegates to the January convention and had been placed on the general ticket by their fellow delegates. Virtually all of the legislators were native-born Tennesseans or long-time residents of the state. The overwhelming majority were antebellum Whigs, a fact commented on triumphantly by the Knoxville *Whig* (April 19, 1865) as showing the "inclinations of the parties in this state to go into the rebellion." The majority were formerly slaveholders, and the occupations of the members fitted a pattern of political activity typical of earlier years. In general, the Brownlow Assembly began with a composition adequate to lend prestige and authority to the new régime, although most of the more prestigious members were gone before the term ended.[17]

[17] The great majority of the legislators had no prior political office-holding experience and would have none after Radical power was broken in the state. One-third of the senators and one-fourth of the representatives were men of considerable experience in state or county offices, a few with long records of political activity. Probably the amount of experience represented by this legislature was equal to that of a customary legislature of the antebellum years. Long service, even a second term, was not the rule for state legislators. A change for the worse occurred before the end of this legislative term of office, however, because many resignations resulted from the bitter struggles on controversial issues; and significantly the men of greatest political experience were the ones most likely to resign.

Governor Brownlow was inaugurated on April 5 and immediately sent a lengthy message to the legislature calling attention to several obvious needs of the state, advising that secession was an abomination that could not be legislated against too severely and that those responsible for the misery of the war ought to be excluded entirely from the government of the state, and urging that the privilege of voting be guarded effectually against the "approach of treason." A working majority in each house followed the bulk of the governor's recommendations. Stringent criminal statutes were adopted in the hope of bringing the postwar crime wave under control. A reward was offered for the apprehension of the secessionist governor of 1861, Isham G. Harris. The Thirteenth Amendment to the United States Constitution was ratified without opposition.

When senators were selected, the choices fell on men not identified with the more extreme Radical attitudes. Judge David T. Patterson, Andrew Johnson's son-in-law, won the seat allocated by custom to East Tennessee. Patterson defeated Horace Maynard, despite Brownlow's support for Maynard, whose extremely vindictive attitude evidently alienated many legislators. Joseph S. Fowler won the Middle Tennessee seat over a man more openly allied with the Brownlow faction, William H. Wisener. In the United States Senate neither man acted to suit Brownlow; Fowler drifted away from Radicalism and refused to vote for conviction of Johnson in the impeachment trial, and Patterson was from the beginning a Conservative in the Senate. Disquieting tendencies were therefore evident to Brownlow from the beginning of his administration. It is probable that the state legislators were willing to follow the governor's lead whenever they were convinced that the party's control of the state government was in jeopardy. When, on the other hand, the loaves and fishes were to be distributed, less subservience was to be expected. Furthermore, in antebellum Tennessee politics, the governor had customarily been expected to be reasonably neutral in the intraparty senatorial contests in caucus meetings.

The elective franchise bill was the key to Radical control of the state. An effort to deny voting privileges to all former Confederates appeared to have little organized opposition in the Senate, but encountered sufficient resistance in the House to force a tempering. Edmund Cooper of Middle Tennessee, soon to be elected to Congress, led such a determined opposition to disfranchising former Confederates that for a time it seemed improbable that such a measure could clear the House. Even the speaker, William Heiskell, was opposed to a Radical measure. A persuasive argument with the Unionists, however, was that without such disfranchisement the state would not be readmitted to its place in Congress, and, as a result, Tennessee loyalists would not be able to get damages for property taken by federal forces during the war. Loyalists' claims were many and large and played a powerful role in political maneuvering in Tennessee.

The bill which finally did pass was a Radical one, albeit not as Radical as Brownlow had wanted. A retroactive principle was applied so that the mass of former Confederates were disfranchised for five years and their leaders for fifteen. The suffrage for the moment was limited to men "publicly known to have entertained unconditional Union sentiments from the outbreak of the rebellion until the present time"; men reaching twenty-one after March 4, 1865, providing that they had not engaged in armed rebellion; citizens of proven loyalty from other states; citizens serving as United States soldiers or honorably discharged from such service; Union men forcibly drafted into the Confederate army, on testimony of two admitted voters; and men who had voted in the elections of November, 1864, or February or March, 1865, or who had already taken the oath of allegiance to the United States and would have voted in any of those elections had they been held within reach.[18] A system of voter registration by county court clerks was established in the act, with proof under oath that the applicant qualified required before the issuance of a certificate. The legislature took care to reserve to its subsequent session or sessions the authority granted in the constitutional amendment to this legislature alone to adjust the voting requirements.

The first election after the adoption of the franchise act was one held in August of 1865 for United States representatives. Conservatives had no further justification for boycotting the political procedure and little hope that the Brownlow movement could be set aside as fraudulent. Registration was encouraged, therefore, and a group of notable men sought the seats in Congress. The election was almost entirely a Whig affair. Twenty-three candidates received support worthy of mention; seventeen were well-known Whigs, one was a prominent Democrat, and five were not classifiable as to antebellum political affiliation (three, at least, had not participated in political activity before the war). None but Whigs came close to victory. It appears that the great bulk of Democrats were disfranchised through acceptance of disunion and that their leaders could see nothing to gain by seeking election.

During the course of the congressional campaign, positions were somewhat clarified. An extreme Conservative position denied the

[18] *Acts* of Tennessee, Brownlow Assembly, 1st sess., 32–36.

validity of the Brownlow régime and proposed to replace it with a legitimate one at the first opportunity. A moderate Conservative view conceded the legitimacy of the existing state government but was opposed to disfranchisement or any proscriptive legislation. Even Radicalism was not easily defined. Some extreme Radicals followed Brownlow's lead closely and apparently favored the most proscriptive policy possible. Other shades of Radicalism less extreme than Brownlow's were represented by candidates for Congress. The popular vote in the congressional contests was certainly not limited to a Conservative versus Radical dichotomy. War records, experience, and simply familiarity with a candidate's name were obviously important.

The outcome of the elections was disappointing to Brownlow because less than a majority of the votes cast went to candidates approving his policies. One-fifth were cast for candidates openly opposed to his entire program, and another two-fifths were for candidates less Radical than Brownlow and potentially his political opponents. Of the eight men elected, only three acted consistently with the Radicals in Congress. One, Benjamin Hawkins, was on the fence; and four proved to be outright Conservatives in Congress. The governor had been able to save a seat for one of the Radicals only by investigating alleged violations of the franchise law and throwing out the returns from enough boxes to reverse the original outcome in the Sixth District. Samuel M. Arnell, author of the franchise act, had lost out to an extreme Conservative, Dorsey B. Thomas, and could be rescued only by these extraordinary steps. The August elections, therefore, demonstrated to Brownlow that he had no adequate control of the electorate and that the registration procedure was not, in his judgment, trustworthy.

The legislature reassembled in October of 1865, seriously depleted in experienced leadership by resignations. Governor Brownlow again presented a typically wide array of state problems that he thought required legislative action. He encouraged enticements for immigrants, especially from Germany, as a far better way to regenerate the South than the "sudden and compulsory admission of the blacks to the ballot box." He pleaded for pay increases for judges and other state officers to halt a wave of resignations. He outlined the problems of railroads and banking institutions, and the needs of state institutions, and advocated a relief law to protect debtors faced with mortgage foreclosures. His proposed solution for intemperance was a prohibitory tax on alcoholic beverages.

Brownlow's keenest concern was to have the franchise act appropriately amended, and he condemned those who mistook submission to necessity for true repentance among former Confederates. The Governor specifically advised against enfranchising Negro men, offering the usual arguments concerning incompetence and adding mention of his fear that rural Negroes would be influenced by landowners, most of whom were formerly Confederate sympathizers in the counties where Negroes were most numerous. He did advise scrutiny of all laws pertaining to Negroes so as to adjust these to new conditions, particularly with regard to allowing Negro testimony in court, which he favored. Brownlow devoted considerable space to his premonition that the two races could not live together satisfactorily and expressed a hope that some Negro state could be organized, perhaps in Texas. He explicitly advised that the determination of voting requirements was a state power that could not be taken over by the federal government. As for advice from the North, he thought that the condition of Negroes in many Northern states suggested that those states had best attend to the beams in their own eyes first.[19]

The legislature was reluctant to respond to the more controversial aspects of the governor's recommendations, and the fall passed with little significant legislation. Negro testimony was finally authorized, but only after Brownlow personally intervened to urge passage in order to rid the state of Freedmen's Bureau courts and to satisfy Negro people and thereby, he hinted, forestall Negro suffrage by federal government action. The Governor also maintained that the measure was right in itself, in addition to being politic for other reasons. The most stubborn opposition came from East Tennessee members, whose constituents had little cause to be alarmed by the few Freedmen's Bureau activities there and hence had less to gain.

National developments formed a significant frame of reference for the legislative struggle over tightening the franchise act. During the late winter President Johnson came to an open break with the congressional Radicals with his veto of the bill to extend the life of the Freedmen's Bureau. Conservatives in Tennessee were jubilant at this evidence that Johnson was taking their side and called a mass meeting in Nashville on Washington's Birthday, 1866, to endorse the President's stand. That this meeting came at the height of the legislative battle over voting requirements was certainly no coincidence, nor did Brownlow consider it to be such. The regular elections for county officers in March, 1866, alarmed Brownlow greatly because Conservatives made a clean sweep in Middle and West Tennessee counties. Revision of the franchise law was now more urgently required than

[19] Tennessee *House Journal*, Brownlow Assembly, 1st Adjourned sess., 5–26.

ever, in Brownlow's opinion, because the county officials registered voters and conducted elections.

In February the Conservatives had filibustered as long as they could against the franchise bill amendments and then had reduced the House below a quorum by resignations. In special elections called to fill the vacancies, four new Radical representatives were selected under questionable electoral circumstances in their counties. The House mustered a bare quorum thereby, expelled the dozen Conservatives who had resigned and been re-elected, and passed the franchise bill on April 12, 1866. Crying fraud, Conservatives made every effort to block passage of the bill through the Senate, but, under threat of a "new" state" movement in East Tennessee that bore evidence of manipulation, enough senators quailed to let the bill through. A Conservative state circuit judge ruled the law unconstitutional but was overruled by the Brownlow-appointed state supreme court.

The new law practically placed the privilege of voting under direct control of the governor. All previous registrations were voided, and commissioners appointed by the governor were to hold all registrations. The opportunity for registration by those claiming that they would have voted in November, 1864, or February or March, 1865, was deleted. No ambiguity was left about the requirement that two witnesses from among recognized voters were necessary to substantiate the right to register claimed by anyone who was challenged by a voter. The law furthermore authorized commissioners to hear proof contravening the proof offered by an applicant and made the commissioners judges of the weight of conflicting testimony. The opportunity to register and vote was thereby made largely dependent on decisions by men appointed by Governor Brownlow. Furthermore, all former Confederates, even nonparticipating sympathizers, were disfranchised permanently.[20]

The major cities of the state were a concern to the Governor both because of crime waves and because of political opposition to his programs. At his request the legislature created metropolitan police districts for Memphis, Nashville, and Chattanooga, under the control of powerful boards appointed by the governor. Knoxville apparently was well enough governed to be left alone, especially since it was in Radical Congressman Horace Maynard's district and was the home of Brownlow's paper, the *Whig*.

The second session of the Brownlow Assembly had only recently adjourned when it had to be recalled to consider ratification of the

---

[20] *Acts* of Tennessee, Brownlow Assembly, 1st Adjourned sess., 42–48.

Fourteenth Amendment. Fusion between national and Tennessee Conservatives was nearly complete by July 4, 1866, when the called session convened, and Brownlow was openly allied with congressional Radicals. Conservatives failed to block ratification in the state senate, but enough absented themselves from the house to prevent assembling of a quorum. On order from the house, two absent members were finally apprehended and brought to Nashville. Before a writ of habeas corpus could be served, the majority of the house overruled the speaker, counted the two prisoners present to reach a quorum, and passed the ratification resolution. Jubilantly Brownlow wired the clerk of the United States Senate that the battle was won, adding: "My compliments to the 'dead dog' of the White House."[21] The irate legislators impeached, removed from office, and disfranchised Judge Thomas N. Frazier, who had issued the habeas corpus writs in the attempt to extricate from house arrest the two detained legislators.

After word reached Washington of the ratification action by Tennessee's legislature, the state's representation to Congress was finally seated. An effort to hold up seating of the Tennessee delegation until voting privileges had been granted to the state's Negro men did not gain much support on the roll-call votes authorizing admission.

The last session of the Brownlow Assembly convened in November of 1866 with a working majority of Radicals in both houses as a result of some special elections to fill vacancies. The new franchise law had worked well enough to guarantee Radical victory in these elections, and Conservatives could no longer break a quorum by absenteeism or resignation. Brownlow advised the session that several aspects of state affairs required action, with salaries for judges, needs of state institutions, and state support of railroads again in the spotlight. Negro suffrage was the main order of business, however, because this was the last opportunity to amend the voting requirements without a constitutional amendment, which could not have been adopted and ratified against Conservative opposition. Brownlow frankly stated that Tennessee Conservatives had such powerful support from national Conservatives, led by President Johnson, that he feared a plot to overthrow his administration by force.

Some of the extreme Conservatives in Tennessee, publicizing their views through the press, especially the Memphis *Avalanche,* gave the

---

[21] Several versions of this telegram got into newspapers. One is in Nashville *Press and Times,* July 2, 1866; another is in Knoxville *Whig,* July 25, 1866, quoted in Coulter, *Brownlow,* p. 315.

Governor ample ammunition to use in his charge of a conspiracy to unseat him. Denouncing every measure of the Brownlow administration as void, some of these extreme Conservatives had advocated a grass-roots citizens' movement of all adult white men to send a convention to Nashville, adopt a state constitution, and submit it to Congress for acceptance—just as though a new state were being created. Brownlow now advised that only by the assistance of Negro votes could the loyal men of the state prevent a triumph by rebels. He also referred to what he believed to be the drift of national opinion on the subject of Negro voting, a greater aptitude among Negroes than had been anticipated, and a disheartening persistence of disloyalty among former Confederates. But his chief reason was political self-preservation.[22]

Before taking up the question of Negro suffrage, the legislature made nonqualification for voting a ground for challenge as to the competency of any juror. Radicals argued that this step was necessary because convictions for violation of the franchise law, which the Governor claimed would be numerous, could not be obtained from juries that included the disfranchised. The effect was to exclude former Confederates from most juries and thereby to militate against their chances for justice in cases where passions were aroused.

When the legislature had not enacted a bill for Negro suffrage by mid-January, 1867, the Governor prodded with another message stating categorically that without Negro votes the state would pass into disloyal hands in the coming August elections. The strongest opposition among Radicals came from East Tennessee. Brownlow addressed himself assiduously to overcoming this resistance, denying that the privilege of voting implied racial equality and asking his East Tennessee supporters: "Think of some low white man in your community you would not dine with—does his casting a ballot make him your social equal?"[23] The legislators ultimately saw the hopelessness of their party position without Negro voting support and passed the measure, but East Tennessee members were lukewarm. Furthermore, the privileges of sitting on juries and holding political office, normally accorded voters, were explicitly denied to Negro voters in this bill.[24]

Tennessee became the first state in which large numbers of Negroes voted and, indeed, decisively controlled the outcome of state elections. The question naturally arises whether the enfranchisement of the

[22] Tennessee *Senate Journal*, Brownlow Assembly, 2d Adjourned sess., 10–22.
[23] Knoxville *Whig*, Jan. 30, 1867.
[24] *Acts* of Tennessee, Brownlow Assembly, 2d Adjourned sess., 27–33.

freedmen in Tennessee was the result of local considerations or a reflection of the surging tide in Congress and among Radical Republicans of the North. Governor Brownlow had roundly denounced those of the North who would seek to interfere in the internal affairs of Tennessee, and he had expressed the gravest doubts about the capacity of freedmen to participate in the political system of the country. Nevertheless, he had from time to time during 1865 and 1866 made public pronouncements that seemed to leave open the door for a change of position on his part. When in the winter of 1866–67 he asked the legislature for the extension of voting privileges to Negro men, he was surely influenced by a number of considerations both within and outside Tennessee.

In the first place, after September of 1866 he unhesitatingly and often affirmed candidly that the Republicans could not retain control of Tennessee in state general elections without the help of Negro voters. This conviction alone would have been sufficient to cause him to desire Negro enfranchisement, but not sufficient to bring him to sponsorship of a hopeless endeavor. Other Radical Republicans in Tennessee had to share his belief that without the votes of Negroes the Conservatives and Democrats would win control of the state government. Furthermore, unless a large portion of Brownlow's following became convinced that to permit Negroes to vote was somehow respectable and in the national mainstream of developments, the Governor would have been hard pressed to force Tennessee into a uniquely Radical posture. Developments in the North, then, as well as internal Tennessee circumstances, were probably each indispensable to the success of his proposal.

Brownlow was probably relieved when he was able to come out in open hostility toward Andrew Johnson. The interlude of co-operation on Unionism grounds was, after all, an exception to the lifelong political hostility of the Whig editor toward the Democratic party chieftain. When Brownlow announced his return to the role of Johnson-baiter, he placed his decision substantially on the basis that Johnson was evidently attempting to rejuvenate the old, hated Democratic party.[25] After Johnson and the Radical Republicans were openly at war, and after Johnson's backers promoted the Philadelphia National Union Convention of August, 1866, to seek coalescence around the President's Reconstruction policies, Brownlow with all of his antebellum and wartime gusto led a large Tennessee delegation

[25] Thomas B. Alexander, "Strange Bedfellows: The Interlocking Careers of T. A. R. Nelson, Andrew Johnson, and W. G. (Parson) Brownlow," East Tennessee Historical Society's *Publications*, no. 24 (1952): 68–91.

to the Radical counterattack, the Southern Loyalist Convention in Philadelphia in September of 1866. There he was repeatedly placed in the limelight and cheered as lustily as during his wartime speaking engagements.

The Southern Loyalists present at this convention were, of course, openly allied with Radical Republicans and could see no hope of gaining control of their home states unless the vote could be extended to the Negro men. Hence, somewhat to the discomfort of many of the Northern Republicans present as "honorary" delegates, they fervently advocated Negro suffrage. In this infectious atmosphere, Brownlow espoused the objective and promised to bring it to pass in his home state the following winter. He then participated in an extended speaking tour through the North in the campaign to counter President Johnson's "swing around the circle." Damning Johnson was old hat for Brownlow, and to do it to the delighted cheers of Northern Radical audiences was a kind of ratification of a lifetime stand.[26] By the time he returned to Tennessee, Brownlow had probably consumed in the crucible of white-hot polemics all his mental reservations about Negro voting. His recognition of the political advantage of Negro voting was emotionally vindicated, and he was ready for action.

Tennessee legislators were not as ready as their governor, however. They were fully aware that this was their last opportunity to amend the voting requirements, because only this first legislature, elected under the amended constitution, had been given that right. The succeeding legislature could not take the action on Negro suffrage advocated by Brownlow. Only a constitutional amendment (manifestly impossible) could accomplish the purpose after the expiration of the terms of the sitting legislators. Still, the absolute necessity of an action these men were deeply reluctant to take had to be demonstrated. Brownlow had something to say on the subject beyond the mere prediction of failure at the polls. He described what he understood to be a conspiracy, of which the President was a chief manipulator, to overthrow the Brownlow régime by force. His request that the legislature authorize the enlistment of several regiments of a state guard to protect the political authorities underscored how seriously he was viewing his administration's jeopardy.

Brownlow probably believed that such a conspiracy was afoot. His recent experiences in the North had inundated him with charges

[26] Coulter, *Brownlow*, pp. 318–22; James M. McPherson, *The Struggle for Equality: Abolitionists and the Negro in the Civil War and Reconstruction* (Princeton, 1964), pp. 360–63.

from all sides that Johnson was engaged in a national conspiracy. And the extreme Conservative press in Tennessee provided fuel for the fires of his imagination through a succession of indiscreet editorials. As early as April of 1866, after their defeat in the electoral franchise struggle of that month, Tennessee Conservative legislators met in caucus and adopted a plan to ask President Johnson to permit the selection of a state constitutional convention in an election in which no antebellum voters would be disfranchised. This convention was then to restore a state government in total disregard of the Brownlow régime. This same caucus at a second meeting backed down from the proposal, but its first action had aroused fears.[27] After the ratification of the Fourteenth Amendment by the Tennessee legislature, the idea of a popularly selected convention to supersede the existing state government was renewed. The Memphis *Commercial* (July 20, 1866) and other extreme Conservative papers editorially sponsored such a plan. President Johnson and his Conservative advisors wished to avoid any action in Tennessee that might damage Conservative chances in the 1866 congressional elections in the North and managed to put a stop to the effort. Yet Tennessee papers continued to carry reports that Northern Conservatives and the national administration would sustain Tennessee Conservatives if in August of 1867 they should nominate a man for governor and elect him in an extra-legal election in which the voting restrictions of the Brownlow régime should be ignored.

In judging whether Brownlow actually believed that his administration was in any danger of being supplanted by such a *coup*, one should not overlook the tone of the extreme Conservative editorials. The Memphis *Avalanche* pronouncements matched in lack of restraint those of Brownlow's own *Whig*. On January 7, 1866, the *Avalanche* carried a description of the legislators as "men scraped together from all the ignorant and unworthy parts of society—the scrubs, the curs, 'the bats'—for the single merit that they advocate the proscription of their countrymen, and can vote in the coarse interest of revenge." The *Avalanche,* in reply to charges of fomenting revolution, declared on February 9:

It is true, in speaking of the mean and cowardly Radicals in the Tennessee Legislature and in the Congress of the United States, who are seeking to humiliate and disgrace the rebel soldier, we have spoken in no honied words. The worm in the dust will squirm when the heel is upon its head, and this

---

[27] J. B. Bingham to Andrew Johnson, May 17, 1866, Andrew Johnson Papers, Division of Manuscripts, Library of Congress (LC), describes these caucus meetings fully.

complaint of the South at the proposed persecutions by the Radicals is the natural outgushing of human nature. A remonstrance against the cruelty and oppressions of blind fanatics is not getting up a revolution.

On April 22, 1866, the following editorial comments were published:

If the Radicals in West Tennessee had the power, they would adopt the same atrocities, and the rebels here would be assassinated or driven from their homes, as has been done in East Tennessee. . . . Since they cannot in this part of the State, assassinate, kill and murder rebels, and take possession of their property, they propose to give a greasy, filthy, stinking negro the right to crowd them from the polls, to exercise those rights of franchise which belong not to indians and negroes, but to white men. . . . For a while they were deceived as to their strength. . . . The late elections in this county undeceived them. Only one hundred and one men were found base enough to vote for the Radical ticket. We have held up the names of a portion of these men, and written small pox over their doors in order that our people might shun them. Now that trade has forsaken them, and they see that the people they propose to degrade are not cravens enough to feed and fatten them, they curse the *Avalanche,* and resort to that stale devise of worsted foes—PERSECUTION!

The following was published on May 23, 1866, in answer to the question as to why Radicalism thrived in cities and towns but not in rural areas: "The Radicalism *per se* will not venture to settle among a brave people who, though law-abiding, will suffer no innova-, tions upon their social forms. Radicals never go beyond the reach of the negger [*sic*] Bureau, and, therefore, as they cannot spit their venom in the country without having their filthy jaws slapped by Southern (gentlemen,) they take care to remain within the protection of the ebony line."

Tennessee legislators and Governor Brownlow might have been convinced that President Johnson would somehow back Tennessee Conservatives in overturning the existing Tennessee government. The stunning defeat encountered by Johnson supporters in the autumn 1866 congressional elections, however, must have raised grave doubts about Johnson's capacity to furnish any effective assistance to such an endeavor. Tennessee's representation in Congress had already been seated, furthermore, so that the state was very unlikely to be included under any of the plans for congressional Reconstruction that were being debated in Congress between December, 1866, and March, 1867.

To remain in office and control the governmental structure is a normal enough motive for even extraordinary political actions on the part of a party. To precipitate an upheaval of the customary political system, such as was involved in admitting Negro men to voting privileges, required, one is inclined to believe, something more than the normal desire for victory at the polls. Several Northern states had only recently rejected proposals to permit Negro men to vote, and Congress showed no intention of imposing Negro suffrage on Tennessee. The Fifteenth Amendment, that would prohibit race as a discriminator in voting requirements, was not unthought of in February, 1867, but was no more than a fond dream of the leading reformers, decidedly not a politically viable prospect. Tennessee legislators would be introducing into their own state what no other Southern or Northern state legislature outside New England had been willing to do if Negro voting were approved in Tennessee.

Among the influences to be weighed on the side of such a development must be included the inexperience of most of the legislators in juxtaposition to the dominating role of Governor Brownlow. His desire to be a reputable member of the Radical Republican element and his conviction that it was the wave of the future were relayed to the legislators, reinforced by the congressional election debacle of the pro-Johnson elements in 1866. Nevertheless, identification with the home-state political terrain was very probably a necessary prerequisite to moving the legislators on such an issue.

Here it became critically important that what Brownlow called "the inclinations of the parties in this state to go into the rebellion" had eventuated in an almost all-Whig political organization following Brownlow, the long-time clarion voice of Whiggery. Although Conservative Unionist opposition to Brownlow was also preponderantly of Whig background, the chief enemy in the struggle, as Brownlow was able to define it, was none other than "Andy" Johnson, Tennessee Democrat supreme and object of Whig animosity and distrust for as long as most of the legislators could even remember. And what was this villain bent upon doing other than restoring the old Secession Democracy to its former position of power? In the interest of partisan aggrandizement, then, Johnson was allegedly willing to belie his own stanch Unionism and betray his Unionist associates into the hands of the rebels. Despising Democrats and hating rebels, hardly distinguishing between the two any longer, Tennessee legislators might agree to fight fire with fire and, as Brownlow himself expressed it, "a loyal negro is more eminently entitled to suffrage than a disloyal white man."[28]

Even intrastate sectionalism was involved, for East Tennesseans were basking in an unfamiliar role of dominance over the state and were willing to take some chances with the 10 per cent Negro vote

[28] Tennessee *Senate Journal*, Brownlow Assembly, 2d Adjourned sess., 11.

in their section, despite the bitter racist attitudes of their own voting constituents. Middle and West Tennessee legislators rarely counted among their voting constituents the bulk of white men anyway. What might happen to them politically and perhaps personally if "treason" should triumph again in the state was fairly explicit in the images painted so luridly in the Memphis *Avalanche* editorials. After all, a legislator might go far to keep from power those who classed him among the "scrubs, the curs, 'the bats'" of society, promised to write "small pox" over his door, and prepared to slap his "filthy jaws." And even if they were not really concerned about "words" harming them, they also had good reason for assuming the readiness of some "sticks and stones."

Washington developments can hardly be said to have stampeded the Tennessee legislature. Not only was it unlikely that Tennessee would be included under some congressional plan of Reconstruction but also during the legislative delay on the Negro suffrage bill in Tennessee the congressional Radicals in the House could not muster a majority for their plans for Reconstruction and almost lost the opportunity to pass any Reconstruction legislation in time to avoid a pocket veto after the end of the congressional term on March 4, 1867. As late as February 6, 1867, when the Tennessee House passed the Negro voting measure, a stalemate was in effect in Washington, where House Moderates had forced Thaddeus Stevens' Reconstruction bill back into committee. It is true that Negro suffrage was much under discussion, but certainly not true on February 6 that its imposition by congressional act was inevitable.

Five days before the Tennessee senate passed the measure on February 25, however, the compromise congressional plan had passed both houses of Congress, and it was known that Negro suffrage would be effected in the other ten Confederate states.[29] Whether the Tennessee senate would have blocked the measure had Congress not included Negro voting in its plan cannot be determined. Judging by previous readiness of the state senate to go further than the House in support of Brownlow, it would seem highly probable that the senate would have acted favorably on the measure anyway.[30]

[29] David Donald, *The Politics of Reconstruction, 1863–1867* (Baton Rouge, 1965), pp. 32–82.
[30] Negro leaders in Tennessee, assisted by visiting workers from the North, had sought voting privileges almost from the end of fighting. With protection from the Freedmen's Bureau, Negro workers were able to hold meetings and forward resolutions and petitions to the legislature and governor's office. As early as the summer of 1865 a convention of Negro men, assembled in Nashville, was addressed by the Tennessee chief officer of the Freedmen's Bureau, Clinton B. Fisk, and adopted a

Closely related to Negro enfranchisement was the authorization of a state Guard. Governor Brownlow, at the same time that he asked for Negro suffrage, asked the legislature for a military force under his direct control. It is altogether probable that the Governor, in addition to believing that revolutionary efforts to overthrow his régime were afoot, anticipated even greater efforts if Negroes were allowed to vote. The Tennessee State Guard, provided by the legislature at the same time that Negro voting was authorized in February of 1867, would furnish some defensive capacity to Brownlow. Brownlow had already obtained proffers from several Northern governors of the necessary arms and ammunition; but to mobilize the Guard would be expensive. For the moment, therefore, a governor's proclamation was substituted for actual mobilization, in the hope that threats might suffice to overawe political opposition. The proclamation was fierce of phrase, promising faithfully to employ the Guard if outrages did not stop.

Not satisfied that political developments associated with the forthcoming August general elections were proceeding satisfactorily, and fearing that potential Negro voters were subject to too much hostile pressure, Brownlow on March 1 unsuccessfully sought federal troops to preserve order. He then called the Guard to active duty by an order of March 6, 1867. Only men who could take the franchise oath of past loyalty could enlist, so, as intended, the Guard consisted of unconditional Unionists among the whites and of Negro men. Twenty-one companies of an authorized force of one hundred men each were accepted and scattered over the state, under the immediate command of Brigadier General Joseph A. Cooper. Soon after the elections almost all of the Guard was disbanded, and the legislature assembling after the elections repealed the law authorizing it.

Marshaling the new Negro vote for the Republican party in Tennessee was a major undertaking. The Conservative opposition had really very little with which to appeal for Negro support, but made a considerable effort nevertheless. The problems of the Repub-

---

threatening attitude, which included the sending of a petition to Congress praying exclusion of Tennessee Representatives unless the Tennessee legislature acted on a petition for Negro suffrage before the December, 1865, assembling of Congress. Such political activity as this might have influenced Northern politicians to believe that the time had arrived for Negro suffrage, but it could not have been a major influence on the Tennessee legislature—certainly not after Congress had seated the Tennessee delegation with no more than a minor flurry about requiring Negro suffrage.

Alrutheus Ambush Taylor, *The Negro in Tennessee, 1865–1880* (Washington, D.C., 1941), offers careful treatment of all major aspects of this topic.

licans were chiefly in the realm of communication and organization. The Negro voters were almost all illiterate and could not be reached by the customary political newspaper campaign. Speakers could reach audiences but could not assure a turnout of the voters nor guard against tricks to mislead voters who could not read the ballots they were to cast. The Union League was the agency employed to overcome the handicaps inherent in depending on such voters.

The Union League was founded in the North in 1862 as an unconditional Union club. It spread into the upper South with federal army control and enrolled many Tennessee Unionists, who formed local chapters before the war ended. In the reorganization of Tennessee civil government, Union League members were among the most active. In the ensuing division into Conservative Unionists and Radical Unionists it was the Conservatives who dropped out of the central political organization in several stages. The Radicals were therefore left in control of the political clubs, such as the Union League chapters, and by the summer of 1866 were deliberately forming chapters exclusively Radical in membership. Such an organization was nothing new in Tennessee politics, but rather closely paralleled the Democratic or Whig political clubs organized in nearly every antebellum presidential contest in Tennessee. The League was by 1867 simply a political club, composed of local chapters, directed by a state central organization, and furnished campaign materials and some guidance from national club sources. Its employment to control Negro votes was merely an adaptation of an old technique to a new situation. The Tennessee Radicals in 1867 aimed at the ideal of a Union League chapter in every civil district of each county. Although such an objective was unreasonably extensive, organization among both white and Negro voters was remarkably thorough.

The initiation ceremony, which was simple in most of the Northern chapters, was elaborated greatly as an appeal to the Negroes. Oaths, patriotic and religious symbols and songs, and many secret signs went along with an obligation to vote only for League-approved candidates. Imitating a familiar religious practice of teaching by catechism those too young to read, a Union League catechism was circulated widely under congressional frank and through publication in Radical newspapers. It was intended that the catechism should be in the hands of every Radical Republican who could read, for regular use in the Union League chapter meetings. One version of the catechism consisted of forty-six questions and answers, along the following lines:

QUESTION. With what party should the colored man vote?
ANSWER. The Union Republican party.

Q. Why should the colored man vote with that party?
A. Because that party has made him free and given him the right to vote.
Q. What is a Democrat?
A. A member of that party which before the rebellion sustained every legislative act demanded by the slaveholders, such as the Fugitive Slave Law, and the attempt made to force slavery upon the Western Territories.
Q. Would the Democrats make slaves of the colored people again if they could?
A. It is fair to presume they would, for they have opposed their freedom by every means in their power, and have always labored to extend slavery.
Q. Why do they not do unto others as they would be done by?
A. Because they are devoid of principle, and destitute of all sense of justice where the colored man is concerned.
Q. Do all white people belong to a party which would treat us in that way?
A. They do not. There are many who have stood up nobly for your rights, and who will aid you to the end; indeed, all the Republicans are such.
Q. What is the reason that several of the Northern States do not give us the right to vote?
A. Chiefly because they have in the past been controlled by the Democratic party.[31]

Tennessee voters were to select in the 1867 elections a governor, legislators, and representatives to Congress. Brownlow was nominated to succeed himself. The opposition, operating under the banner of the Conservative party and appealing to any former Democrats who could vote, as well as to the former Whigs who were not willing to accept Brownlow's program, held a state convention and nominated Emerson Etheridge, the West Tennessee Union Whig who had become an extreme Conservative in denouncing the Brownlow administration as illegal and fraudulent. Every man seriously con-

[31] Walter L. Fleming, ed., *Documentary History of Reconstruction* (2 vols.; Cleveland, 1906–7), 2:13–19.

sidered for the nomination had been a Whig. The Conservative party platform called for removal of all disfranchisements of white men, accepted Negro suffrage, and praised President Johnson's program of Reconstruction. In the eight races for congressional seats, all of the Radical Republican nominees and at least six of the Conservatives had been Whigs. The only identifiable former Democrat in the contest, W. P. Caldwell, ran the worst race. Almost all of the candidates on both sides were men of considerable political experience; some were outstanding antebellum political leaders, such as Balie Peyton, who had served three terms in Congress, had been appointed by William Henry Harrison to the position of United States district attorney, and had in 1860 been a presidential elector on the John Bell ticket.

The election results were an almost clean sweep for the Radical Republican party. The governor, all eight congressmen, every member of the state senate, and all but three members of the house would be Radicals.[32] The Radicals had been very successful in appealing to the Negro voters and getting them to the polls, usually in organized companies marched to vote under protection against fraud or intimidation. Union League leaders, with assistance from the state Guard units in many places, directed these marches. From an estimated Negro vote potential of between 40,000 and 50,000, more than 35,000 Negroes voted. The white vote dropped slightly as a result of the more stringent registration law and the governor's total authority over registration officials, but the most significant implication of the white vote total was that the earlier registrations had not been notably erroneous or fraudulent in the great majority of the counties.

Even in the sweeping victory of the Radicals in these 1867 elections, however, some ominous harbingers of trouble for Radicals appeared. In three Middle Tennessee counties the Negro turnout was far below expectation and permitted a striking Conservative advantage. In West Tennessee far less than half of the potential Negro vote appeared in some counties that were narrowly lost by the Radicals. In Tipton County the total Radical vote reached only 178 against 1,273 Conservative votes, despite the fact that there were nearly 1,500 potential Negro votes and few white Unionists.

[32] The newly elected legislature was not up to the level of experience of its predecessor. A few experienced men were elected to each house, but the great majority of the legislators had not previously held a state office and would not again hold one. The virtual elimination of conservatives from the legislature removed a substantial proportion of the best qualified members of the Brownlow Assembly. In comparison with typical state legislatures of other periods of Tennessee history, this one was decidedly below par.

In the aftermath of the Conservative debacle of 1867 the opponents of Brownlow's régime swiftly implemented the use of force, fear, and intimidation against Radicals. The Ku-Klux Klan came to represent in the minds of Radicals the pressures they feared, but Ku-Klux activity was by no means the whole of this anti-Radical movement. The object of what may be labeled "Ku-Kluxism" in Tennessee was the overthrow of Radical Reconstruction. Ku-Kluxism flourished from 1867 until that object was accomplished and then rapidly disappeared as a state-wide activity. There was no plot to overthrow the civil government of the state by violent revolution. But Ku-Kluxism was distinctly political in that social, economic, psychological, and even violent pressure was applied to reduce Radical voting strength in the state. Several instances of murder and numerous cases of physical assault were attributable to Klan activity or to men acting under Klan disguise. The greatest weapon, however, was general dread and fear of physical violence, coupled with open social ostracism and threat of economic reprisal. A war of nerves was mounted and waged against Middle and West Tennessee Radicals in which direct violence was not generally required. Scattered shots or whistle calls through the countryside on election eve were often more effective in reducing Radical-voter turnout than was individual assault.

What prepared a large segment of the white population of Tennessee, Unionists as well as former Confederates, to participate in or at least condone such undemocratic and often illegal activity? A bill of indictment of Brownlow's administration must have seemed to a great many to have been so outrageous as to justify ordinarily unacceptable behavior. Former Confederate generals surely did not lightly undertake the risks of dire punishment necessarily involved in such conspiratorial action as that practiced by the Ku-Klux Klan.

Brownlow, himself, was a standing indictment against his own administration in the eyes of most Conservatives and Democrats. His deep and embittered hatred for all who had participated in any way in the attempt to establish the Confederacy seemed to increase rather than dissolve with time. By word and deed he proclaimed that he was governor, not for all of the people, but for his own party alone. Vindictiveness was a deliberate policy, practiced not as a necessary evil to be apologized for but as a virtue in itself. Neither former Confederates nor any who took their part could hope to escape from standing charges of unpunished crimes against humanity as long as Brownlow controlled the state. Three years after Appomattox, Brownlow could castigate returning ministers in such terms as these:

Now these apostate, hypocrytical [sic] preachers come back and push themselves into neighborhoods where they are not wanted, and commence their exercises with the infamous, blistering lie that they took no part in the late rebellion—that their church is non-political. . . . These recreant ministers should hide their faces in utter confusion for their atrocious crimes. They would do so if their moral natures were not leprous with unrepentant treason. God knows them, and honest, loyal men loathe them.[33]

The Conservatives had been forced to stand by and observe the ruthlessness with which Radical leadership took each successive step that became necessary to maintain their control. When it appeared that Brownlow could not command a majority, even among the Unionists who were permitted to vote in the 1865 congressional elections, a new franchise act promptly reduced the white electorate further and made the temporary disfranchisement of former Confederates permanent. When this too did not appear to guarantee continued success, Negro enfranchisement followed, and a private army of Radicals was provided for the Governor's use during campaigning and election time in 1867. The state Guard was again authorized in 1868 for use in the national elections of that year. All registration commissioners were appointed by the Governor, and all election officials were designated by these commissioners. The Governor exercised a power to canvass all returns, hear evidence, and reject the vote of any county or precinct he judged to have been fraudulent. The legislature subsequently legalized such canvassing activity, which was thereafter used freely by the Governor.

The courts might have been a source of relief, for they had power to declare key Radical legislation unconstitutional. But the election of judges, customary in Tennessee from the constitutional revisions of 1834 until the onset of war in 1861, was not resumed for the higher judicial positions until 1869. As a result, the constitutionality of Radical franchise laws was sustained by Brownlow-appointed judges of the state's highest court, with scant attention to the reasoning in contrary opinions from lower courts. Former Confederates were excluded from jury service, and confidence in decisions was not high. Several years after the end of the Brownlow régime, the Conservative judges elected to the state's highest court were still holding invalid many decisions of juries that were judged to have been unrepresentative and biased in nature.[34]

The tax rate in Tennessee rose rapidly. In 1861 the property tax rate was 15 cents on $100 and 35 cents on each poll. In 1869 the rate

[33] Knoxville *Whig*, April 1, 1868.
[34] Alexander, *Thomas A. R. Nelson*, p. 151.

was four times that level—60 cents on $100 and $1.50 on each poll. The public school law enacted by the legislature in 1867 provided some state funds and empowered each civil district in every county to levy additional school taxes. The attempt to establish a racially segregated school system, with two schools in almost every civil district, was ambitious beyond all prospects of financial support, and few civil districts taxed themselves for the purpose. The great majority of landowners in Middle and West Tennessee were disfranchised and were especially frustrated by being subject to taxation without a vote on the subject, whatever the purpose of the expenditure. Exceptionally long legislative sessions and the state Guard were costs to the state not cheerfully borne by the landowners. City rings, operating under Brownlow appointment, paid out large sums, thought to be fraudulently padded. The lending of state bonds to railroads was renewed after the war and got seriously out of hand. Bribery of legislators became scandalous, and much of $14 million worth of bonds was issued to hopelessly insolvent companies and eventually became a liability of the state's taxpayers. Radical politicians were no more active than Conservatives in the railroad scrambles, but the administration in power was most likely to be blamed by taxpayers who became aware of the rapidly swelling state debt.

Traditional white fears that Negroes might get unruly and become dangerous neighbors underlay much of the mounting determination to get Brownlow out of power. Negro voting and the encouragement to overt political activity furnished by white Radical political leaders, reflected in the sometimes militant Union League parading, was incendiary in the thinking of many whites, and the use of Negro men in the state Guard alarmed such men even more. Education for the Negro, provided in some measure by Freedmen's Bureau schools and by the scattered state public schools, was resented and feared by many whites on the grounds that the Negro's appropriate work required no formal education and that he was being taught to distrust and even hate his white neighbors. The most widely reported activities of Ku-Klux groups, therefore, were the seizure of arms from Negro residences and the attempted intimidation of teachers of Negro schools, who were often also among the local Radical political leaders. Probably the justification some of the more sensitive whites found for their extra-legal and illegal activities lay in the theory that neither law enforcement nor trial procedure could any longer be trusted and must be supplanted by vigilante organization among the whites of the community.

Governor Brownlow's pardon record did not go unnoticed in this regard. Professing to believe that one-fourth of the inmates of the penitentiary were there because of their color or Unionism, he pardoned freely. During the early part of 1868 about 250 were released. He was accused of pardoning Radicals as fast as they landed in prison. General Nathan Bedford Forrest, head of the Ku-Klux Klan, testified that the Governor pardoned Negroes convicted on rape charges within a few days. Without passing judgment on the correctness of the Governor's position, it is not difficult to understand how his more violent opposition added his pardon record to their distrust of the processes of justice and to their willingness to believe that vigilante-type crimes were justifiable.

The first general test of Radical Republican strength under duress from Kukluxism in Tennessee came in November of 1868, during the presidential election and the congressional elections, which had been changed from the state election date to the presidential election date by the legislature. Tennessee Conservatives, although led almost entirely by former Whigs, had little difficulty in supporting the Democratic presidential nominee, Horatio Seymour, in preference to a Republican. The state was carried for General Ulysses S. Grant, the Republican nominee, but his total popular vote in Middle Tennessee was barely above one-half that received by Brownlow in the gubernatorial contest of the previous year. Counties of most widely reported Ku-Klux activity were usually those from which returns revealed a disastrous drop in Negro vote. The congressional seats were eventually all occupied by Republicans, but the governor had to throw out many returns to save two of the Republican candidates from their defeat on the face of the returns. Furthermore, in four of the eight districts the Republicans were unable to agree on a single nominee and suffered schism in the general elections.

The denouement of Radical control in Tennessee came with unexpected swiftness and simplicity during the following year, 1869. Governor Brownlow decided to obtain a seat in the United States Senate and did so to the chagrin of several Radicals who had had their eyes on this plum. He resigned the governorship in February of 1869 to the senate presiding officer, DeWitt C. Senter, another East Tennessee Whig Unionist. Three months later, when the Radical state convention met to nominate a gubernatorial candidate, Congressman William B. Stokes would not permit Senter an uncontested nomination. Amid charges that fraud had been perpetrated in selection of delegates to the convention, no consensus was reached, and two rival bodies, each claiming to be the legitimate convention, nominated Senter and Stokes respectively. After some preliminary fencing, Senter apparently concluded that he could not win under the existing voting arrangements and announced his support for removal of all disfranchising requirements. Then, having the power to remove and replace registrars, Senter installed his own appointees in almost every county of the state, evidently with instructions to permit all to register. Early in July President Johnson was informed that the new registrar in Greeneville had signed 1,200 certificates on the previous day and by night would have signed as many as needed. "We mean business now, & will do it up right," added the correspondent.[35]

The Conservatives put no gubernatorial candidate in the field and supported Senter, of course. After the bulk of the former Confederates had been registered, Conservatives did put candidates for the legislative seats in the races that had been between Stokes and Senter partisans. The outcome was entirely predictable before election day: Stokes received about the same vote, county by county, that had gone to Grant the preceding year, while Senter piled up a majority greater than any ever previously seen in Tennessee. The total vote in the state skyrocketed, with two counties, Bedford and Giles, reporting more votes than they had men of twenty-one or older.

In the legislature there were to be only eight members who had supported Stokes, all from East Tennessee. Thirteen Senter Republicans, eight from East Tennessee, won seats. All of the remaining seats were filled by Conservatives, including twenty-one from East Tennessee. The newly elected state senate was dominated by former Whigs, and the house was apparently about two-to-one, former Whig as opposed to former Democrat. It is notable, however, that antebellum Democrats now reappeared in considerable numbers among election victors. Eight of the senators were men of outstanding political experience, and a dozen of the house leaders were men of notable political records. The bulk of the membership was new to politics, especially in the house, so that in experience this legislature cannot be ranked much, if any, above the first legislature elected during the Brownlow period. John W. Leftwich, former Conservative congressman from Memphis, thought highly of the Conservative candidates for the legislature, but had suggested with some anxiety that a few "old heads" join the group "to direct control and maybe restrain younger ones."[36]

---

[35] John Williams to Andrew Johnson, July 6, 1869, Andrew Johnson Papers, LC.
[36] Leftwich to T. A. R. Nelson, July 23, 1869, Thomas A. R. Nelson Papers, McClung Collection, Lawson McGhee Library, Knoxville, Tennessee.

Senter's actions in illegally obliterating the suffrage restrictions can be explained only through conjecture. He came to the governorship and the titular headship of a state party far less secure than its victory at the polls the preceding November would suggest. The pressure of Ku-Kluxism was powerful and was producing considerable effect in some places. Despite ever more severe punishment authorized for such activity, no Ku-Klux member was apprehended and convicted by Tennessee authorities. Brownlow's effort to get names for prosecution through a private detective, Seymour Barmore of Cincinnati, resulted only in the murder of Barmore. After Barmore disappeared, Governor Brownlow mobilized the state Guard; the day Barmore's body was recovered from Duck River Brownlow declared martial law in nine counties. Probably in anticipation of the Governor's rage, Forrest had already issued the order for all Klan regalia to be destroyed and all activity to cease until authorization from a Klan official of the congressional district level or higher. Governor Senter found this situation on his hands and immediately softened the impact of martial law. Ku-Klux demonstrations did not cease, however, and pressure was still on.

A second source of serious weakness of the Tennessee Radical party was the continued defection of leaders at each acceleration of the pace of Radicalism. Every major measure asked by Brownlow of his second legislature met considerable opposition, and eventually the speaker of the house went on record as favoring immediate removal of all restrictions on voting. The state secretary of state, Andrew Jackson Fletcher, long Brownlow's right hand man, deserted the cause of restricted franchise before Brownlow left office. United States Senator Fowler had refused in 1868 to vote for conviction of President Johnson on the impeachment charges. Before the end of 1868 he, too, was openly in favor of enfranchisement of all white men in Tennessee and throughout the South. One segment of the Republican leadership on the national stage had espoused universal suffrage restoration and before 1869 had made this proposal highly respectable as national Republican doctrine. This posture assisted the Republicans in their national campaign in 1868, but it contributed to the overthrow of Republicanism in Tennessee. Brownlow's son, John Bell Brownlow, dourly commented after the 1869 debacle: "Our Northern brethren desired Tenn. to be Republican but were too timid to sustain us in the only measures by which it could be *kept* Republican."[37]

[37] Marginal notation by John Bell Brownlow on LC file of Knoxville *Whig*, Feb. 3, 1869.

A third harbinger of trouble for state Radicalism may be seen in the waning enthusiasm of Negro voters. In additions to fear engendered by Ku-Kluxism, the poor practical returns for Negroes were all too evident. Officeholding at the state level was totally denied Negroes, in practice even after legal prohibition had been ungraciously abandoned. Rarely did county or town offices fall to Negroes, even where they were the majority among voters. Education, greatly desired by the Negroes, was never adequately provided. The public school law did not adequately finance the system for more than a skeleton beginning, and the majority of the Negro youth were not provided with any formal educational opportunity.

The Tennessee supreme court handed down a unanimous decision in May of 1869 that seriously damaged Radical party prospects for winning the next election. The voiding of all prior registrations by the Governor upon appointment of a replacement registrar of voters was held to be unconstitutional. Brownlow had tried to start all over after the first election under the original version of the franchise act—the congressional election of 1865. Now, however, all who had been issued certificates were held to be entitled to vote unless deprived by due process of law. No one could tell how many this would restore to the electorate, but talk of as many as 30,000 alarmed the Radicals.

Intraparty friction was probably the greatest and surely the immediate cause of Radical party downfall. Personal ambitions had clashed from the beginning of Reconstruction. Jealousy between natives and the few outsiders seeking office became an open issue. Civilian Unionists became embittered about the success of Federal soldiers who capitalized on war records. Some Radicals sought support in the Union Leagues by advocating more nominations for Negroes, thereby alienating fellow-Radical office-seekers. Rival rings vied for control of the major cities, especially Memphis. When Senter became governor he led a party that was split in a multitude of ways, not the least being the determined opposition to his own re-election by Stokes and the enmity of the party's central executive committee chairman, A. M. Cate, who had gone so far as to have Senter declared ineligible for office under the Fourteenth Amendment because he had taken an oath under the Confederacy, as a legislator in 1861. Congress had to pass a relief measure for Senter to save him from the consequences of this intraparty feud. The judicial elections for the state supreme court in May of 1869 produced further internal division when two incumbents were denied renomination by the party convention. One of the jettisoned Radical judges ran as an independent in open collaboration with a Conservative candidate. The schism in the 1869 gubernatorial nominating convention was not, then, a startling development. It was the culmination of increasingly intransigent factionalism within the Radical party in Tennessee.

It is altogether probable that Conservative leaders persuaded Senter that Radicalism was crumbling in Tennessee and that he could be the hero instead of the goat. An unprincipled bargain was not necessarily the circumstance. Senter was perturbed after the victory by the drastic acts of the legislature and finally remarked in disgust that it had accomplished one thing anyway—it had made the previous two Assemblies respectable.[38] At the end of his term, Senter retired from politics permanently, always calling himself a Republican. What may have influenced him as much as anything was the Whig tradition in the state and the widespread talk of the time that a revival of Whiggery in some national combination of Conservatives was to be the wave of the future. Senter's correspondence reveals that he was favorably inclined toward the formation of such a new party.[39] That Senter intended to hold the loyalty of his friends among the Republicans is certainly clear, for he made a special trip to Washington to get assurances from President Grant that his friends would not be ousted from federal appointive positions. Whatever Senter hoped for in party realignment never came to pass in Tennessee, because Middle and West Tennessee Whigs ultimately repudiated their refusals to be classed as Democrats in exchange for a lion's share of offices and influence in the post-Reconstruction Democratic party of the state.

One curious enigma is the fact that Brownlow supported Senter in the 1869 election, although privately Brownlow and his son believed that Senter's replacement of registrars and mass registrations were unjustifiable and illegal. Perhaps Brownlow was thinking primarily of his forthcoming senatorial career as a Republican in the midst of what he thought was to be a national policy of universal suffrage. One can hardly escape the conclusion, however, that it was a personal matter. Stokes had opposed Brownlow in the senatorial election and was viewed as a rival. Senter had supported Brownlow and hence was on the right side. Other long-time Brownlow associates found their way into the Senter position as required. The Reverend T. H. Pearne, who had bought the Knoxville *Whig* from Brownlow, first proclaimed that the people of Tennessee would vote

---

[38] Senter to Leonidas C. Houk, June 20, Leonidas Campbell Houk Papers, McClung Collection, Lawson McGhee Library, Knoxville, Tennessee.

[39] *Id.* to *id.*, Aug. 23, 1869, *ibid.*

for universal suffrage when the "rebels" restored to life "the thousands of blue-eyed boys of the Mountains who were starved to death
at Andersonville and other rebel hells."[40] On the same day, however,
Senter announced for universal suffrage in Nashville; and five days
later Pearne turned the necessary backflip and came up praising the
great national Republican ideal, universal suffrage. Leonidas C.
Houk, disaffected Republican recently defeated for Congress by
Horace Maynard, rode the Senter bandwagon around each turn.
After the universal suffrage stand was taken, Houk wrote to Senter's
secretary: "I didn't believe it, but I have learned to talk eloquently,
of the justice of restoring 'the tax-payers of the state,' to 'their
rights.' "[41] Personal factionalism rather than political principle or
policy probably accounted for the limited Senter support among
state Republican leaders.

The legislature elected in 1869 immediately set to work to repeal
most of the key Radical legislation and authorized a state constitutional convention for 1870 to clean up the remainder. In total disregard of the supposedly constitutional restrictions on the privilege
of voting, the legislature authorized universal suffrage for the convention election. A light voter turnout in this election revealed better
than any other single index the general realization that state political
Reconstruction was over except for the formalities.

The Convention of 1870 was composed of generally experienced
men and was led by a number of the outstanding political figures in
the state. Few extremist proposals got more than a perfunctory hearing. Universal manhood suffrage was provided for, although payment
of a poll tax was included as a voting prerequisite. Parsimony in
state expenditures and prohibition of any further lending of state
credit, as in the case of bonds loaned to railroad companies, was a
prime order of business. Revision of the state judicial system made
possible an early election in which Radical Republican judges' tenure
could be terminated. Even state elections were moved from the odd
to the even-numbered years, so as to have a general state election in
1870 instead of 1871. In the 1870 elections the name "Democrat" was
easily interchangeable with "Conservative." The Conservative and
Democratic party won all state supreme court posts and the bulk of
the lower judicial positions in Middle and West Tennessee. John
C. Brown, a former Whig and Confederate general, was elected

[40] Knoxville *Whig*, June 5, 1869, quoted in Philip M. Hamer, ed., *Tennessee: A
History, 1673–1932* (4 vols.; New York, 1933), 2:649; Knoxville *Whig*, June 10, 1869.
[41] Houk to Frank Hyberger, June 16, 1869, DeWitt C. Senter Papers, Tennessee
State Library and Archives, Nashville.

governor; both houses of the legislature became Conservative and Democratic by large margins; and six of the eight congressional seats were recaptured. Though issues not a part of Reconstruction made possible thereafter some Republican success in Tennessee politics, Republicans generally controlled for the succeeding century only East Tennessee.

It is very difficult to perceive in the process of political Reconstruction in Tennessee any profound elements or narrowly missed opportunities to leap a century forward in reform. Idealists and hardheaded reformers abounded in the North, and some saw clearly the contours of the future and struggled heroically to shape the country's policies while they were malleable in the heat of postwar contention. Some in Tennessee were of this ilk, and some others were touched by this dream; but these altogether were no more than an inconsequential voice far in the wings of the political theater. The dominant theme in the drama was simply a struggle for control of the state government between rival groups defined in the tumultuous years preceding Reconstruction. Those who managed to seize control in the final months of the Confederacy maintained that control by disfranchisement of former Confederates and extension of suffrage to Negroes— steps that only the emotionalism of war and its aftermath made feasible. The first disfranchisement measure only contemplated five years of nonvoting for former Confederates (exclusive of leaders). The escalation to permanent disfranchisement was a panic reaction to the prospect of imminent defeat at the polls.

The dwindling Radical Republican party in Tennessee very soon found itself in an untenable position at home and among even the Northern Republican leaders. As Horace Greeley wrote at the time of the Radical debacle in Tennessee in 1869:

It is not possible, in a republic, to deny the right of suffrage to a large and intelligent portion of the community because of their past political transgressions. You can shoot them or hang them in the flush of victory, if you will, though at your own heavy cost; possibly you might confiscate their property and drive their leaders into exile; but you must do either with celerity, and before popular passion has had time to cool. Thereafter, the inevitable drift is toward universal amnesty, and it cannot long be successfully resisted.[42]

The "carpetbagger" and "scalawag" stereotypes have almost no applicability in Tennessee. Only a very few men from other states received political preference, but even this slight inroad met fierce

[42] Reprinted in Memphis *Avalanche*, Aug. 13, 1869.

opposition from Radicals. Native whites who co-operated with the
Radical party through no principle but the desire for spoils cannot
meaningfully be isolated in the Tennessee account. No attempt has
been made by any serious student to treat even the most Radical
unconditional Unionists of the state as "scalawags."

Negroes were surely used by the native Radical whites of
Tennessee. The most Radical leaders were usually the ones most
opposed to Negro office-holding; Governor DeWitt Senter correctly
represented his East Tennessee constituents when as senator he refused
to the end to vote to permit Negroes to hold office. Little effective
demand for office came from Negroes, outside a few scattered locali-
ties. Negro voters were in large majority in many counties and in
some congressional districts. One Negro in Middle Tennessee
pointed out this fact and announced for a legislative seat, but his
Negro constituents ignored him and voted for a white Radical. The
freedmen as voters under Radical aegis were actually remarkably
tractable, considering the amount of racist comment traceable to
their own political party leadership. To view Reconstruction as a
missed opportunity because it was not radical enough may have applicability somewhere else, but not in the internal political process in
Tennessee. The white men of Tennessee were no less racist in their
convictions than were their white fellow countrymen in Indiana or
Illinois, California or Connecticut. No permanent, profound change
in race adjustments was going to be achieved from within Tennessee.

Advanced educational concepts were involved in the public school
legislation of 1867 and 1868. The principle of state taxation for
public education had, however, been achieved by Andrew Johnson's
gubernatorial administration in the 1850s. The Fourteenth Amendment would, in any case, have compelled support for Negro schools
in any postwar system. The Tennessee laws provided for segregated
schools, and for so many as to negate the intent of the law. Adverse
court rulings on the principle of district school taxes soon emasculated the concept, and the first legislature after Radical downfall
established county option for public education. Only afterward was
state support restored and a state superintendent's office re-created.
There is little solid evidence that the educational legislation of the
Radical period won more converts than it created opponents for
public education. What Tennessee began in the 1870s appears to
have been in the general stream of educational reform in the region
and the nation rather than a delayed after-image of Reconstruction
legislation.

Economic forces were always at work in Tennessee Reconstruction. Railroad promoters were among the most obvious of the influence wielders. Some of the money for Senter's gubernatorial campaign in 1869, perhaps that which bought the Nashville *Press and Times* from Stokes' supporters to turn it into a Senter organ, came from hopeful railroad promoters who were bragging that they would get $5 million from the succeeding legislature. Taxes on property were not high in comparison with levels of a century later, but multiplication of the tax rate by four was not acceptable to property owners who had no enthusiasm for the objectives of state expenditures. As a matter of practical assessment, it should be recognized that state government customarily had so little direct influence on the life of the ordinary citizen in the 1860s that not many could get excited about who was at the helm, except for the two points at which Brownlow activity impinged—taxation and race relations. No economic lords, moving political chessmen about, can have been the key to the Reconstruction process, although some delved into the troubled waters with considerable success, as well in Tennessee as in New York or Washington.

The significance of the political reconstruction of Tennessee after the Civil War cannot be read in terms of twentieth-century issues. The record of those events can reveal much about the conditioning effects of region, party, wartime antagonism, and racism operating on people cut loose from familiar moorings by the sword of war. It is in these aspects of the story that one may best seek the insights into human behavior furnished by this particular segment of history.

CHAPTER THREE

Crisis Politics in West Virginia, 1861-1870
Richard O. Curry

In November, 1870, an anonymous correspondent of the Cincinnati *Gazette,* who called himself Stylus, sadly reported that "West Virginia has reversed her political record completely, and gone over to the Democratic side."[1] In 1870, West Virginia elected "the entire Democratic State ticket, . . . a large majority in the lower house of the Legislature, . . . two Democratic Congressmen out of three," and, as a result of these victories, the Democrats, in January, 1871, undoubtedly would replace United States Senator Waitman T. Willey who had served in the Senate since West Virginia's admission into the Union in 1863.

Stylus consoled himself, however, with the conviction that the Republican party, the great pioneer of "moral ideas," was now required to "pay the penalty" exacted by society from those "who have led mortals upward." "Certain it is," he wrote, that

whether or not the Republican Party of West Virginia has a future or not, its existence has not been in vain. It has left an imperishable record of good behind it. It broke the bonds of white and black slavery in this State. It helped save the government of our common country. It has given the State a magnificent school system and supplied the light of education to tens of thousands who beforetime sat hopelessly in the valley and shadows of darkness. Compared with the record of the Democratic Party in the days when there were sixty thousand white adults in Virginia who could neither read nor write, its glory is that of the full orbed sun at high noon.

Yet, Stylus, despite his disillusionment with human frailty, was a shrewd political observer who clearly recognized that Republican ascendancy in West Virginia (1863–70) had been an accident of history, dependent upon conditions and circumstances that no longer existed.

A small portion of my article "A Reappraisal of Statehood Politics in West Virginia," *Journal of Southern History* 28 (Nov., 1962): 403–21, has been incorporated (with changes) into this chapter, by permission.

[1] Newspaper clipping in Archibald W. Campbell Papers, W. Va. Univ. Library, Morgantown.

"In the first place," Stylus wrote, "let me premise that West Virginia, at the breaking out of war, was Democratic, and has, therefore, simply resumed her *status quo ante bellum*." Western Virginia, after all, had voted for Breckinridge by substantial majorities in the presidential election of 1860. Lincoln received only 1,929 votes in the entire state of Virginia, of which 1,198 were cast by voters in the northwest panhandle—a rather "slim nucleus, was it not, those 1,929 Republican votes," for the party destined, during the war, to become the dominant political force in the state.

In West Virginia, as in other border states, secession destroyed old political alignments, and loyal Union men of all parties joined together to form what afterward became "the Union Republican party." "The pressure of the war," Stylus continued, "the armed occupation of our soil by Union soldiers, the question of a separate State, the enlistment of our young men, and the 'cohesive power of public plunder,' kept this aggregation from the old parties in homogenous shape through most of the war, even despite the emancipation of the Negroes and their enlistment in the army." But alas, "this homogeneity was more apparent than real." What Stylus termed a "sloughing off" process began as early as 1864. While Lincoln defeated McClellan decisively (23,152–10,438), dissatisfaction with the war policies of the Lincoln administration caused a schism in Unionist–Republican ranks that posed a serious threat to Republican ascendancy after the war—a threat that neither disfranchisement nor other proscriptive policies could turn aside. Therefore, if we are to fully understand the meaning of Stylus's observation that, in 1870, West Virginia "simply resumed her *status quo ante bellum*" by returning the Democratic party to power, it becomes necessary to analyze the forces, factors, and circumstances which led to the creation of the state of West Virginia in 1863. Only then can later developments during the Reconstruction era be understood.

First of all, it needs to be emphasized that the state of West Virginia was a child of the Civil War. The war itself created the circumstances which made the dismemberment of the Old Dominion possible. Yet, most writers on West Virginia statehood have observed that the creation of this state represented, in one sense, the culmination of more than fifty years of sectional conflict within the state of Virginia. These writers contend that West Virginia, whose political and economic interests coincided with those of the industrialized, free-soil North, chafed for decades under the domination of conservative, slaveholding, eastern Virginia. Thus, with the outbreak of war in 1861, western Virginians repudiated secession, urged and aided

McClellan's invasion of trans-Allegheny Virginia, and launched a movement to create a new state, loyal to the Union.[2]

The passage of a secession ordinance by the Virginia Convention of 1861 on April 17 served as a signal for organized resistance in the northwest. Only five days later, a Union mass meeting of some 1,200 people met at Clarksburg in Harrison County to plan a course of action to meet "the present, fearful emergency." Called by John S. Carlile, the guiding spirit behind the new state movement in 1861 and later a United States senator from West Virginia, this assemblage unequivocally denounced secession and issued a call for the next gathering which became known as the May Convention or, more commonly, the First Wheeling Convention.[3]

At the First Wheeling Convention, of May 13–15, northwestern Unionists failed to adopt Carlile's "New Virginia" plan for immediate separation from the Old Dominion, but they resolved to organize a provisional government loyal to the Union, should the Virginia electorate ratify the proposed secession ordinance on May 23.[4]

When the secession ordinance was adopted as anticipated, on May 23, the Second Wheeling Convention of June, 1861, repudiated it and formed the Reorganized Government of Virginia under the leadership of Francis H. Pierpont, Union war governor of the Old Dominion.[5] Pierpont wired Washington, asking official recognition of the Reorganized Government as the *de jure* government of Virginia. This was extended by Lincoln on July 4 in his message to Congress. "These loyal citizens," Lincoln stated, "this government is bound to recognize, and protect, as being Virginia."[6] In August, 1861, the adjourned session of the Second Wheeling Convention, secure in the knowledge that a semblance of legality would be maintained by securing permission from the Pierpont government to create a separate state, passed a dismemberment ordinance—the first in a long series of acts which led to the creation of the state of West Virginia.

[2] Charles H. Ambler, *Francis H. Pierpont, Union War Governor of Virginia and Father of West Virginia* (Chapel Hill, N.C., 1937); George E. Moore, *A Banner in the Hills: West Virginia's Statehood* (New York, 1963); James G. Randall, *Constitutional Problems under Lincoln* (New York, 1926); James C. McGregor, *The Disruption of Virginia* (New York, 1922).

[3] Wheeling *Intelligencer*, April 26, 1861.

[4] Virgil A. Lewis, ed., *How West Virginia Was Made; Proceedings of the First Convention of the People of Northwestern Virginia at Wheeling, May 13, 14 and 15, 1861, and the Journal of the Second Convention of the People of Northwestern Virginia at Wheeling, Which Assembled June 11th, 1861 . . .* (Charleston, W.Va., 1909), pp. 35–76.

[5] *Ibid.*, pp. 77–182.

[6] *Congressional Globe*, 37th Cong., 2d sess., Appendix, 1–4.

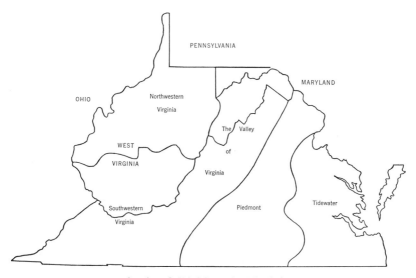

Sectional Divisions in Virginia.

The state-making process consumed nearly two years. The West Virginia constitutional convention convened in November, 1861; a constitution was ratified by voters in Union counties in the spring of 1862; the Wheeling legislature granted permission for dismemberment in May, 1862; the United States Senate passed a statehood bill in July of the same year, and the House passed it the following December. On December 31, 1862, President Lincoln signed the bill admitting West Virginia into the Union, subject to one condition: the inclusion of the Willey Amendment in her constitution, a gradual emancipation proviso demanded by Radicals in Congress. This amendment was approved by Union voters in March, 1863, and West Virginia was admitted into the Union on June 20, 1863.

Thus, the presence of strong Unionist sentiment in West Virginia cannot be controverted, nor can one overemphasize the importance of half a century of sectional conflict in crystallizing that sentiment. But a crucial point, ignored by most writers on West Virginia statehood, is this: the territory included in the new state was not confined to Unionist strongholds of the northwest, but included at least twenty-five counties whose inhabitants strongly supported secession and opposed the disruption of Virginia.

Of fifty counties ultimately included in West Virginia, thirty-five comprised the section then known as the northwest; six were in the Shenandoah region; and nine were considered southwestern. Unionist

County-by-County Voting Pattern on the Secession Ordinance Referendum in (West) Virginia, May 23, 1861.

strength lay in the northwest. In fact, there were no important Union strongholds outside an area confined to twenty-four of the thirty-five counties of the northwest—those counties located along the banks of the Ohio river, the Pennsylvania border, and the tracks of the Baltimore and Ohio. These Unionist counties comprised about one-third of the land area of West Virginia, and, with a white population of 210,000, they included about 60 per cent of the state's population. With at least 85 per cent of the residents opposing secession, the voters in these counties rejected the secession ordinance on May 23 and thereafter supported all measures designed to dismember the Old Dominion.

As indicated above, the situation that existed in the rest of West Virginia was in marked contrast to the Union solidarity demonstrated by the twenty-four northwestern counties. The remaining twenty-six West Virginia counties not only opposed breaking away from Virginia but were overwhelmingly secessionist and Confederate in outlook. The pro-Confederate counties, half the total in the state, included nearly two-thirds of the state land area and 40 per cent of its population. As one would expect, Confederate strength centered mainly in the southwestern and valley counties;[7] but even in the northwest there was a sizable area that remained loyal to Virginia and the South. Eleven northwestern counties—Barbour, Braxton, Calhoun, Clay, Gilmer, Nicholas, Pocohontas, Randolph, Roane, Tucker, and Webster—voted to ratify the secession ordinance and militantly opposed withdrawal from Virginia.[8]

In short, Unionism was confined to an area in northwest, trans-Allegheny Virginia. The arbitrary inclusion of a large Confederate minority within the limits of West Virginia was a key factor in the history of statehood politics and provides a major frame of reference in explaining the bitter partisanship which characterized West Virginia politics in the Reconstruction period. Once this is recognized—the fact that Union solidarity in West Virginia is nothing more than a myth—at least two fundamental questions arise. First, why did the inhabitants of half the counties in the new state oppose its establishment and remain ardently attached to Virginia and the Confederacy? Second, why were so many Confederate counties included in West Virginia?

[7] For evidence of secession sentiment in southwestern and Valley counties see: Henry M. Mathews to Governor John Letcher, April 21, 1861, and W. H. Syme to Letcher, April 25, 1861, both in John Letcher Executive Papers, Virginia State Library, Richmond; Robert Hagar to Governor Francis H. Pierpont, July 30, 1861, and H. W. Crothers to Pierpont, both in Francis H. Pierpont Executive Papers, Virginia State Library; J. B. Anderson to J. B. Moorman, May 25, 1861, and "May" to "Jackson," May 23, 1861, both in George B. McClellan Papers, Series I, Manuscripts Division, LC; Fayette County Court Minute Book, June, 1857–July, 1861 (County Clerk's Office, Fayettesville, W.Va.); Richmond *Dispatch*, May 28 and June 1, 1861; Richmond *Enquirer*, May 28 and June 28, 1861; Kanawha Valley *Star*, May 14 and May 21, 1861; Oren F. Morton, *A History of Monroe County, West Virginia* (Staunton, Va., 1906), appendix, pp. 422–60; David E. Johnston, *A History of Middle New River Settlements and Contiguous Territories* (Huntington, W. Va., 1906), appendix, pp. 462–500; Willis F. Evans, *History of Berkeley County, West Virginia* (Wheeling, W. Va., 1928), pp. 112–19; Hu Maxwell and H. L. Swisher, *History of Hampshire County, West Virginia* . . . (Morgantown, W. Va., 1897), pp. 591–643.

[8] For evidence of secession evidence in northwestern counties see: Thomas M. Harris to H. H. Withers, June 18, 1861, in George B. McClellan Papers, Series I; _____ to Pierpont, n.d., _____ to Pierpont, July 29, 1861, Spencer Dayton to Pierpont, Aug. 24, 1861, and Authur I. Boreman to Pierpont, Sept. 20, 1862, all in Francis H. Pierpont Executive Papers, Va. State Library, Richmond; Sarah J. Maxwell to Mary K. Swisher, May, 1861, in Maxwell-Bonnifield Typescripts, W. Va. Univ. Library, Morgantown; Lot D. Morrall to Samuel Woods, June 29, 1861, in Samuel Woods Family Papers, W. Va. Univ. Library; Charles H. Ambler, Francis H. Atwood, and William B. Mathews, eds., *Debates and Proceedings of the First Constitutional Convention of West Virginia, 1861–1863* (3 vols.; Huntington, W. Va., 1939), 2:33–34, 219, 648; 3:135–43, 204–24, 501–26; and "Voting Results on the Secession Ordinance Referendum in (West) Virginia, May 23, 1861," in Richard O. Curry, *A House Divided: A Study of Statehood Politics and the Copperhead Movement in West Virginia* (Pittsburgh, 1964), pp. 141–47.

The answer to the first question lies in the history of sectional conflict in Virginia in the period from 1830 to 1861. It cannot be denied that sectional grievances were largely responsible for producing a new state movement in 1861. But most writers have not correctly understood the nature of the sectional divisions which were operating in Virginia on the eve of war. It must be recognized that sectional conflict in Virginia during the antebellum period was characterized by its changing pattern. Before 1830, Valley and trans-Allegheny counties stood together in opposition to political domination by the Tidewater and Piedmont sections. Both western regions came to demand the adoption of such reforms as universal manhood suffrage, proportional representation in the General Assembly, the popular election of governor and the governor's council, substantial appropriations for internal improvements in western counties, and a more equitable tax structure. At the Constitutional Convention of 1830, however, Valley counties deserted their former allies from trans-Allegheny Virginia and began to move into the proslavery orbit. By 1830 slavery had begun to take deep roots in the Valley. Tidewater and Piedmont delegates who controlled the convention were now more than willing to conciliate Valley counties by granting them a larger number of delegates in the General Assembly and by promising liberal appropriations for internal improvements. On the other hand, trans-Allegheny delegates received no concessions in the way of increased representation or financial aid. Nor were their feelings soothed by the attitude of Tidewater aristocrats, as betrayed by Benjamin Watkins Leigh: "Now what real share as far as the mind is concerned," Leigh declared, "does any man suppose the peasantry of the West . . . can or will take in the affairs of state?" Thus, the Constitution of 1830 was a triumph for conservatism, and trans-Allegheny delegates returned from Richmond bitterly disillusioned.[9]

An editorial which appeared in the Winchester *Republican* on December 3, 1830 not only illustrates the drift of the Valley away from the trans-Allegheny counties but also casts light on the persistent sentiment for dismemberment that the events of 1830 would create in trans-Allegheny Virginia. After noting that the General Assembly was scheduled to meet in a few days, the editorial stated:

The preservation of the state, we believe, will depend upon this Legislature. Dispute the claims of the Trans-Allegheny counties to what they may deem a proper share of the fund for internal improvements and *a division of the*

---

[9] *Proceedings and Debates of the Virginia State Convention of 1829–1830* (Richmond, 1830), p. 158.

state must follow—not immediately perhaps, but the signal will be given for the rising of the clans, and *they* will rise. . . . The northern counties demand to be separated from the state with a view of attaching themselves to Maryland or Pennsylvania; the southwestern counties go for a division of the state into two commonwealths. . . . Of the two projects spoken of, that which would be least injurious to the Valley and the state at large, would be to part with the northwestern counties. Let them go. Let us get clear of this disaffected population. Then prosecute the improvements called for in the southwest, and that portion of our state, deprived of its northern allies, would give up its desire for a separation.

The prediction that the "disaffected population" of the northwest would never be reconciled and that the people in southwestern counties could be converted into "good Virginians" found fulfillment in the thirty years remaining before the Civil War and provides a key for understanding why southwestern counties remained loyal to Virginia and to the Confederacy. The Virginia Constitution of 1850 satisfied many of the political demands made by the trans-Allegheny southwest in 1830. The new constitution provided for universal manhood suffrage, popular election of the governor, and proportional representation for the lower house. Furthermore, a substantial program of internal improvements, which included, for example, the completion between 1850 and 1856 of the Virginia and Tennessee Railroad, served to channel southwestern trade toward the Valley and Richmond. The institution of slavery continued to grow in the southwest after 1830; the inhabitants were largely Southern in origin, and the press and pulpit were proslavery in orientation. Thus, by 1861, the Valley and the trans-Allegheny southwest had been conciliated by the east and had drawn closer to the Tidewater and Piedmont because of its evolving pattern of life and trade.[10]

At the time this was happening, the trans-Allegheny northwest continued to be dissatisfied and was in fact drawing farther away from the rest of Virginia. Not content with the reforms of the Constitution of 1850, northwestern Virginians continued to resent tax discriminations in favor of slave property and demanded that representation in the state senate as well as in the lower house be based on white population. Northwestern trade centered in the Ohio River Valley and in Baltimore and Philadelphia. All rivers in the region flowed westward into the Ohio, and the Baltimore and Ohio

[10] *Ibid., passim;* Charles H. Ambler, *Sectionalism in Virginia, 1776–1861* (Chicago, 1910); Ambler, "The Cleavage Between Eastern and Western Virginia," *American Historical Review* 15 (July, 1910): 762–80; Maud F. Callahan, *The Evolution of the Constitution of West Virginia* (Morgantown, W.Va., 1909); David L. Pulliam, *The Constitutional Conventions of Virginia* (Richmond, 1901); and Curry, *A House Divided,* pp. 20–43.

Railroad channeled northwestern trade to Baltimore and Philadelphia rather than to Richmond and Norfolk. A system of internal improvements to tie the northwest to the rest of the state was never undertaken. Furthermore, the northwest, partly as a consequence of this pattern of trade, had become industry-minded in marked contrast to the agricultural orientation of the rest of Virginia. The cities of Wheeling and Wellsburg, on the Ohio River, became growing industrial centers; an iron industry thrived in the Monongahela River valley, and a salt industry was located in the Kanawha region.[11] Finally it must be remembered that the northwest, in contrast to the southwest, had thousands of people of Northern origin and a strong Methodist Episcopal Church. One contemporary put it this way: "It must be recollected that our intercourse is almost entirely with the West and North, we have none with the central and eastern portions of Virginia. We are not slaveholders, many of us are of Northern birth, we read almost exclusively Northern newspapers and books, and listen to Northern preachers."[12]

Although an understanding of the changing pattern of sectional conflict makes clear the reasons for the cleavages between the inhabitants of western Virginia in 1861 and explains why the division of loyalties fell into the geographical pattern it did, it does not tell us why so much Confederate territory was included in the state of West Virginia. Unfortunately, its inclusion cannot be attributed to something as clear-cut as McClellan's invasion, or to the geography of Virginia which prevented the Old Dominion's defending Confederate counties in the west.

The strangest thing about this is that the enemies of statehood *within Union ranks* were largely responsible for the inclusion of southwestern and Valley counties in West Virginia. Our emphasis upon the numerical and geographical divisions between Unionists and Confederates has perhaps tended to obscure the fact that the Unionists were divided among themselves over the question of statehood. Contrary to tradition, the Unionists of northwestern Virginia

[11] Ambler, *Sectionalism in Virginia*, pp. 305–19; Barton H. Wise, *The Life of Henry A. Wise of Virginia, 1806–1876* (New York, 1899); Isaac F. Boughter, *Internal Improvements in Northwestern Virginia: a Study of State Policy Prior to the Civil War* (Pittsburgh, 1934); Catherine B. Smith, "The Terminus of the Cumberland Road on the Ohio," *West Virginia History* 14 (April, 1953): 193–264; M. F. Maury and William Fontaine, *Resources of West Virginia* (Wheeling, 1876); Samuel T. Wiley, *History of Monongalia County, West Virginia* . . . (Kingwood, W. Va., 1883); and *Journal, Acts and Proceedings of a General Convention of the State of Virginia Assembled at Richmond* (Richmond, 1850).

[12] Robert Johnston to John Letcher, May 9, 1861, in John Letcher Executive Papers, Virginia State Library, Richmond.

were by no means in agreement about the desirability of creating a new state. The voting masses in Union counties overwhelmingly supported the separate-state movement, but a small, effective minority of the delegates to the Second Wheeling Convention and to the constitutional convention were opposed and used obstructionist tactics at every opportunity to defeat the statehood movement. Unionists opposed to statehood persistently demanded that all Virginia west of the Blue Ridge Mountains be included in West Virginia. Since the effect of this would have been to put the Unionists in a minority, the strategy of the obstructionists, had it succeeded, would have seriously embarrassed, and in all probability would have defeated the new-state project. The opponents of statehood never publicly admitted that they opposed the creation of West Virginia, for they knew it was strongly favored by their constituencies. Instead, they talked in terms of dismemberment at the "proper time" when the new state could have a "proper boundary." In August, 1861, when the chips were down, the opponents of statehood, having failed in their efforts to extend the boundaries to the Blue Ridge, voted against the dismemberment ordinance passed by the Second Wheeling Convention. After the passage of the ordinance, the opponents attempted to have the referendum on dismemberment postponed indefinitely but were voted down by a two to one majority. Thirty-nine counties, with a white population of 272,759, were named in the ordinance. Twenty-four of these, with a total of 211,643 inhabitants, were Unionist in outlook.[13]

Despite the passage of the ordinance, the boundary question was not resolved at the Second Wheeling Convention. It plagued the proceedings of the constitutional convention which convened at Wheeling on November 26, 1861. Obstructionists now called for the inclusion of seventy-one counties in the new state. Of these, forty-five, having a white population of 316,308, were loyal to the Confederacy and unquestionably opposed to dismemberment. And most of these counties lay outside Union lines. Unionists would have been hopelessly outnumbered. Is it any wonder, then, that Granville Parker, an ardent advocate of the new state, proclaimed: "With far more probability of an alliance might we go to the emperor Napoleon and ask him to annex his empire to our little state." The "adoption of this report," James W. Paxton remarked, "will embarrass, retard, and in all likelihood will defeat the whole new state project." Even "the bandit guerilla [Albert Gallatin] Jenkins," quipped another, "may

[13] Lewis, ed., *How West Virginia Was Made*, pp. 77–182; Ambler *et al.*, ed., *Debates and Proceedings*, 1: 73–76.

be made governor of the new state of West Virginia by this operation." Finally, on December 13, 1861, the territorial limits of West
Virginia were fixed at fifty counties, a total of eleven more than were
included in the dismemberment ordinance passed by the Second
Wheeling Convention. Even so, obstructionists made one last attempt
to further enlarge the boundaries of the new state. On February 11,
1862, James H. Brown of Kanawha county made a motion calling
once again for the inclusion of all counties west of the Blue Ridge.
This motion inspired one delegate to comment sardonically that the
"gentleman from Kanawha" was "entirely too modest" in making
his proposal. "You just ought to take in the whole state," he said.
After a brief exchange, Brown's proposal was defeated, twenty-eight
to thirteen.[14]

Of the original thirty-nine counties included in West Virginia at
least fifteen were pro-Confederate, but their geographic location made
the inclusion of these fifteen imperative. The reasons why new-state
advocates compromised with obstructionists and added eleven
counties to the original thirty-nine are not clearly established. It is
possible that the inclusion of Valley secession counties at the constitutional convention can be explained by the wish of new-state advocates to take the Baltimore and Ohio completely out of Virginia. But
at no time were the new-state men willing to jeopardize statehood
for West Virginia by adopting the "large state" plan, which called
for the inclusion of all of Virginia west of the Blue Ridge. Nor were
they deceived by efforts to postpone consideration of statehood, a
stratagem which opponents of statehood unsuccessfully attempted
once their "large state" plan was defeated. In any case, it is clear that
had obstructionists not attempted to defeat the statehood movement
by proposals for territorial enlargement, the state of West Virginia
would have been limited to thirty-nine counties, with eleven fewer
counties loyal to the Confederacy.

As it turned out, of course, the arbitrary inclusion of the twenty-
five Confederate counties did not block statehood, despite the difficulties over the Willey Amendment in 1862. Their inclusion, however,
was to have far-reaching effects upon Reconstruction politics in West
Virginia. Although the Rebel minority, roughly 40 per cent of the
state's population, was in no position to dominate the state's political
life after the war—the Rebel minority in conjunction with conservative Unionists, with whom they formed a coalition in 1866, was in a
position to challenge Republican ascendancy.

[14] *Ibid.*, 1:73–76, 408, 367, 379; 3:410, 415.

What has not been previously recognized is that dissension over statehood within Union ranks in 1861 and 1862 gave rise to a Copperhead movement in West Virginia. In 1862 many of the men who the year before had been in the forefront of the fight for separate statehood withdrew their support and joined those Conservatives who had been in opposition from the beginning. Although the motives of the Union minority who originally attempted to block statehood in 1861 are not totally clear it is perfectly plain why many prominent newstate leaders withdrew their support in 1862. Such men as John S. Carlile, John J. Davis, Wheeling legislator John C. Vance, and ex-Congressman Sherrard Clemens reversed themselves and began to oppose the statehood movement when Congress required as a condition for admission into the Union the passage of the Willey Amendment, providing for the gradual emancipation of slaves.[15]

The influence of these men, especially of Carlile, had been so great in 1861 that it is doubtful that the dismemberment ordinance would have passed in the second session of the Second Wheeling Convention without their support. Carlile, who was demanding dismemberment as early as May, 1861, when other leaders hesitated, is referred to by pro-Union writers as the "Judas Iscariot" of the new-state movement because of his apparent desertion of the cause in the United States Senate in 1862, but they are at a loss to explain his motives. These men—Carlile, Davis, Vance, Clemens, and others like them—as well as those leaders who had earlier opposed statehood, were all strong and consistent supporters of the Union and opponents of the Confederacy. As in other parts of the nation, especially the middle west, West Virginia Copperheads favored the preservation of "the Constitution as it is" and the restoration of "the Union as it was." They condemned with equal fervor the "nigger bills" passed by Congress, the emancipation proclamation, the suspension of the writ of *habeas corpus*, arbitrary arrests, and the attachment of an emancipation clause to the West Virginia constitution. It is clear that Copperheads viewed themselves as patriots and Unionists and looked upon Radicals as fanatics and dis-Unionists who were leading the United States down the road to military despotism. And certainly, John S. Carlile, who had been the most outspoken and vilified of all northwestern Unionists at the Virginia convention of 1861, was neither a lukewarm Unionist nor a quasi-secessionist. Carlile, as did other West Virginia

[15] *Congressional Globe*, 37th Cong., 2d sess., 3320; 3d sess., 59.

Conservatives, consistently called for a vigorous prosecution of the war to suppress rebellion.[16]

The statehood movement, the Willey Amendment, and the war policies of the Lincoln administration created a schism in Union ranks that was not to be healed. "Unconditional Unionists"—that is, those who were willing to accept statehood on any terms—in time became Radical Republicans. As the war worked on toward Appomattox, the Radicals pushed through the West Virginia legislature a proscriptive program, which during the Reconstruction years they enforced, often making little distinction between Rebels and conservative Union Democrats.

Compared to the complexities involved in interpreting Civil War politics in West Virginia, the political patterns that developed during Reconstruction are clearcut—the lines having been drawn in advance by the "state-makers" themselves as a result of the boundaries they chose for the state of West Virginia, and their support of the war policies of the Lincoln administration, especially in regard to slavery. Thus it was that in 1865 the Unionist–Republicans found themselves faced by the unenviable prospect of being consigned to political oblivion. At no time during the war, on any issue, did the "Unconditional Unionists" or Radicals muster more than 28,000 votes. In contrast, the southwestern and Valley secessionist counties contained in 1860 some 20,600 white males of voting age. Moreover, at least 4,000 voters in northwestern counties cast ballots in favor of the secession ordinance of 1861. Add to this total the potential voting strength of the conservative Unionists, or Copperheads, of the northwest. No totally accurate tabulation of Copperhead strength exists, but some indication is provided by noting that Lincoln's majority over McClellan in the election of 1864 stood at 23,152–10,438.[17] Little wonder then that Radicals reacted to their predicament by enacting proscriptive measures into law—measures that they rigorously and successfully enforced for nearly five years.

[16] See Richard O. Curry, "The Union As It Was: A Critique of Recent Interpretations of the 'Copperheads,'" *Civil War History* 13 (March, 1967): 25–39; F. Gerald Ham, ed., "The Mind of a Copperhead: Letters of John J. Davis on the Secession Crisis and Statehood Politics in West Virginia, 1860–1862," *West Virginia History* 24 (Jan., 1963): 93–109; Peter G. Van Winkle Letters in Waitman T. Willey Papers, W. Va. Univ. Library; Arthur I. Boreman letters in Francis H. Pierpont Executive Papers, Va. State Library, Richmond; speeches of John S. Carlile in *Congressional Globe*, 37th Cong., 2d sess., 864–69, 964–66, 968, 972, 1157–62, 3313–14; Clarksburg *Patriot*, March 20, 1863; Clarksburg *National Telegraph*, 1862–65; Wheeling *Press*, 1862–63; and Morgantown *Monitor*, 1862–64.

[17] County by county voting results on all major political issues in West Virginia, 1861–64, can be found in Curry, *A House Divided*, pp. 141–52.

The first proscriptive acts were passed in February, 1865—most notably, the voters' test oath, which required all persons whose loyalty was challenged to swear, under oath, to both past and future loyalty. While such a device was effective enough in disfranchising ex-Confederates in predominantly Union areas, it had little or no effect in southwestern and Valley counties that were not occupied by federal troops. For example, Henry Mason Mathews, an ex-Confederate army major (later to be governor of West Virginia, 1877–81), was elected to the state senate in 1865; and Samuel Price, who had served in Richmond during the war as lieutenant-governor of Virginia, was elected judge of the Ninth Judicial Circuit, which included his home county of Greenbrier, as well as Pocohontas, Monroe, McDowell, and other southern border counties. Mathews was refused his seat by the Senate, and Price was denied his commission by Governor Arthur I. Boreman. But such developments led Boreman, in his annual message to the West Virginia legislature in 1866, to demand sweeping proscriptive measures to subdue the "spirit of insubordination" manifested by Rebel elements in the state.[18]

The legislature responded to Boreman's recommendations by passing "iron-clad" oath laws applicable to voters, attorneys, suitors, jurors, and teachers. But the heart of the Radical program, which assured Republican control until 1870, was provided by the registration law of 1866 which effectively disfranchised 20,000–25,000 people. This law, which was accompanied by the ratification of a constitutional amendment that validated it, placed the registration of voters under the control of county registration boards appointed by Governor Boreman. The boards were empowered, subject to no appeals whatever, to refuse to register and to strike from the voting roles the names of any persons even suspected of disloyalty—whether or not such persons were willing to take the "iron clad" oath, and whether or not they offered evidence attesting to their fidelity to God and the Union. The boards alone, by virtue of evidence, whim, intuition, or revelations from God, decided what constituted satisfactory proof of loyalty or disloyalty. In some instances, actions for damages against registrars were attempted by persons who claimed that they

[18] *Acts of the Legislature of the State of West Virginia* (1865), pp. 37, 47–48; *Journal of the House of Delegates of the State of West Virginia* (1866), pp. 7–10; *Journal of the Senate of the State of West Virginia* (1866), pp. 31. Hereafter referred to as *Acts, House Journal,* and *Senate Journal.* Four ex-Confederates besides Mathews were refused seats by the West Virginia legislature in January, 1866, *House Journal* (1866), p. 82.

had been wrongfully deprived of their rights. But such suits, under an act of 1866, were summarily dismissed.[19]

In addition to legislative proscription, which deprived ex-Confederates of their right to vote and denied teachers and attorneys their right to earn a living,[20] punitive damages were assessed by the West Virginia courts against scores of ex-Rebels in war trespass cases in which Radical judges, upheld by the state supreme court, repudiated the doctrine of belligerent rights. In the case of *Allen T. Caperton* v. *Nicholas Martin* (4 W.Va. 138), for example, Martin was awarded $600 in damages because Caperton, acting in his capacity as Confederate provost marshal for Monroe County, arrested the plaintiff and transported him to Richmond where he was imprisoned by Confederate authorities. And in the case of *Hood, et al.* v. *Maxwell* (1 W.Va. 219) the plaintiff was awarded $1,516.25 in damages from Hood and three other ex-Confederate soldiers who, during the war, seized from one John Maxwell for the use of state troops "1,041½ bushels of wheat, 30 bushels of corn, 15 barrels of flour, 1 brown horse, 1 wagon, harness, bridles, etc., and provisions sufficient for meals for thirty persons." Hood's plea of belligerent rights—that is, his argument that "it is a well settled doctrine that an officer contracting for government is not liable to be sued personally upon such contract"— was rejected by the court on the ground that *de facto*, not *de jure*, extension of belligerent rights was granted to the Confederacy by the Lincoln administration. Individuals, therefore, were personally responsible for acts authorized by Confederate authorities.[21] No useful purpose can be served here by detailing the results of dozens of similar cases; but in at least two instances state judges who refused

[19] *Acts* (1866), pp. 19, 25, 44, 122–23, 130. The voters' test oath amendment was ratified by the electorate, 23,157–15,921 (Wheeling *Intelligencer,* July 12, 1866). See Governor Boreman's instructions to "County Boards of Registration, Township Registrars, and Supervisors and Inspectors of Election, March 13, 1867," in Arthur I. Boreman Executive Papers, State Dept. of Archives and History, Charleston, W.Va.

[20] Some ex-Confederates were able to form unofficial partnerships with Unionist lawyers. For example, Samuel Woods "did the office work and prepared the cases" while his partner appeared in court. See Ruth Woods Dayton, *Samuel Woods and His Family* (Charleston, W.Va., 1939).

[21] Reports of similar cases are found in John M. Hagans (comp.), *Supreme Court of Appeals of West Virginia, 1863–1874* (7 vols.; Morgantown, W.Va., 1906). The West Virginia courts pointedly ignored rulings by the U.S. Supreme Court in *Ex parte Garland* (4 Wallace 333) in which the federal test oath for lawyers was declared unconstitutional, and in *Cummings* v. *Missouri* (4 Wallace 267) which banned loyalty oaths for ministers. In fact, the West Virginia legislature asserted the doctrine of state sovereignty in an act of Feb. 17, 1866, which declared: "The circuit courts and the supreme court of appeals of West Virginia are alone authorized to interpret and determine the constitutionality of any of the legislative acts of this state." *Acts* (1866), p. 25.

to go along with the Radical program were arbitrarily removed from office by the state legislature.[22]

Radical proscriptive policies can be explained in part by political expediency and by the passions engendered by war, especially guerrilla warfare waged throughout the conflict by Confederate raiders.[23] Equally important were fears held by Radicals regarding the perpetuity of West Virginia itself. These fears produced a crisis psychology and were not totally assuaged until the United States Supreme Court demonstrated that it had no intention of challenging the constitutionality of the state-making process (78 U.S. 39). "It is not to be disguised," declared Archibald W. Campbell, editor of the influential Wheeling *Intelligencer*, "that within the State of West Virginia there is a reactionary party, not only as regards National politics, but as regards the very existence of the State of West Virginia. The party calling itself 'Democratic' in this State opposed the formation of the new State, and . . . we are not at all surprised to see men who have been in the rebellion, and others who sympathized with it . . . intimating a desire to get back into the old state."[24]

Such fears first found expression in the presidential election of 1864. For example, state judge Ralph L. Berkshire wrote to Senator Willey that the Copperheads would make "great exertions" in the coming elections to win over "a portion of the Union men by insidiously appealing to their ancient party affinities." "That they will fail most signally," he concluded, "there is no shadow of doubt, yet in our infant state . . . there never was a time when it behooves genuine Union men to be more vigilant and active, for I . . . can have no faith or hope whatever, if we are again . . . to lapse into Democracy and be ruled and controlled mostly by known secessionists."[25] Unionist–Republican orators reiterated this theme throughout the campaign. "An effort has been organized in secret conclave to wipe out West Virginia," Senator Willey declared. "And we stand in this contest

[22] Judge John W. Kennedy was removed from office by the legislature in 1865 and Judge William L. Hindman in 1868. *Acts* (1865), p. 88; *House Journal* (1865), pp. 2–5; Wheeling *Register*, March 9, 1865; *Acts* (1868), pp. 170–71; *Senate Journal* (1868), pp. 34–36.

[23] See Richard O. Curry and F. Gerald Ham, eds., "The Bushwhackers' War: Insurgency and Counter-Insurgency in West Virginia," *Civil War History* 10 (Dec. 1964): 416–33. See also "Paroled Prisoners," in Wheeling *Register*, May 23, 1865; "Meeting in Taylor County," Wheeling *Intelligencer*, May 3, 1865; John S. Hoffman to Gideon D. Camden, May 19, 1865, Walter P. Cooper to Camden, May 24, 1865, and S. M. Somers to Camden, July 14, 1865, all in Gideon D. Camden Papers, W. Va. Univ. Library, Morgantown.

[24] Wheeling *Intelligencer*, Jan. 27, 1866.

[25] Ralph L. Berkshire to Waitman T. Willey, March 15, 1864, in Waitman T. Willey Papers, W. Va. Univ. Library, Morgantown.

to combat that effort." "The McClellan party in West Virginia," another Radical leader contended, "is made up of those who actively or passively sympathize with the South, and who never have been and are unwilling to be reconciled to the new State."[26]

Lewis Baker, editor of the Wheeling *Register,* the leading Democratic newspaper in the state, not only ridiculed charges of disloyalty made by Campbell, Willey, and others, but argued that "the Conservatives of West Virginia are not making war upon the new State, nor do they intend to do so." Only the United States Supreme Court could do that. "A large number of conservatives," Baker continued, "and perhaps all, desired a new State." "But," he added sarcastically, "our Abolition friends labored to defeat the manner proposed by the Conservatives for its formation, and succeeded in doing so; they formed it in their own way, and now they seem wonderfully alarmed by its perpetuity."[27]

Baker was dead right. Alarmed they were and alarmed they continued to be throughout the early Reconstruction years. Lincoln's death, the passage of re-integration resolutions by the Virginia General Assembly in 1865, petitions drawn up that same year by ex-Confederates in some border counties demanding re-annexation to Virginia, and the unsuccessful attempt made by the Old Dominion to reclaim the Valley counties of Berkeley and Jefferson in 1866–67 affected the attitudes of West Virginia Republicans in regard to both state and national politics.[28] "Our perpetuity as a state," Senator Willey declared in December, 1865, "to say nothing of the Union itself . . . depends upon the unity of the Republican party and its ascendancy for some years to come. That unity is in extreme danger. Let us be careful to do nothing to imperil it further."[29] The attitude of Congressman Chester D. Hubbard is even more revealing. On February 22, 1866, he wrote to his son:

> you are probably a little surprised at my vote on the last declaration of the Com. of Fifteen [Joint Committee on Reconstruction] knowing my

---

[26] Speech on Oct. 5, 1864, in Wheeling *Register,* Oct. 7, 1864.

[27] Wheeling *Register,* Oct. 10, 1864.

[28] See Wheeling *Register,* Dec. 30, 1865; Wheeling *Intelligencer,* June 27, 1866; newspaper clipping from Richmond *Enquirer* on "Proposed Reunion of Virginia and West Virginia," in Archibald W. Campbell Papers, W. Va. Univ. Library, Morgantown; and *Diary* of Waitman T. Willey, W. Va. Univ. Library.

[29] Waitman T. Willey to Henry Dering, *et al.,* Wheeling *Intelligencer,* March 19, 1865. See also Willey's *Diary,* 1, p. 167. Willey's son William, a conservative Unionist who served as co-editor of the Morgantown *Monitor* during the war, was an object of great embarrassment to his father during the Reconstruction period. See John Marshall Hagans to Willey, March 8, 1868, in Waitman T. Willey Papers, W. Va. Univ. Library, Morgantown.

willingness hitherto to vote for the admission of the members from Tennessee, and where they could take the oath from other states. But I was not quite ready to go over to the Democratic party, where I think the President is going without let or hindrance [sic]. And besides it is essential, that the State should hang on to the majority by some hook however, feeble, if we expect any favorable legislation. . . . Set this down as a fact. We have nothing to hope as a State from the Democracy. They would not have suffered our Coat of Arms to be placed in the ceiling with those of the other states if they could have helped it. They seek occasion to place themselves on the record against the state and if they attain to power within the next ten years and the legislature of both States are favorable, we will be put back into the old State.[30]

Two years later, Senator Willey was being urged by some alarmed Radicals to vote for Andrew Johnson's conviction on the ground that "If the President is acquitted . . . all is lost." "We cannot carry the presidential election," one Radical leader declared, if Johnson emerges "triumphant over Congress, the people! If we lose the Presidential election, we shall lose the next Congress, and then farewell to West Virginia. A Copperhead Congress would not admit our representatives, and then what becomes of us? . . . God help us!"[31]

In retrospect, such fears, while real enough in the minds of Radicals themselves, seem exaggerated. Neither in 1867 nor in 1871, in the case of *Virginia* v. *West Virginia* (78 U.S. 39), did the United States Supreme Court even review the constitutional issues involved in West Virginia's formation. Rather, the Court validated West Virginia's claims to two counties, Berkeley and Jefferson, which were not included in the original statehood bill passed by Congress. And no evidence exists to suggest that the Democratic party, either on state or national levels, was prepared to challenge the constitutionality of statehood for West Virginia, even if it had been in a position to do so.

In time, West Virginia Radicals came to realize that the only real threat they faced was that posed by the coalition formed by conservative Union Democrats and ex-Rebels within the state itself. Disfranchisement, buttressed by the use of federal troops to enforce it, proved to be nothing more than a stop-gap measure that could not indefi-

---

[30] Chester D. Hubbard to William P. Hubbard, Feb. 22, 1866, in Hubbard Family Papers, W. Va. Univ. Library, Morgantown. See also C. D. Hubbard to W. P. Hubbard, May 6 and Dec. 4, 1865, in *ibid*. See also Richard O. Curry, ed., "A Note on the Motives of Three Radical Republicans," *Journal of Negro History* 47 (Oct. 1962), pp. 273–77.

[31] Ellery R. Hall to Waitman T. Willey, May 14, 1868, in Waitman T. Willey Papers, W.Va. Univ. Library, Morgantown. See also J. M. Hagans to W. T. Willey, April 10, 1868, and A. B. Schuyler to W. T. Willey, April 21, 1868, in *ibid*.

nitely postpone defeat at the hands of resurgent Democrats.[32] By 1869, many Republican leaders had reached the conclusion that if the party was to survive as a major political force in West Virginia the "war screws" had to be loosened. Horace Greeley, in a letter aimed at extreme Radicals who "vowed that the 'bleeding and purging' treatment must go on" assessed the situation in West Virginia this way: "Every year one thousand of your rebels die, and one thousand or more of their sons become of age,—you can't disfranchise them. You now have [a] five thousand majority. Six years will convert this into a rebel majority of one thousand. The rebels will be enfranchised in spite of you. Go your own way and see if the rebels don't have you under their feet. I speak from a large experience when I tell you that your house is built upon the sand. Now you can amnesty the rebels—Soon the question will be, shall they amnesty you? Look at Kentucky and Maryland and read your certain fate in theirs."[33]

Liberal or "let-up" Republicans in West Virginia fully realized that serious risks to Republican ascendancy were involved if proscriptive measures were relaxed, but concluded with Greeley that total disaster awaited them if immediate steps were not taken toward reconciliation. Granville D. Hall, successor to Archibald W. Campbell as editor of the influential Wheeling *Intelligencer*, acutely summarized the Liberal position in a letter to Charles Sumner that deserves lengthy quotation. "It is the opinion of our wisest and best Republicans," Hall began,

that as a matter of party sucess we simply must relax the extreme rigor of our policy toward our ex-rebels in order to maintain ourselves as a party in the state. . . . In the border and interior counties, where most of the ex-rebels are to be found, the feeling is still very bitter and both parties are willing to proscribe each other to the utmost. But in this the more populous part of the state we shall lose ground very rapidly by maintaining the system of tests demanded by the smaller number of Republicans in the border counties, and will inevitably lose the next general election. This feeling is strengthened among our friends in this section by the knowledge that our system of

---

[32] For evidence on the use of federal troops in West Virginia during the Reconstruction see: Major Joseph C. Conrad to Governor Arthur I. Boreman, May 6, 1867; Conrad to Boreman, Oct. 9, 1868; William E. Stevenson to Boreman, March 8, 1869; Jonathan S. Witcher to Boreman, Sept. 7, 1869; all in Arthur I. Boreman Executive Papers, State Dept. of Archives and History, Charleston, W.Va.; Lt. Col. W. F. Drum to Joseph Conrad, June 15, 1867; Drum to Conrad, June 24, 1867; Conrad to General Nathan Goff, Jr., April 6, 1869; all in Nathan Goff, Jr., Papers, W. Va. Univ. Library, Morgantown; annual messages, 1867–68, of Governor Boreman to the West Virginia legislature, *House Journal* (1867), pp. 3–7; *Senate Journal* (1868), pp. 7–11; annual message of Governor Stevenson to the West Virginia legislature, *Senate Journal* (1869), pp. 6–9.

[33] Wheeling *Intelligencer*, May 12, 1869.

registration (the entire machinery being in the hands of the Governor) has been used arbitrarily and improperly in many counties and still is: the officers taking advantage of the power it puts in their hands to promote personal ends or gratify private hatreds.

It is but natural, therefore, that the movement that has been inaugurated by the more disinterested and far-seeing Republicans should meet the bitter opposition of those holding the minor offices, who would resist any movement to abridge their powers or weaken their hold on the petty control they now exercise. It does encounter the hostility of this class throughout the state; but I fear if our policy is to be controlled and the status of our party fixed by that class, we cannot command the respect and support of the disinterested portion of our party.

The enfranchisement of the ex-rebels will require an amendment to our State constitution, and this amendment must be proposed by two successive legislatures (we elect yearly) and ratified by the people. So that by this process, it could not become operative and the rebels could not vote until 1872. Our only hope of perpetuating Republican ascendancy in the State is by a magnanimous policy which shall bring a portion of the ex-rebels into co-operation with us when they become voters. A very large number of them were old line Whigs before the war. They do not like the Democracy and they would come to us if we gave them the ballot. But if we wait for the Democrats to enfranchise them, they will of course fall into that party.[34]

The position of "bitter end" Republicans, typified by the editorial reactions of the Ravenswood *News,* the Morgantown *Post,* the Martinsburg *Berkeley-Union,* the Parkersburg *State Journal,* and the Fairmont *West Virginian,* could not be changed. The tide, however, was running against Radicalism, as in the annual elections to the state legislature in the fall of 1869, thirteen Liberal Republicans, four Radical Republicans, and five Democrats were elected to the state senate. Moreover, the "let-uppers" completely controlled the House of Delegates. But the fact that the Democrats won twenty-three of fifty-six available seats must have given even Liberal Republicans pause for reflection, as the schism in Republican ranks permitted the Democrats to make larger gains in the lower house than the Liberals had anticipated.[35] Nevertheless, this legislature, which convened in January, 1870, repealed the test oaths applicable to lawyers, teachers, and suitors, and passed the Flick Amendment—which, to the chagrin

---

[34] Hall to Sumner, Sept. 14, 1869, typescript in Granville D. Hall Papers, W. Va. Univ. Library, Morgantown. See also Hall to Carl Schurz, Oct. 5, 1869, and Cyrus Newlin to Messrs. Hagans, Low & Co., June 19, 1869, in *ibid.*; and the "Address to the Republican Voters of Ohio County," Aug. 26, 1869, in Archibald W. Campbell Papers, W. Va. Univ. Library, Morgantown.

[35] Wheeling *Intelligencer,* Nov. 5, 1869 and April 15, 1870; *Senate Journal* (1870), p. 259; *House Journal* (1870), p. 260; and John Marshall Hagans to Waitman T. Willey, Jan. 17, 1870, in Waitman T. Willey Papers, W. Va. Univ. Library, Morgantown.

of most Democrats and some Republicans, linked the removal of voting curtailment to Negro enfranchisement. Opposition to Negro enfranchisement was based on racial, rather than practical grounds, however, as potential Negro voting strength in the state did not exceed 3,500—a small price to pay, most Democrats concluded, in exchange for the enfranchisement of nearly 20,000 ex-Confederates, if and when the Flick Amendment was passed by two successive legislatures and ratified by the electorate.[36]

Liberal Republican strategy was doomed, however, as the triumph of the Democratic party was closer at hand than anyone suspected at the time. The Democratic sweep in the fall elections of 1870, despite disfranchisement, exceeded the fondest hopes of most Democrats and the worst fears of most Republicans. As it turned out the Liberals offered too little, too late. What they needed was time and the gradual removal of voting curtailment, if they were to successfully woo ex-Rebels, who had been "old line Whigs," into the ranks of the Republican party. But they did not have time, and time alone, even if "let-up" policies had been inaugurated earlier, provided no guarantee that their wooing would have worked. Even so, as Liberals clearly recognized by 1869, any positive policy that seemed to offer a chance for success was preferable to the impossible task of trying to keep the "Chinese shoe" on the foot of the Democrats.

A touch of irony existed in the Democratic triumph of 1870, however, which Liberal Republicans could hardly have found amusing. The ratification of the Fifteenth Amendment, and the passage of the Enforcement Act by Congress in 1870 proved to be a weapon in the hands of the Democrats, rather than the Republicans—a weapon that helped pave the way for a Democratic victory far sooner than either Liberal Republicans or Democrats themselves had anticipated.

Simply stated, the U.S. commissioners appointed by United States District Judge John J. Jackson to enforce the Fifteenth Amendment used their powers to undermine the authority of the county voter registration boards appointed by Governor William E. Stevenson. The havoc caused by Judge Jackson's appointees, Jackson being a conservative Union Democrat elevated to the federal bench by Lincoln in 1861, is well-reflected in a letter by Governor Stevenson to Nathan Goff, Jr., U.S. Attorney for West Virginia. "There is a certain fool," Stevenson wrote,

called C. A. Sperry who is U.S. Commissioner, and a most complete tool for the most bitter unreconstructed rebels in Greenbrier Co. I don't know how

---

[36] *Acts* (1870), pp. 16–17, 34, 158; and Wheeling *Intelligencer*, Feb., 1870, *passim.*

many election officers he has arrested and held to bail; the other day (the 8th inst. I think) he arrested the Board of Supervisors and put a portion of them in jail for two days and then held them in $5000 bail each to appear at the U.S. District court at its next session in Charleston. . . . These men appeal to me for protection—protection from the *very tribunal* that ought to defend them. . . . The State law will be powerless unless backed by U.S. bayonets if this man is permitted to carry on in this violent way.[37]

In the face of such pressures, Governor Stevenson advised his county registrars, in an "Official Circular Relating to Registration," that "Your duty is . . . plain. Execute the law relating to the registration of voters as formerly instructed, fearlessly and impartially; not permitting yourselves to be deterred by intimidation, threats of violence or persecution."[38]   And the state's attorney general, A. B. Caldwell, in a widely distributed circular, argued that "a registrar or board of registration cannot be sued or indicted in the District Court of the United States, under said act, for any infraction of duty, except *a refusal to register 'on account of race, color, or previous condition of servitude.' "*[39]

Judge Jackson's interpretation of the Enforcement Act was the one that counted, however, and seriously weakened the Radicals' position. "I presume," Jackson wrote, "that most of the difficulties that have occurred with 'registrars' acting under the laws of the State, arise from the fact that they suppose they are invested with the exercise of a discretion in the execution of them." The Enforcement Act, Jackson concluded, "qualifies the state law by taking away from the officer acting under it all discretion affecting the rights of citizens in the exercise of the right of suffrage."[40]

It will be recalled that under West Virginia law registration boards were empowered, subject to no appeals, to refuse registration to any individual, and to strike from the list of registered voters the name

[37] Stevenson to Goff, Nov. 13, 1870, in Nathan Goff, Jr., Papers, W. Va. Univ. Library, Morgantown. See also Lewis Stuart, *et al.* to Goff, Aug. 11, 1870; J. F. Caldwell to U.S. Attorney General, Aug. 11, 1870; M. F. Pleasants to Goff, Aug. 20, 1870; Thomas H. Talbot to Goff, Aug. 24, 1870; Arthur I. Boreman to Goff, Jan. 27, 1871; A. T. Sherman to Goff, Feb. 4, 1871; Goff to Boreman, Jan. 31, 1871, all in *ibid.*; W. E. Stevenson to W. T. Willey, April 8 and Nov. 22, 1870, in Waitman T. Willey Papers, W. Va. Univ. Library, Morgantown; and Morrow to A. B. Fleming, Aug. 4, 1870, in Aretas B. Fleming Papers, W. Va. Univ. Library, Morgantown.

[38] Wheeling *Intelligencer*, Sept. 23, 1870.

[39] Caldwell to Stevenson, July 18, 1870, in Broadsides collection, W. Va. Univ. Library, Morgantown.

[40] "Enforcement Act of March 31, 1870 Construed" (2 Hughes 518). See also "The Registration of Voters Under the Act of Congress to Enforce the Fifteenth Amendment," in Broadsides collection, W. Va. Univ. Library, Morgantown.

of any person even suspected of disloyalty. Such discretionary powers, under Judge Jackson's ruling, were no longer valid. As state judge James H. Ferguson, in his charge to a Wayne county grand jury phrased it: "It is a mistake to suppose that in the registration of voters whose loyalty is questioned, the burthen of proof is by law forced on the applicant for registration." Unless concrete evidence, admissible in a court of law, could be produced by the boards themselves, registration could not be denied. Nor could a county board of registration "strike a man's name from the list merely because charges have been made against him." Until proved guilty of the charges, he must "be considered innocent."[41]

It is not my purpose to suggest, however, that the intimidation of Republican voting registrars under the provisions of the Enforcement Act was the only factor involved in the Democrats' triumph. In a few predominantly Unionist–Republican (or anti-secessionist) counties, notably Marshall, Wood, Ritchie, Monogalia, and Preston, Republican voting strength declined appreciably between 1868–70,[42] and this decline was attributed by some Republican editors to racial prejudice—the unwillingness of "a great many Republicans" to accept Negro suffrage.[43] On balance, however, the Republicans did not lose the election of 1870 because of substantial losses in their voting strength. In 1868, Governor William E. Stevenson polled 27,348 votes and won the election by a 5,100 majority. In 1870, Stevenson polled 26,683 votes, but lost the election to John J. Jacob by a majority of 2,000. A net loss, therefore, of roughly 650 votes, attributable in part to the ratification of the Fifteenth Amendment could not have been the critical factor explaining Stevenson's defeat. In 1870, the Republicans virtually held their own, whereas the Democratic party increased its strength by nearly 6,500 votes.[44]

The Democrats scored significant gains in all sections of the state. In those twenty-four Unionist–Republican counties of the northwest, the Democrats increased their voting strength by 3,300. In this area Republican registrars had often disfranchised conservative Union Democrats as readily as ex-Rebels. Under Judge Jackson's ruling, they now did so at their peril. Equally important, the Democrats

[41] "Judge James H. Ferguson's Charge to a Wayne County Grand Jury on the Enforcement of the Registration Law and the Duty of Registrars," in *ibid*.

[42] Voting Results in West Virginia elections of 1868 and 1870, in Arthur I. Boreman Executive Papers, State Dept. of Archives and History, Charleston, W.Va.

[43] Wheeling *Intelligencer*, Nov. 15, 1870. See also *Diary* of Waitman T. Willey, 1, p. 252, W. Va. Univ. Library, Morgantown.

[44] Voting Results, 1868 and 1870, Arthur I. Boreman Executive Papers, State Dept. of Archives and History, Charleston, W. Va.

broke the Republican stranglehold in those twenty-six northwestern, southwestern, and Valley counties that had been predominantly secessionist in outlook in 1861. In these counties (eleven northwestern, nine southwestern, and six Shenandoah Valley) the Republicans polled 5,691 votes in 1868 compared to only 4,487 for the Democrats. In 1870, the Republicans actually increased their voting strength in these counties by more than 600 votes, but the Democratic total skyrocketed from 4,487 in 1868 to 8,408 in 1870. Considering the fact that these twenty-six counties had contained 27,876 eligible voters in 1860, it is clear that even in 1870 Republican voter registrars succeeded in holding the vote down. Only 37 per cent of the potential electorate (based on 1860 census figures) cast ballots in the election of 1868. In 1870, the percentage increased only to 50 per cent. But it was large enough to permit the Democrats to carry these areas by a 2,100 vote majority.[45]

Thus, Reconstruction in West Virginia came to a dramatic and sudden end. In 1871, the Flick Amendment was passed by the West Virginia legislature for the second time and was ratified by the electorate. In 1872, a new state constitution was drawn up which virtually reduced the governor of the state to a figurehead, which denied the legislature control over the election laws of the state, and omitted registration as a requirement for voting. And the West Virginia courts, now staffed by Democratic judges, reversed the convictions of ex-Confederates in war trespass cases.[46]

In conclusion, it must be pointed out that while Reconstruction in West Virginia was characterized by partisan strife, violence, personal vindictiveness, and ultimately by Liberal Republican attempts at accommodation, the only real political question at issue was that of loyalty versus disloyalty. Otherwise, West Virginia politics in the postbellum period, with the exception of the establishment of a public school system, may be characterized as the politics of negative liberalism. The Republican party in this state refused to consider Negro enfranchisement before the ratification of the Fifteenth Amendment, and only faltering, inconsequential steps were taken toward providing public education for Negro children, and this, in

[45] *Ibid.*

[46] *Acts* (1871), pp. 17, 152–53, 261, 273–74, 277. The West Virginia constitution of 1872 is printed in *ibid.* (1872–73), pp. 1–48. The Samuel Woods typescripts in the Charles H. Ambler Papers, W. Va. Univ. Library, Morgantown, provide keen insights to the workings of the convention by one of its leading members. For accounts of cases reversing war trespass convictions see Hagans (comp.), *Supreme Court of Appeals of West Virginia*, vols. 4–7, *passim*. See also *Pierce et al. v. Carskadon* (16 Wallace 234).

segregated schools.[47] The only other social service provided by the West Virginia legislature for her Negro citizens was an arrangement with the state of Virginia to care for indigent and insane Negroes. West Virginia had no such facilities and was not about to provide them.[48] Racism and a commitment to the Jacksonian ideal of "rugged individualism"—as reflected by the West Virginia constitution of 1872—continued to have a strong appeal for the Appalachian mind. And so, West Virginia, like the rest of the nation, entered the "Gilded Age" woefully unprepared to meet the social, political, and economic problems caused by the transportation and industrial revolutions.

[47] "Fourth Annual Report of the Superintendent of Free Schools of the State of West Virginia," *West Virginia Public Documents* (1868), pp. 16–17.

[48] *Acts* (1872), pp. 277–78; *ibid.* (1873), p. 287. See also: Reuben Sheeler, "The Negro in West Virginia Before 1900" (Ph.D. diss., W. Va. Univ., 1954); and Walter B. Posey, *The Negro Citizen of West Virginia* (Institute, W.Va., 1934).

CHAPTER FOUR

Kentucky: "Pariah Among the Elect"
Ross A. Webb

Howard K. Beale, speaking to the Southern Historical Association in Lexington, Kentucky, in November, 1939, suggested that "further studies and changed points of view [are] necessary to a full understanding of Reconstruction." "We need," said Beale, "to restudy Reconstruction in each state, freed from preconceptions of the right and wrong of Reconstruction and determined to discover just what lasting influences Reconstruction exerted."[1] In 1959 Carl N. Degler attacked the generally accepted "myth" of Reconstruction history by asking the mundane question: "How Black was Reconstruction?" After asserting the need of a "balanced picture," Degler concluded that "the tragedy" of Reconstruction was that it failed.[2]

No major attempt has been made to re-evaluate Kentucky's postwar years since Professor E. Merton Coulter's monumental *The Civil War and Readjustment in Kentucky* in 1926. While well-researched and scholarly, Coulter's book continued the "myth" of Kentucky as a pro-Confederate state that Secretary of War E. M. Stanton considered "a pariah among the elect." Coulter treated his subject with the devotion of a Southern scholar, sometimes losing sight of the true nature of Kentucky's postwar attitudes and sentiments.[3]

As sectionalism gradually triumphed over nationalism in the late 1850s and civil strife became inevitable, both North and South courted the border states. For Kentucky, such a conflict meant that it would become "the battlefield" of the Union, in which the armies of the two contending ideologies would lay waste to its fields and ruin its emerging industrial economy.

Kentucky had strong binding ties with both sections. In common with the South, the state possessed a way of life based upon slave labor and "Bourbon" aristocratic rule. Her early settlers had come to this "dark and bloody ground" predominantly from Virginia and the Carolinas. Filling up the fertile lands of the Bluegrass and the

---

[1] Howard K. Beale, "On Rewriting Reconstruction History," *The American Historical Review* 45 (July, 1940): pp. 807–27.

[2] Carl N. Degler, *Out of Our Past* (New York, 1962), pp. 217–37.

[3] E. Merton Coulter, *The Civil War and Readjustment in Kentucky* (Chapel Hill, N.C., 1926).

Pennyroyal, they established a culture of a distinctive Southern regional character, with miniature plantations operated by slave labor and a gentried class that tended to dominate society, economically and politically. Many of these "Bourbons" enjoyed the luxury of "winter plantations" in the South, and conversely many Southerners made their annual summer trek to the increasingly famous "watering places" of Kentucky. This produced a familiarity, as well as an identity, with Southern culture. The Kentucky–Ohio–Mississippi river system also tended to orient trade southward. The South, with its basic one-crop economy, welcomed the diversity of produce which came out of Kentucky: mules, horses, hogs, sheep, cattle, slaves, flour, hemp, sugar, and tobacco. Over the years "the Mississippi trade" had grown by leaps and bounds.

Although Kentucky was proud of the Union, after her admission in 1792 she battled consistently for the sovereign right of statehood. The Kentucky Resolutions of 1798 attested to her strong states' rights philosophy. Throughout the antebellum period continuous minor clashes occurred between the federal government and Kentucky over tariff, tobacco and liquor legislation, not to mention the profitable domestic slave trade. From this standpoint, Kentucky was sympathetic with the Southern states' rights cause.

But Kentucky was not so culturally uniform as many historians have assumed. In the Appalachian Plateau of eastern Kentucky and in the knobs of the northern and western regions the soil was relatively sterile. Here the pioneer struggled valiantly against nature to eke out his living. As settlers arrived, either by the Cumberland Gap or by the Ohio River, finding the fertile lands of the Bluegrass and the "Pennyrile" taken up, they were forced into these less productive regions where they developed a rugged, individualistic, small-farming economy, operated with few if any slaves. Out of their "fundamental" religious tradition they placed high value on the dignity of human worth and tended to regard their "Bourbon" neighbors with disdain. In many ways Kentucky was a microcosm of conflict between the Bourbon and the yeoman, the slaveholder and the independent farmer, the agriculturalist and the commercialist, and the "states-righter" and the Unionist.

As a result of Kentucky's economic diversity, her prosperity was not so intricately tied into the Southern economy as was previously believed. The varied nature of her produce allowed her the ambivalence of choice with regard to market. If the Southern market were threatened, she could always sell her products to the North, which, as the impending struggle became more ominous, was anxious to secure them. Like the river port of Cincinnati, which began shifting its trade from a Southern to an Eastern orientation during the stormy decade of the 1850s, so with the trade of Louisville and other Kentucky river towns.

Kentucky's population had also been undergoing a marked transition during the first half of the nineteenth century. Kentucky was a population *entrepôt* for transmigration to the West and Northwest. Her "sons and daughters" were among the pioneer settlers of Indiana, Illinois, Missouri, Iowa, and Minnesota.[4] These in general were considered "Northern" states whose political, economic, and social philosophy had been molded, in part, by former Kentuckians. As conflict threatened, a vast number of Kentuckians with relatives in these neighboring Northern states pondered whether they could war against their own flesh and blood.

Much has been made of the fact that Kentucky ranked ninth among the sixteen Southern states in the number of slaves within her borders. As of 1860 there were approximately 38,645 slaveholders who controlled a slave population of 225,483 Negroes. Furthermore, Kentucky was the center of a lucrative slave trade. Thus when Northern tocsins sounded the cry of liberation, Kentucky slaveholders immediately regarded this as a threat to their property, as in reality it was. But it must be remembered that Kentucky was predominately a state comprised of small farmers who operated their farms with few if any slaves. Of some 83,000 farms in Kentucky in 1860, 74,000 of them were small farms averaging between 20 and 50 acres. Only 200 farms possessed more than a thousand acres.[5] While the Bourbon gentry found slavery profitable in the maintenance of their large acreage, the small farmer found slavery a questionable economic asset. Abolition societies had existed in Kentucky at an early date, and conscious efforts had been made by the "illustrious" Henry Clay to promote the migration of freed Negroes to the overseas colony of Liberia. Still, as ardent abolitionists of the variety of Cassius Marcellus Clay stumped the Kentucky countryside, the threat of economic loss as well as of Negro insurrection frightened the slaveholder to stubborn resistance. Since the gentry exercised strong control over both the economy and politics of the state, historians have tended to regard Bourbon sentiment as indicative of the true attitude of Kentucky. Upon more careful examination it becomes apparent that the issue of slavery was in reality more emotionally

[4] In 1860 there were nearly 332,000 former Kentuckians residing in other states. *Eighth Census, Population,* 1860, p. xxxiii.

[5] *Eighth Census, Agriculture,* 1860, pp. viii–clxx.

involved with domestic or states' rights than in humanitarian or apologetic principles. This was reflected in Kentucky's representative in the Thirty-sixth Congress, Francis Marion Bristow. In the "fruitless efforts" of the House of Representatives to elect a speaker, a passionate debate occurred on slavery. Reminding his colleagues that Kentucky was "deeply interested" in that institution and that his own congressional district owned more "of that property than any other district in the state," he charged that his constituents were both "conservative" and "law-abiding" citizens. Despite the efforts of "fanatical and lawless abolitionists" who threatened the "domestic peace" of the state, Kentucky had "never looked to a dissolution of this Union as a remedy for these evils." Still, he warned that Kentucky had "a right to expect . . . a faithful regard to her constitutional and legal rights."[6] No one worked more earnestly for conciliation than did Bristow,[7] but when "the descent to folly" occurred, Bristow took the lead in the formulation of the Bowling Green Resolves of May 22, 1861, which declared that Kentucky would remain a member of the federal Union, that "no just cause for secession" existed, and "that Government is ordained of God, for the benefit of mankind, and that no Government ought to be overthrown without a cause for revolution."[8] Significantly these Resolves were issued in the heart of pro-Confederate country where only a few miles away, at Russellville, a Confederate government was soon to be established.[9]

Kentucky's decision to remain neutral was respected by the federal administration. President Lincoln assured the state that he would not send in troops and reminded his "fellow Kentuckians" that the war was being fought to preserve the Union and not to free the slaves. This was responsible for the conversion of many a states'-rights-oriented Kentuckian to the cause of federalism in the early years of the struggle. Further support for the Union came when in September, 1861, a Confederate invasion of Kentucky began: neutrality had been broken not by Union arms, but by the Confederacy. This gave to General U. S. Grant the excuse he had been waiting for and he crossed immediately from Illinois into Kentucky to seize Paducah.

If Kentuckians were as pro-Southern as has been suggested, why did they not support the Confederate invasion? The opportunity was never more favorable. Yet with the violation of Kentucky's neutrality,

[6] *The Congressional Globe,* Part I, 36th Cong., 1st sess., 579.
[7] See Ross A. Webb, "Francis Marion Bristow, A Study in Unionism," *The Filson Club History Quarterly* 37 (April, 1963): 146–55.
[8] The Louisville *Journal,* May 27, 1861.
[9] A convention meeting at Russellville established a Confederate government for Kentucky on Nov. 18, 1861.

the bulk of her youth flocked to Union rather than to Confederate colors. Of approximately 100,000 Kentuckians who saw service in the Civil War, approximately 30,000 enlisted in the Confederate Army as compared to 75,760 in the Union Army.[10] The Unionist captain, Thomas Speed, wrote: "Every part of the State was Union in sentiment, except the extreme west end, and it was from all the other portions of the State where Union sentiment prevailed, including the Blue Grass, that the main body of the Union troops came."[11] The Confederate lawyer and journalist, Colonel J. Stoddard Johnston, in his *Confederate Military History* (1898), confirms Speed's statement: "Whatever may be said of the character of the men whom Kentucky furnished to the Confederate army, the federal statistics of the war show that, judged by all the known physical tests, the federal troops from Kentucky excelled those of all other States."[12]

Despite Presidential assurances that the war was to preserve the Union and not to free the slaves, Kentuckians were becoming wary of the federal government as a result of the passage of the Confiscation Acts of 1861, 1862, and the abolition of slavery in the District of Columbia (April, 1862) and in the territories of the United States (June, 1862). Was the next step uncompensated liberation of the Negroes in the loyal states? Kentuckians suddenly began to fear that even "Father Abraham" had deserted them when in September, 1862, he issued his Preliminary Emancipation Proclamation followed by the formal decree of January 1, 1863, freeing all slaves in areas rebellious against federal authority. What did the future hold for Kentucky if such patent intervention in the domestic affairs of the states were continued?

A greater source of antagonism toward the federal government was the imposition of martial law upon Kentucky, under Brigadier General Jeremiah T. Boyle. This was explained as an effort to suppress treasonable activity within the state and as a measure of protection against the recurring raids of Confederate guerrillas. While a stinging rebuke to proud Kentuckians, as late as December, 1863, Governor Thomas E. Bramlette declared in his message to the legislature: "The Union is indispensable to us, and we are indispensable

[10] *The War of the Rebellion: A Compilation of the Official Records of the Union and Confederate Armies* (Washington, 1880–1901), ser. 3, 4, p. 1269; ser. 4, 1, p. 962.
[11] Thomas Speed, *The Union Cause in Kentucky, 1860–1865* (New York, 1907), pp. 159–61.
[12] As quoted in E. Polk Johnson, *A History of Kentucky and Kentuckians* (3 vols.; Chicago, 1912), 1: 387.

to the Union. We cannot, therefore, separate, but must preserve our unity which gives us our Nationality."[13]

Kentucky had complied with her quotas for the Union Army, but irrespective of this, early in 1864 the federal government began recruiting Negro regiments in the state. The arming of slaves represented not only an invasion of private property but presented the oblique threat that they might be used to suppress other freedoms. Strong opposition ensued. At Lexington, for example, the daring federal Cavalry officer, Colonel Frank L. Wolford, aroused public sentiment to such a pitch that he was promptly arrested and imprisoned.[14] The resignation of Boyle as military commander brought little relief, for Major General Steven G. Burbridge proved even more dictatorial.

The significant factor in this growing discontent with the federal government was the persistence of a number of determined Unionists of various political stripes, who despite the strong anti-administration sentiment worked to preserve the bonds of federal union. Outstanding among them were John J. Crittenden, Garrett Davis, James Speed, Edgar Needham, Benjamin H. Bristow, William C. Goodloe, John A. Prall, R. T. Baker, and Robert J. Breckinridge. It was to this group that Lincoln turned for support; it was this group which he courted, and they did not fail him.

Kentucky's loyalty to the Union therefore can be explained by its ability to reorient its versatile trade northward, by its filial connections with the northwest, by its realization that slavery was a questionable economic asset, by the fact that the Emancipation Proclamation did not apply to Kentucky, by the vicious and destructive activities of Confederate guerrillas, by the presence of the Union Army as an awesome reminder of choice, and by the political activity of numerous Union men in local, state, and national government who worked earnestly to keep Kentucky within the Union.

A "grandfather's myth" has grown up regarding the great attachment of nineteenth-century Kentuckians to "the lost cause." Over the years the glamour and romance surrounding the Confederacy has mounted, and with it the conviction by new Kentuckians that their common heritage was a part of that gallant, unsuccessful effort. Professor E. Merton Coulter has written: "As between the North and the

[13] *Journal of the Adjourned Session of 1863–64 of the Senate of the Commonwealth of Kentucky* (Frankfort, Ky., 1865), p. 21.

[14] Lewis and Richard H. Collins, *History of Kentucky* (2 vols.; Frankfort, Ky., 1966), 1:132.

South the finer feelings of sentiment bound the State to the latter."[15] It is unquestionably true that the bulk of the Bourbon aristocracy was pro-Confederate, as well as a small common element who believed in, and gave of themselves, for the cause. While it would be unfair to decry their devotion to the Confederacy, *they were by no means the majority of Kentuckians.*

With the outbreak of the fratricidal struggle in 1861 a coalition of existing political parties occurred in Kentucky under the name of "Unionists." This political oddity was successful in all three elections held in 1861. Under the skillful leadership of the fiery editor of the Louisville *Journal,* George D. Prentice, the Unionists won nine of the ten congressional seats in the special election of June 20.[16] The States' Rights party was successful only in the First Congressional District, an area in and around Paducah. Concentrating on the state elections of August 5, the Unionists won control of 76 of the 100 seats in the House and 27 of the 38 seats in the Senate. Kentucky was in "safe" hands, but it was not in any sense Republican oriented. Its opposition to secession rested upon the predilection that a full union of states against the present Republican administration would lead to redress of grievances and recognition of the domestic rights of the states.[17] As threats to Kentucky's slave property mounted, as military rule worsened, as Negroes were enlisted into the Union Army, strong opposition mounted, *but with the oft-repeated explanation that the criticisms were aimed at the Republican administration and not at the Union.*[18]

Meanwhile Prentice began espousing the idea of a single national party. If a coalition had been able to save Kentucky from secession, a national coalition in which Republicans and Democrats would abandon their sectional and Radical aims might repair the breach and restore the Union.[19] The growth of Union parties in the North, coupled with reports of increasing Conservative victories over Republicanism seemed encouraging evidence that the scheme might work.[20] However, Prentice's idea proved to be a pipe dream, for within Kentucky the actions of the military as well as the utterings of such "radicals" as Cassius M. Clay (recently returned from his diplomatic post in Russia), urging Negro emancipation, gave abundant evidence

[15] Coulter, *Civil War and Readjustment in Kentucky,* p. 17.
[16] The Louisville *Journal,* April 12, 1861.
[17] *Ibid.,* Jan. 14, 1861.
[18] *Ibid.,* March 20, 1861.
[19] *Ibid.,* April 9, 1862.
[20] *Ibid.,* Oct. 13, 1862.

that the Republican party was not about to forsake its national objectives. Furthermore, the issuance of the Emancipation Proclamation of 1863 indicated that the President was "pro-Radical" in his thinking. Kentucky's narrow domestic philosophy would not allow the state to grasp the wider implications of this action as a means of courting European humanitarian sentiment for the Union. The editor of the Frankfort *Commonwealth* railed: "This proclamation is a nullity" and urged legal resistance against this interference with the domestic institutions of the South.[21] Although Prentice damned the Proclamation as "a grand mistake," he urged continuing support of the President, in view of "the varying fortunes" of war,[22] but the legislature showed less restraint as it formally deplored the Chief Executive's action.

The political arena was strongly anti-Republican as Kentucky prepared for the all-important August elections of 1863: the governorship, the legislature, and the congressional representatives were all in dispute. Reaction had set in destroying the ephemeral political unity that had earlier existed. The coalition was now divided into Unionists and Democrats. Conscious of the results should "the right men" not be elected, military and state authorities used every precaution. Late in July, Governor James F. Robinson issued a proclamation restricting the franchise, while General A. E. Burnside declared the state under martial law to protect "the rights of loyal citizens and the freedom of election."[23] The victory was complete: the Unionist candidate, Thomas E. Bramlette, was elected governor over the Democratic candidate, Charles A. Wickliffe, by a majority of over 50,000 votes; Unionists were elected over Democrats and States' Rights candidates (Independent Union) in almost every instance. Nevertheless, it was charged that some 55,000 voters had been kept from the polls either by military intimidation or threat of arrest.[24]

In the contest, a further division in the ranks of the Unionists had occurred. At the state convention held in Louisville on March 18–19, a debate had erupted over support for the declaration of the "Union as it was." Numerous Unionists took exception to this, chief of whom were Mortimer M. Benton, David Goodloe, William H. Campbell, George and Edward Denny, and General Green Clay Smith. Several of these objectors were later nominated by their constituents for the legislature and for Congress with the promise of "unconditional"

---

[21] The Frankfort *Commonwealth*, Jan. 5, 1863.
[22] The Louisville *Journal*, Jan. 9, 1863.
[23] *The War of the Rebellion*, ser. 1, 23, pt. 2, p. 572.
[24] Collins, *History of Kentucky*, 1:127–28. Charles Kerr, ed., *History of Kentucky* (5 vols.; Chicago, 1922), 2:897. The Louisville *Journal*, Aug. 8, 1863.

support to the national government as opposed to the "half way" measures of the Louisville platform. Although these men claimed the title "Unconditional Unionists," in reality they were to become the founders of a revitalized Republican party in Kentucky.[25]

One of the leading "lights" of the new political order was the Reverend Robert J. Breckinridge, Presbyterian minister, former superintendent of public instruction for Kentucky, and professor of theology at the Danville Seminary.[26] Using the influential Seminary publication, the *Danville Review,* he urged continuing support of the President. However, it was not until the Frankfort *Commonwealth* began espousing the cause of the administration, that the Unconditional Unionists had any major means of influencing the electorate of Kentucky.[27]

At the outset the legislature showed its strong Unionist make-up by commending Generals Grant and Burnside for their victories at Stone River, Chickamauga, Lookout Mountain, and Missionary Ridge, by ordering the "Stars and Stripes" to be raised in front of the capitol, by empowering the Governor to raise a military force of 5,000 men for a period of three years to cope with the Confederate guerrillas, by passing several measures intended to increase enlistment, and by forbidding the further importation of slaves into Kentucky under penalty of a $600 fine for each slave illegally brought in.[28] Efforts also were made to improve public education, the mental asylums, internal navigation, and the banking system.

Meanwhile strong opposition to the federal government's continued enlistment of Negroes into the Union Army arose in Kentucky. Whereas Governor Bramlette had originally backed the administration, he now repented "of all the promises of support he had ever made to the Lincoln government."[29] Since the Union party did not consider itself a "Lincoln or Republican party," it agreed to participate in the state Democratic convention which met at Louisville on May 25, 1864. After instructing its delegates to the Chicago convention to support General George McClellan for President and Thomas E. Bramlette for Vice President, a dissident group comprised of Benjamin H. Bristow, Curtis F. Burnam, Rufus K. Williams, Albert

[25] See Edward Isaiah Malberg, "The Republican Party in Kentucky, 1856–67," (Master's thesis, University of Kentucky, 1967), pp. 52–54.

[26] Kerr, *History of Kentucky,* 3:17.

[27] The Frankfort *Commonwealth,* Dec. 28, 1863.

[28] *Ibid.,* Jan. 12, 19, 21, Feb. 2, 16, 20, 1864. *Journal of the Senate,* 1863, pp. 269–71, 282, 429–49. Efforts also were made to improve public education, the mental asylums, the locks and dams on the Green and Barren rivers, and the banking system. Collins, *History of Kentucky,* 2:130.

[29] Coulter, *Civil War and Readjustment in Kentucky,* p. 179.

G. Hodges, and Lucien Anderson, frustrated that they had been unable to capture Union support for the Baltimore convention, summoned a convention of their own. To everyone's amazement 109 delegates from 56 counties showed up in Louisville, where they voiced approval of administrative policy and instructed their delegates to the Baltimore convention to support Lincoln's renomination.[30] Unconditional Unionism increased in strength as a result of this further rift in the Unionist ranks.

However, during the summer of 1864 the Unconditional Unionists were injured severely by Major General Steven G. Burbridge's interference in local elections. When Burbridge ordered the name of Alvin Duvall, a Southern States' Rights man running for judge of the Court of Appeals, stricken from the polling books, he hoped that the Unconditional Union candidate, Mortimer M. Benton, would be elected. "Conservative" Unionists immediately nominated the popular former chief justice, George Robertson, as a compromise candidate. Despite the presence of the Union Army, which so intimidated the people that only 11,000 votes were cast out of a possible 45,000, Robertson was elected. As if the army intervention were not enough, a series of arrests of prominent individuals considered pro-Confederate in their sentiments further antagonized Kentuckians.[31]

Burbridge made his greatest political blunder in October when he issued his famous "hog order." Supposedly motivated by the needs of the Union Army, he instructed Kentucky livestock producers to sell their surplus hogs to the United States government at fair market value. While this appeared innocuous, on November 7, 1864, the Louisville *Democrat* charged that only certain packing houses were enjoying the profits, while other packing plants were suffering from loss of product. Burbridge was accused of favoritism at the expense of the meat packers as well as the farmer who was forced to sell his product below the average selling price. Here was excellent election material. Burbridge's chicanery in no small way handed the state to the Democrats in the November presidential election. Despite the pressures of the military, McClellan received a majority of nearly 35,000 over Lincoln.[32]

[30] Robert J. Breckinridge and Francis Marion Bristow were named as delegates to the Baltimore convention. Collins, *History of Kentucky,* 1:133–34.
[31] Chief Justice Joshua F. Bullitt of the Court of Appeals was forced to flee the state at this time. Collins, *History of Kentucky,* 1:137.
[32] Despite these reverses, the Unconditional Unionist could take some comfort from the fact that in the eighth district Lincoln claimed ten of the fifteen mountain counties as well as Fayette, Kenton, and Campbell counties. While the loss of Louisville was disturbing, nearly one-quarter of the votes had been cast for Lincoln. The Louisville *Journal,* Aug. 30, 1867. Malberg, "The Republican Party in Kentucky," p. 77.

Lincoln's failure to carry Kentucky obviated the need to placate the state. When Governor Bramlette protested the "hog swindle" to the President, not only was the objectionable order revoked but Burbridge was replaced by the former Kentuckian, General John M. Palmer, with the hope that he would be more acceptable to the state.[33]

In an effort to achieve a stronger organization, the Unconditional Unionists held a convention at Frankfort on January 4, 1865. Under the leadership of William C. Goodloe, Benjamin H. Bristow, and W. R. Kinney the party appealed to all loyal men of the state to adhere to the Baltimore platform of 1864, to support the proposed amendment to the Constitution abolishing slavery, and to vigorously combat Confederate guerrilla activity in the state.[34]

Simultaneously the legislature convened. Despite the pleas of the Unconditional Unionists to ratify the Thirteenth Amendment, the legislature, still smarting from military intervention, overwhelmingly rejected it.[35]

But while the legislature quibbled, the war came to a rapid close. When news of Lee's surrender at Appomattox Courthouse reached Frankfort, the *Commonwealth* carried the headlines: "VICTORY Surrender of Lee 'Glory to God in the Highest' !" But the celebrations ended abruptly five days later when news of the assassination of President Lincoln reached Kentucky. The same press reported the tragedy: "The terrible news was received by our community, on Saturday morning, with feelings of the most profound grief. Nearly every countenance was depicted with the deepest sorrow."[36] The legislature reflected similar sentiments and promptly drafted resolutions lamenting the passing of the martyr President, ranking him among the greatest "patriots and statesmen of the nation and the world."[37] Attempting to capitalize on this sentiment, the Unconditional Unionists tried to force a legislative review of the Thirteenth Amendment, but to no avail. While Kentuckians mourned the passing of Lincoln, the right to deal with domestic questions was still theirs.[38]

---

[33] Collins, *History of Kentucky*, 1:144, 153. The Louisville *Journal*, Feb. 21, 1865.

[34] The Frankfort *Commonwealth*, Jan. 6, 1865. The Louisville *Journal*, Jan. 5, 1865.

[35] The Frankfort *Commonwealth*, Feb. 28, 1865. Collins, *History of Kentucky*, 1:155.

[36] The Frankfort *Commonwealth*, April 11, 1865.

[37] *Ibid.*, April 18, 1865. *Acts of Kentucky*, 1865, Resolution No. 78, 159; Resolution No. 82, 161.

[38] The Frankfort *Commonwealth*, June 6, 1865.

The war at an end, Kentuckians now worked to secure the return of freedoms denied them during the war, to rehabilitate their returning native sons, and to prevent "Radical" Republican domination from Washington. While a political "tug of war" existed at the national level between the Radical Republicans and Lincoln's successor, Andrew Johnson, for mastery of the large Conservative vote of the country, Kentucky was a microcosm of a similar conflict. Two political identities, the Democrats and the Unconditional Unionists, vied for control of the large Conservative element in the state. The Democrats were a strange combination of "Union Democrats," who had supported the federal cause during the war years both politically and militarily, and "Southern Democrats," as the returning pro-Confederate politicians and ex-Confederate veterans were called. A common meeting ground for the two elements existed in their antagonism to congressional reconstruction, their insistence upon strict construction of the Constitution, and their belief in states' rights. The issue that had originally divided them—secession—was now settled and the two factions could once again agree on public issues. However, with the removal of all proscriptive measures in December, 1865, the "Southern Democrats" tended to dominate the party under the leadership of men like John W. Stevenson and Preston H. Leslie. Significantly, the reason for this was not, as Professor Coulter has suggested, that Kentucky had at last revealed her pro-Confederate sympathies, but rather that these ex-Confederate Democrats had been prominent political leaders before the war and were now reclaiming their popular support. Their pro-Confederate sympathies were consistently played down, although they were actively interested in the return of the Southern states to their rightful place in the Union. On the other hand, the Unconditional Unionists were wed to national Republicanism. While demanding support for the federal administration, they had misgivings about congressional Reconstruction. Although a "right" or Radical wing existed in Kentucky, it was never dominant for the party accepted "moderate" leadership from men like James Speed and Benjamin H. Bristow. Moderate Republicans made their appeal to the electorate on the grounds that they were the party of political and economic liberalism. The Conservatives, who were organized politically, consisted of old-line Whigs disenchanted with Republican Radical Reconstruction, Independents opposed to the centralization of power in Washington, Union Democrats frustrated by the increased political influence of "Southern Democrats" over the party, and a large element of indifferent Kentuckians simply not aware of the political issues of the day. The Conservatives had distinguished leadership from prominent individuals like Thomas E. Bramlette, R. T. Jacob, and J. H. Harney.

If the Democrats were going to recoup their political fortunes after the war, it became obvious that they must make a strong appeal to the Conservatives by emphasizing that Reconstruction was "base usurpation" which violated "the Constitution of the United States" and "the rights of the people." They demanded that the Southern states be restored to the "free and unrestrained exercise of their privileges and prerogatives" within the Union, since a republican system of government could only be retained "by the recognition of the equality of the States composing the Union." They damned the centralization of power in Washington, condemned the tariff as "intolerable" because it discriminated in favor of New England, and insisted upon "cheap money" as a means of inflating the economy. Led by such outstanding Kentuckians as Garrett Davis, Lazarus W. Powell, Robert Mallory, John Helm, Charles Wickliffe, and W. F. Bullock,[39] the Democrats made a strong appeal to a sensitive Kentucky electorate and won the support of a majority of the Conservatives.

At a meeting of the State Central Committee of Unconditional Unionists held in Frankfort on May 23, 1865, that party declared its full suport of the national administration and the Thirteenth Amendment. While encouraging a policy of magnanimity toward returning Confederates, they opposed repeal of the state's Expatriation Act, which would keep "traitors" from exercising their political rights. Anyone not in agreement with these principles was declared a member of the Democrat party.[40] By purging their rolls, the Unconditional Unionists drove many a sympathetic Conservative into the ranks of their opponents.

Meanwhile the election of August, 1866, was in the offing. As was expected, the ratification of the Thirteenth Amendment became the primary issue. The Unconditional Unionists urged adoption on the grounds that slavery was dead and must be so recognized. The Democrats with their Conservative allies countered that slavery was a domestic institution over which the federal government had no jurisdiction, therefore the amendment was unconstitutional. Much was made of the continuing presence of the Union Army in Kentucky and of the interference of General Palmer in state affairs. Despite the presence of the military at the polls, the Union Democrats and Conservatives captured five of the nine congressional seats and won a

---

[39] The Frankfort *Daily Kentucky Yeoman*, Dec. 4, 5, 1865, Feb. 7, 9, June 7, 1866.
[40] *Ibid.*, May 26, 1865. The Louisville *Journal*, June 1, 1865.

majority of two in the Senate and twenty in the House.[41] When several of the elections were challenged because of undue military interference, twelve legislators lost their seats and several of the military were prosecuted for interfering with the elections. This gross violation of the act of Congress of February 25, 1865, forbidding military interference with elections, resulted in President Johnson's ordering an end of martial law in Kentucky on October 12, 1865.[42]

The Democrat–Conservative coalition was "in the saddle." To increase their support from the pro-Confederate element, they proceeded not only to repeal the Expatriation Act but defeated an attempt by the Unconditional Unionists to require an oath of allegiance on the grounds that the allegiance due by the citizen to his state was subordinate to the paramount allegiance due to the government of the United States. When it was suggested that the Kentucky Democrats were infested with "Rebels," that party was quick to respond. "We have buried the tomahawk here in Kentucky, and our noble Legislature has gained infinite honor by wiping away the political disabilities of her sons, and has set an example of magnanimity which might well be followed by other bodies having legislature function."[43]

The promulgation of the Thirteenth Amendment on December 18, 1865, and the extension of the Freedmen's Bureau to Kentucky in January, 1866, stimulated the pen of "Old Kentucky" to vituperate: "Let out your spite, Messrs. gentlemen abolitionists; you may not always have the power. The day may come, as it did to Danton, Robespierre, and Marat, in the French Revolution, when the knives you are whetting for others may take off your own heads."[44]

While the Freedmen's Bureau had been created primarily for the rehabilitation and protection of Negroes in those areas formerly in rebellion against the United States, General Clinton B. Fisk, Assistant Commissioner of the Bureau in Nashville, Tennessee was instructed from Washington to name Bureau officials for Kentucky.[45] Radical supporters argued that the establishment of the Bureau in Kentucky was necessary because the Legislature had not been unable to prevent coercion and injury to freedmen.[46] These were not adequate answers

[41] Collins, *History of Kentucky,* 1:163. The Louisville *Journal,* Aug. 11, 1865. The Frankfort *Commonwealth,* Aug. 11, 1865.
[42] Coulter, *Civil War and Readjustment in Kentucky,* pp. 282–86. Collins, *History of Kentucky,* 1:164. The Frankfort *Commonwealth,* Aug. 15, 25, 26, Sept. 12, 1865, Jan. 19, 30, Feb. 9, 1866.
[43] The Frankfort *Daily Kentucky Yeoman,* Feb. 2, 3, 1866.
[44] *Ibid.,* Dec. 21, 1865.
[45] The Frankfort *Commonwealth,* Jan. 2, 1866.
[46] *Ibid.,* Jan. 8, 1866.

to the emotional Kentuckian who was prone to concur with the sentiments of "Old Kentucky": "The right of the Negro to hold office or to vote in this State has always been denied, and we trust ever will be. Now, we ask, whether there is any necessity under the circumstances above suggested to introduce into this State the Freedman's Bureau. If the laws of the State protect the Negro in all his civil rights, as we have stated, and if there is a prevailing disposition upon the part of the whites to encourage the colored people in the pursuits of industry, is not this enough? What more can the Freedman's Bureau do for the Negro?"[47]

As was expected, the leadership of the Bureau was entrusted to civilians who were more often than not Unconditional Unionists. Of the forty-one superintendents appointed during the first month, the majority were identified with either the Republican or the Unconditional Unionist party.

Frightened by the implications of this new federal intervention, the Legislature in February, 1866, granted Negroes virtually all civil rights enjoyed by whites except that Negro testimony could not be used as evidence against whites. Nevertheless Negroes were competent witnesses in civil suits where only Negroes were concerned and in criminal cases where the Negro was the defendant.[48]

General aversion to the Freedman's Bureau resulted in a unique political movement to revive the old Union party in the hope that a united front would force an end of congressional intervention in Kentucky. In addition to this, many a Union Democrat, fearing the loss of political leadership as his party became infiltrated with returning ex-Confederates, sensed that it was politically opportune to attempt to revitalize the Unionist concept as an instrument to maintain power. On January 17, 1866, a number of Unionist-minded legislators met in caucus to draft a group of resolutions designed to appeal to men of varying Union sentiment. A third party movement was clearly under way in Kentucky. After expressing gratitude to the Union Army for the suppression of rebellion, they endorsed President Johnson's Reconstruction program as the basis of a sound rehabilitation policy. The loyal spirit of states previously in rebellion was praised as a promise of speedy reunion. Affirming allegiance to the national government, they asked that the Freedmen's Bureau be removed from the state, for they were confident that Kentucky would

[47] The Frankfort *Daily Kentucky Yeoman*, Jan. 2, 1866.
[48] Collins, *History of Kentucky*, 1:170.

pass the necessary legislative measures to insure the rights of the Negro.[49]

The Democratic proponents of this coalition were regarded as "Sallee-Busters." One Southern Democrat remarked of this "unholy" combination: "Ye gods! Would not old Hickory kick your Sallee-Buster higher than a kite." Nevertheless, these were highly respectable men, among whom were R. T. Jacob, John H. Harney, John H. Harlan, George D. Prentice, and Hamilton Pope.[50]

This effort at coalition appeared relatively successful when moderate Unconditional Unionists joined Union Democrats and Conservatives in supporting President Johnson's veto of the new Freedmen's Bureau Bill of February, 1866. The Chief Executive gave as his reasons that Congress had no power to legislate with eleven states of the Union unrepresented. Furthermore, the provisions for military trials violated the Fifth Amendment.[51] The editor of the *Daily Kentucky Yeoman* exclaimed: "Thank Heaven, Andrew Johnson, under Divine Providence has saved and shielded us from the last engine of tyranny and oppression."[52]

Further antagonism toward congressional Reconstruction was evoked by the passage of the Civil Rights Act of April 9, 1866. This measure bestowed citizenship upon the Negro; asserted the right of the federal government to intervene in state affairs to protect its citizens; gave to federal Courts exclusive jurisdiction over offenders; and made available the military and naval forces of the United States as enforcement agencies. Again President Johnson exercised his veto of this measure as an unwarranted invasion of states' rights, but as was in the case with the Freedmen's Bureau Bill, Congress repassed the measure. The Chief Executive's actions endeared him to Kentuckians who were in complete accord with his states' rights philosophy.

"The Crowning Infancy," as the Democratic press in Kentucky called it, was the passage of the Negro Homestead Act, opening public lands in Mississippi, Louisiana, Arkansas, and Florida to be taken up in eighty-acre homesteads by actual settlers. The Freedmen's Bureau was ordered to inform Negroes of this and to urge them to take advantage of it. "Not satisfied with Negro equality, these hell-hounds are determined to force Negro superiority upon the people of the

[49] The Louisville *Journal*, Jan. 19, 1866. The Frankfort *Commonwealth*, Jan. 19, 1866.

[50] The Frankfort *Daily Kentucky Yeoman*, May 24, June 28, 1866.

[51] The Louisville *Journal*, Feb. 26, 1866. The Frankfort *Commonwealth*, Feb. 23, 1866.

[52] The Frankfort *Daily Kentucky Yeoman*, Feb. 24, 1866.

South," bemoaned the editor of the *Daily Kentucky Yeoman*. This congressional action was another stimulant to a possible fusion of the Unconditional Unionists, Conservative Unionists, and the "Sallee-Busters" into one party.[53]

The first evidence that such a coalition was taking form occurred at the state convention of Union soldiers and sailors held in Louisville on April 6, where a permanent organization called the "Union Soldiers' Association of Kentucky" was established.[54] When the meeting turned out to be apolitical, efforts were made to hold a convention at Louisville on May 30. However, the Unconditional Unionists opposed the stringent criticisms of Congress and for the most part withdrew, whereupon the Union Democrats and Conservative Unionists organized themselves into the Conservative Union Democrats. After endorsing President Johnson's policies they proceeded bitterly to attack congressional Reconstruction. Since the immediate need was to nominate a candidate for the clerkship of the Court of Appeals, Colonel Richard R. Bolling was selected.[55] When Bolling refused the nomination, John Seaton volunteered his services, but recognizing that Seaton could not "carry the day," the prominent Union General, Edward H. Hobson, was chosen.[56]

Meanwhile the Democrats in convention nominated Alvin Duvall for the clerkship. Duvall was a pro-Southern man who, in 1864, had been forced by General Burbridge to flee the state.[57] The Louisville *Journal* charged that this political contest was "squarely" between "those who fought for the Union, and those who fought for the revolt all through the war."[58] Charges of congressional intimidation were voiced. The Democrats claimed that Congress was so interested in Hobson's election that they were dangling a subsidy of "Five Million Dollars to Kentucky Depending Upon the Defeat of the Secession Party." "Let the people of Kentucky remember," scolded the editor of the *Daily Kentucky Yeoman*, "that they have been robbed of more than *one hundred millions* of slave property by the . . . party . . . of which General E. H. Hobson was a prominent and distinguished leader."[59]

[53] *Ibid.*, June 20, 1866.

[54] The Frankfort *Commonwealth*, May 4, 1866.

[55] *Ibid.*, April 20, 1866. The Louisville *Journal*, April 21, May 31, 1866.

[56] The Frankfort *Commonwealth*, May 8, 11, June 5, 12, 1866. The Louisville *Journal*, June 27, 28, July 9, 1866. Collins, *History of Kentucky*, 1:172.

[57] The Frankfort *Daily Kentucky Yeoman*, May 15, 1866. Collins, *History of Kentucky*, 1:137.

[58] The Cincinnati *Gazette*, June 28, 1866, as quoted in Coulter, *Civil War and Readjustment in Kentucky*, p. 911.

[59] The Frankfort *Daily Kentucky Yeoman*, July 5, 26, 1866.

The newness of the coalition, coupled with the threat of congressional intervention, resulted in Hobson's defeat. Duvall's overwhelming victory (a majority of over 37,000 votes) was generally regarded as "an all out rebel victory." Many historians have made a strong case for this interpretation ignoring the fact that Duvall was symbolic in the Kentucky mind not so much with "the lost cause" as with federal military oppression.[60]

As Kentucky attempted to achieve some form of political unity to back the administration in its fight against Radical congressional Reconstruction, so did the President attempt to create a national party of moderates throughout the country. Late in August, 1866, it was announced that the President would make a "swing around the circle" and would visit Kentucky. Arriving in Louisville on September 12, Johnson was enthusiastically received. Warming to the occasion, he urged support of the platform of the National Union Convention, the third party being called into existence to support his reconstruction policies.[61]

When the call was issued to all Union veterans "favorable to the President's policy" to meet in convention at Cleveland on September 17, Kentucky responded by electing 79 delegates of various political hues, among whom were Governor Thomas E. Bramlette, Major General L. H. Rousseau, General W. C. Whitaker, and Colonel B. H. Bristow. At Cleveland, Governor Bramlette offered the expected resolution endorsing the policies of the President. The convention then approved the platform of the Philadelphia National Convention as the only course open to those who desired to preserve the Constitution and the Union.[62]

The alliance of Conservative and Unionist Democrats was severely tested in the election of a United States Senator early in 1867. The Union Democrats consistently voted for Lazarus W. Powell, while the Conservatives kept balloting for Garrett Davis. The Unconditional Unionists finding themselves unable to support either candidate ultimately settled upon the moderate, Benjamin H. Bristow. However, the Union Democrats quickly agreed to support Davis, thereby swallowing the Conservatives "body, bones, and breeches." The third party movement had failed. When the Democratic state convention met on February 22, 1867, to select its candidates for the pending state elections, it was a large and powerful body that nominated John L. Helm

[60] Professor Coulter claims: "Kentucky was now in complete accord with her Southern traditions." Kerr, *History of Kentucky*, 2:912.

[61] The Louisville *Journal*, Sept. 10, 12, 1866. The Frankfort *Daily Kentucky Yeoman*, Sept. 11, 13, 20, 1866.

[62] The Louisville *Journal*, Aug. 31, Sept. 13, 20, 1866.

for governor. The platform condemned congressional Reconstruction as an attempt to reduce ten states "to mere territorial dependencies," damned the "high and odious protective tariff," and criticized the corruption of public offices. It pledged support to the President for "his veto of those iniquitous and unconstitutional bills known as the Freedmen's Bureau Bill and the Civil Rights Bill, as well as for his vetoes of other bills."[63] The rump of the Conservative party subsequently met in Louisville and nominated W. B. Kinkhead for governor. But this third party movement (referred to as the Jacob-Harney Society) had little hope of success, for those Conservatives not swallowed up by the Democrats went over into the ranks of the Unconditional Unionists now openly referred to as Republicans. The most outstanding of the converts was a young Kentucky lawyer named John Marshall Harlan.[64] The Republicans gathered in Frankfort in mid-February, where after some deliberation, they nominated Sidney M. Barnes for governor. Significantly, however, the assembly listened to the moderates of the party (James Speed and B. H. Bristow) as it drafted its platform. Support of the extreme measures of congressional Reconstruction were suppressed to the disappointment of the Radical wing.[65]

The issue of the campaign was the Fourteenth Amendment, which threw the cloak of federal protection around the Negro by granting him equal civil rights with whites. While the Republicans supported it, the Democrats attacked it as a further invasion of states' rights. A test of political power came in the May congressional elections when the Democrats made "a clean sweep"—electing nine congressmen. Still the outcome of the August state elections was considered to be more conclusive. To the great distress of the Republicans, the Democrats not only elected Helm governor, but overwhelmingly carried the state. The Republicans secured only seven of the thirty-eight seats in the Senate and ten of the one hundred seats in the House.[66] The editor of the Frankfort *Commonwealth* lamented: "The 'Lost Cause' is found again in Kentucky."[67] Historians have picked up this phrase and assumed that the Democrats were now thoroughly pro-Confederate. But the Democrats, while emphasing states' rights, consistently declared their devotion to the Union and the Constitution. It was anti-congressional antagonism not pro-Confederate sentiment that motivated the Kentucky Democrats. This was the first major election free from the

[63] The Frankfort *Daily Kentucky Yeoman*, Feb. 26, 1867.
[64] *Ibid.*, Jan. 26, 30, 1867.
[65] *Ibid.*, Feb. 28, March 1, 1867.
[66] The Louisville *Journal*, Aug. 6, 1867.
[67] The Frankfort *Commonwealth*, Aug. 9, 1867.

influence of the Union Army, and Kentuckians seized the opportunity to declare their dissatisfaction with the shabby treatment of the state by the Republicans.

Another significant factor influencing the August election of 1867 was the move in Congress by Radical Republicans to refuse to seat the newly elected Kentucky representatives and to appoint a congressional committee to inquire into the question of the loyalty of Kentuckians.[68] While the excitement soon died away and all the congressmen except John D. Young were seated, this unfortunate investigation was not forgotten.[69] The Democrats claimed that their success heralded "a new era" in American politics. The editor of the *Daily Kentucky Yeoman* wrote: "The Democracy of Kentucky set the example, Connecticut followed, California and Montana came on in line, and now come Pennsylvania, Ohio, Indiana, and Iowa. New York and the rest will follow in November—'revolutions never go backward'—and the platter will be swept."[70]

When Governor Helm died after only five days in office, a special gubernatorial election coincided with the presidential election of 1868. The Democrats nominated John W. Stevenson, the incumbent governor, and backed Horatio Seymour for the presidency. The third party movement in the meantime had disappeared, for those Conservatives not absorbed by the Democrats had found their way into the Republican party. The Republicans selected R. T. Baker for governor and by acclamation supported U. S. Grant for president. Playing down the radical nature of the party, they attempted to appeal to moderates of every political complexion. Unlike the Democrats who castigated the Radicals on the impeachment proceedings against President Johnson, Kentucky Republicans purposely remained silent.[71]

The Republicans did little campaigning in the state election, for Stevenson was extremely popular. Rather they chose to throw all of their efforts into swinging the state into Grant's column. Moderates, like Bristow and Speed, attempted to characterize their party as one

[68] This was the work of Samuel McKee, Steven Burbridge, and Sam Johnson who were disappointed Radical Republican candidates for Congress. The Frankfort *Daily Kentucky Yeoman*, May 30, 1867. The "Congressional Smelling Committee," as it was called by the editor of the *Daily Kentucky Yeoman*, met in Lexington on October 19, 1867. See U.S. House of Representatives, Kentucky Elections, Misc. Docs., 40th Cong., 1st sess., no. 47, Washington, 1867. *The Congressional Globe,* 40th Cong., 1st sess., 4681.

[69] The Louisville *Journal,* Nov. 28, 1867.

[70] The Frankfort *Daily Kentucky Yeoman,* Oct. 10, 1867.

[71] The Louisville *Journal,* Feb. 18, 1868. The Frankfort *Daily Kentucky Yeoman,* Feb. 29, 1868.

that promoted "the progress and advancement of man." They tried to interpret Grant as not only "the hero of forty battles" but the "gracious saviour of the Union." Despite this appeal, the Democrats were successful in electing Stevenson, in carrying the state for Seymour, and in electing a full delegation to Congress.[72]

During the ensuing winter and spring of 1868–69 the controversial issue in Kentucky was the Fifteenth Amendment. The Democrats viewed this measure as an attempt by the Republicans to regain political strength by appealing to the grateful Negro. Certainly the enfranchisement of the Negro would help a battered Republican party overcome losses sustained in the elections of 1867 and 1868. While Kentucky Republicans argued that the love of liberty was inherent in human nature and to stifle it by refusing the franchise to the Negro would result in great danger to the state, such arguments were weak alongside those of Garrett Davis who charged that the amendment was unconstitutional since it violated the "inherent sovereignty" of the states.[73] It was a foregone conclusion that the Democratic legislature, possessed of strong racial prejudices and personal antagonisms against federal authority, would reject the amendment, as it did on March 13, 1869.[74]

While there were numerous newspapers trumpeting the cause of the Democrats in the state, few Republican presses[75] with any extensive circulation could match the unusually outstanding Democratic editors of the Louisville *Daily Journal*, the Louisville *Daily Courier*, and the Louisville *Democrat*: George Prentice, Walter N. Haldeman, and John H. Harney. With the consolidation of the *Courier* and the *Journal* under Haldeman as president, Prentice as editor, and the ambitious Henry Watterson as editorial manager,[76] the Republicans determined to establish a journal which would foster their policies and philosophy. On December 29, 1869, the first issue of the Louisville *Daily Commercial* appeared. This newspaper was not only noted for its "safe and sane" reporting, but for its "moderate" Republican philosophy. Simultaneously, leading Republicans such as Benjamin H. Bristow, John H. Harlan, and James Speed began exploiting their party as "progressive" and "liberal." They pleaded with Kentuckians

[72] Stevenson received a majority of 88,965 over Baker, while Seymour secured a 75,000 majority over Grant. Collins, *History of Kentucky*, 1:192.

[73] The Frankfort *Daily Kentucky Yeoman*, March 23, 1869.

[74] Collins, *History of Kentucky*, 1:195.

[75] The most important Republican newspaper in the state was the Frankfort *Commonwealth*, under the able editorship of Colonel Albert G. Hodges.

[76] J. Stoddard Johnston, *Memorial History of Louisville from Its First Settlement to the Year 1896* (2 vols.; Chicago, 1896), 2:71.

"to cut loose from the prejudices of the past" and to conform to the new "spirit of progress" and the "liberal ideas" of the present.[77]

This well could have reshaped Kentucky politics had not the aggressive Henry Watterson begun advocating a "new departure" from historic Democratic philosophy. Using the *Courier–Journal*, "Marse Henry" put forward the concept of a "new South" which called for acceptance of the Fourteenth and Fifteenth Amendments, recognition of Negro suffrage, fostering of industrial development, and legislative subsidization of railroads. Watterson argued that if the South was to take its rightful place in the Union, it must accept the results of the war, whether it liked them or not.[78] This was a revolutionary step for the Democrats to take, but after eyeing the political record, Watterson was convinced that it was better to swallow the pill, no matter how bitter, than to allow the Republicans a monopoly on progressive liberal philosophy. While Watterson may have been sympathetic to, and possibly even derived his ideas from the Republicans, he was certain that the Democratic party was the instrument of progress and advancement. Using the press as a powerful propaganda agency, he set out to convert his party to the "new departure."

The removal of the Freedmen's Bureau in 1869 ended a major source of federal antagonism in the state. Opposed as an insult and injury to both the loyalty and sovereignty of Kentucky[79] and charged with gross violations of the rights of white Kentuckians, it had nevertheless accomplished much. It did some creditable work among the Negroes by sending them back to work at a wage fixed by the Bureau, by setting up schools for them,[80] by encouraging the habit of saving,[81] and by attempting to secure them justice in the courts.

The faults usually attributed to the Freedmen's Bureau were the result of the failure of state political leadership to co-operate with its programs. Mutual suspicion on the part of the Bureau and native white Kentuckians frustrated many of its programs. For example, the efforts made to stabilize labor at a uniform wage of $100 to $150 per year for males and $50 to $100 for females failed primarily because of an unwillingness of white employers and the Bureau to co-operate.

[77] Speech of B. H. Bristow on behalf of James Speed's candidacy for Congress, as reported in the Louisville *Commercial*, Oct. 24, 25, 1870.

[78] Thomas D. Clark, *History of Kentucky* (Lexington, 1960), p. 412.

[79] Frankfort *Daily Kentucky Yeoman*, Jan. 17, 1866.

[80] By mid-1866 the Freedmen's Bureau had set up thirty-five Negro schools with fifty-eight teachers. There were 4,122 pupils and an average attendance of 3,215. Coulter, *Civil War and Readjustment*, p. 357. The Cincinnati *Gazette*, Oct. 19, 1866.

[81] In 1873 the branches of the Freedman's Saving and Trust Company, located in Louisville and Lexington, contained $171,000 in savings belonging to Negroes. House of Representatives, Misc. Docs., 43d Cong., 2d sess., no. 16, 61. Temple Bodley and Samuel M. Wilson, *History of Kentucky* (3 vols.; Chicago, 1928), 2:358.

White "tenancy" also struck severely at the efforts of the Bureau to rehabilitate the freedman on the land.

In the face of all this, some positive move had to be made in Kentucky on behalf of the freedmen. In 1866, General Fisk announced that Freedmen's Bureau courts would be established for the protection of the Negro. Prompt action resulted; no less than eighty-nine persons were arrested in 1867, charged with crimes against the Negro, and handed over to the federal courts for trial.[82] Although the legislature had refused to ratify the Thirteenth Amendment after its adoption in 1865, Kentucky passed a Civil Rights Act (February, 1866) which repealed the old slave code. This measure to no small extent was the result of congressional refusal to remove the Freedmen's Bureau from the state until Negroes had been granted civil rights. While the act gave freedmen virtually all the civil rights enjoyed by white persons, it still withheld the right of Negroes to sit on juries and testify against whites.[83]

Reaction on the part of the rival white laborer was immediate. Bands of individuals, at first called Regulators and afterward Ku-Klux Klan, took upon themselves the right to punish offenders of state law. A rule of terror developed in Marion, Boyle, Jessamine, Lincoln, Mercer, Nelson, Nicholas, and Franklin counties. Kentucky was faced with the threat of mob rule as the Ku-Klux Klan rode through the countryside, armed and disguised, whipping, torturing, and stealing without discretion.[84]

But the man exercising federal authority in Kentucky was equal to his responsibility. The United States district attorney for Kentucky at this time was the moderate Unconditional Unionist, Benjamin H. Bristow. Determined that the recently passed federal Civil Rights Act of April 9, 1866, would be enforced, Kentucky became the legal testing ground of that measure. The refusal to Negroes of the right to testify was a denial of a civil right and therefore justified the use of writs of *habeas corpus* to transfer cases involving Negroes from state courts to federal courts.[85] Two celebrated cases, the *United States* vs. *Rhodes* and the *United States* vs. *Blyew and Kennard* attested to the constitutionality of the Civil Rights Act of 1866.[86] However, in January,

---

[82] Coulter, *Civil War and Readjustment,* p. 348.

[83] Collins, *History of Kentucky,* 1:170.

[84] See W. E. B. DuBois, *Black Reconstruction* (New York, 1935), p. 568.

[85] The Louisville *Journal,* Oct. 3, 1866. *The United States* v. *Rhodes,* Fed. Cas. 785 (no. 16,151) (C. C. D. Ky. 1866). *The United States* v. *Blyew and Kennard,* 80 U.S. (13 Wall.) 642 (1872).

[86] See Ross A. Webb, "Benjamin Helm Bristow, The Man Who Walked in Front of Destiny," *The Filson Club History Quarterly* 41 (April, 1867): 107–14.

1869, Governor Stevenson called the attention of the legislature to these obvious violations of the right of the state to exercise criminal jurisdiction and urged a legislative appropriation to test the constitutionality of the federal Civil Rights Act. Motivated by increasing congressional intervention in the state, the legislators readily agreed. However, several years were to pass before the Supreme Court was to rule on the matter.[87]

In the interim Bristow and his successor, Gabriel C. Wharton, with the backing of the Attorney General continued to successfully sustain the Civil Rights Act as a measure of federal protection to the exploited freedman. When numerous lawyers urged the legislature to pass more liberal laws for the Negro in order to relieve the state from "the unequal and oppressive" Civil Rights Act of Congress,[88] a maddened legislature not only quashed a resolution to this effect, but rejected as well the Fifteenth Amendment to enfranchise the Negro. However, under the continuing pressures of Watterson's "new departure" the legislature in January, 1872, finally amended the law of evidence to allow "parties in interest, persons of color" the right to testify in Kentucky courts. This action undoubtedly affected the decision of the United States Supreme Court when in April of the same year it reversed the decision of the United States circuit court of Kentucky in the Blyew and Kennard Case on the grounds that this court had no jurisdiction in the crime of murder "merely because two persons who witnessed the murder were citizens of the African race, and for that purpose incompetent by the law of Kentucky to testify in the courts of that State." They were not persons affected by the cause, which was the only basis for transfer of the case from a state to a federal court.[89]

The adoption of the Fourteenth and Fifteenth Amendments encouraged the Republicans to anticipate a recoup of their political fortunes. It was estimated that 100,000 votes would be added to the Republican column in Kentucky alone. With the adoption of the Fifteenth Amendment in March, 1870, picnics and celebrations were held throughout the state, where Republicans made stirring speeches in an effort to court Negro support. One such occasion, held in Paris, Kentucky, was attended by 6,000 Negroes,[90] but the most ambitious move to organize the Negroes occurred in Frankfort in February, 1870. Freedmen from almost every county gathered for the "First

[87] The case was not settled until 1872 when the Supreme Court reversed the decision of the United States Circuit for Kentucky.
[88] Collins, *History of Kentucky*, 1:194.
[89] *The United States* v. *Blyew and Kennard*, 80 U.S. (13 Wall.) 590–600 (1872).
[90] Collins, *History of Kentucky*, 1:204. DuBois, *Black Reconstruction*, p. 569.

Republican Convention of the Colored Citizens of the State of Kentucky." Although they were refused the legislative rooms and forced to hold their meetings elsewhere, under Republican sponsorship they passed resolutions condemning the importation of Chinese labor, endorsing Republican policies, and denouncing the Democrats.[91]

As preparations were being made for the county elections in August, 1870, the Democrats resorted to various devices to stifle the Negro vote. Town charters were changed to leave out the areas of Negro settlement, lengthy residence requirements were imposed, and propaganda machines told the Negro that suffrage would bring only trouble. If they wished to continue their jobs with their Democratic patrons they must exercise their franchise accordingly. Negroes were also urged to demand of their Republican brethren patronage equal to their support. Republicans, fearful of antagonizing their white supporters, did not dare fulfill these demands or place Negroes on their tickets, and so alienated the freedman. While the Democrats carried the August elections it was with a reduced majority. They polled a total vote of 88,000 to 57,000 for the Republicans.[92] It was clear to both parties that Negro suffrage would be an important factor in future elections.

There were other vital problems in the state besides Negro suffrage. No institution had suffered more during the war than the public schools of Kentucky. Although Kentucky's "common-schools" went back to 1798 when the legislature granted 6,000 acres of land to each county to establish "seminaries of learning," the beginnings of "public education" did not really occur until 1830 when the legislature authorized the county courts to create school districts supported by a levy of 6¼ cents on $100 worth of property and a poll tax of fifty cents. Since the state school fund was never adequate, school terms were short and teachers were badly educated and poorly paid. A number of private academies existed for those able to afford them, but in most cases, they were not "quality" institutions. Kentucky, however, was proud of its institutions of "higher education, such as Transylvania University which had been founded in 1780 as Transylvania Seminary. By 1818 it was one of the most important schools in the West, if not in the nation.

In 1838 the legislature passed further legislation "to establish a system of public schools in Kentucky," but general indifference, the lack of taxable resources, sparsity of population, "conservative reaction, religious fundamentalism, and republican invidiousness" stunted

[91] The Frankfort *Daily Kentucky Yeoman*, March 2, 1870.
[92] Collins, *History of Kentucky*, 1:207.

the efforts. The appointment of the Reverend Robert J. Breckinridge as superintendent of public instruction (1847–53) marked a turning point in public education. This highly influential man successfully had aroused communities to a sense of educational need when the Civil War broke out.[93] However, the state was so thoroughly demoralized by contending armies and guerrillas during the war years that public schools were for the most part suspended, while many of the private and denominational colleges closed their doors.[94] In March, 1863, a concerned legislature made special provision for the reestablishment of common school districts and appropriated five cents per $100 of assessable property, the fines for gamblers, and a paltry dog tax.[95] In December, 1863, Governor Bramlette again called the attention of the legislature to the necessity of fostering public education in the state and a bill was introduced to establish a state school for the training of teachers. Senator W. C. Whitaker urged the passage of the measure: "Year after year we have imported teachers (of course, rarely the best) . . . until (in) some localities the peculiar charms of Kentucky character have been nearly superceded by Yankee notions. This can only be remedied by Kentucky teachers, by teachers who have learnt the difficult art of developing the body, heart, and mind of the young in an institution under our own control." Unfortunately a difference of opinion developed between the two houses as to whether the tax increase should be used to support a normal school or the public schools. For this reason the measure failed.[96] However, at the next session of the legislature, Colonel John B. Bowman proposed that the state take advantage of the Morrill Act of 1862, granting public lands to the states for the establishment of agricultural and mechanical colleges. He proposed moving Kentucky University (Bacon's College) from Harrodsburg to Lexington and consolidating it with Transylvania College. By establishing agricultural and mechanical schools, the newly formed Kentucky University could secure the federal land scrip. Although a sharp debate ensued on the location of the proposed university, enabling legislation was passed in 1865 creating a state university.[97]

The public schools did not achieve any significant attention until Zach F. Smith was elected superintendent of public instruction in 1867. Enthusiastic and determined, he pressured the legislature to

[93] Arthur K. Moore, *The Frontier Mind* (New York, 1963), p. 236.

[94] Coulter, *Civil War and Readjustment*, pp. 254, 400–1.

[95] Clark, *History of Kentucky*, p. 354. Collins, *History of Kentucky*, 1:121.

[96] *Journal of the Senate of Kentucky*, 1863, pp. 7–23, 269–71, 282, 429–49. The Frankfort *Commonwealth*, Jan. 12, 19, 21, Feb. 2, 20, 1864.

[97] *Acts of Kentucky*, 1865, p. 67.

action. In December, 1867, he made a "special report" to the General Assembly recommending an additional tax of 15 cents on the $100 assessable property "as the basis of an effective and vigorous" public school system. At Smith's insistence an act was passed on January 23, 1869, which permitted the electorate to vote on a twenty-mill increase. The increase was approved and on March 2 the legislature enacted the additional levy into law, but with the provision that it "be collected off the property of white persons only, and expended exclusively for the education of white children."[98]

Progress was soon evident: school revenue increased by $600,000 in the next two years; the number of districts was increased by 700; and the number of students by 29,000.[99] While this was a remarkable feat, Kentucky still lagged, for in 1871 there were 40,000 adult white males in the state who could neither read nor write.[100] Smith's resignation in 1871 resulted in a decline of leadership which, coupled with numerous educational experiments, produced a lack of stability in Kentucky education between 1871 and 1900.

Formal Negro education was not begun until the advent of the Freedmen's Bureau in Kentucky. Under pressures from that agency the legislature on February 16, 1866, appropriated a small percentage of the taxes on Negro property and dogs to the support of colored schools, which were placed under the control of the state superintendent.[101] With the increase of the common school fund and the growth and improvement of white schools under Superintendent Smith, the Negro began demanding equality of educational opportunity by threatening to resort to the courts.[102] A separate school fund and system was set up for the Negro in 1874, which was supported principally from taxes paid by Negroes and a poll tax of one dollar on each Negro male over twenty-one years of age. The schools were to be managed by colored trustees. It was specifically provided that Negroes could not attend white schools nor could whites attend Negro schools.[103] Unfortunately Negro schools were never of the quality of white schools for no normal school training was provided for Negro teachers until 1889, when the legislature created the

---

[98] Collins, *History of Kentucky*, 1:183, 197, 202.

[99] *Ibid.*, 1:505.

[100] Coulter, *Civil War and Readjustment,* p. 402.

[101] *Acts of Kentucky*, 1867, p. 4.

[102] The Frankfort *Daily Kentucky Yeoman,* Dec. 6, 1871.

[103] A tax of forty-five cents on each $100 worth of Negro property was levied. Separate schools must be at least one mile distant from each other in the country and 600 feet in the towns. *American Annual Cyclopedia and Register of Important Events* (New York, 1874), pp. 440–41.

"Kentucky Normal School for Colored Persons" (Kentucky State College) which opened in Frankfort the following year.

An effort was made in 1865 to provide the Negro with an opportunity for higher education. In that year Berea College received a new charter from the legislature and opened its doors to seventy-five whites and three Negro students. However, when the white students discovered this, two-thirds of them withdrew. Undeterred the administration continued to admit Negroes until the legislature prohibited it in 1904.[104] Because of this and its mission to Appalachia, Berea attracted significant support from Northern and Eastern philanthropists.

Coincidental with the revived interest in education were marked social changes in Kentucky. The freeing of the slaves resulted in a widespread movement to encourage foreign laborers, including Chinese coolies, to settle in Kentucky. However, during the decade following the war less than 3,500 foreigners came to the state to settle primarily in Louisville. Shortages of farm labor caused by the immigration of the Negro to the urban centers resulted in the development of "tenancy" farming. "Poor whites" were encouraged to move to the more fertile areas, while landless whites from neighboring states to the north were lured into the state as workers in the growing tobacco industry. Soon "the white tenant" won the reputation of being a more "trustworthy" hand than the Negro.[105] This new social element proved valuable, not only economically but politically as well. Utilizing its voting potential the former bourbon slaveholding aristocracy was able to continue its monopoly over local, county, and state government.

Some interesting social movements arose in Kentucky in the postwar years. Before the war the majority of Kentucky distilleries were small, each catering to its own locale, but after the war they became national distributors and their product increased four-fold. This resulted in marked intemperance and the growth of a nation-wide temperance movement. Kentucky was not to be spared from the evangelical work of the temperance reformer. Pressures were exerted on the legislature to control the sale of liquor in the state, but the most that could be achieved was the granting of the right of local county option and the prohibition of the sale of alcohol to minors and inebriates. Nevertheless, the Order of Good Templars and the Womens Christian Temperance Union urged sobriety in the state to the great annoyance of the distilling industry.[106]

[104] Coulter, *Civil War and Readjustment*, p. 403.
[105] Clark, *History of Kentucky*, p. 351.
[106] *American Annual Cyclopedia*, 1874, p. 440. Clark, *History of Kentucky*, pp. 396–99.

Closely associated with the temperance movement was the issue of women's rights. When the issue of Negro suffrage was threatening Democratic domination of the state, a Mrs. Blackwell of New York argued before the legislature that the women's vote would offset the Negro vote. Assemblymen both humorously and seriously argued that if the Negro were enfranchised, Kentucky should place equal confidence in women.[107] Despite heavy opposition the movement survived to bear fruit in the twentieth century.

Prosperity returned to the state in the postwar years. The livestock business slowly revived, production being evaluated at almost $55,000,000 by 1870; mineral wealth was discovered; and increased appropriations were made for the improvement of river navigation as a stimulus to trade and commerce.[108]

The Civil War did not destroy sectional interdependence. Although the river trade revived rapidly after the war, the era of the steamboat was past and the era of railroads had arrived. St. Louis, Cincinnati, and Louisville were the main trade distributors to the South from the interior. As trade *entrepôts,* if they were to continue their domination of the interior they must become centers of railroad development. Louisville's trade had changed in nature from a predominately distributive trade before the war to a productive commerce in dry goods, tobacco, liquor, and meats after the war. Because of this, Kentucky politicians consistently damned Republican tariff policy as "intolerable" and discriminatory, and cursed the threat of specie redemption as tantamount to depression. Recognizing the importance of Southern trade, they urged the return of the Southern states to their "ancient and respected position" in the Union as quickly as possible.[109]

The importance of the railroad to Louisville's monopoly of Southern trade had been proven before the war. In 1851 a million dollars was subscribed to help build a railroad from Louisville to Nashville, which from the time of its opening in 1859 had proved a financial success. In 1860 the line was extended to Memphis—the gateway to Mobile and New Orleans—and numerous feeder lines were built to Lebanon in 1857, to Bardstown in 1865, and to Richmond in 1868.[110]

By 1868 Louisville not only had established her rail connections to the South but had "through car service" to New York.[111] Cincinnati was not content to allow Louisville a monopoly of the Southern trade. Recognizing her dependence upon the L. & N. Railroad, Cincinnatians

---

[107] The Cincinnati *Commercial,* Feb. 9, 1867.
[108] Kerr, *History of Kentucky,* 2:921.
[109] The Frankfort *Daily Kentucky Yeoman,* Feb. 7, 9, June 12, 1866.
[110] Kerr, *History of Kentucky,* 2:928–29.
[111] *Ibid.,* p. 930.

began planning a Southern railway that would run south through Paris, Lexington, and Richmond to East Tennessee.[112] Tennessee granted a charter to the company immediately and authorized $10,000 per mile to build the road from Chattanooga to the Kentucky border. After a stormy debate, the Kentucky legislature eventually chartered the Cincinnati, Lexington, and East Tennessee railroads and granted permission for the company to acquire the Kentucky Central, which ran from Cincinnati via Lexington to Nicholasville. However, when the Kentucky Central refused to amalgamate, the project came to a halt.[113] Cincinnati in the meantime had secured a change in the Ohio constitution permitting the city to tax to provide for $10,000,000 worth of bonds to construct the road. All that was needed was the necessary enabling legislation from the Kentucky General Assembly.[114] When a new bill was introduced into the Kentucky legislature in January, 1870, the L. & N. lobby descended upon the capitol, where it damned the measure as one favoring Ohio over the interests of Kentucky. Amid lavish entertainment of the legislators by both the Louisville and Nashville and the Cincinnati Southern the General Assembly dawdled for nearly two months before defeating the measure.[115] Angry Central Kentuckians claimed they had been outraged by their own legislature, but Louisville was extremely relieved that her monopoly of the Southern trade had not been broken.

Undeterred, Cincinnati now attempted to secure federal incorporation of "the Cincinnati and Chattanooga Railroad." On March 15, 1870, Senator John Sherman of Ohio introduced a bill in the Congress "to promote commerce and to cheapen the transportation of the mails and military and naval stores between Cincinnati and Chattanooga by building an interstate railroad South." Despite the backing of Representative James A. Garfield, who argued that the "great Northwest" would "have the right of way across the State of Kentucky" to the market of the South, the obstructionist tactics of such Kentucky politicians as Representative James M. Beck and Senator Garrett Davis resulted in delay and inactivity. While the House eventually passed the bill in March, 1871, the Senate ended its extra session on April 20, having taken no action on "the Southern Railroad Bill."[116]

[112] Kerr, History of Kentucky, 2:951–52.

[113] The Cincinnati Commercial, March 12, 18, April 16, 1867. See Edward A. Ferguson, Founding the Cincinnati Southern Railway (Cincinnati, 1905), p. 76.

[114] The Cincinnati Commercial, Dec. 2, 10, 1869, Jan. 20, 1870.

[115] Collins, History of Kentucky, 1:201–2.

[116] John Sherman, Recollections of Forty Years in the House, Senate and Cabinet (2 vols.; New York, 1895), 1:475–76. Collins, History of Kentucky, 1:203. The Congressional Globe, 41st Cong., 2d sess., 1948.

This proved to many Kentuckians that Congress was still ready to violate the domestic rights of a state.

Federal antagonism had in the meantime been aroused by Attorney General Amos T. Akerman's ordering of a vigorous prosecution in Kentucky of violators of the Fifteenth Amendment and the Enforcement Act of May 31, 1870.[117] Since these measures were designed to keep secessionist politicians out of high public positions, Kentucky Republican Radicals (Steven G. Burbridge and Thomas L. Jones) attempted to indict Governor John W. Stevenson, with a view to having him excluded from his seat in the United States Senate. The legislature had elected him to that post in December, 1869, but he was not to take his seat until March 4, 1871.[118] However, when the United States district attorney, G. C. Wharton, advised that there was insufficient evidence for such an indictment and Kentucky's United States senator, Thomas C. McCreary, secured the passage of an act (March, 1871) granting relief from political disability under the Fourteenth Amendment to seventy-three leading Kentuckians, chief among them being Stevenson.[119] On February 13, 1871, Stevenson resigned the governorship and Lieutenant Governor Preston H. Leslie succeeded him.

As Republicans readied for the state gubernatorial contest in August, the issues were clearly defined: the right of Negro testimony, Ku-Klux Klan activity, public education, and the Southern Railroad Bill.[120] At the Republican convention in Frankfort on May 17, 1871, the young, ambitious Louisville lawyer, John M. Harlan, was nominated unanimously for governor.[121] Under the skillful guidance of James Speed, a "ten point program" was adopted which condemned Democratic policy as "prejudiced" and "outmoded," while claiming Republican programs to be "progressive" and "liberal."[122]

The Democrats selected the incumbent governor, Preston H. Leslie, as their candidate. What they lacked in platform was offset by a well-organized party and an ample treasury. Leslie, only recently relieved of his war disabilities, was unable to forget the preceding decade and campaigned on the major theme that congressional tyranny would

---

[117] 16 Stat., 140, secs. 14, 15, May 31, 1870. Homer Cummings and Carl McFarland, *Federal Justice, Chapters in the History of Justice and the Federal Executive* (New York, 1937), p. 231.

[118] Collins, *History of Kentucky*, 2:199.

[119] *Ibid.*, 1:213.

[120] William Brown to B. H. Bristow, April 20, 1871, John M. Harlan Papers, the Law Library, University of Louisville.

[121] The Louisville *Commercial*, May 18, 1871.

[122] The Louisville *Courier-Journal*, May 24, 1871.

befall the state if a Republican were elected. Leslie also attacked Harlan's earlier political career, referring to him as a "political weathercock."[123] Harlan damned Democratic policy as "suicidal and ruinous." By failing to develop the resources of the state, by not supporting the Southern Railroad Bill the Democrats had not opened up central Kentucky to vast material improvements. The Louisville and Nashville railroad monopoly too long had controlled the destinies of Kentucky and of the Democratic party. As New York had rolled in the filth and corruption of the New York Central and the Erie, so had Kentucky wallowed under the domination of the L. & N.[124] Harlan also courted the Negro vote by urging "complete legal and political equality" for the colored population of Kentucky, but his inability to recognize their "social equality" lost him many a Negro vote.[125]

While an able orator, Harlan was no match for Leslie, who won the election by a majority of better than 37,000. Still the Republicans had made remarkable gains since the last contest in 1868, when Stevenson had won by a majority of nearly 89,000 votes.[126] Although the Republicans lost in 1872, the Louisville *Commercial* crowed that they had "carried every important city in the State except Louisville, Covington, and Owensboro." Republican majorities had been recorded in Newport, Maysville, Paris, Lexington, Danville, Nicholasville, Frankfort, Hopkinsville, and Paducah.[127]

While the Republicans had polled more votes than ever before, they recognized that they had not secured the Negro vote as extensively as had been expected. This, the first gubernatorial election under Negro suffrage, saw freedmen confused and waivering in their political allegiance, the result of the appeals of Watterson's Democratic "new departure" and the failure of the national Republican party to extend federal patronage to them. Nevertheless, in the twenty-five of one hundred and sixteen Kentucky counties carried by the Republicans, the Negro vote had proved the deciding factor.[128]

The newly elected legislature consisted of thirty-five Democrats and three Republicans in the Senate and eighty-two Democrats and

---

[123] John S. Goff, "Justice John Marshall Harlan of Kentucky," *The Register of the Kentucky Historical Society* 55, 2 (April, 1957): 115–16. The Louisville *Journal*, June 3, 1871.

[124] *Ibid.*, May 24, June 28, 1871. The Louisville *Commercial*, July 29, 1871.

[125] During the campaign Harlan commented on Negro equality: "No law ever can or will regulate such relations. Social equality can never exist between the two races in Kentucky." The Louisville *Journal*, July 29, 1871.

[126] Collins, *History of Kentucky*, 1:192.

[127] The Louisville *Commercial*, Aug. 15, 1871.

[128] Collins, *History of Kentucky*, 1:216.

eighteen Republicans in the House.[129] That many of the legislators had made commitments to support the Cincinnati Southern Railroad Bill was apparent when, on the second day of the session, a new and considerably changed Southern Railroad Bill was introduced. The election of the pro-Cincinnati Southern legislator, James B. McCreary, as speaker of the House further encouraged belief that the bill would be passed. However, a bitter fight ensued and although the measure passed the House, a tie resulted in the Senate which forced Lieutenant Governor John G. Carlisle to cast the deciding vote. To his party's disgust, Carlisle voted for the bill.[130] Unfortunately, during the legislative debate the Cincinnati Southern Railroad Bill was called up in the United States Senate as an ominous reminder that Congress would act if Kentucky did not pass the bill. Although the federal bill was dropped,[131] here was further proof that Congress still intended to continue federal intervention in state affairs.

Stringent restrictions were placed upon "the Southern" railroad by the Kentucky legislature. It could not remove a legal suit from state to federal courts, neither could it bring suit against Kentucky. To offset any advantage which Cincinnati might have in Southern markets, the state levied a one per cent tax on every 100 pounds of freight passing through the state, as well as a twenty-five to fifty cents levy on every passenger using the railroad within the state.[132] Despite these restraints, the road was begun in 1873 and completed in 1880. Louisville's monopoly of trade was effected sharply by the opening of the Southern, for "the Falls City" lost a large portion of its trade in central Kentucky.

Ku-Klux Klan activity in Kentucky continued to disturb federal–state relations. The Attorney General urged G. C. Wharton, the United States district attorney, to use every means to break up the Klan.[133] If the state could not, or would not, suppress this irresponsible organization, then the federal government would have to take positive action.[134] One of the cases pressed by Wharton involved the sons of certain highly influential Kentuckians (Rich Crittenden, Howard

---

[129] *Ibid.*, 1:216.

[130] The Cincinnati *Gazette*, Dec. 8, 1871, Jan. 30, 1872. Collins, *History of Kentucky*, 1:224. *Acts of Kentucky*, 1871, pp. 23–32.

[131] *The Congressional Globe*, 42d Cong., 2d sess., part I, 380; part 3, 1950.

[132] Collins, *History of Kentucky*, 1:224.

[133] Department of Justice, Papers of the Attorney General, Letter Book I, National Archives, RG 60.

[134] William Brown wrote B. H. Bristow, the Solicitor General of the United States: "Ku-Klux outrages have been as numerous since the election as at any period during the war." William Brown to B. H. Bristow, Sept. 21, 1871, Bristow Papers, Library of Congress (LC).

Smith, James Alley, and others), who were involved in the hanging of two Negroes at Frankfort. Special monies were dispatched from Washington to make this case an example to Klansmen. As a result, two of the four offenders were indicted on a charge of murder.[135] The United States marshal, W. A. Meriwether, summed up the importance of the case when he wrote the solicitor general, B. H. Bristow: "When you strike a Crittenden, you strike the State of Kentucky and his friends will never consent to have justice meted out to him." The Crittenden case had broad implications judicially and politically, for it involved the issue of Negro testimony. Meriwether wrote Bristow that this case would insure that the legislature would pass a law "giving" the colored people the right to vote.[136] In his December message Governor Leslie urged the legislature to apply some remedy to the disorders and disregard for the law within the state by passing laws to strike at the "secret vengeance of evil-disposed persons." While much of the lawlessness had been provoked by "the unwarranted interference of Federal authority" in local affairs and "its intrusive assumption of jurisdiction" in administering the laws of the Commonwealth, blame also must be placed upon the state for refusing the right of Negro testimony. At the behest of a number of influential state lawyers and judges, the legislature amended Kentucky's law of evidence on January 30, 1872, to allow "parties in interest, persons of color" to testify.[137]

Another grievance against the federal government was its failure to pay a long-standing debt which had been incurred by Kentucky in the "raising, maintaining and equipping" of volunteers during the Civil War. This had be authorized by the Congressional Act of July 27, 1861, and while the national government at first met its financial obligations, payments had dwindled until by March, 1869, $1,323,234 was still owing Kentucky. Various missions to Washington resulted only in a rebuff. When Congress repealed the Act of 1861, effective June 30, 1871, Governor Leslie sent the quartermaster-general, Fayette Hewett, to Washington to press Kentucky's claim before the limit should expire. Although the Secretary of War finally authorized payment, Secretary of the Treasury George Boutwell, after "mature consideration," rejected the claim and cancelled the warrant. Leslie had no recourse but to apply to the Supreme Court for a writ of *mandamus* to compel the Secretary of the Treasury to honor the

---

[135] J. M. Harlan to B. H. Bristow, Sept. 27, 29, 1871. G. C. Wharton to B. H. Bristow, Oct. 1, 1871, Bristow Papers, LC.

[136] W. A. Meriwether to B. H. Bristow, Nov. 8, 1871, Bristow Papers, LC.

[137] Collins, *History of Kentucky*, 1:222.

claim. When this was denied, Leslie appealed to Congress for relief. Under the skillful guidance of Kentucky's Congressmen, a War Claims Bill was passed in June, 1872, which appropriated $1,000,000 "to pay any proper claims of Kentucky for money expended for state forces after August 24, 1861."[138] Satisfaction had been secured, but not without a great deal of effort and money.

During the legislative session of 1871–72 Kentucky Republicans hoped to "create a diversion" strong enough to prevent the election of a Democrat to the United States Senate. Anticipating a division in the Democratic ranks between supporters of Thomas C. McCreary and James M. Beck, Republicans put forward the candidacy of John M. Harlan. However, the Democrats "out foxed" them by holding a legislature caucus which named McCreary as their candidate. In the ensuing legislative election McCreary received 112 votes to Harlan's 20.[139] This was a serious blow to Republican prestige; still General John W. Finnell believed that a "bold manly canvass" would carry the state for Grant in 1872 providing that "a proper, judicious, and perfectly legitimate use of the Federal patronage in Ky. could be effected."[140]

Finnell's optimism waned quickly, for a breach developed in the party over a second term for Grant. Headed by such prominent Republicans as Sam McKee, M. Boland, Bob Johnston, and E. W. Kennedy, an attempt was made "to pack the ward meetings" against Grant.[141] Despite this divisive element, the Republican state convention met in Louisville on March 13 and pledged its support to the national nominees of the Philadelphia convention. It was obvious to Kentucky "liberals," as to others throughout the country, that any progressive reform from within the party was impossible. Under the careful sponsorship of Carl Schurz, Lyman Trumbull, J. N. Cox, Charles Francis Adams, B. Gratz Brown, and others an independent convention was called at Cincinnati where "Liberal Republicans" nominated Horace Greeley for the presidency and the former Kentuckian, B. Gratz Brown, as vice president. Harlan was alarmed that this movement might "assume large proportions," and the Republican state central committee immediately began tightening up its organization.[142] Kentucky Republicans were hopeful that the breach

[138] *Ibid.*, 1:199, 230. *The Commonwealth of Kentucky* v. *George Boutwell*, 80 W.S. (13 Wall.) 526 (1872).

[139] G. C. Wharton to B. H. Bristow, Dec. 12, 1871, Bristow Papers, LC. Collins, *History of Kentucky* 1:221.

[140] John W. Finnell to B. H. Bristow, Nov. 2, 1871, Bristow Papers, LC.

[141] Edgar Needham to B. H. Bristow, Feb. 14, 1872, Bristow Papers, LC.

[142] G. C. Wharton to B. H. Bristow, April 19, 1872. John W. Finnell to B. H. Bristow, April 26, 1872, Bristow Papers, LC.

might be healed if a Kentuckian could be nominated as Grant's running mate at the Philadelphia convention and pressed Harlan's cause. But the necessity to placate Charles Sumner of Massachusetts and the Radicals forced the selection of the "Natick Cobbler," Henry Wilson of Massachusetts, as the vice presidential nominee.

The Democrats did not hold their state convention until June 20. At Frankfort they selected their delegates to the national convention at Baltimore. Despite the efforts of the "old-line" Democrats to oppose Greeley's nomination at Baltimore, the beckoning finger of victory was too strong and Greeley became the Democratic nominee for the presidency. In Kentucky, however, the "unholy" union of Democrat and Liberal Republican was not universally acceptable. "Straight-out" Democrats refused the "union" ticket and called a convention in Louisville on September 3, where they nominated (over his protest) Charles O'Conor for President and Charles Francis Adams for Vice President. Confidently they invited support of their ticket.[143]

But the "watchfulness" of Republicans in the South, together with their "the bloody shirt" appeal in the North, resulted in Grant's victory. Still Harlan's concern over the Liberal Republican movement in Kentucky proved real, for the Liberal Republican–Democratic ticket carried the state. However, upon analysis the Republicans discovered that there had been a falling-off of Democratic votes by better than 23,000 since the August elections of 1871.[144] They could look forward with some degree of confidence to the gubernatorial contest of 1874.

In the midst of this optimism came the Panic of 1873. Though there was much individual loss, Kentucky wisely chose this moment to invest the *sinking fund* in five-twenty United States gold-bearing interest bonds, which not only helped to stimulate the national economy, but strengthened the economic base of the state.

In the midst of depression the third geological survey was ordered by the legislature to determine the mineral wealth of the state. Governor Leslie appointed a former Kentuckian, Nathaniel Southgate Shaler, professor of geology at Harvard University, as chief of the survey corps. While Kentuckians were conscious of productive soil and an abundance of timber resources, Shaler's survey brought an awareness of new and hidden wealth in iron ore, coal, and oil.

[143] Collins, *History of Kentucky*, 1:230, 231.
[144] *Ibid.*, 1:235.

By 1884 seventy mines in Kentucky were producing 1,550,000 tons of coal annually. A new base had been added to Kentucky's economy.[145]

Paralleling the opening of coal and timber resources was the growth of railway mileage. By 1880 there were more than 1,500 miles in operation. All of this was made possible through the encouragement of capital investment in Kentucky's industry and railroad development. Chambers of commerce circulated pamphlets advertising the state as "a land of unlimited promise." This, with generous tax exemption and special privileges, was responsible for the expansion of Kentucky's timber, coal, distilling, and tobacco industries.

Kentucky farmers were slow to adjust to the new industrial order. After 1865, Kentucky fell victim to a one-crop economy—tobacco. As cotton had been the chief money crop of the antebellum South, so tobacco became the major money crop in Kentucky. When the Panic of 1873 struck, tobacco prices fell to an all-time low, land values collapsed, and farm mortgages were foreclosed by over-extended banks. Although the federal government attempted to stabilize the monetary system by demonetizing silver ("the crime of '73") and called for the resumption of greenbacks in gold by 1879 (the Redemption Act of 1875), Kentucky farmers joined the Patrons of Husbandry (the Grange) movement as a means to combat the money evil and to stimulate inflation. They did not intend a third party movement, rather they hoped to exert sufficient influence in elections to pressure state and national attention to their needs.[146]

The Grange movement was too new to have any decided effect upon the congressional contest of 1874. While the Republicans were able to elect one representative[147] to Congress, Democratic strength seemed relatively unimpaired. In the election instead of the Republicans waving "the bloody shirt," as was the case in the North, in Kentucky it was the Democrats who continued to remind the electorate of the ignominies and sufferings which the state had endured under federal "Radical" Republican rule. By attacking recent federal treatment of Louisiana and the South in general, they warned Kentuckians to be ever on the alert against "black hearted" Republicans. The Republicans on the other hand attempted to divert attention away from war and postwar policies by calling attention to the necessity for improving educational programs and stimulating industrial development.[148]

---

[145] Elizabeth S. Kinkead, *A History of Kentucky* (New York, 1898), p. 211. Kerr, *History of Kentucky*, 2:997–98.

[146] These counties were in the dark tobacco belt and were among the first to feel the brunt of the Panic of 1873. Clark, *History of Kentucky*, pp. 413–14.

[147] J. M. Harlan to B. H. Bristow, Oct. 30, Nov. 13, 1874, Bristow Papers, LC.

[148] *American Annual Cyclopedia*, 1873, p. 403. *Ibid.*, 1874, p. 441.

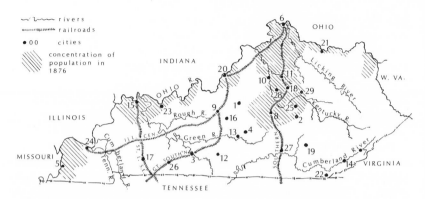

Map of Kentucky. *Key:* 1 Bardstown, 2 Berea, 3 Bowling Green, 4 Campbellsville, 5 Columbus, 6 Covington, 7 Cumberland, 8 Danville, 9 Elizabethtown, 10 Frankfort, 11 Georgetown, 12 Glasgow, 13 Greensburg, 14 Harlan, 15 Henderson, 16 Hodgenville, 17 Hopkinsville, 18 Lexington, 19 London, 20 Louisville, 21 Maysville, 22 Middleboro, 23 Owensboro, 24 Paducah, 25 Richmond, 26 Russellville, 27 Somerset, 28 Versailles, 29 Winchester. (*Map prepared by Paula J. Treder.*)

As the gubernatorial election of 1875 approached, Republicans were worried over the defection of the Negro from the party. Kentucky Negroes warned Republican leaders that the suspension of the Freedmen's Bank had locked up their hard earned savings, and the failure of the party to recognize the Negro as "an integral part" of the patronage system was responsible for the declining Negro vote.[149] Despite the efforts of B. H. Bristow (then secretary of the treasury) and John M. Harlan to allay Negro animosity, it was becoming increasingly clear that "Marse" Henry Watterson's efforts to pit the Negro and the Republican party against one another on the patronage question were succeeding.

At the Democratic state convention, J. B. McCreary was nominated for the governorship. After condemning federal intervention in state affairs, a platform was adopted which called for increased measures of internal economic development. The Republicans, rent with division caused by the increasing corruption in the federal government, as well as by the ominous threat that Grant would seek a third term, ultimately united behind John M. Harlan. Undeterred by his defeat in 1871, Harlan was confident that "with proper aid from the North" he could "*startle the country*" in 1875.[150] The Republicans demanded

[149] Horace Morris, George Brown, Madison Minnis to B. H. Bristow, Jan., 1875, Bristow Papers, LC.
[150] J. H. Harlan to B. H. Bristow, May 15, 1875, Bristow Papers, LC.

increased aid to education, economic support to industry, and encouragement of immigration. They damned the Democrats for not suppressing the Ku-Klux Klan and for failing to provide adequate aid for the development of the states' resources. Pleading with the electorate to forget their prejudices and to unite behind a party able "to rebuild the waste places, to promote the general welfare, and to advance by all proper means the greatness and prosperity of our common country," the Republicans eagerly awaited the contest.[151]

Every effort was made to court the Grangers. Writing to the Chairman of the Republican State Executive Committee, Secretary Bristow urged the party "to get control of the Agricultural paper in Louisville" and to assure the farmer that it was the Republicans who were seriously interested in "cheap transportation and benefits to the Western farmers" and not the Democrats.[152] Believing that Harlan's success would have an "immense influence" on the Ohio and Pennsylvania elections, Bristow secured some $35,000 from Washington, New York, and Philadelphia supporters to "smite the enemy with the weapons of the Lord."[153]

Despite this outside backing, levies upon officeholders, promises to the Grangers, and Harlan's vigorous canvass, the Democratic nominee carried the election: McCreary received 126,976 votes to Harlan's 90,795. Two factors explain McCreary's relatively close victory: the Democrats became alarmed and put out their speakers and large amounts of money a week before the election, urging Kentuckians "to stand firm" in view of the pending elections in Ohio,[154] and a serious flood which inundated the state just prior to the election extensively destroying farm property. This promise of "hard times" upset the political calculations of the Republicans, for fearful of any political change that might threaten rehabilitation Kentuckians voted Democratic.[155]

---

[151] *Address of the Hon. B. H. Bristow, Delivered on the Ooccasion of the Decoration of Soldiers' Graves at Cave Hill Cemetery, Louisville, Kentucky, May 29, 1875* (Washington, 1875), pp. 3–8.

[152] B. H. Bristow to W. A. Meriwether, June 9, 1875, Bristow Papers, LC.

[153] Even the iniquitous Orville E. Babcock "kicked in" and promised to "set cross legged for luck" on election day. Horace Porter to B. H. Bristow, June 12, 1875. O. E. Babcock to B. H. Bristow, June 16, 1875, Bristow Papers, LC.

[154] The political struggle in Ohio turned on inflation vs. contraction. The Democrats here under Governor William Allen was advocating "soft-money," while Rutherford B. Hayes championed "hard-money." If Hayes won the governor's chair, the prospects of his party becoming a "sound money" party were assured, while if Allen won, the opposite result would follow. Hayes won by a narrow margin. See Harry Barnard, *Rutherford B. Hayes and His America* (Indianapolis, 1954), pp. 275–76.

[155] B. H. Bristow to Buford Wilson, Aug. 7, 1875, Bristow Papers, LC.

Republicans were not despondent as the presidential contest of 1876 approached. Kentucky possessed a presidential possibility in the person of the secretary of the treasury, Benjamin H. Bristow. Synonymous in the public mind with reform as a result of his triumph over the whiskey and railroad magnates, with sound national financing as a result of his encouragement of economy in government and specie resumption,[156] it was also known that he favored a policy of amelioration toward the South. In his Cave Hill address of May 29, 1875, at Louisville, Kentucky, Bristow noted that ten years had passed since the civil conflict had ended. The time had come to lay aside prejudice, for it required "no prophet to foretell that sooner or later the South must enter upon a career of unexampled prosperity" under the influence of "free institutions" and boundless resources. The issues of the war had become historical anachronisms. It was not the past, but the future which must be grasped. "God speed the time when the men of the North and of the South shall vie with each other in efforts to rebuild the waste places, to promote the general welfare, and to advance by all proper means the greatness and prosperity of our common country."[157] While Bristow lost the Republican nomination to Rutherford B. Hayes, he played an active role in the campaign and to some extent helped formulate the basis of the Compromise of 1877, which won the presidency for Hayes.[158]

The "Compromise of 1877" brought Reconstruction officially to an end. Yet, Governor J. B. McCreary had proclaimed its demise in Kentucky in his inaugural address of 1875: "I wish to see the records of secession, coercion and reconstruction filed away forever, and the people of the whole country earnestly advocating peace and reconciliation, and all looking to the Constitution as the guarantee of our liberties and the safeguard of every citizen."[159]

Reconstruction in Kentucky was not as bleak as it has been made out to be. While it is true that Kentucky labored momentarily under the military, lost the protection of the right of *habeas corpus,* felt the full impact of the Freedmen's Bureau, and suffered the ignominy of congressional investigation, significant advances were made. Democracy and egalitarianism made some real progress in Kentucky during these years. The rights of the Negro were protected by the federal courts under the Civil Rights Act of 1866. The assumption by the

[156] The Redemption Act of 1875 was passed by Congress at Bristow's instigation.
[157] *Address of Hon. B. H. Bristow . . . at Cave Hill Cemetery . . . May 29, 1875,* pp. 3–8.
[158] The New York *Times,* Oct. 7, 1876. The Cincinnati *Commercial,* Oct. 9, 1876.
[159] The Louisville *Courier–Journal,* Sept. 1, 1875. *American Annual Cyclopedia,* 1875, p. 417.

federal courts of jurisdiction over criminal cases involving Negroes forced the legislature to grant this privilege in 1872. Because of the pressures of the Freedmen's Bureau, a serious effort was made to found schools for the Negro. While "separate but equal" schools were never achieved in Kentucky, nevertheless as the legislature expanded the public school system through increased taxes, additional monies were expended upon Negro education. From slave state to free state was a marked transition for Kentucky to make and prejudice ran high, but free public education was sponsored for white and black alike. The demand for state constitutional reform in order that *all* people might be brought into "full control of their government" began as early as 1873. While momentarily stalemated, a new constitution was drafted in 1890, which reflected "the new order" created during the Reconstruction period in Kentucky history. The breaking down of "bourbon" domination of Kentucky's politics by a broadened and more active electorate, conscious of its needs and ready to take political action through third party movements, forced not only new policies of social and welfare development, but resulted in a gradual decline of "normal" Democratic majorities.[160] Any discussion of Reconstruction must point out that congressional intervention in Kentucky produced the strong desire to protect the domestic rights of the state from being absorbed by the federal government. It was this reaction that prompted historians to call Kentucky "pro-Confederate" in the Reconstruction period, when in reality it was anti-administration and anti-congressional in its sentiment.

[160] Following the Civil War the coalition of Bluegrass and Pennyroyal "Bourbons" dominated the state, but gradually there evolved a large faction of small farmers who found such domination intolerable. Their political shiftings from the Democrats to the Populists in the 1890s ultimately allowed not only the election of a Republican governor in 1895 but permitted William McKinley to be the first Republican president to carry the state in 1896. This gradual decline in the "normal" Democratic majority continued until the Great Depression of 1929 when it was reversed by the political reaction of the Kentucky coal miner and the Negro. See John H. Fenton, *Politics in the Border States* (New Orleans, 1957), pp. 64–65.

CHAPTER FIVE

Redemption or Reaction?—
Maryland in the Post-Civil War Years

Charles L. Wagandt

Emancipation Victorious

The bells tolled as Baltimoreans awakened to the roar of cannon. The time was sunrise, the date November 1, 1864.[1] The guns spoke not in anger but in celebration of a great moment in Maryland history— the abolition of slavery. In just two years this seemingly invulnerable institution had been battered into oblivion. Its destruction did more than free the slaves. It also cut a strong link with the rebellious states. Some citizens, however, saw no glory in the historic event. To them emancipation meant a revolutionary confiscation of an estimated thirty million dollars worth of property.

These losses bore heavily upon the southern part of the state, an area quite different socially, economically, and politically from the north and west. The differences arose in part from geographical contrasts. Maryland, small in size but rich in diversity, thrust its long arm from the shores of the Atlantic westward to the watershed of the Mississippi. Ocean, bay, and river; lowland, valley, and mountain carved their patterns into the state, helping to sculpture its unusual shape. Here came together north and south, east and midwest.

In Southern Maryland tobacco flourished. Seafood and general farming provided a living for the Eastern Shore. These two sections, separated by the Chesapeake Bay but generally within the coastal plain, offered the state a conservative, relatively stable, agricultural society with a homogeneous white population. Significantly, the proportion of Negroes ran high, more than 40 per cent, and exceeded 50 per cent in some Southern Maryland counties. In the latter, slavery and Confederate sympathies had been most strongly entrenched.

Such was not the case in Baltimore and the northern counties, where Union sentiment dominated. In this area Negroes accounted for only 13 per cent of the population. Just one-fourth of them had been slaves in 1860. But what the region lacked in numbers of Negroes, it filled

---

[1] *Baltimore Clipper*, Nov. 2, 1864, and *Baltimore American*, Nov. 2, 1864.

through white immigration. About 18 per cent of its inhabitants in 1870 were foreign-born. That same percentage represented the population increase of the area from 1860 to 1870. During this period the population of the rest of the state registered a gain of only a few percentage points. This meant that in 1870 the people of the north numbered more than twice those of the other two regions.[2]

A heterogeneous people enriched this land with farms, mines, and towns. The cash value of improved farm land rose significantly between 1860 and 1870, reaching a level 80 per cent higher than in the southern and eastern counties. Commerce and industry expanded, creating another disparity with the rest of the state. The north turned out over 90 per cent of the value of Maryland's manufactured products in 1870. Most of this production flowed from the Baltimore area, whose port, railroad facilities, and water power accelerated development.[3]

Such dissimilarities to the tidewater country almost inevitably generated friction. The burgeoning areas struggled for more equitable representation in the state legislature, while curious compromises were devised to accommodate sectional differences. For instance, the Constitution of 1851 divided the state into three gubernatorial districts: (1) Southern Maryland and the city of Baltimore; (2) Eastern Shore, including Cecil County; (3) six counties in the north and west of the state. Every four years the governor had to be chosen from a different district so that in any twelve-year period each region would have its own man serving a full term in the gubernatorial chair. Geography also played a role in the selection of United States senators. The law required one from the Eastern Shore and the other from the Western Shore.

While sectional differences profoundly affected Maryland, one institution tended to cross regional lines and draw the entire state toward Southern culture and customs. That was slavery. It exerted a disproportionate influence upon social, political, and economic life. It

[2] Statistics in this paragraph are based on census reports: *Population of the United States in 1860; Compiled from the Original Returns of the Eighth Census* (Washington, D.C., 1864), *A Compendium of the Ninth Census (June 1, 1870)* (Washington, D.C., 1872), pp. 56 and 417. For the purpose of this essay, Cecil County is considered part of northern Maryland rather than the Eastern Shore. Northern Maryland embraces all of the counties bordering Pennsylvania plus the city of Baltimore. Western Maryland is thereby included in northern Maryland.

[3] Statistics in this paragraph are based on census reports: *Agriculture of the United States in 1860; Compiled from the Original Returns of the Eighth Census* (Washington, D.C., 1864), p. 72; *Manufactures of the United States in 1860; Compiled from the Original Returns of the Eighth Census* (Washington, D.C., 1865), p. 228; *A Compendium of the Ninth Census,* p. 826; *The Statistics of the Wealth and Industry of the United States,* Ninth Census (Washington, D.C., 1872), 3, p. 172.

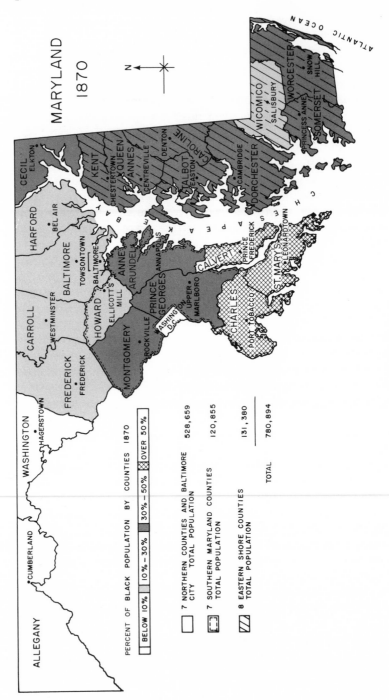

Map of Maryland

steered Maryland on a reactionary course, as abolitionists mounted their attacks in the pre-Civil War years.

In 1860 a law was enacted to prevent the slaveholder from freeing his Negro even if he wished to do so. Possession of certain antislavery literature was punishable by imprisonment. This attack on human rights buttressed the social system against the insidious doubt as to the basic right of one man to own the body and services of another, a doubt which gnawed at more than a few consciences. So many Marylanders had emancipated their slaves by 1860 that more free blacks could be found in Maryland than in any other state of the Union.[4] They nearly equaled the slaves in numbers.

The slave question was caught in the surge of emotion that threatened to sink the Union by the end of 1860. When the nation plunged into war, Maryland for a brief moment in April, 1861, teetered on the brink of secession, but quickly regained firm footing within the Union. This did not, however, lessen the worship of the god of slavery. In fact, the new Unionist governor of Maryland, Augustus W. Bradford, implied in his inaugural in January, 1862, that Maryland would remain loyal to the Union only so long as slavery was left alone. He spoke confidently of the emancipation movement swirling out of the North as "the last spasm of an expiring faction."[5]

But that spasm became a mighty convulsion. Lincoln recognized the rising clamor and knew the country could not long endure half slave and half free. He contemplated striking a strong, psychological blow at the embattled Confederacy by having the loyal slave states abolish slavery, with the help of federal compensation. The offer went forth as a war measure which would save money and lives by shortening the conflict.

The conservatives would have none of it. The plan smacked of bribery and governmental interference. They questioned the constitutionality of appropriating money for such purposes and argued that the country could not afford the expense. These states' rightists spoke for freedom, the freedom of a privileged group to rule as it chose. In later years, when it looked as though there would be neither slaves nor compensation, the slaveowners forgot their earlier scruples and pleaded for dollars to mitigate their losses.

The President's offer broke the subtle censorship that gagged the Maryland press and made every other interest subservient to slavery.

---

[4] In 1860 free Negroes numbered 83,942 while the slaves totaled 87,189. See *Population of the United States in 1860*, p. 211.

[5] Document F, *Maryland House Democrats 1861–1862* (Annapolis, 1862). Address can also be found in newspapers.

This break did not at first weaken the power structure of the Union party, which gathered together Republicans, most ex-Whigs, and the relatively few Democrats who remained loyal. The hierarchy of this Union party tried desperately to brush the "side issue" of slavery under the political carpet. But the slave issue had an annoying habit of not staying put. Step by step, the institution began to crumble under the multi-pronged assaults of Northern abolitionists, national legislation, military action, and the realists who could see no point in continuing an institution that had so bitterly divided the nation.

Inevitably, some Marylander would step forward to capitalize on the situation and exploit it for political advantage. He would have other issues working for him, among them the under-representation of the north and west in the legislative halls. Henry Winter Davis grasped the opportunity. A masterful orator and a brilliant, arrogant fighter, he determined to overthrow the conservative leadership of the Union party. To do so, the Davis partisans attacked slavery as "the domination of an interest over free men . . . of aristocratic privilege over republican equality, of a minority over a majority."[6] They appealed to the middle class of the north and west and to white laborers and plain farmers throughout Maryland.

Thrown on the defensive, the exponents of the status quo stirred the white man's fears by portraying the freed Negro as shiftless, vicious, drunk, and degraded. Emancipation would result in burdening the alms-houses, prisons, and taxpayers. Conversely, stories circulated of free Negroes driving wages down.[7] But the most powerful rallying cry of all was the appeal for racial purity.

Winter Davis exploded this treacherous issue by sarcastically urging all those who were afraid of marrying a Negro to petition the legislature to punish them in case they should succumb to this weakness. He also turned the racially charged question of Negro soldiers to his advantage by shrewdly calling the black man the poor man's substitute. This reduced the slaveowner's credibility, putting him in the awkward position of opposing the enlistment of slaves, while often buying his own way out of military service.[8]

The Davis men found support for their efforts among a number of politically oriented army officers. The local commander, Major General

---

[6] Address of the Unconditional Union State Central Committee to the People of Maryland, September 16, 1863 (Baltimore, 1863). The Baltimore American and other papers printed the address.

[7] For example, it was reported that Negroes worked for as little as ten cents a day in Chester County, Pennsylvania. Evening Journal, as cited in Montgomery County Sentinel, July 4, 1862.

[8] Abolition was also supported as a tool to end Negro competition with white men. No longer would the black be backed by the capital and influence of the slaveowner. Address of the Unconditional Union State Central Committee.

Robert C. Schenck, ordered military detachments to "protect" the polls in the important election on November, 1863. This action violated Maryland law and created a favorable climate for a rash of corrupt election activities. These malpractices struck hardest at the Eastern Shore and helped sweep an emancipationist majority into legislative office. Though tarnished, the victory achieved such proportions that it seems safe to say that most Marylanders favored some form of abolition.[9]

But Davis then moved on to more radical ground, becoming one of Lincoln's foremost antagonists. His views and those of his Maryland associates generated a strong reaction among a people historically of rather conservative bent. Only by the disfranchisment of many voters did the new Constitution of 1864 squeeze through to victory.

This Constitution cut the Negro's bonds and swept away the old power structure. Southern Maryland and the Eastern Shore found their legislative power greatly reduced. They got only twenty-seven of eighty seats in the lower house, a ratio that fairly accurately represented the total population. In the Senate the southern areas maintained a preponderance, despite the addition of two seats for the city of Baltimore.

The new Constitution breathed life into a number of reforms. A new, improved, public school system came into being. Out went the rotation of the gubernatorial chair among three geographical districts. In came the office of lieutenant-governor and a system for registering voters. But war fever and political expediency decreed one provision that rankled a host of Marylanders and provoked a rising storm of discontent after the war. That was the disfranchisement of those who had ever sympathized with the Southern cause.

With abolition victorious, the ranks of those who had fought longest and hardest for its achievement collapsed in disarray. Henry Winter Davis did not even seek re-election in 1864.[10] Unionists turned from Davis in order to rally around President Lincoln. Davis, an admirer said, "is a glorious fellow; but confound him! he ruined us as a party in the very hour of our triumph."[11] The "Softs" among the Unionists, having been forced to embrace the radical position on abolition, now gained a commanding place in the party. Thomas Swann, an old

---

[9] See Charles L. Wagandt, *The Mighty Revolution: Negro Emancipation in Maryland, 1862–1864* (Baltimore, 1964), Chapter 11. General Schenck was also an Ohio congressman-elect.

[10] Davis wrote, "I think the demoralization is so great that I do not feel inclined to go through the labor it would require to make it successful." Henry Winter Davis to Samuel Francis Du Pont, Oct. 19, 1864, Samuel Francis Du Pont Papers, Eleutherian Mills Historical Library, Wilmington, Del.

[11] Peter G. Sauerwein to Edward McPherson, Oct. 22, 1864, Edward B. McPherson Papers, Library of Congress (hereafter referred to as LC).

antagonist of Davis, got the nomination for governor, and conservative Unionist Charles E. Phelps ran in Davis's place in Baltimore's third congressional district.

The Unionists won the state for Lincoln by 40,171 to 32,739.[12] Though the President suffered a substantial defeat in Southern Maryland and on the Eastern Shore, his margin in Baltimore and the northern counties carried him to victory. Total votes numbered 72,910, a more than 20 per cent drop from the 1860 figure of 92,502. The disfranchising clause of the new Constitution apparently affected some areas severely, such as Baltimore city and Talbot County. Obviously, the provision proved less effective in the hotbed of rebel sentiment, Charles County. The tally there dropped from 1,197 to 988. Just twenty-seven of these votes were cast for Lincoln.[13]

Out of the election came victory for Swann, but incumbent Congressman John A. J. Creswell, a Davis protegé, suffered defeat on the Eastern Shore. The Unionists easily carried the House of Delegates, but were less fortunate in the Senate, where the Democrats claimed a 13–11 edge. This margin quickly evaporated as Senator-elect William Holland of Dorchester County, fearing arrest as a Southern sympathizer, resigned.[14] A new election was held and Unionist Thomas King Carroll elected. The Senate margin then shifted to a 13–11 Unionist edge, when another senator was unseated for disloyalty and replaced by his Republican opponent.[15]

With Lincoln's second term in the offing, the perennial struggle for office and power centered upon the top prize, Collector for the Port

[12] *Baltimore American*, Nov. 29, 1864.

[13] *Baltimore American*, Nov. 14, 1861 and Nov. 29, 1864. The returns showed Baltimore city—1860: 30,146; 1864: 17,937; and Talbot County—1860: 1791; 1864: 845. Some irregularities occurred in the elections. For example, Senator Thomas H. Hicks charged that in the Parson's Creek election district of Dorchester County the secessionists took control of the polls. (See Thomas H. Hicks to General Wallace, Nov. 12, 1864, Middle Dept., Letters Received, RG98, National Archives [hereafter referred to as NA]). On the other hand, the army ordered the arrest of Eastern Shoremen who brought suit against loyal election judges who denied them the ballot. The army also proclaimed a similar fate for persons threatening Unionists or openly declaring disloyalty. See Oliver Matthews to Brig. General Henry Hayes Lockwood, Nov. 5, 1864, Middle Dept., Letters Sent, RG98, NA.

[14] William Holland to Governor James Black Groome, June 3, 1874. Executive Papers, Hall of Records, Annapolis, Maryland.

[15] William Starr Myers, *The Self-Reconstruction of Maryland, 1864–1867* (series 27, no. 1–2, in The Johns Hopkins University Studies in Historical and Political Science) (Baltimore, 1909), p. 17. Another Eastern Shore state senator-elect, Levin L. Waters of Somerset County, was arrested and jailed, allegedly for having flown the Rebel flag in 1861. He was later released and took his seat in the Senate. Roy P. Basler (editor), *The Collected Works of Abraham Lincoln* (New Brunswick, N.J., 1953), 8: 198.

of Baltimore. One popular scheme would have sent Thomas H. Hicks, ill and in need of money, straight from the floor of the United States Senate to the collector's job. That would open the way for Montgomery Blair, former postmaster general under President Lincoln, to pick up the Senate seat. Of course it meant ousting Collector Henry W. Hoffman, a Davisite now in bad odor with his leader.[16]

The scheme miscarried. Hicks breathed his last on February 13, 1865, and the legislature rejected Blair's aspirations. Instead, it gave the senatorial seat to defeated Congressman John A. J. Creswell. Davis delighted in the triumph, calling it a *coup de grâce* to his Maryland enemies.[17] The collectorship went to Congressman Edwin H. Webster, who played a double game by appealing for support from both conservatives and radicals. Davis did not view the appointment optimistically. He now correctly considered Webster to be in the other camp.[18]

On December 30, 1865, pneumonia stilled Henry Winter Davis's tempestuous genius. No one could fill his controversial role, though Judge Hugh L. Bond of Baltimore came closer than anyone else. His death and those of Hicks and Lincoln healed no wounds, but closed an era of unparalleled divisiveness and bitterness in Maryland history.

Thus did Maryland slavery die. In the muck of self-interest and a bloody Civil War the emancipation movement had achieved victory. It seemed, however, as though good could achieve great conquests only with the help of evil, for necessity, fear, and party strife had forced reforms "which no sense of right" could have impelled.[19] Maryland thereby became the first loyal slave state to rid itself entirely of the "peculiar institution."

The Freed Negro and the White Marylander

The slaves greeted the striking of their bonds with dignity. No rowdy celebration marked the occasion. Instead Negroes welcomed their new status with some uncertainty, for ahead lay the unchartered realm of an undiscovered world. Quiet and orderly, the blacks appeared desirous of making an honest living. Many employers and employees seemed satisfied. In fact, the Negro laborers at Hoods Mills in Carroll County must have performed too well. A number of whites sought to drive them away for fear that they would depress wages.[20]

[16] Wagandt, *Mighty Revolution*, p. 266.

[17] H. W. Davis to S. F. Du Pont, March 12, 1865, S. F. Du Pont Papers.

[18] Wagandt, *Mighty Revolution*, p. 267. Edwin H. Webster was appointed by President Andrew Johnson.

[19] Journal of Dr. Samuel A. Harrison, March 21, 1865, Maryland Historical Society.

[20] Lieutenant S. N. Clark to Colonel John Eaton, Sept. 12, 1865, Executive Papers.

But not all whites reacted with fear or vindictiveness and malice. Some accepted the new order with kindliness and forbearance, even hopefully. A number of aristocrats learned a new dimension of life—labor. For instance, the once wealthy family of General Tench Tilghman, one of Maryland's oldest and most respectable, confronted the dilemma "of large property, large debts, large pride, large wants," but only small income. Necessity caused the young Tilghman ladies to milk the cows while the general held an umbrella over their heads to ward off the rain. The ladies even carried the chamber pots from the rooms, for white servants considered this "nigger-work."[21]

Confronted by such circumstances many former slaveowners clung tenaciously to the last glimmer of the old order. They hurried to the Orphans Court to get Negro children bound to them. "There seems to be," confided one observer to his diary, "an ill defined belief, a vague hope, that . . . slavery will again be resurrected."[22] The courts co-operated by forcing an estimated 3,281 children into this vestigial form of slavery.[23] Not surprisingly, apprenticing was concentrated in many of the old slave counties.

Negro parents protested, claiming they were able to support their children.[24] Their pleas found a sympathetic hearing before Judge Hugh L. Bond, who presided over the Criminal Court of Baltimore city. He liberally issued writs of *habeas corpus* to free the apprentices, but his writs failed on occasion to bring results.[25] Nor did the General Assembly look favorably upon the Judge's actions. In 1867 the legislators passed a bill to stop him from issuing writs of *habeas corpus* in apprenticeship cases.[26]

But Bond was not the blacks' only source of help. Major General Lew Wallace, later to achieve fame as author of *Ben Hur,* moved quickly to the Negro's support. Just eight days after Maryland emancipation he issued General Orders No. 112 from his headquarters in

---

[21] Harrison Journal, Nov. 13, 1864, and Dec. 25, 1864.

[22] *Ibid.,* Nov. 2, 1864.

[23] Baltimore *Sun,* Oct. 17, 1867.

[24] Legally, apprenticeship was permissible only if the parents were unable to care for their children. See *Baltimore American,* Jan. 9, 1867, and Bartus Trew, deputy provost marshal in Kent County, to Major William M. Este, Nov. 15, 1864, Middle Department, Letters Received, RG98, NA.

[25] In some cases masters "refuse to obey the writ, and in others prosecute the parents who sue it out." *Baltimore American,* Jan. 9, 1867.

[26] Baltimore *Sun,* Oct. 17, 1867. See also W. A. Low, "The Freedmen's Bureau and Civil Rights in Maryland," *The Journal of Negro History* 37 (1952): 242. In 1865 the Court of Appeals, Maryland's top judicial body, found the apprenticing of Negro minors to be legal, but noted that the requirements of the law must "be studiously observed in their true spirit and design." *Baltimore American,* No. 4, 1865.

Baltimore. Wallace pointed to "evil disposed parties" who would obstruct emancipation by forced apprenticeship and noted that the freedmen, unaware of any legal rights they might have, sometimes encountered unfriendly law officers. To alleviate these conditions, the General placed the freedmen under military protection—to continue until the Maryland legislature could make such protection unnecessary.

Simultaneously, the General created a Freedman's Bureau for his department and ordered the seizure of the exclusive Maryland Club in Baltimore, a stronghold of aristocratic sympathizers of the South. Little imagination is needed to contemplate how galling Wallace's act must have been to the pride of many a Maryland gentleman. Renamed "Freedman's Rest," the club was to provide a resting place for "the sick, helpless and needy." Wallace determined to support it with donations and fines, and, if necessary, a levy upon Baltimore's rebel sympathizers. The Freedman's Bureau expired less than three months later and turned over its papers to the lower house of the General Assembly.[27]

Neither Judge Bond nor General Wallace halted apprenticing, but their efforts forced the Orphans Courts to move more cautiously. At least for a time after Wallace's order, the Orphans Court of Prince Georges County stopped acting on applications for apprentices.[28] In Baltimore County the court decided to bind only with parents' consent, unless the parents obviously could not provide for the children.[29] In the southern part of the Eastern Shore unstable conditions prompted the move of Brigadier General Henry Hayes Lockwood's headquarters to Cambridge, a town destined to be the scene of racial violence a century later. His responsibilities included protecting white Unionists and freedmen and breaking up apprenticeship without parents' consent. Where support was not available and parents desired it children

[27] *Communication from Major Gen'l. Lew Wallace, in Relation to the Freedman's Bureau, to the General Assembly of Maryland* (Document J., House of Delegates, Annapolis, 1865), pp. 4–5. The correspondence in this document is replete with the problems arising from binding Negro children. Wallace's bureau used the singular in spelling "Freedman," whereas the later federal bureau used the plural.

[28] *Marlborough Gazette*, cited in *Baltimore American*, Nov. 18, 1864.

[29] *Baltimore American*, Dec. 2, 1864. Dr. Samuel A. Harrison, a former slave-owner in Talbot County, remarked, "I understood that the negro children were generally, indeed universally bound to their former masters. . . . there were cases where the masters took the children who were large enough to be of service, and left the infants & smaller children to be cared for by the mothers & fathers. The negroes (the parents) manifested much feeling during the proceedings. There seems to be a general impression among loyal and moderate men that the O. [Orphans] Court is not acting justly to these poor creatures." Harrison Journal, Nov. 11, 1864.

could be sent to Baltimore for care. But Lockwood was urged to keep families together and to discourage emigration at this time.[30]

In October of 1867 Chief Justice Salmon P. Chase entered the fight. Sitting in the United States Circuit Court, he observed that a Negro apprentice, unlike his white counterpart, was not entitled to education and could be transferred from one master to another. These discriminatory provisions violated the new Civil Rights Act of 1866.[31] The system also transgressed the Thirteenth Amendment to the U.S. Constitution. Chase's knock-out blow followed a battering that had overwhelmed Negro apprenticeship. Apparently twenty-three hundred, about 70 per cent, of the bound children had already won their freedom, some through Judge Bond but most by their master's discharge upon yielding to pressure by a new Freedmen's Bureau or threats of a court suit.[32]

This Freedmen's Bureau got its start from the congressional act of March 3, 1865, which created the Bureau of Refugees, Freedmen, and Abandoned Lands. Unlike Wallace's earlier, short-lived invention, it extended generally throughout the old slave states. Its legislative demise did not occur until 1872, but the Bureau in Maryland concluded all but its educational and claims work in the summer of 1868.[33]

While fully active in Maryland, the Freedmen's Bureau investigated complaints about the mistreatment of Negroes and the apprenticing of their children. It provided rations to the needy and help in processing veterans' claims. The agency also sought facilities for Negro education and became interested in the socio-economic planning of First Lieutenant Edward F. O'Brien, who superintended three confiscated farms in Southern Maryland. Black labor successfully farmed the land, on which lived 534 persons. An army officer proudly claimed that nothing had been left undone to elevate the Negro's self-respect and self-reliance. The undertaking, he stated, disproved the idea that a

[30] Saml. B. Lawrence to Brig. Gen. H. H. Lockwood, Dec. 2, 1864, *The War of Rebellion: A Compilation of the Official Records of the Union and Confederate Armies* (Washington, 1880–1901), series 1, vol. 43, pt. 2, pp. 728–29. The postmaster at Prince Frederick in Calvert County charged that some Negro parents suffered beatings because they would not consent to having their children bound. The Court refused to hear their protestations. Postmaster at Prince Frederick, Maryland, to A. Lincoln, Jan. 11, 1865, Robert Todd Lincoln Collection of the Papers of Abraham Lincoln, LC.

[31] *Easton Star* (Talbot County, Md.), Oct. 22, 1867. During this era Supreme Court justices served also in the federal circuit courts.

[32] Baltimore *Sun,* Oct. 17, 1867.

[33] C. H. Howard to O. O. Howard, Oct. 10, 1868, Records of the Bureau of Refugees, Freedmen, and Abandoned Lands, RG105, NA.

Negro would not work unless watched by a white man. The rare cases of laziness were effectively remedied by stopping wages.[34]

Many planters in Southern Maryland did not share this enthusiasm for Negro labor. They complained about Negro indolence, impudence, and insubordination and blamed the Negro for an increase in crime. These whites also accused Negroes of refusing to hire themselves by the year. This disturbed the landowners who were accustomed to a ready supply of black labor, but who now looked upon fallow fields. So many Negroes had left the plantations that the cultivated acreage of three Southern Maryland counties was said to be cut in half.[35] Even the emancipationist Frederick *Examiner* expressed concern. One of its commentators warned that society would not tolerate "drones and vagrants."[36]

On the other hand, the freedmen grumbled about ill-treatment and the refusal of employers to pay them. Many planters would not hire Negroes who had relatives in the United States service. Nor could black property or persons be protected by civil authority. An army officer reported hearing the cynical remark, "we have civil law—we can take care of the 'niggers,' " repeated many times.[37] In one case Lieut. Edward F. O'Brien took the affidavit of a cruelly beaten Negro to the civil authorities to obtain a warrant for the arrest of the white offender. The local justice of the peace, George Alvey, refused to issue the warrant. The indignant Lieutenant asked the Governor to suspend Alvey's commission and expressed the hope that for humanity's sake Maryland did not have "so odious a law" that a man could not obtain justice "because he happens to be black." To this fervent cry the Governor drily replied that the law prohibited Negro evidence in any matter concerning a white.[38]

---

[34] Lieutenant S. N. Clark to Colonel John Eaton, Aug. 24, 1865, Executive Papers. The farms, property of Maryland Rebels, were seized by the military in May, 1864. Education on the farms was provided by the New York Society of Friends in a school of eighty-seven pupils.

[35] Lieutenant S. N. Clark to Colonel John Eaton, Jr., Aug. 21, 1865, Executive Papers. The counties were Prince Georges, Charles, and St. Mary's.

[36] Most supporters of abolition had been motivated, the journal observed, by a desire for the general welfare rather than a distaste for slavery. Frederick *Examiner*, Nov. 2, 1864.

[37] The officer believed that the Negro, denied justice, might seek it through a "bloody outbreak." Clark to Eaton, Aug. 21, 1865. See also Testimony of John W. Start, Jan. 29, 1867, Maryland Investigation, Papers of the House of Representatives, RG233, NA.

[38] First Lieutenant Edward F. O'Brien to Governor Bradford, July 24, 1865, Executive Papers; Governor Bradford to Edward F. O'Brien, July 29, 1865, Governor's Letterbook, Hall of Records, Annapolis, Md.

As further commentary upon the inability to assure justice, one Republican journal reported upon the case of a white man who was found by a jury *"not guilty"* to the charge of premeditated murder of a Negro. The Western Maryland weekly headlined the article, "No Crime to Kill a Negro," and claimed that the black man possessed no rights a Democrat had to respect.[39] An Eastern Shoreman, Dr. Samuel A. Harrison, contemplated the same problem. He said, "The Negro can neither have justice nor humanity shown him: and a white man dare not interfere in his behalf without having the finger of scorn, of public censure, and it may be violence aimed at him."[40]

Harrison epitomized many a sensitive Marylander's ambivalent feelings toward the Negro. He wrestled inwardly over the evolving status of the blacks as old concepts vied with new insights. Harrison confessed his racial bias and referred to the black "as a debased creature, hardly human."[41] Yet he decried with profound feeling the white man's injustice to the Negro and deplored the system that condoned such inhumanity.

This inhumanity prompted a Negro minister from one of the old slave counties to complain to Judge Bond of the persecution suffered by his people. It was impossible, Bond said, to get a clergyman along the bay shore even to hint that a Christian obligation existed to be kind, "much less just, toward the colored people." He called for a revival of a Christianity that did not fear persecution and did not merely reflect public opinion.[42]

Prejudice took many forms in tearing at the economic and social fabric of the state. For example, the British Consul in Baltimore wrote home, in the fall of 1867, that hostility for the Negro was threatening to interfere with British shipping. Formerly Negroes and whites went to sea on the same vessels. Now the shipping masters and boarding-house keepers would not provide a white man for a vessel that had a Negro on board. This created a problem when a British ship arrived in Baltimore and several men deserted, as frequently happened. An excellent Negro seaman was forced to leave the vessel so that replacements could be recruited.[43]

There was talk of white men's clubs and the Ku-Klux Klan in Maryland. A Democratic newspaper, the *Easton Star,* believed that a branch

[39] *Civilian and Telegraph* (Cumberland, Allegany County, Md.), Oct. 7, 1869.
[40] Harrison Journal, Oct. 8, 1864.
[41] *Ibid.,* Oct. 21, 1864.
[42] *Baltimore American,* Jan. 7, 1867.
[43] Harry Rainals to the Right Honorable Lord Stanley, Nov. 11, 1867, Correspondence of the British Consul at Baltimore, Foreign Office Papers, Public Record Office, London, England. Endorsements on Rainals' letter indicated British official disapproval of the Consul's removal of the Negro sailor.

of the secret order had been established in its area. Though unsympathetic to Negro progress, the journal warned against the KKK and pointed to attempts being made to locate their meeting place and "their diabolical secrets." The whole group, said the *Star*, could shortly find itself in jail.[44] The KKK apparently never established a significant foothold in the state.

Nevertheless, the Assistant Commissioner for the Freedmen's Bureau in Maryland was unwilling to rely solely on the local courts. He recommended the creation of Freedmen's courts to investigate and dispense justice whenever blacks could not obtain it in civil courts.[45] But he recommended in vain. Justice absented itself when a religious camp meeting near Elkridge Landing, Anne Arundel County, collapsed in a wave of white terrorism directed at the segregated quarters of the Negro participants.[46] Nor was justice apparent in the fires that had destroyed a dozen Negro schools by 1867. Half were in Kent County on the Eastern Shore. Only one other county suffered more than one such conflagration. That was Queen Annes, just to the south of Kent. Most of the schools served also as churches, many of which had been built by Negroes under the guidance of the Methodist Episcopal Church.[47]

Education was a prime goal for freedmen and their white friends. Before the war, only a relatively few Negroes got some formal education. Reportedly, 1,616 attended school in 1850, but only 1,355 in 1860.[48] Emancipation brought an upsurge, helped by financial support from the North. In about two years the freedman's aid societies of Boston gave almost thirty thousand dollars to the education and im-

[44] *Easton Star,* June 16, 1868. A letter dated April 4, 1871, in the Executive Papers indicated there were also Klansmen in the area of Hagerstown, Washington County. For Unionist fears generated by the forming of a white man's club, see Will. H. Lowdermilk to Gov. Swann, April 14, 1866, Executive Papers.

[45] Bvt. Maj. Gen. E. M. Gregory to Maj. Gen. O. O. Howard, Nov. 3, 1866, Records of the Freedmen's Bureau.

[46] Testimony of William H. Downs, Jan. 29, 1867, and others, Maryland Investigation. The camp meeting took place in Aug., 1866.

[47] Testimony of Fielder Israel, Feb. 15, 1867, Maryland Investigation. A number of churches connected with the northern Methodists, who entertained liberal racial views, were broken into, and a religious corporation bill was passed to permit frequent contests over the picking of trustees and to allow local congregations to take control of church property. Its enactment could have created chaos in many church bodies. The governor pocket-vetoed the bill. See Thomas Swann Notebook, April 2, 1868, Mrs. Sherlock Swann, Baltimore, Maryland; Charles Hoffman, *et al.* to Governor Swann, March 29, 1868; Methodist clergymen to Governor Swann, March 31, 1868; Members of the First Presbyterian Church of Baltimore (who protested against the bill) to Governor Swann, March, 1868; John M. Frazier to (addressee not shown), March 31, 1868, Executive Papers.

[48] *The Statistics of the Population of the United States, Embracing the Tables of Race, Nationality, Sex, Selected Ages, and Occupations* (Washington, D.C., 1872), p. 395.

provement of Maryland Negroes.[49] Some gentlemen in Baltimore also contributed. Judge Hugh L. Bond privately expressed his determination and that of others to give the Negro the "opportunity to get out of the slough."[50] But generally very little, if anything, came from the white residents or county governments to support Negro schools.[51]

Most white people rebelled at the idea of being taxed to educate Negroes. One newspaper expressed shock at the help provided by the Freedmen's Bureau in building schools for blacks, because this was a government agency supported by white taxes.[52] The Rev. Libertus Van Bokkelen, superintendent of public instruction under the Constitution of 1864, had to plead with state legislators in order to get them to agree to segregate black taxes for use in Negro schools.[53]

In 1870 Negro enrollment reached 7,674—3,307 of whom were in Baltimore.[54] Negroes in the counties usually paid the teachers' board and incidental expense, totaling an estimated $7,000–$8,000 in 1866.[55] Most of the teachers were colored, and some of them suffered physical abuse. Attacks sometimes also harassed the student. Even a white teacher from New England was warned by an "indignation meeting" to leave, but she pluckily declined.[56]

The viciousness displayed in school burnings ebbed. The buildings were rebuilt by the Negroes, and interest grew in their education.[57] Good experience with "educated free labor," accompanied by a scarcity

[49] Hugh L. Bond (?) to (no addressee), Nov. 10, 1866, Hugh L. Bond Papers, Maryland Historical Society.

[50] Hugh L. Bond to Kate Bond, Jan. 1, 1865, Bond Papers.

[51] Testimony of Fielder Israel, Feb. 15, 1867, Maryland Investigation.

[52] Easton Star, Sept. 24, 1867. The Baltimore Association for the Moral and Educational Improvement of the Colored People proved particularly helpful in educational work. See Charles McDougall to W. H. Wiegel, Nov. 1, 1866, Records of the Freedmen's Bureau. To get school aid from the Freedmen's Bureau, several conditions had to be met: a minimum of thirty students, a site for the school, funds for constructing the schoolhouse, and agreement to pay teacher's board. Benevolent societies generally provided the teacher's salary. "The Bureau then usually supplied the lumber and sometimes all of the material, and in behalf of the aid societies, engaged to send a teacher whose salary should be paid for at least one term," wrote C. H. Howard to O. O. Howard, Oct. 10, 1867, Records of the Freedmen's Bureau.

[53] Testimony of the Reverend Libertus Van Bokkelen, Nov. 14, 1867, Maryland Investigation.

[54] Statistics of the Population of the United States (1870), p. 415.

[55] Testimony of Fielder Israel. W. A. Low in "The Freedmen's Bureau and Education in Maryland," Maryland Historical Magazine 47 (1952): 35, used the estimate of ten thousand dollars as the total contribution of Negroes in Maryland to their schools in 1866.

[56] Testimony of Fielder Israel.

[57] Testimony of John A. Hopper, Nov. 14, 1867, and Richard M. Janney, Feb. 15, 1867, Maryland Investigation; Baltimore American, Jan. 16, 1867.

of other labor, helped improve white attitudes.[58] The Assistant Commissioner of the Freedmen's Bureau for Maryland said, perhaps over-enthusiastically, that the condition of the Negro in October of 1867 was "most excellent."[59]

Maryland, as in the past and future, only flirted with extremism. In varying degrees, nonetheless, racial prejudice infected all parts of the state. Certainly more than a few isolated incidents of persecution and injustice marred race relations in the old slave counties, though little overt action against the Negro occurred in the northern counties. White behavior generally was kindly toward the Negro as long as he kept his so called "place." The bully and social misfit, however, could safely vent his venom upon the Negro.

Enfranchising the Rebels

Meanwhile the war had ended. Rebel soldiers began their homeward trek. The anticipation of seeing their families doubtlessly salved the bitterness of defeat. But in Maryland the Confederate warrior was not welcome to the many loyalists who had long suffered the ill will of Southern sympathizers. Even a moderately disposed Unionist signed a request to the Commanding General in Baltimore to prevent the Rebels, who had supposedly lost none of their arrogance, from returning home and disturbing the peace of the loyal citizens.[60] Unionists must have been as deeply gratified as Rebels were anguished when they learned that presidential amnesty did not extend to persons who had left the jurisdiction of the federal union in order to aid the rebellion. The proscription, however, did not last long. Soon Maryland's Confederate veterans were returning to their families.

For a while, it looked as if the Rebels could not hope to regain the benefits of citizenship. But Southern sympathizers, who had watched the arbitrary imprisonment and exiling of many friends and relatives, refused to wait patiently or penitently. They clamored for their "rights" and soon got them. With their lives and property secure, the Rebels and their sympathizers agitated for the vote. Not even a year had elapsed since the war's end, when through the land was heard again, "No taxation without representation." Of course these people

[58] E. M. Gregory to O. O. Howard, Oct. [no day given], 1867, Records of the Freedmen's Bureau.
[59] E. M. Gregory to O. O. Howard, Oct. [no day], 1867, Records of the Freedmen's Bureau. This report did not include a few counties in Southern Maryland, where progress was a little slower. See C. H. Howard to O. O. Howard, Oct. 22, 1867, and Oct. 10, 1868, Records of the Freedmen's Bureau.
[60] Harrison Journal, May 22, 1865.

did not embrace the tax-paying Negro in their plea, for they vigorously opposed extending the franchise to the black man and shouted "outrage" at attempts to infringe upon the white man's right to infringe upon the Negro's rights.

Politically, these people adhered to the Democratic party—the party that had been tainted by treason and shattered by war. During the conflict, candidates had sometimes campaigned under a variety of banners rather than risk the Democratic label. In 1863 no state-wide Democratic candidate ran, but in 1864 the party revived. Stimulated by the prospects of a presidential election and a detested constitutional convention, the Democrats began organizing in earnest. On June 15 the party held a state convention. They fought Lincoln and the Constitution of 1864 and soon were seeking Rebel enfranchisement.

To further their cause, the Democrats were reported to be conspiring to call a new constitutional convention, apparently counting on two factors—no interference by the army and the support of a new ally, Governor Swann.[61] But the Radicals wielded a major counter weapon— the Registry Law. Winter Davis in December, 1865, looked to it to hold back the rising tide of Democrats until the Negro could get the vote. He would make the removal of the Negro's disabilities the condition for restoring the ballot to the Rebel.[62]

The Registry Law executed the disfranchising portions of the Constitution of 1864. The bill, which empowered the governor to appoint three registrars for each election district or ward, had been passed in the months just prior to General Lee's surrender. That General Assembly also approved the Thirteenth Amendment to the U.S. Constitution, elected Creswell to Hicks's Senate seat, wiped out much of the Black Code of the state, created a system of free public schools, and provided for the soldiers' vote.

Concerned over who would be appointed registrars, former Congressman John W. Crisfield, a conservative Unionist, urged Governor Bradford to avoid violent partisans. While it was right to disfranchise those who had actively engaged in rebellion, it was wrong to deny the ballot to someone who had done no more than make an intemperate remark. Wholesale proscription would create a large class, "formidable for evil," who would plot to overthrow the government. Allowed the vote, they would be absorbed and neutralized.[63]

---

[61] H. Winter Davis to John A. J. Creswell [Dec. 22, 1865], John A. J. Creswell Papers, LC.

[62] H. Winter Davis to Charles Sumner, Dec. 5, 1865, Charles Sumner Papers, Harvard College Library.

[63] John W. Crisfield to Governor Bradford, April 30, 1865, Governor's Letterbook.

Undoubtedly, Crisfield was disappointed in Bradford's appointments. On August 2, 1865, the registrars met in convention in Baltimore. They agreed upon a catechism of twenty-five questions that recalled a similar interrogation in 1863. Among the questions to be asked a prospective voter were: "Have you ever in any manner adhered to the enemies of the United States . . .? Have you ever on any occasion expressed sympathy for the Government of the United States during the rebellion?"[64] The names of all white, adult, male residents, applying or not, were to be placed on the books. Anyone disqualified could henceforth become a voter only if two-thirds of the General Assembly agreed, or if he joined the army or navy.

A rising tide of dissent protested the registration act, but legal attempts to subvert it collapsed in the courts. Partisan registrars disfranchised sufficient numbers to assure a Union party victory in the November 1865 election. Baltimore city registered only 10,842,[65] roughly one-fourth of the white male citizens over twenty-one. Of the registered, about half voted. The disfranchisement was therefore far more complete than in 1864 when, despite the strict requirements of the new Constitution, nearly eighteen thousand Baltimoreans had managed to vote for President.

Thomas Swann assumed the office of governor on January 10, 1866. His message to a special session of the legislature supported the registration act. If that law seemed radical, so much more so was the struggle to break up the Union. Should changes be desired, they could be reflected in the legislators chosen in the fall elections. Swann also backed President Johnson's Reconstruction policy, a reorganization of the state militia, and admission of Negro testimony in the courts. Not surprisingly, he opposed Negro suffrage.[66]

During Swann's first year in office the campaign against the registration act, initiated in 1865, reached a crescendo. To enfranchise the disloyal would require the defection of many Unionists, for Democratic registration was too small to do the job. The defections were neither long in coming nor small in numbers. Old enemies became new allies.

With the end of the war and the safety of the Union assured, many Unionists felt free to follow their conservative leanings, forget wartime animosities, and indulge their racial fears. Some had left their party during the war as abolition became a war aim. This failed to detract

---

[64] Myers, *Self-Reconstruction*, pp. 31–32.
[65] *Baltimore American*, Nov. 8, 1865. The estimated population of Baltimore was 240,000.
[66] Myers, *Self-Reconstruction*, pp. 40–41.

significantly from a popular showing against slavery in the November, 1863, election. But military intervention in elections, Radical excesses, rigid voter proscription of Southern sympathizers, and the confiscation of slave property without compensation caused large desertions from the party. Even an emancipationist like Reverdy Johnson attacked the Constitution of 1864 and backed McClellan for President. Now many conservative Unionists accepted the Democratic position of white supremacy and support of as much of the old order as could be salvaged from war.

The most famous Marylander to desert the Unconditional Unionist cause was Montgomery Blair, who had left Lincoln's cabinet in September of 1864. He addressed a Howard County meeting on August 27, 1865. Blair railed at Secretary of War Edwin M. Stanton and the registration act.[67] Nor did he relax his efforts. He addressed by letter a mass meeting held in Talbot County on October 17, 1865. In it he related disfranchisement in Maryland to Northern Radical schemes to disfranchise the South. Dipping his pen into the vitriol of which he was so fond, Blair raged about "public plunder," "a gang of scoundrels," and "unnumbered crimes." The real objective of the registration act, Blair charged, "is to screen from punishment the lawless men, who under the cover of transcendant [sic] loyalty have really been the greatest offenders against the cause of the Union."[68]

This was the kind of intemperate talk expected from a Democrat who had opposed the war to maintain the Union. It was hard to believe that Blair could swing so far. Yet he and the Radicals had long shared a mutual hatred. With his goals of Union and emancipation achieved, he could comfortably gravitate to a more conservative position.

Less given to partisan pyrotechnics, United States Senator Reverdy Johnson wrote to the same Talbot County meeting. He pointed to the incongruity of Confederate servicemen's being granted the franchise in the South while a Marylander, if he ever uttered a disloyal thought or gave to a relative in the Southern service, was disfranchised. The meeting approved the inevitable resolutions. They argued that the registration law was "anti-Republican, illegal and unconstitutional" and had been adopted during a period of great excitement. Now many of the law's advocates regretted this action. Only those seeking the perpetuation of their power allegedly desired its continuance.[69]

[67] *Civilian and Telegraph,* Aug. 31, 1865.
[68] *Easton Star,* Oct. 24, 1865.
[69] *Ibid.* Reverdy Johnson's comparison with the Confederate states was not fully relevant because Maryland retained her position in the Union.

In January, 1866, the Democratic leadership of the state called a convention of all who opposed the registration law. Held on January 24, its members elected Blair president. A committee was dispatched to the special session of the General Assembly, but the legislators remained unmoved. Nor did they respond favorably to a flood of petitions calling for repeal of the registration law.

For a time Democrats, conservative Unionists, and radical Unionists supported the President. This anomaly did not last long. The battle lines became more clearly defined when Johnson successively vetoed the Freedmen's Bureau and Civil Rights bills, only to have the latter bill overridden by Congress. As support of McClellan and opposition to the Constitution of 1864 had marched side by side, so now did support of Johnson and opposition to the registration law. The pro-registration forces linked with the congressional Radicals, though they tacked to a more conservative bearing in order to dodge the unpopular question of Negro suffrage, which they called a false issue. The important question, they claimed, was whether Rebels should be allowed to vote.

The Unionists early debated the merits of giving the Rebel the ballot. Just prior to the meeting of the 1866 General Assembly, Governor Swann talked to several prominent politicians. Congressmen Webster and Phelps said the franchise had been kept long enough from the Rebels. The party which gave them the ballot would be the strongest. Congressman John L. Thomas and Mayor John Lee Chapman of Baltimore disagreed.[70]

Internal dissension inevitably erupted into public debate. At a meeting on May 1, the Unconditional Union party executive committee split openly and irrevocably into conservative and radical factions. For a while both sides staked claims to the name of Unconditional Union although the conservatives in general soon moved into coalition with the Democrats, while the radicals became Republicans. The radical minority of the executive committee took their case to the people through the press and called for a state convention in Baltimore on June 6.[71]

Governor Swann opposed. Yet he asserted that the views expressed in his annual message of January 1 to the legislature remained unchanged; he still wanted the government controlled exclusively by loyal men. As for the Negro vote, he regarded that question and congressional control of suffrage in the states as virtually subordinat-

---

[70] Testimony of John Lee Chapman, Oct. 17, 1867, Maryland Investigation.
[71] *Civilian and Telegraph*, May 10, 1866.

ing the white race to domination by the Negro.[72] Swann avoided any explanation as to how the Negro vote would enable a minority, "inferior" race to take over Maryland.

A surprised *Civilian and Telegraph* lamented the Governor's action. Incomprehensible, agonized the editor, as he contemplated Swann's cutting loose from the party that elected him. The journal fancifully assumed that the Rebels would not accept Swann, which meant he would be left with only a few friends for support.[73] The editor reckoned without a full knowledge of Swann's astuteness. The Governor was eyeing the United States Senate seat held by Creswell. His longing was not likely to be realized as long as the Radicals controlled the legislature, for they could be expected to re-elect Creswell in 1867. Therefore Swann had to turn to the Democrats and Conservatives, whose political views he doubtlessly preferred anyway. To get them into power necessitated the appointment of understanding registrars, who would qualify as voters many previously excluded citizens. With the legislature controlled by Conservatives and Democrats, the registration law could be repealed and Swann elected to the Senate. Such a bargain repelled the more squeamish, but the practical-minded did not consider the price too high. Once the vote was gotten, said one observer, "we can regulate things to suit ourselves."[74]

Swann replaced Bradford's registrars with new men. Frequently they were Conservatives who had supported the Union, but the partisan mayor of Baltimore, John L. Chapman, labeled the city's new registrars as generally Rebel sympathizers.[75] With the evasion of the law and the Constitution, registration soared. Qualified voters increased in Somerset County from 1,804 to 3,273, in Dorchester County from 1,365 to 2,295, in Baltimore from less than 11,000 to over 24,000, and in Allegany County from 3,186 to 5,214.[76]

Strengthened by the flood of new voters, Conservatives and Democrats donned the mantle of true Unionism. They denounced abolitionists as disunionists and smeared their opponents with claims that they

[72] *Baltimore American*, May 12, 1866.
[73] *Civilian and Telegraph*, May 17, 1866.
[74] J. H. Franklin to George Gale, July 7, 1866, George Gale Papers, Maryland Historical Society. See also George Vickers to George Gale, June 25 and July 20, 1866, Gale Papers.
[75] Testimony of John Lee Chapman, Oct. 17, 1867, Maryland Investigation. See also testimony of Thomas Hodson, Nov. 16, 1867, Henry W. Straughn, Nov. 16, 1867, and Dr. Charles H. Ohr, Feb. 25, 1867. Ohr reported that twelve of Swann's sixteen registrars in Allegany County were known as disloyal throughout the war.
[76] One observer estimated forty to fifty per cent of the increase was due to the registration of persons not entitled to vote. See Testimony of Thomas S. Hodson, Nov. 16, 1867, and Henry W. Straughn, Nov. 16, 1867, Maryland Investigation; Myers, *Self-Reconstruction*, p. 76; Edward R. S. Canby to U. S. Grant, Oct. 23, 1866, U. S. Grant Papers, LC; and *Civilian and Telegraph*, Oct. 25, 1866.

favored Negro suffrage and equality. Radical success in November, claimed the coalition, would give the victors permanent power and assure the continued disfranchisement of a majority of the people. One Democratic journal ominously predicted the formation of a Negro militia that would suppress any popular uprising against the Radical program. Negroes and Radicals would run the state. But the evocation of such horrors did not exclude the time-honored exploitation of local issues. The oystermen were told that the Radicals had tried to levy a five cent tax per bushel on oysters, only to have the Democratic legislators defeat it.[77]

National politics intertwined with local as agitators talked bitterly of new conspiracies and a second civil war. Rumors even circulated of a Johnson *coup d'état* aided by Swann's Maryland militia.[78] Conservatives and Democrats pulled together but not always harmoniously. Old suspicions and new ambitions did not lie quietly. The coalition threatened to split in some counties over legislative candidates, but the need for one another proved strong enough to overcome these disruptive tendencies.[79]

The President obviously gave his blessing to the work of the Conservatives and Democrats. His helping hand extended into the unending power struggle that swirled around the federal patronage. Collector of Customs Webster, who had exploited Radicals in his quest for office, called for the ouster of the Radical assessor of the Third District. Webster considered this post one of the three most highly prized federal offices in the state. Webster got his wish. A more conservative district attorney also went into office.[80]

Gravely weakened by treachery and desertion, the tattered remnants of the old Union party lay in the hands of the Radicals. They worried the voter in 1866 with the fear that the Conservative–Democrat coalition would give state compensation to the ex-slave owners. That would saddle the taxpayer with a large financial expense. This would be particularly burdensome to the northern counties, where there had been few slaves. The issue gave the Radicals a platform from which to attack. They needed all the support that could be mustered as they tried to shake loose from the haunting specter of Negro suffrage. Creswell turned the argument around by telling the electorate that it was not a

[77] *Easton Star,* June 19, 1866 and Nov. 6, 1866.

[78] *Civilian and Telegraph,* Oct. 3 and 31, 1867. *Easton Star* of April 10, 1866, believed that the Civil Rights bill of 1866 might lead to Johnson's impeachment and a new civil war.

[79] Richard Paul Fuke, "The Break-up of the Maryland Union Party, 1866" (M.A. thesis, University of Maryland, 1965), pp. 83–86.

[80] Edwin H. Webster to the Secretary of the President, June 9, 1866, Andrew Johnson Papers, LC.

question of giving the black man the vote but rather a determination "that the Rebels shall not vote for the negro."[81] There was truth in this partisan claim because the Democrats would have the blacks counted for representational purposes, but not allow them the ballot. But the Radicals were indulging in a game of "make believe" in conveying to the voter the idea that the Negro suffrage issue had been settled by the Maryland Constitution and was therefore not germane to the election. The attempt proved to be an exercise in futility.

The legality of the registration law and the rights of the judges of election stirred debate as opposing forces jockeyed for a strong position on election day. A preliminary race took place in the Baltimore city election on October 10. Reverdy Johnson and J. H. B. Latrobe unsuccessfully sponsored the view that the registration law did not apply to a municipal election. The Democrats also attempted to use the expanded 1866 registration list but failed as Attorney General Alexander Randall contended that the 1865 list would still be the legal one on October 10. The 1866 list was not considered complete by that date. The judges of election accepted this interpretation. The official decision tended to quiet a potentially explosive situation,[82] enabling the Unconditional Unionists to sweep Mayor John Lee Chapman back into office with a Radical city council.

The triumphant Radicals had tasted their final victory. In November the new list of eligible voters would be in effect, but this did not eliminate the anxiety of the Conservatives and Democrats. They feared skulduggery by the Radical judges of election in Baltimore city. To replace them would require new police commissioners, because they appointed the judges. Governor Swann obligingly removed Messrs. Samuel Hindes and Nicholas L. Wood and gave their positions to William T. Valiant and James Young.

Now it was the turn of the Radicals to demonstrate their resourcefulness. They were not found wanting. Hindes and Wood refused to surrender their offices. Valiant and Young countered by ordering the Sheriff to summon a *posse comitatus*. Not to be outdone, Judge Bond issued warrants for the arrest of the new Commissioners and the Sheriff, charging them with conspiracy. Rather than give bail, Valiant and Young went to jail.[83] An angry mob hooted around the Court

[81] *Baltimore American,* May 19, 1866.

[82] Alexander Randall Diary, Oct. 20, 1866, Maryland Historical Society.

[83] *Baltimore American,* Nov. 5, 1866. The third police commissioner was Mayor John Lee Chapman. Valiant and Young were ordered to give security for keeping the peace and to desist from attempting to exercise the office of commissioner until they could prove their claim. Valiant and Young won their right to act as police commissioners shortly after the election.

House, but no serious incident occurred.[84] About this time Bond received a threatening letter that denounced him as a "black hearted nigger loving son of a bitch" and concluded with a hearty "God damn you."[85] Bond, however, seemed to thrive on excitement.

There would be plenty of it if fears were realized. Talk of insurrection intensified feeling as a flurry of activity gave credence to the rumors. A Union veterans group and the Union Leagues combed the city for help. Over five thousand readied to support the old police commissioners.[86] Brigadier General Edward R. S. Canby was ordered to Baltimore. He reported to General Ulysses S. Grant that the city was quiet but tense. Since the judges of election were subject to legal action for any wrongdoing, Canby regarded the attempt to replace the incumbents as an effort to gain power indirectly by admitting votes unacceptable under the Constitution. This was the scheme stirring many Baltimoreans to resist.[87]

Swann hurried to Washington after the jailing of the new commissioners and reportedly talked to the President, Secretary Stanton, General Grant, and Attorney General Henry Stanbery. The Governor returned to Baltimore with Grant, who wired on Monday that a "collision looked almost inevitable" that morning. Later in the day hope for peace substantially improved.[88]

Negotiations took place for the appointment of one Conservative judge and one Conservative clerk in each precinct, but the arrangement collapsed.[89] Nevertheless, the fearful predictions failed to come true. Comparative quiet prevailed on election day. The voters gave the Conservatives and Democrats an overwhelming endorsement. Ironically, this success came at a time when the nation was reacting to the South's behavior and Johnson's policy by increasing Radical power in the Congress. But in Maryland the victors swept the legislature by more than two-thirds in each house. This was the constitutional margin needed to enfranchise those white men previously denied the ballot.

The General Assembly convened in early January. Its membership included former Governor Philip Francis Thomas, future Governor

[84] Bond claimed that his action prevented "a most tremendous riot, and rivers of blood. [General Ulysses S.] Grant thinks the President would have . . . caused him to interfere and that half of Penna. would have been here in 48 hours—to resist him." Hugh L. Bond to Mrs. Thomas Bond [Nov. 1866], H. L. Bond Papers.

[85] Civic to Judge Bond, Nov. 1866, H. L. Bond Papers.

[86] *Baltimore American,* Oct. 22, 1866.

[87] Edward Canby to U. S. Grant, Oct. 23, 1866, U. S. Grant Papers.

[88] Baltimore *Sun,* Nov. 5, 1866; *Baltimore American,* Nov. 5, 1866; Myers, *Self-Reconstruction,* p. 75.

[89] Baltimore *Sun,* Nov. 6, 1866, and *Baltimore American,* Nov. 6, 1866.

Oden Bowie, and future United States Senator George Vickers. To one historian this was the Reform Legislature of 1867,[90] a questionable term at best. Mistrust, political intrigue, and the dubious use of large sums of money conspired with reactionary forces to thrust their will upon a legislature hardly worthy of the term "reform."

To get Swann elected United States senator required political leger-demain. By the eccentricities of Maryland law and geography this Senate seat belonged to the Eastern Shore. Swann came from the Western Shore. Therefore the time-honored agreement must be set aside. The Conservative–Democratic coalition could get no assurance from Radical state Senator Charles H. Ohr that he would vote for the repeal of the Eastern Shore law; so he was thrown out of the Senate.[91] This was done by rejecting on a technicality the votes of an election district that had given Ohr his narrow majority.

The General Assembly put together a series of interrelated acts that repealed the Eastern Shore law and then re-enacted it for future use, elected Swann to the U.S. Senate, restored full citizenship to the dis-franchised, and passed a bill to provide for the calling of a constitu-tional convention. The bill ordered a special election, at which time the voters would decide on a convention and vote for delegates. The legislature pushed the number of delegates for some counties beyond the existing General Assembly allotment in order to strike at the more populous and loyal areas. Baltimore city delegates, Conservatives and supporters of Swann, willingly submitted to this partial emasculation of their power, no doubt because it was part of the agreement.

These acts pertaining to the convention were unconstitutional, but the precedent had been set. Every one of Maryland's constitutions has come into being through illegal means. When strictly legal procedures were followed in 1966–68, the proposed constitution went down to defeat. So Maryland's record of illegitimate constitutions remains gloriously unblemished.

During the legislative session the Conservative–Democrats passed a new militia bill since the old law had lapsed in 1866. They rejected the Fourteenth Amendment to the United States Constitution and tried to get a bill passed for immediate new elections in Baltimore. Frightened jobholders in the city levied a 7 per cent or 8 per cent contribution[92] upon their salaries in order to buy enough state legislators to defeat that bill and the constitutional convention proposal. Only the lamp-

[90] Myers, *Self-Reconstruction*, Chapter IV, pp. 80–112.
[91] Testimony of Dr. Charles H. Ohr, Oct. 23, 1867, Maryland Investigation. See also *Civilian and Telegraph*, Jan. 24, 1867.
[92] Testimony of D. P[inckney] West, Oct. 25, 1867, Maryland Investigation.

lighters, because of their small salaries, were exempt. Mayor Chapman paid $210 into the fund, which, according to reports, reached $15,000.[93] The city council also appropriated $20,000 for legal fees to fight the election bill. Because of legal and political problems plus the alleged bribery, the Baltimore bill never became law. The reprieve proved brief, for the new Constitution of 1867 provided a swift means for overthrowing the Baltimore Radicals.

With victory in his grasp, Swann prepared to resign his gubernatorial powers, but rumors made him pause. Charges of corrupt bargains unsettled the political climate, while a petition was framed to request the United States Senate to refuse Swann a seat. Maryland's other Senator, the able but unpredictable Reverdy Johnson, was reportedly furious because the repeal and re-enactment of the Eastern Shore law made it possible for him to be re-elected. He told Montgomery Blair that Swann would be excluded from the Senate. A worried Blair wrote Swann in a confidential letter that his resignation would expose Maryland to seizure by the Radicals. Blair pleaded with Swann to hold his gubernatorial chair in order to squelch the conspiracy.[94] Obviously, Blair considered Lieutenant Governor Christopher C. Cox an unsafe politician.

Cox was to be inaugurated on February 26. But instead of a new governor taking office that day, there was a note from Swann saying he could not resign without further deliberation. On March 1, Swann formally declined the office, using the occasion to say he did so in the public interest. It would have been far better if he had omitted from his remarks that the honor had been bestowed upon him "without any agency or solicitation on my part."[95] That statement was either a bold lie or a rash attempt at self-delusion.

As Swann's substitute the General Assembly chose ex-Governor Philip Francis Thomas, a man of doubtful loyalty to the Union. The United States Senate rejected Thomas but accepted the legislature's next offering, George Vickers, a former Conservative Unionist who had opposed emancipation. Vickers won the high office after several days of balloting early in March of 1868.[96]

---

[93] Testimony of John Lee Chapman, Oct. 17, 1867, Maryland Investigation.

[94] Montgomery Blair to Governor [Thomas Swann], Feb. 22, 1867, Blair Family Papers, LC.

[95] *Journal of the Proceedings of the Senate of Maryland, January Session, 1867* (Annapolis, 1867), March 1, 1867, pp. 375–76.

[96] *Easton Star,* March 10, 1868. That paper (see June 9, 1868) would have preferred to re-elect Philip F. Thomas and risk his rejection again, but the question of impeaching the President was before the nation. Both Maryland senators were necessary to save Johnson; so the legislature turned to Vickers.

Two and a half months after Cox's aborted inauguration, the Maryland voters approved a constitutional convention. The date was April 10 and the totals 34,534 to 24,136.[97] The Convention opened on May 8. One gentleman, John F. Dent of St. Mary's County, bore the distinction of serving in his third constitutional convention, for he had previously been a member of the 1851 and 1864 delegations. Presiding over the session that lasted more than three months was Judge Richard B. Carmichael, who achieved notoriety in the Civil War by being dragged from the bench by the military.

The new document reflected the tastes of its Conservative membership. Dropped was the heady phrase that "all men are created equally free" and out went the office of lieutenant governor. All state officeholders lost their jobs, except Governor Swann. The Constitution further provided for a new election in Baltimore city in order to rid that metropolis of its Radicals. A more complete sweep of one's antagonists could not have been devised.

The new document erased the restrictive test oaths. Now all rebel sympathizers could vote without constitutional restraint. Officeholders henceforth would take a simple oath or affirmation that they would support the federal constitution and bear allegiance to Maryland. The governor got the veto power, and the judicial system underwent some changes. The legislature lost any power to suspend the writ of *habeas corpus* but won the right to change the school system. To stop the radical argument that the General Assembly would compensate the slaveowners, the Constitution expressly forbade this, as had its predecessor. But the 1867 version fancifully encouraged false hope for the financial losers by mandating the legislature to seek federal compensation.

Considerable debate centered upon giving the Negro the opportunity to testify in court. No specific race issue, other than Negro suffrage, stirred more Maryland controversy in the postwar years. The justification for excluding Negro testimony sprang in part from the relationship between master and slave. Many Marylanders wished to continue this exclusive tradition. To do otherwise would hurl a firebrand amid the people, for it would grant unusual privileges to political aliens and raise the Negro to political equality. At least that was one interpretation. Delegate J. Montgomery Peters (Baltimore) added his own flourish by charging that the Negro testimony clause would carry out the "infamous" Civil Rights Act. This he scathingly rejected as "a mean cringing to the Yankee Congress."

[97] *Baltimore American*, Sept. 30, 1867.

Calmer heads reminded the Convention that the Negro was trusted in daily dealings with whites and was "intelligent, honest and conscientious." These delegates insisted on the need for Negro testimony. Otherwise, great crimes could be committed in the presence of blacks without fear of punishment. Besides, the Negro had a natural right, distinct from his political right, to testify.

Delegate William M. Merrick (Howard County) drew applause by calling a white man's sense of nobility so flimsy that it "should be torn from him" if he felt lowered by being associated with a Negro on the witness stand. The more practical members advocated yielding on Negro testimony and fighting on the main issues of equal rights and suffrage. Former United States Senator Anthony Kennedy, in a speech somewhat reminiscent of his plaintive remarks in the national capitol, talked of revolution overturning the foundations of society and said that there was only a small "remnant of American constitutional liberty left us." Marylanders should adapt to present circumstances and adopt those laws necessary to their protection. In accordance with this, Negro testimony should be admitted.[98]

Since the courts had confirmed the legal right of the Negro to testify, the debate was a futile dialogue on the part of those delegates who wished to reject reality. They were not alone in this attitude. For instance, Judge Daniel R. Magruder of the circuit court for Anne Arundel and Calvert counties had received a warrant for his arrest on the charge of violating Negro civil rights by refusing Negro testimony.[99] Now the constitutional convention resolved its differences on the issue by providing for Negro testimony but allowing the legislature to reverse this provision.

The delegates spurned the democratic principle of equitable apportionment by swinging the power balance toward the old slaveholding counties in the southern part of the state. The latter picked up seven additional delegates, while the rest of Maryland lost one. That gave Baltimore and the northern counties 52 delegates or one delegate for every 8,552 persons (of whom 7,416 were whites) while the southern

---

[98] Philip B. Perlman (compiler), *Debates of the Maryland Constitutional Convention of 1867* (Baltimore, 1923). The sources for the quotations and general statements on Negro testimony can be found on pp. 158, 161–62, 340–43, 345–46.

[99] Testimony of Isaac Brooks, Jr., Feb. 14, 1867, Maryland Investigation. Richard J. Bowie, chief justice of Maryland's highest court, rendered a decision "that, under the amended Federal Constitution and the Civil Rights law, negroes are competent witnesses in any court in Maryland against white persons." *Easton Star*, July 17, 1866. Magruder apparently was never brought to trial, which prompted an official of the Freedmen's Bureau to remark that this was "one of the many instances proving that the law in Maryland is administered in the interest of a privileged class." C. H. Howard to O. O. Howard, Oct. 10, 1868, Records of the Freedmen's Bureau.

counties boasted 34 delegates or one delegate for every 7,127 persons (of whom 3,832 were whites). Unlike the 1864 document, the new constitution apportioned on the basis of black and white population, even though the Negro was excluded from the vote. To assure rural supremacy, the delegates slammed a lid on representation once a county or city legislative district reached the six delegates allocated for 55,000 population. In the senate the southern preponderance continued and in fact soon increased when Wicomico County came into being. That gave the area 15 senators or one for every 16,155 persons (of whom 8,685 were whites) while the north had 10 or one for every 44,472 persons (of whom 38,564 were whites).[100]

Radicals denounced the overrepresentation granted the southern counties and criticized some judicial changes and their costs.[101] The constitutional abolition of the existing school system further incurred their wrath, which was hardly mollified by accusations that they wanted to open the white schools to Negro children. "Then," asked one Eastern Shore Democratic journal, "what decent poor white man would send his children to them?"[102]

Another Democratic newspaper warned that defeat of the document would be interpreted as a readiness on Maryland's part to accept the congressional yoke and to become ripe for mongrelism.[103] Meanwhile, the *Easton Star* shored the Convention's defenses against a possible conservative attack on the question of Negro testimony. It called the clause a "crumb of comfort" to the minority. One benefit would ensue in that Negro witness would make it possible to catch white scoundrels inciting Negroes to insurrection.[104]

Another journal triumphantly touched a happy note by pointing to the relatively brief period required to get revenge; "Three short years enable us to destroy forever the most insufferable tyranny that was ever attempted over freemen."[105] Such tidings of joy were not long in winning voter approval. The Constitution swept to victory on September 18, by more than two to one, 47,152–23,036, and went into effect on October 5.[106]

---

[100] See 1860 census figures and the Constitution of 1867. In 1872 the legislature created the new county of Garrett in extreme western Maryland.

[101] *Civilian and Telegraph*, Sept. 12, 1867, printed a report that the new judicial system would cost an additional $40,200 annually.

[102] *Easton Star*, Sept. 10, 1867.

[103] *Centreville Observer*, cited in *Easton Star*, Sept. 10, 1867.

[104] *Easton Star*, Sept. 17, 1867.

[105] *Prince Georgian*, cited in *Easton Star*, Sept. 10, 1867.

[106] Thomas Swann Notebook. The constitutional convention election had been closer, 34,534 to 24,136. *Proceedings of the State Convention, of Maryland, to Frame a New Constitution, Commenced at Annapolis, May 8, 1867* (Annapolis, 1867), pp. 1–2.

Enfranchising the Negro

The issue of Negro suffrage assumed major proportions after emancipation was won. The last of the Rebels had yet to surrender when Cumberland's Unionist weekly addressed itself to the problem, "What shall we do with the negroes?" The answer, said this Western Maryland journal, lay in the dropping of "preconceived ideas and old prejudices." Provide the Negro with knowledge, pay for his labor, and reward him with the ballot.[107]

During the same month Winter Davis called for the Negro vote in a letter to a friend. He said that he had little sympathy for premature agitators; "They are cocks which crow at midnight; they do not herald the dawn, but merely disturb natural rest by untimely clamor. But," he added, "this is a question of political dynamics, which presses now for solution, and on it depends the chief fruits of the war."[108] Otherwise, another generation would pass before an answer could be found, and then possibly only with civil disturbances. Later that year he publicly expressed the same concept in a different way. It was insane, he argued, to believe that the South would bestow suffrage or equality. There were just two alternatives—"an oligarchy of loyal whites or an aristocracy of hostile whites. The one is loyal, but is not republican; the other is neither loyal nor republican."[109]

Many Maryland Radicals did not welcome the issue, though they recognized its importance for the restoration of the nation.[110] They knew too well that Negro suffrage smacked of Negro equality, a concept repugnant to most Marylanders. Of course in 1861 slavery had appeared even more firmly entrenched in Maryland than did opposition to Negro suffrage in 1865. Yet the miracle did happen—most Marylanders favored emancipation in 1863.

But one miracle, conceived in the name of humanity but wrought in the anguish of hate and war, was enough for one generation. The arguments for emancipation could be twisted into an appeal to the self-interest of the whites. The arguments for Negro suffrage could not be so readily turned to the white Marylander's benefit, unless he held or longed for a political job under the sponsorship of the Radical faction.

---

[107] *Civilian and Telegraph*, May 18, 1865.

[108] *Speeches and Addresses Delivered in the Congress of the United States, and on Several Public Occasions, by Henry Winter Davis* (New York, 1867), p. 563. The date of these remarks was May 27, 1865.

[109] *Ibid.*, pp. 586 and 596. The date of these remarks was Oct., 1865.

[110] Peter G. Sauerwein to Edward McPherson, Aug. 1, 1865, Edward McPherson Papers.

The *Civilian and Telegraph* and Henry Winter Davis had jumped dangerously far in front of the thinking of most citizens of the state. Davis realized how tough the issue was. He looked to the nation's Republicans to require the Rebel states to adopt Negro suffrage. Then, if the administration would get "off our backs," he would try to carry the issue in Maryland.[111] And doubtlessly he would have, but fate decreed otherwise, as death ended his career.

This flurry of interest in the black vote subsided during the campaign of 1866 as the Radicals tried to refute accusations that they favored Negro enfranchisement. Badly defeated in that election, the Radicals plotted a new course. They grasped for the issue from which they had publicly recoiled—Negro suffrage. As the Baltimore *Sun* noted, the election relieved them of "further duplicity" on the question.[112]

The Republican party of Maryland petitioned Congress for a republican form of government in accordance with the principle of Negro suffrage. In other words, the party wanted federal intervention in the state. The resolution went further, calling for the defeat of the proposed constitutional convention and the rejection of any participation in the selection of delegates. Should the convention win, then the Republicans should seek another constitutional convention, with universal manhood suffrage prescribed for the election of delegates.[113] The threat never materialized.

In the meantime Congressman Hamilton Ward of New York had introduced a resolution to direct the Committee on Elections to ascertain whether the federal laws and Constitution had been violated in the 1866 election in Maryland.[114] On March 18, 1867, Congressman Francis Thomas asked the Committee on Judiciary to complete the Maryland inquiries.[115] Hearings were held in 1867, but no action was taken by Congress to intervene in Maryland.

In 1867 a battered Republican party looked to November with dim prospects. The party picked Judge Bond for its gubernatorial candidate and summoned the faithful to turn out a full vote in order to show Congress that Maryland would have given the Radicals a large majority if equal rights had prevailed. Hopefully, Congress would

---

[111] H. Winter Davis to Charles Sumner, Dec. 5, 1865, Sumner Papers.

[112] Baltimore *Sun,* Nov. 8, 1866.

[113] *Civilian and Telegraph,* April 4, 1867.

[114] *Baltimore American,* Jan. 16, 1867.

[115] Francis Thomas, a former governor of Maryland, wanted to ascertain whether Marylanders had a "government republican in form" that Congress could "recognize and guaranty." *Congressional Globe,* March 18, 1867, 40th Cong., 1st sess., vol. 38, p. 193.

intervene and by March 1 install a republican form of government, with Judge Bond as governor.[116]

Certainly lust for power helped motivate the plea. Yet these Radicals were not without a case. Perhaps Congressman Schuyler Colfax, speaker of the House of Representatives, expressed it as well as anyone in declining an invitation to attend a border state convention on September 12:

> If a State which *enfranchises* by the tens of thousands every man who bore arms to destroy the nation . . . and at the same time *disenfranchises* by the tens of thousands other men who are . . . unmistakably loyal—if such a State has a republican government, I would like some learned jurist to inform us what would be an anti-republican government. If a State where loyalty is more odious, and devotion to the Union in its darkest hours . . . is punished by ostracism, outrage and dishonor—and the bitterest enmity and bloodiest hostility to the Republic is the surest passport to social distinction, to public honors and to official trust—if *that* kind of Government is one that the United States is to guarantee— . . . our Revolutionary fathers must have sadly misunderstood the meaning of the language they placed . . . in the Constitution.[117]

Congressman Francis Thomas hammered out the same theme in his quest for congressional intervention and Negro suffrage. Using the hyperbole of the era, Thomas told his congressional colleagues that he had been denying for thirty years that Maryland had a republican government. One-fifth of the white population controlled the legislation for the state, because no law could be passed or repealed without its consent. The majority could not rule. No free people should submit to this "tryanny and oppression."[118] So Thomas enshrined himself as one of those voices in Maryland which throughout its history have called for equitable representation. Entrenched political forces have paid little heed.

Congressman Phelps looked at the world quite differently. He regarded Thomas's move as an attempt to subvert the legal government of the state and force Negro suffrage upon the people "at the point of the bayonet."[119] In a later speech Phelps warned against the gathering of too much power in a despotic Congress and attacked the presidential impeachment movement as a design "not to vindicate justice but to grasp power."[120] Phelps displayed the politician's astute-

---

[116] Baltimore *Sun*, Nov. 1, 1867, and *Easton Star*, Nov. 5, 1867.

[117] Schuyler Colfax to John L. Thomas, Jr., Sept. 7, 1867, *Civilian and Telegraph*, Sept. 26, 1867.

[118] *Congressional Globe*, March 28, 1867, 40th Cong., 1st sess., vol. 38, p. 416.

[119] *Ibid.*, Dec. 17, 1867, 40th Cong., 2d sess., vol. 39, pt. 1, p. 231.

[120] *Ibid.*, Feb. 22, 1868, 40th Cong., 2d sess., vol. 39, Appendix, p. 247.

ness of spotting the mote of his opponent's eye but overlooked the mote in his own eye as he failed to see the injustices perpetrated by those he would defend.

The *Baltimore American* charged Congressman Phelps with encouraging the burning of Negro churches by showing that he did not feel deep concern for these crimes. This leading Republican daily proclaimed, "We are the partisans of humanity, justice and right."[121] But it was not alone in showing that more than self-interest spurred many Republicans. John R. Kenly, a Maryland lawyer breveted a major general for his service to the Union, spoke for Negro suffrage, "because I believe in the brotherhood of man."[122] Judge Bond pondered the problem. He observed that God did not create all persons equal. Some were taller; some were more intelligent than others. Should he consider himself superior to the blacks, "it is no reason that I should stop the avenues of their egress from beastliness toward humanity in order to preserve my superiority." Bond personalized his attitude by pointing to those New Yorkers who considered themselves his superior. He would hate to have them make laws discriminating against him.[123]

Maryland Negroes did not rely entirely on the whites to forward their interests. A group of blacks in December, 1865, asked for the vote, for admission of their testimony in court, for appointment of Negro teachers in Negro schools as long as schools were segregated, for repeal of the existing system of Negro apprentices, and for legal protection in entering the professions and trades.[124]

In 1866 three hundred Baltimore Negroes urged President Johnson to sign the Civil Rights bill. They argued their case by emphasizing several facts. Not a single culprit had been punished for burning their schools and churches. Justice was obstructed by disqualifying Negro testimony concerning the fires. Nor could teachers of Negroes expect protection against brutal assaults and mistreatment. But this was not all. Negro homes were invaded and children were seized and forcibly bound to white masters. The Negroes lacked the sympathetic assistance of Christians; therefore protection could come only from the law

---

[121] *Baltimore American*, Jan. 12, 1867.

[122] S. B. Nelson (publisher), *History of Baltimore, Maryland from its Founding as a Town to the Current Year 1729–1898* (n.p., 1898), p. 123.

[123] Hugh L. Bond to Kate Bond [1866?], Bond Papers. Although Senator Reverdy Johnson echoed the conservative position by calling the Negro as safe in Maryland as in Massachusetts, he rejected the popular thesis that the Negro was inferior or even sub-human. Johnson told his fellow senators that the black race was just as capable of creating a high civilization as the white. He had seen among Negroes as much "native talent" as among whites and anticipated their becoming "valuable citizens." *Congressional Globe*, Jan. 23, 1866, 39th Cong., 1st sess., vol. 36, p. 373.

[124] Baltimore *Sun*, Dec. 29, 1865.

"till the followers of the common Master shall cease to be corrupted or overawed by treason."[125]

Though the President did not heed the petitioners, Negroes did make progress. Negro leadership, the help of men like Judge Bond, and the national civil rights movement broke down many barriers. The black code crumbled under legislative changes. The system of penal slavery, whereby a Negro could be sold for a crime, received the inevitable *coup de grâce* from the General Assembly in 1867. It was inevitable because the federal Civil Rights Act of 1866 outlawed legislation that authorized different punishment for Negro and white offenders.

Discrimination was dealt another blow in a case involving the prohibition of a Negro's sitting on street cars. Riding on the exposed platform of the vehicle could be a disheartening experience. To gain protection from the elements, a black woman sometimes borrowed a white child, which entitled her to sit inside. A New York Negro did not take kindly to this discrimination. Arrested for sitting in a Baltimore street car, he sued the Passenger Railway Company and got ten dollars in damages.[126] The Negroes thus won, in 1870, the right to equality of service. For a while, the railway ran Jim Crow cars, but another court case in the following year ended segregation. This, as a *Baltimore American* headline proclaimed, made "THE CARS FREE TO ALL."[127]

Although Maryland Negroes had not been able to participate actively in the emancipation movement, they openly campaigned for the vote. On May 14, 1867, Negroes appeared for the first time as equals in a Maryland political convention. Nearly all of the county delegations to this Republican meeting included blacks.[128] At the border state convention in Baltimore later that year, Dr. Henry J. Browne, a Negro, ridiculed racial prejudice. He attacked the concept of compensating slaveowners and militantly claimed that the South owed the Negro the wages for 250 years of bondage.[129] A number of Negro meetings were also held. Among them was an interstate convention that met in Baltimore in August, 1868. The members supported Grant and planned to urge suffrage upon Congress in December.[130]

[125] Newspaper clipping in Creswell Papers, vol. 11, p. 2185.
[126] Grace Hill Jacobs, "The Negro in Baltimore, 1860–1900" (M.A. thesis, Howard University, 1945), pp. 82–83; *Baltimore American*, April 30, 1870.
[127] *Baltimore American*, Nov. 14, 1871. See also the issues of Nov. 11 and 13, 1871.
[128] *Civilian and Telegraph*, May 23, 1867.
[129] *Baltimore American*, Sept. 13, 1867.
[130] *Easton Star*, Aug. 18, 1868.

But in Maryland the Republican ticket of Grant and Colfax lost by a two to one margin. The quest of some radicals for the reconstruction of Maryland met an equally unsuccessful fate, as would have Maryland Negro suffrage if national goals had not been involved.

This was made obvious when, in January of 1869, Oden Bowie became the first Democrat in eleven years to hold the gubernatorial reins. His inaugural address followed the party line—restoration of the South, suffrage left to the states, white supremacy, etc. The war for the Union had been won, but the old power once again resided in Annapolis. Not a single elected Republican officeholder remained to mar the Democratic sweep. Support of the Rebel cause now became part of the credentials of many aspirants for appointed posts.[131]

The General Assembly, already totally Democratic in its 1868 session, appeared at first to be about to reward Thomas Swann with the senate seat then held by Reverdy Johnson. But such was not the case. A resurrected Democratic powerhouse, William Thomas Hamilton of Western Maryland, got the prize.[132] But Swann had some compensation, for in the 1868 elections he had won a congressional seat.

When the Fifteenth Amendment to the United States Constitution came before the General Assembly, the legislators did the expected,[133] rejecting the idea of granting Negro suffrage, just as it had earlier refused to accept the Fourteenth Amendment and Negro citizenship. Maryland representatives in Congress proclaimed the same sentiments. Senator George Vickers asserted that Negroes and whites could not properly be associated together in the state and general governments. He underscored the point by quoting an 1860 speech of an Ohio Senator that pictured the two races as incapable of living happily and prosperously in the same place. "That was in 1860, and what was

[131] Bowie attended to a variety of state problems, including support of the Pennsylvania Railroad in its struggle with the Baltimore and Ohio. Railroads were politically active during this era, but William B. Catton, who is currently writing a biography of John Work Garrett, president of the Baltimore and Ohio during the Civil War and Reconstruction, has found no evidence that Garrett interfered in politics except in railroad matters. Interview with William B. Catton, Feb. 28, 1969.

[132] In 1868 Reverdy Johnson resigned in the final months of his senatorial term in order to accept the ambassadorship to Great Britain. On July 13, 1868, Swann appointed a potent Democratic figure to the vacancy, William Pinkney Whyte (Thomas Swann Notebook). It was Whyte whom Hamilton replaced.

[133] The Fifteenth Amendment got a dress rehearsal in the bill to grant Negro suffrage in the District of Columbia. This action recalled the successful war-time move to undermine slavery through emancipation in the district. Both efforts were denounced by many Marylanders, whose state inevitably experienced shock waves from events in the district.

true then is true in 1868," Vickers declared.[134] But that was where he and his conservative allies were wrong. As in the emancipation movement, Vickers could not keep up with the revolution that was occurring. The political center moved toward the left, as people were pushed or pulled toward granting the Negro more rights.

Swann called himself a friend of the Negro,[135] but the Negro could well have done without such professed support. The former railroad president, mayor, and governor told his congressional colleagues, "you have invited him [the Negro] to your railroad cars, to your public institutions, to your work-shops, to your halls of legislation, but here your power ends. . . . You have not converted the people."[136] In speaking several months later against a bill to enforce the Fifteenth Amendment, Swann reverted to the oft-repeated scare of the 1860s. The bill, he said, was the first move in beginning a race war. He pointed to the Anglo-Saxon's pride and the Negro's demoralization and asked for a pause in the revolutionary program.[137]

During that month Senator Hamilton attacked the same legislation. He spoke of "the spirit of coercion" that was abroad in the land and charged that the rights of the states were being violated. Maryland's registration law would be subverted by the proposed legislation. Hamilton went further, saying that the bill would restrict a white man in what he could say to a Negro voter. For instance, he might urge a black man not to register or vote by telling him to "stay out of this conflict, where there is so much passion, prejudice, and interest; . . . stay at home and work; . . . it will be better for you now and better for you in the future!" Talking to a Negro in such a way under this bill might be risky. The Negro could go to a commissioner and make the accusation that intimidation had been used to keep him from voting.[138]

Other Maryland legislators joined in the fight against any federal effort to achieve equality for the Negro. Senator Vickers disliked "the leveling principles of universal suffrage" and seethed with revulsion at efforts to abolish the caste system.[139] School integration and social equality obviously were not for him. In 1872 Vickers attacked a civil

[134] *Congressional Globe*, June 8, 1868, 40th Cong., 2d sess., vol. 39, Appendix, pp. 329–33.

[135] *Ibid.*, May 27, 1870, 41st Cong., 2d sess., vol. 42, Appendix, p. 433.

[136] *Ibid.*, Dec. 21, 1869, 41st Cong., 2d sess., vol. 42, Appendix, pp. 23–24.

[137] *Ibid.*, May 27, 1870, 41st Cong., 2d sess., vol. 42, Appendix, pp. 431, 433, 435.

[138] *Ibid.*, May 18 and 19, 1870, 41st Cong., 2d sess., vol. 42, Appendix, p. 355.

[139] *Ibid.*, February 24, 1871, 41st Cong., 3d sess., vol. 43, pt. 2, p. 1637. Vickers also charged that the consolidation of power would destroy state "sovereignty, and lead to monarchy, aristocracy, anarchy, or revolution."

rights proposal of Senator Charles Sumner. Because a man has the right to travel a public road, that does not give him, Vickers said, the right to enter the property of another.[140] In other words, an innkeeper should be able to restrict his clientele.

With the Democratic party all powerful, the Conservative Unionists either merged with their new allies, as did Swann, or wandered between parties as did Bradford. The war-time Governor allied himself to the Conservative–Democrat movement of 1866–67, but supported Grant in 1868. Disenchanted, he joined the Liberal Republicans for the 1872 campaign. In 1876 he apparently gave his vote to the regular Republican nominee, Rutherford B. Hayes.

Men like Bradford objected to Republican plans for reconstructing the South. They wanted Grant's administration to follow a more conciliatory course. Since Negro suffrage had been achieved, why not remove all of the South's political restrictions?[141] These Conservatives longed for the Republicans to adopt such a course, for the Democrats rankled them by glorifying the rebellion and demonstrating their preference for the most obnoxious of its supporters.

The Democrats no longer needed Bradford's kind, but the Republicans did. Creswell, who had been appointed by Grant to his cabinet, recognized the fact. He hoped to co-operate with Bradford and agreed that universal amnesty should follow manhood suffrage. On the other hand, a fearful Creswell warned of "terrible calamities" that would follow Democratic supremacy. Therefore, patriots must work out reforms within the confines of the Republican party.[142]

Obviously, Liberal Republicanism was anathema to Creswell. But the Eastern Shoreman need not have worried. The movement, whose national ticket won Democratic support, attracted only a few of the old radical element, such as Henry W. Hoffman, former congressman, and Joseph J. Stewart, former assessor of internal revenue. This coalition, headed by Horace Greeley for President, stirred no enthusiasm among many Democrats. Greeley carried the state by less than 1,000 votes, a remarkably poor showing considering Maryland's Democratic strength during that period.

In the meantime the small Radical or Republican party engaged in the risky luxury of schism. Both sides of the party denounced Governor Swann and President Johnson as traitors and called for Negro suffrage. But they splintered on the current role of the Negro in the party.

[140] *Ibid.*, Feb. 8, 1872, 42nd Cong., 2d sess., vol. 45, Appendix, p. 42.
[141] Augustus W. Bradford to John A. J. Creswell, Nov. 7, 1870, copy in Augustus W. Bradford Papers, Maryland Historical Society.
[142] John A. J. Creswell to Augustus W. Bradford, Nov. 28, 1870, Bradford Papers.

In 1868 the dominant faction, led by Creswell, reduced the blacks to the role of consultants, while the Bond forces welcomed the Negro to full participation in all party affairs. The Bond men that year sent a rival delegation to the Republican National Convention in Chicago, but it was not seated. Their position was hardly enhanced by Grant's appointment of Creswell to his cabinet.

Anna Ella Carroll, who had achieved some notoriety as an advisor to Lincoln, disliked Creswell. She accused him of abusing the federal patronage and seeking to keep the party small in order to maintain his leadership. Miss Carroll warned that Negroes would look elsewhere for political enfranchisement and were doing so.[143] Henry W. Hoffman sympathized with her views. He predicted in March, 1870, that astute Democrats would seek Negro support by pointing to "the hollowness and insincerity of the present Republican leaders."[144]

Hoffman's fears of Democratic astuteness went largely unrealized. In some counties, it is true, the Democrats did seek the black vote in 1870; for example, in Baltimore's Third Congressional District and the Fifth Congressional District in Southern Maryland. Elsewhere in the state the Democrats adhered to their time-honored racist traditions.

The registering of Negroes assumed remarkable proportions. The law provided only three days in the counties and six days in Baltimore, yet over 35,000 blacks qualified out of a possible 39,120.[145] This was particularly significant when compared with the 1868 election results. Grant lost the state by less than 32,000 votes. The upsurge assured the Republicans of strong support in Southern Maryland, a region formerly barren of Republicans. Wholeheartedly, Negroes supported the party even though they had not been treated well by the Creswell faction.

All white Republicans were not, however, happy with their new comrades. In Allegany County, in Western Maryland, where the Negro vote was small, the white backlash beat down Republican strength. The local weekly hopefully believed "a little calm reflection" would

---

[143] Anna Ella Carroll to the Republican senators (of Maryland), [1869?], Anna Ella Carroll Papers, Maryland Historical Society.

[144] Henry W. Hoffman to Anna Ella Carroll, March 7, 1870, A. E. Carroll Papers. From 1868–70 Negroes were excluded from active participation in Republican primaries, etc. Ratification of the Fifteenth Amendment re-opened the doors.

[145] Margaret Law Calcott, *The Negro in Maryland Politics, 1870–1912* (Baltimore, 1969), p. 24. With registration nearly complete, the *Baltimore American* of Oct. 17, 1870, gave figures that totalled 36,084 for the number of qualified Negroes. In the 1870 election 134,525 voted out of 169,845 male citizens over twenty-one. See *Baltimore Sun*, Nov. 11, 1871, and *The Statistics of the Population of the United States* (1870 Census), 1:629.

overcome white prejudices.[146] Meanwhile, the *Cecil Whig* charged the opposition with redoubling their efforts to libel the Negro in order to intensify prejudice.[147]

Acting under a new law, federal officials were present to assure a fair election as blacks and whites went to the polls on November 8, 1870. The election proceeded quietly.[148] Seventy-nine per cent of the male citizens of voting age cast ballots, with the highest turn-outs in areas with large numbers of Negroes. Though the Republicans failed to carry a single congressional district, they came close in two contests. Eventually Western Maryland returned to its natural political home, the Republican party. A recent study reveals that the four westernmost counties, three Southern Maryland counties, and one Eastern Shore county usually voted Republican from 1870 to 1895.[149]

The Negro enabled the two-party system to achieve respectability in Maryland, with indications of a high Negro turn-out at elections.[150] But the Negroes did not uncomplainingly walk the Republican road. In February, 1870, some Negro politicians urged that governmental department chiefs appoint blacks and noted that their people, like the whites, wanted encouragement. These politicians opposed the dissolution of the Colored Republican State Central Committee until Negroes were taken more fully into the political fellowship.[151] Such appeals failed to produce for the Negro his fair share of party patronage or offices.

Three years after getting the vote, Negroes held only two of the twenty positions allotted to the city of Baltimore on the Republican State Central Committee. A higher proportion, one-fourth, was black on the entire state-wide committee. Dissatisfaction spurred some Negroes to talk of a separate, black political organization, but an attempt in 1873 to achieve this collapsed under opposition from more moderate Negroes.[152] They knew that black persons won far more recognition in the Republican party than in the Democratic party.

The biggest obstacle to Republican success was the city of Baltimore, which the Democrats converted into their stronghold. Republicans

---

[146] *Civilian and Telegraph,* Nov. 17, 1870.

[147] *Cecil Whig,* July 2, 1870.

[148] Baltimore *Sun,* Nov. 9, 1870.

[149] Calcott, *Negro in Maryland Politics,* pp. 39 and 67.

[150] *Ibid.,* p. 218.

[151] Nelson, *History of Baltimore,* pp. 177–79. Resolutions also recommended the National Freedmen's Savings Bank in Baltimore for Negro deposits and pleaded the cause of the Cuban republic and the organization of labor unions.

[152] Jeffrey R. Brackett, *Notes on the Progress of the Colored People of Maryland Since the War* (*Johns Hopkins University Studies in Historical and Political Science*) (Baltimore, 1890), pp. 17–18.

did little to improve their competitive position in that city. They seemed less interested in corralling votes than in factional squabbles over federal patronage plums.[153] In April, 1872, one faction of embittered Republicans attacked the primary election tactics of their colleagues from the Custom House. Three-fourths of the judges of elections, who were appointees of the ward presidents, held jobs in the Custom House, or actively sympathized with the same political organization. This opened the way to ballot-box stuffing, dishonest vote counting, and the movement of voters from polling place to polling place in order to vote several times. As a consequence, the chairman of the Republican State Central Committee, Andrew W. Denison, recommended that Baltimore's twenty-one delegates to the Republican State Convention not be seated.[154]

At the same time many Democrats were becoming dissatisfied with their own party. One journal warned its readers about the Maryland legislative lobby and county rings—if these rings were not broken, the Democratic party in the state would become as corrupt as the Republican party in the North. The editorial charged that Maryland political morality had been tending downward, while the power of the Annapolis lobby had been rising.[155] In 1873 independent and fusion tickets appeared in some counties, but 1875 saw the biggest effort on the part of reform Democrats to lock arms with the Republicans. These two years brought forth Republican platforms that avoided the party's usual appeal to the Negro.[156] The omission was a quest for more Democratic support.

Severn Teackle Wallis, a prominent Democrat running for attorney general on the Reform ticket, enlivened the contest of 1875 with his ridicule. In attacking the opposition, he noted how the political machine worked: "One does the morality and another the immorality; one sees that the sentiments are lovely, while another looks after the ballot-boxes and the 'boys'; one sets the traps, and another covers them up, but there they all are, on the spot, each at his post, and each keen for his share of the game."[157]

In October Henry M. Warfield, Reform candidate for mayor of Baltimore, narrowly missed victory. The November state-wide elections gave the Reform ticket a majority in the counties, but corrupt prac-

---

[153] Calcott, *Negro in Maryland Politics*, p. 71.

[154] *J. Philip Sindall et al. to Andrew W. Denison, April 20, 1872* (no publishing data for this pamphlet), Bradford Papers.

[155] *Easton Star*, June 22, 1869.

[156] Calcott, *Negro in Maryland Politics*, p. 78.

[157] Severn T. Wallis to the Voters of Maryland, Oct. 9, 1875, *Civilian and Telegraph*, Oct. 21, 1875.

tices by the frightened ring in Baltimore puffed such a large majority for the Democrats that they carried Maryland by a safe margin. To achieve this result, ring ruffians assaulted Negroes and white reformers and used "pudden" tickets. These were small tickets made of thin paper. They were folded inside a larger ballot. In one precinct 542 persons voted, but 819 ballots were counted.[158]

Wallis wrote the Governor that "fraud, intimidation and violence" voided the election in Baltimore. Because he had a majority of the votes in the counties, he obviously considered himself entitled to the office.[159] But he protested in vain. As usual, fraudulent ballots counted as much as legal ones in deciding a political contest.

The 1870s saw politics turn from an obsession with the Negro question to other issues. Racism, according to one student of the period, played an important role in Democratic strategy in only three of the campaigns from 1871 to 1894.[160] Corruption, tariff, and other economic issues attracted attention in the 1870s. But the Negro question continued to possess all the potential power of an inactive volcano. In the late 1890s racism erupted in one of its most virulent forms and culminated in the early 1900s in a tenacious but unsuccessful drive to disfranchise the Negro.

From 1861 to 1867 Maryland suffered but endured. The ravages of war scarred her land, embittered her heart, and disturbed her spirit. Within the tumult mingled the base and the beautiful, the ignoble and the ideal. Out of the fusion of these elements came a new birth of freedom, not only freedom for the Negro but also freedom for the white man from the devastation of an institution he so perversely cherished. Thus did Maryland become the first border state to abolish slavery. Hand in hand with that achievement went the overthrow of the old political order.

But radicalism pushed too far in abusing power through military force and disfranchisement. Besides, emancipation was a little bit too heady a substance for conservative Maryland. So with the nation once again united, Marylanders could safely indulge their distaste for radical policies and their revulsion at Negro advancement. They turned to the custodians of the old order, the Democratic party, whose

[158] Warfield lost the mayoralty by 28,136 to 25,471 (Baltimore *Sun*, Oct. 28, 1875), but J. Morrison Harris, Reform candidate for governor, was overwhelmed in the city by 36,958 to 21,863 and lost the state 85,362 to 72,553, *Baltimore American*, Nov. 10, 1875. See also *Baltimore American* and Baltimore *Sun* of Nov. 3, 1875.
[159] Severn Teackle Wallis to Governor James Black Groome, Nov. 16, 1875, Executive Papers.
[160] Calcott, *Negro in Maryland Politics*, p. 54.

hierarchy was steeped in sympathy for the South. By the end of 1867 the counterrevolution was complete. It sought to assure its future success by malapportioning the state. Political intrigue accompanied the maneuverings, but Swann lost his senatorial prize because he could not practice his legerdemain so readily upon the United States Senate.

The dissolution of the Union party made way for a strong Democratic party and a small Republican party that grasped for Negro suffrage as its one hope for new life. In 1870 the Fifteenth Amendment gave the Republicans their wish and made it possible for Maryland to boast of a reasonably strong minority party. That fact enabled the state to avoid some of the excesses of the South. The Negro generally voted rather freely.

With the 1870s came an acceptance of the Negro voter, a downgrading of the importance of the race issue, and rising concern over economic issues and corruption. The Negro question, of course, was never fully resolved. It remained, to trouble the passions and consciences of later generations.

Thus the violence of the 1860s had uprooted the institution of slavery and given physical freedom and the ballot to the Negro. The promise of this nation came one step closer to fulfillment. And though the revolution stopped short of equality for all peoples, it laid the foundation for a new thrust forward a century later.

CHAPTER SIX

Reconstruction in Delaware
Harold B. Hancock

Reconstruction in Delaware differed markedly from that in the Deep South. Political control by the Democratic party, which had been established in the late 1850s and confirmed during the Civil War, lasted almost undisputed until 1888. The Constitution of 1831 governed the state until 1897. Carpetbaggers, scalawags, occupation forces, and the Ku-Klux Klan were not features of Delaware politics; nor were wholesale corruption and lavish expenditures, though some dishonesty and election irregularities persisted, just as they had before and during the war. Through 1880 governmental expenditures and receipts were less than $200,000 annually, and the state debt was less than $2,000,000. Education was mainly supported by local districts, and there was no state penitentiary nor state institution for the care of the blind, insane, and deaf. Such matters were left to the governments of Delaware's three counties, New Castle, Kent, and Sussex.[1]

An important common bond linking Delaware to the South was the Negro, and determining his status, education, and civil rights provided the most important political topic. Democratic politicians championed Andrew Johnson's policies, attacked congressional plans for the South, and condemned the federal invasion of states' rights, while the Republicans took the opposite side of these questions. Political happenings within and without the state determined that the state would remain Democratic.

Until the end of the Reconstruction period Delaware remained Democratic, political control being secured in part by the use of a notorious assessment law. Negroes took the first steps toward citizen-

---

[1] "Delaware," *American Annual Cyclopedia*, 1880 (New York, 1881), p. 202. Some editions are called *Appleton's Annual Cyclopedia*. The estimated receipts in 1880 were $168,000, and estimated expenditures $97,000. In addition, the state had invested in railroad bonds $673,000 for general purposes and $448,000 invested in bank stock for the benefit of public schools, the return being $31,000. State and local government expenses totaled $6.32 per person in 1890, which was a greater expenditure per person than any southern state spent, except Maryland and the District of Columbia, but less than that spent in the middle atlantic states and New England; U.S. Census, *Compendium of the Eleventh Census*, 1890, part 3 (Washington, 1894), p. 971.

ship in these years. The majority of the inhabitants depended for a livelihood on farming, using traditional methods and raising traditional crops, but some successfully experimented with the raising of fruits, berries, and truck crops. Wilmington and the adjacent section of New Castle County became increasingly industrialized and the leader of the state in culture, education, and wealth.

Delaware is a small state, only one hundred miles long and varying in width from nine to thirty-five miles. On two sides it is bounded by Maryland, on the north by Pennsylvania, and to the east by the Delaware River and Delaware Bay. In 1860 the population totaled 112,216, New Castle County with the city of Wilmington containing almost as many inhabitants as the other two counties combined.[2]

In the postwar period most of the inhabitants continued to earn their living by raising wheat and corn by traditional methods as they had before the war. Orchard products and truck crops became of increasing importance after the completion in 1860 of a railroad running the length of the state. In Wilmington and its immediate vicinity there were important powder mills, shipyards, and machine shops.

South of the Delaware and Chesapeake Canal most of the population was of British origin and Protestant background. The majority of the Negroes also lived here. In northern Delaware, Irish and Germans were added to the original stock in the early part of the nineteenth century, and the Catholic church had established a few parishes.[3]

The economic differences among the three counties are clearly shown by the federal income tax returns during the Civil War. Residents of New Castle County in 1863 paid almost four times as much income tax as those from the two lower counties combined. Fifty per-

[2] U.S. Census, *Population of the United States in 1860* (Washington, 1864), pp. 46–48. Population in Delaware in 1860:

Kent	27,804
New Castle	54,797
Sussex	29,615
	112,216

[3] *Ibid.*, pp. 46–48; U.S. Census, *Population*, 1900 (Washington, 1901), 1:xviii. In 1860 the free Negro population totaled 19,829 and the slaves numbered 1,798. Negroes comprised 19.3 per cent of the population in 1860, but by 1900 this figure was only 16.6 per cent, even though they had increased numerically to 30,697.

Income Taxes Paid by Counties in 1863

New Castle	$221,155
Kent	46,885
Sussex	9,126

Incomes in 1864	New Castle	Kent	Sussex
$10,000 up	50	5	0
$5–10,000	88	14	3

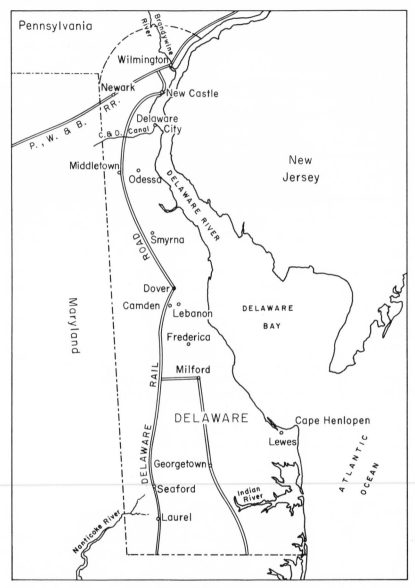

Map of Delaware.

sons in New Castle County in 1864 paid taxes on incomes of $10,000 or over, most of them being manufacturers. Only five persons in Kent County, and none in Sussex County, earned such a figure.[4]

Census returns emphasize the same disparity. In 1870 the assessed value of real estate in New Castle County was as great, and the assessed value of personal property three times as great, as that of the other two counties combined. The total of farm wages and the value of farm products equaled those from the rest of the state. In manufacturing, the capital invested, the wages paid, the value of the articles produced in New Castle County were ten times those of Kent and Sussex Counties.[5]

Culturally and educationally Wilmington was far in advance of the rest of the state, with good schools, active beneficial and reform societies, and energetic religious and business leaders. It benefited from its prosperous business enterprises, a traditional interest in culture, and its location on the main line of the Philadelphia, Wilmington, and Baltimore Railroad. The pace of life in Kent and Sussex Counties was more leisurely, though the building of a railroad initiated economic and social changes. A former resident remembered rural conditions in Sussex County as they existed on April 11, 1861, as "a slow age—an age of oxen, sandy roads, big farms, and crude machinery," in which the farmer was largely self-sufficient. Schools were poor, cultural influences from the small towns and villages limited, and many energetic youths sought better opportunities in cities or moved to the west.[6]

Culturally the state was oriented more toward the South than the Middle Atlantic states or New England. With some exaggeration a bitter critic wrote in the *Boston Herald* in 1867:

[4] "Annual Assessment of Incomes, Carriages and Plate for 1863 and 1864 in Delaware," Fiscal Section, National Archives (NA).

[5] *American Annual Cyclopedia*, 1878, p. 237.

[6] Anna T. Lincoln, *Wilmington: Delaware; Three Centuries under Four Flags* (Rutland, Vt., 1937), *passim*; Joseph A. Conwell, "A Sussex Farmer Boy Sixty-Five Years Ago," *The Conwell Family* (St. Paul, Minn., mimeo., n.d.), pp. 110–15; Dorothy Welch White, ed., *Memoirs of Mary Parker Welch* (New York, 1947), *passim*; Walter A. Powell, *Annals of a Village in Kent County, Delaware* (Dover, n.d.), *passim*. Because the head of the State Normal School in Wilmington sent an unfavorable report on Delaware schools to the United States Commissioner of Education in 1870, the charter of the institution was repealed by the legislature. His report read in part: "The school system of Delaware has remained unchanged for more than forty years, and consequently the progress of popular education has been exceedingly slow. For the past five years several districts have been entirely without public schools, and many which have had such schools have had incompetent teachers. In the rural districts the teachers are paid but about $100 a year, and the schools are in session only four or five months." See *American Annual Cyclopedia*, 1871, p. 232.

It is doubtful if any one of the extreme Southern or Southwestern States is so far behind the average civilization of the age as the little State of Delaware. Properly speaking, Delaware is not a Southern state, but no greater insult could be offered its citizens than an intimation that they are Northern, or belong even to the middle range of Commonwealths. In all matters pertaining to education, in public spirit, and in average culture, Delaware is sadly behind her Sister states of all sections but noticeably distanced by her immediate neighbors.

The writer believed that by geographic latitude Delaware should probably be placed with the Middle Atlantic states, but in sympathy and refinement he ranked her a century behind her sister states. In the use of the whipping post for whites and blacks, both men and women, he placed the state two centuries behind the teachings of Christianity and the practices of gentlemen.[7]

While the majority of Delawareans lived in bountiful, but rural simplicity, a small group like the du Ponts, Ridgelys, and Bayards had the financial means to travel, to send their sons to college, and to enjoy pleasant, leisurely lives. In sharp contrast were the conditions of poor whites who lived in the swamps and forests of lower Delaware, or in the slums of Wilmington. Negroes lived mainly on farms or in segregated sections of towns or villages.[8]

The General Assembly of Delaware was small, consisting of nine senators and twenty-one representatives. The people of New Castle County felt that they did not have a fair share of representation, since that county contained half of the population of the state but elected only one-third of the legislature. The population of Wilmington alone was greater than that of either of the lower counties, and yet it was not even the county seat, which remained in the old town of New Castle until 1881. The counties and the local subdivisions, called "hundreds," were important governmental units.[9]

Politically Delaware had been in the hands of the Democrats since the 1850s. The majority of Delawareans felt at home in this party, which was dominated nationally by Southerners and Southern sympathizers. It reflected well their agrarian interests. Senator James A.

[7] *Smyrna Times*, April 10, 1867, quoting the *Boston Herald*.

[8] For an example of genteel living, see Leon de Valinger and Virginia E. Shaw, eds., *A Calendar of Ridgely Family Letters* (Dover, 1948–61), 1, 2, 3:*passim*. When an army captain investigated an assault upon a Negro congregation in Baltimore Hundred in Sussex County in 1865, he reported, "As a general thing I found the people of that section of the county the most ignorant & illiterate of any people with whom I ever met." See Capt. W. H. Wenie to Lt. W. B. Norman, May 18, 1865, Letters Received, Secretary of War, RG 108, NA.

[9] Jeannette Eckman, "Constitutional Development, 1776–1897," in H. Clay Reed, ed., *Delaware: A History of the First State* (New York, 1947), I: *passim*.

Bayard was one of the leading figures in the party. The backbone of the party in the state were the farmers of Kent and Sussex counties, who shared the political views of their neighbors on the Eastern Shore of Maryland. Slaveowners knew that their interests were protected, and Irish workmen in Wilmington applauded when the lion's tail was pulled. For these reasons, Delaware remained Democratic during the war and for many years afterward.[10]

The Bayards of New Castle County and the three Saulsbury brothers from the lower counties shared party leadership. Senator James A. Bayard first won election to the Senate in 1850, following in the footsteps of two other members of his family. Through patronage, oratory, and legal ability he had built up a considerable following. His ambitious son, Thomas F. Bayard, who was a rising young lawyer in Wilmington, was his first lieutenant. With the aid of the "Customhouse squad" and other federal officeholders, Senator Bayard controlled New Castle County and secured strong backing from influential persons in lower Delaware. In 1863 after making a speech against the "ironclad oath" in the Senate and then taking the oath, he had resigned in protest and was succeeded by George R. Riddle, a Wilmington manufacturer. Later Senator Bayard was appointed to fill a vacancy in 1867. His son's long senatorial career began in 1869.[11]

Willard Saulsbury began a family political dynasty in 1859 by being elected to the United States Senate. Generally considered the most brilliant member of the Sussex bar, he had previously served a term as the state's attorney-general. After two terms his drinking habits had attracted unpleasant notoriety, and his brother-in-law, Governor Ponder, reputedly appointed him Chancellor, in 1873, upon his promise to reform. Upon the death of Governor William Cannon in 1865, Gove Saulsbury, by virtue of being president pro tem of the state senate, became governor and won election in his own right in 1866. Upon a fourth ballot in Democratic caucus in 1871 Eli Saulsbury won the nomination for senatorship from his two brothers and began the first of three terms.[12] In retrospect it seems miraculous that members of this family managed to cling to political power for so many years. Perhaps it was a combination of brains, patronage, and corruption. Their political addresses reflected perfectly the attitudes of their constituents on national issues and the Negro.

[10] Harold Hancock, *Delaware during the Civil War* (Wilmington, Del., 1961), p. 12.

[11] *Ibid.*, pp. 12–13. Officeholders were required to take the ironclad oath by which they pledged allegiance to the Constitution and swore that they had never voluntarily borne arms against the Union or aided the Rebellion. See Mark M. Boatner, ed., *The Civil War Dictionary* (New York, 1959), p. 428.

[12] Hancock, *Civil War*, p. 13.

The Republican party was strong in New Castle County, especially among Wilmington manufacturers and their employees. Frequently legislators from that county and the municipal government of Wilmington were Republicans. After Negroes were enfranchised by the Fifteenth Amendment they also joined the Grand Old Party, but no outstanding Republican leader emerged. At various times Wilmington lawyer Anthony Higgins, ex-Congressmen George P. Fisher and Nathaniel B. Smithers, and Wilmington ward politicians, H. F. Pickels and C. H. Gallagher, claimed to speak for the party. Victories were few, and factional strife over petty matters and patronage hindered party unity.[13]

In spite of the use of federal troops at polling places, the Republicans had had little political success in the state during the Civil War. In 1860 the opponents of the Democrats had combined to elect George P. Fisher, former attorney-general, to Congress. In 1862 in a close election for governor the Union party elected William Cannon, a wealthy landowner and former Democrat. Historians dispute as to whether his change of party was because of his desire to preserve the Union or because of disappointment at not being nominated for important office by Democrats. When the death of United States Representative William Temple in 1863 necessitated a new election, the Democrats boycotted the election to protest the use of federal troops at polling places and required oaths of allegiance. Only thirteen Democrats had voted in the entire state; hence the Union party candidate, Nathaniel B. Smithers, was elected in a landslide. The Democrats controlled all other political offices in the state. Both electors and senators were Democrats, and the party continuously controlled the legislature.[14]

When the Civil War ended, it was uncertain which way Delaware would go politically. In sentiment, the majority of the people were attached to the South, but economic leadership rested with the North, and the manufacturers of New Castle County enjoyed many affiliations with these interests. While the Democrats had won most elections, the Union party, as the Republicans and their allies called themselves from 1862 to 1866, had put up a strong fight, and some of the Democratic victories had been by close margins. In proportion to its size Delaware had provided more troops for the Union armies than any state, and if the soldiers voted "as they had shot," and if the Negro was enfranchised, the result would seemingly not be in doubt. The Democrats found the same devices effective in the postwar period that

[13] *Ibid.*, p. 18.
[14] *Ibid.*, *passim.*

had won them elections during the war. They reminded voters that their opponents were responsible for arresting peaceable citizens, for the use of federal troops at polling places, and for attacking states' rights. Above all, they stressed that the Black Republicans intended to give Negroes equal rights in schools, churches, restaurants, juries, and in marriage.

These differences between Republicans and Democrats were demonstrated when the question arose after Appomattox as to how the defeated South and its leaders should be treated. In general, Democrats favored a forgive-and-forget policy, while Republicans advocated the severe punishment of leaders. Surprisingly, ex-Representative Nathaniel B. Smithers, a Republican, pleaded for leniency at a victory celebration in Dover.[15] More typical of Republican feeling was the opinion of Governor Cannon's son-in-law, who advocated hanging Jefferson Davis as "the foulest malefactor, upon whose soul is the blood of a million men."[16] An editorial entitled "Shall They Be Punished?", which appeared in the *Delaware Journal,* expressed fear that the Rebels everywhere were plotting to seize control of the government and claimed that Union men, who had been maimed for life by Rebel bullets or had been starved in Southern prisons, demanded the punishment of Lee and Davis as well as many of the rank and file.[17] A correspondent of the *Delaware Republican* in Wilmington believed that Southern atrocities had ruled out any notion of leniency, and he recalled that:

From the first battle of Bull Run to the exit of Jeff in petticoats, the most devilish cruelty that humanity could invent has been practiced by them. Carving the bones of our soldiers into trinkets to adorn southern beauty. Starving our prisoners by the thousands. Introducing the yellow fever. Burning our cities by the incendiary's torch. Search history in vain for the savage nation that has ever practiced such barbarities.

On the other hand, Democratic newspapers such as the *Gazette* in Wilmington and the *Delawarean* in Dover pleaded for forgiveness for a defeated people, who had shown themselves to be truly repentant and humbled.[18]

Although in January, 1865, Governor Cannon had recommended to the General Assembly ratification of the Thirteenth Amendment, its

---

[15] *Delawarean,* June 23, 1865.
[16] Charles Heydrick, Diary, May 15, 1865, Delaware State Archives.
[17] *Delaware Journal,* Sept. 12, 1865.
[18] *Delaware Republican,* Aug. 17, 1865; *Delawarean,* May 26, 1865; *Gazette,* Aug. 17, 1865.

members had expressed "their unqualified disapproval."[19] Governor Gove Saulsbury, his successor, in his inaugural address in June reprimanded Congress for interfering with the institution of slavery. The true position of the Negro, he claimed, was as a subordinate race excluded from all political and social privileges. History had repeatedly demonstrated that blacks were incapable of the highest order of intellectual and moral development and that the superior group would only be debased by mingling with the inferior. "The finger of the Almighty has traced in indelible lines the distinction between the Negro and white races, and any attempt to obliterate that distinction is the result of either a blind fanaticism or a wicked and perverse infidelity," he concluded.[20] Not unexpectedly, the Democratic and Republican press took opposite sides on the issue. When the amendment became effective, in December, it probably freed fewer than 1,200 Delaware slaves, as some had already been emancipated by their owners.[21]

Democratic and Republican opinions concerning President Johnson rapidly changed. At the time of his inauguration in March, 1865, an editorial writer in the Democratic *Gazette* had asked, "Is He a Miserable Drunkard?" and had denounced the conferring of political honors upon a man of such immoral character. Within a month after Lincoln's death the *Gazette* found the new president to be "a statesman equal in originality to most of the great men of his day, while as an executive officer he has scarcely an equal."[22] The *Delawarean*, the mouthpiece of the Saulsbury brothers, also supported Johnson, and in December praised his message to Congress "as much in advance of anything Mr. Lincoln ever wrote," and an indication that he was "no radical." The Republican press maintained a dignified silence during the summer and fall, while it waited for Congress to meet.[23]

Democratic politicians and the Democratic press enthusiastically applauded Johnson's subsequent vetoes of the Freedmen's Bureau and Civil Rights Bills, and a measure to enfranchise the Negro in the District of Columbia. In addition to taking note of the unsatisfactory nature of the relations of the states and the federal government, Governor Saulsbury in his message to the legislature on January, 1866, commented upon the lack of wisdom of white men reducing them-

[19] *Journal of the House of Representatives of the State of Delaware, 1865* (Dover, Del., 1866), pp. 8–17, 450; *Laws of the State of Delaware*, 12:683–84. (Hereafter referred to as *House Journal* and *Delaware Laws*.)

[20] *House Journal*, 1865, p. 20.

[21] Hancock, *Civil War*, p. 165.

[22] *Gazette*, March 16, May 2, 1865.

[23] *Delawarean*, July 29, Dec. 9, 1865.

selves to the level of the Negro. While he could sympathize with the Negro as an inferior and dependent race, he did not feel that as a people they were entitled to vote.[24] The legislature responded by passing resolutions which criticized the failure of Congress to permit representatives from the South to take their seats in Congress and eulogized Johnson's efforts to check the Radicals. In connection with condemning the conferring of the franchise upon Negroes in the District of Columbia, the legislature resolved:

> That the immutable laws of God have affixed upon the brow of the white races the ineffaceable stamp of superiority, and that all attempt to elevate the negro to a social or political equality of the white man is futile and subversive of the ends and aims for which the American Government was established, and contrary to the doctrines and teachings of the Father of the Republic.[25]

Republicans in the legislature voted against these resolutions, thus appearing to favor enfranchisement for the Negro. The writer of an article on "Delaware" in the *American Annual Cyclopedia* believed that if the resolutions had dealt specifically with granting the franchise to Negroes in Delaware, the Republicans would have assumed the same attitude as the Democrats.[26] Delaware Republicans were not ready to accept the enfranchisement of the Negro until their party took a stand nationally. In addition, they also knew that many voters in the state were opposed and that some Republicans would abstain from voting in protest and others would join the Democratic party rather than calmly accept the enfranchisement.

After Johnson's veto of the Freedmen's Bureau Bill, Governor Saulsbury telegraphed the President: "Your veto message has been received with profound gratitude and joy by the people of Delaware on whose behalf I thank you for the preservation of their peace and security. It has inspired unbounded confidence in your administration. You will be fully sustained here and I trust and believe everywhere."[27]

To express approval of Johnson's veto, 4,000 citizens assembled in a "Union" meeting in Wilmington, passed complimentary resolutions, and forwarded as gifts sides of beef and mutton.[28] Democrats con-

---

[24] *Journal of the Senate of the State of Delaware* (Dover, Del., 1866), p. 33. (Hereafter referred to as *Senate Journal.*)

[25] *Delaware Laws*, 13:86–88.

[26] *American Annual Cyclopedia*, 1866, p. 264.

[27] Governor Gove Saulsbury to President Andrew Johnson, Feb. 27, 1866, Andrew Johnson Papers, Library of Congress (LC).

[28] W. H. Gear, Chairman to President Andrew Johnson, Feb. 27, 1866, and accompanying undated resolutions, Andrew Johnson Papers, LC.

sidered that Johnson had again "covered himself all over with glory" by vetoing the Civil Rights Bill.[29] Delaware congressmen joined in the chorus of approval.[30] To Republicans it seemed as though his actions had brought forth Copperheads as does the sun. He was denounced for keeping bad company and labeled a "Benedict Arnold."[31]

In the summer of 1866 against the background of political strife in Washington, the time came for the selection of candidates for governor and representative, as well as for the legislature. Both Governor Sauls-bury and Representative John A. Nicholson secured renomination. The Democratic platform praised Johnson, criticized the Radicals, and censured the passage of the Freedmen's Bureau and Civil Rights Bills.[32] The "Republican Union" convention nominated James Riddle, New Castle cotton manufacturer and local Methodist preacher, and the Reverend John McKim, bank teller and Episcopal clergyman, for governor and representative respectively. The platform reserved for Congress the right to organize the Southern states, recommended that Congress pass additional laws to secure the rights of the newly emancipated millions, and endorsed the Fourteenth Amendment.[33]

The main subject of discussion at county and hundred meetings was the Negro. In Kent County a Methodist clergyman at a Democratic rally portrayed the horrors of sitting by a Negro on a train, in church, or in a restaurant, and, worse still, of intermarriage with the degraded race. At another Kent County meeting resolutions labeled the members of the Radical Republican party "Revolutionists, Disunionists, Consolidationists, and political Amalgamationists" because of their stand on Negro equality.[34] A meeting in New Castle County invited attendance by "every white man who loves the white man in preference to niggers, for now is the time to strike the final blow at the damn white niggers who are trying to give the niggers the right to vote, the right to marry the white, and the right to fill your schools with nigger children, and also to fill your Jury Boxes, your Courts and Legislatures with niggers."[35]

In reply the Republicans waved the bloody shirt and claimed that their opponents were mainly "Secesh" rebels, pointing out how they had failed to display "the old flag" over the state capitol at the begin-

---

[29] *Delawarean*, March 31, 1866.

[30] Charles F. Tansill, *The Congressional Career of Thomas F. Bayard* (Washington, 1946), p. 22; Wayne S. Smith, "The Senatorial Career of Williard Saulsbury, 1859–1871" (M.A. thesis, Univ. of Del., 1966), pp. 51–56.

[31] *Delaware Republican*, March 1, 1866.

[32] *Gazette*, Aug. 17, 1866.

[33] *Delaware Journal*, Aug. 14, 1866.

[34] *Delawarean*, Sept. 8, 1866; *Gazette*, Sept. 21, 1866.

[35] *Gazette*, Sept. 21, 1866.

ning of the rebellion, denied aid to destitute families of volunteers, and refused to give honorable burial to the sons of Delaware after Gettysburg.[36] Saulsbury and Nicholson won easily by 1,200 votes, although the members of the General Assembly from New Castle County remained Republican.[37]

The most important political topics in Delaware in 1867 were the continuing struggle between the President and Congress and the status of the Negro. At the beginning of 1867 two Republican newspapers in Wilmington called for the removal of the President on the grounds of "high crimes and misdemeanors," while a third in Kent County remained neutral.[38] One Democratic newspaper counseled the President and people to meet the radical threat of impeachment with "firmness" and another defended the record of "the noblest and most sincere man of all the statesmen who participated in the war for the abolition of slavery and the destruction of the rights of the States."[39] Thomas F. Bayard considered the acts of Congress in overriding state institutions and in precipitating Negro suffrage as a "revolution" and did not believe that a "clash of arms" could be far away.[40]

At the January session of the legislature, in 1867, Governor Saulsbury asked for new legislation concerning free Negroes, since the passage of the Thirteenth Amendment and the Civil Rights Bill had changed their legal status. Believing that Negroes who immigrated into the state were mainly fugitives from justice, he asked for a law forbidding their admission. "Every consideration of justice, patriotism, and humanity," he thought, demanded the rejection of the Fourteenth Amendment.[41] During its session the legislature condemned the Fourteenth Amendment and passed a law providing that the punishment inflicted upon Negro and mulatto criminals should be the same as that received by whites for similar offenses.[42]

Republicans in Delaware had at first denied that they favored the enfranchisement of Negroes, but in September, 1867, the *Delaware Republican*, a newspaper in Wilmington, predicted that by constitutional amendment or act of Congress the colored people of the state would be granted the right to vote by November, 1868. It declared that this would place the Union party in Delaware in a majority position

---

[36] *Delaware Journal*, Sept. 14, 1866.
[37] *Smyrna Times*, Nov. 14, 1866.
[38] *Daily Commercial*, Jan. 12, 1867; *Delaware Republican*, Feb. 11, 1867; *Smyrna Times*, March 15, 1867.
[39] *Delawarean*, Sept. 28, 1867; *Gazette*, June 25, 1867.
[40] Tansill, *Bayard*, p. 21.
[41] *House Journal*, 1867, p. 20.
[42] *Delaware Laws*, 13:304.

rather than a minority, and added, "The advantages that will accrue
from the control of the State Government reconcile us to any un-
pleasantness that may attach to going to the polls with black men, and
we think the members of the Union party will generally be influenced
by the same consideration."[43]

A "black and tan" convention in Wilmington in September claimed
that Delaware did not have a republican form of government and
asked for congressional intervention, since Negroes were denied the
right to vote and New Castle County was not given its fair share of
representation.[44] Thomas F. Bayard considered the meeting a deliberate violation of state law against the attendance of political meetings
by Negroes and mulattoes and considered "that a war of the races
must soon come, and it will be a wretched conflict."[45]

In response to these protests, hearings were conducted by a subcommittee of the Judiciary Committee of the House of Representatives, in October, and seven Delaware Republicans testified. A Wilmington lawyer was of the opinion that "the majority of the people in
Kent and Sussex Counties are decidedly opposed to Negro suffrage,
Negro education, and Negro political and civil equality." To prove
his point, he mentioned the burning of several Negro schoolhouses,
the mobbing of several Negro teachers, and the lynching of a Negro
suspected of arson. He denied that the Republican party within the
state was "primarily" interested in Negro suffrage in order to gain
political control. Anthony Higgins, who was later to become United
States District Attorney and United States Senator, emphasized the
exclusion of Negroes from civil rights. Much of the partisan testimony
related to "disloyalty" within the state during the Civil War, as the
Republicans viewed it, though most of the disloyalty consisted of talk
and threatened action rather than of actual incidents. Delaware had
an estimated five hundred men who served in the Confederacy. Witnesses also paid attention to the unfairness of legislative apportionment, which left New Castle County with its large population under-
represented in the legislature. One vote in the lower counties, it was
claimed, equaled two votes in the upper county. The subcommittee
decided that Delaware did not have a republican form of government,
but the main committee did not take action.[46]

[43] *Delaware Republican*, Sept. 9, 1867.

[44] *Gazette*, Sept. 6, 1867.

[45] Tansill, *Bayard*, p. 21.

[46] Testimony of John P. Nields and Anthony Higgins, Oct. 6, 7, 1867, "Reports of
the Judiciary Committee Relating to the Investigation of Conditions in Delaware,"
House of Rep., 40th Congress, Legislature Section, RG 233, NA; Hancock, *Civil War*,
p. 175.

During Johnson's impeachment in 1868, Democrats and Republicans followed the lines laid down by their national leaders. The *Delawarean* denounced General Grant as a "Jerry Sneak and Radical tool," labeled Stanton a "miserable tyrant and star-chamber statesman," and stated that the purpose back of the plot was to "carry out vile schemes for Africanizing the Southern States and placing the white people in the South under negro rule."[47] A mass meeting of Democrats in Wilmington lauded the chief executive as the champion of the rights gained by our Revolutionary forefathers and the sole safeguard of the liberties of the people against "the wicked acts" of the "Radical Rump" Congress.[48]

In letters, Thomas Bayard regretted that he had just purchased a home and wished that his family and investments were out of the country until reason regained its throne. In his judgment the only course open for Johnson was "boldness"; if the chief executive refused to recognize the revolutionary acts of the Radicals and called upon the people, he would be supported "at the polls and in the field."[49] In view of his "unquestionable guilt," the *Daily Commercial* advised the Senate to do its duty by removing him from office,[50] and another Republican newspaper in the city concurred.[51] Less sure was the *Smyrna Times,* which doubted the legality of the proceedings and reported the trial without editorial comment.[52] Senators Willard Saulsbury and James A. Bayard voted for his acquittal.[53] Democrats voiced relief at the verdict, and the *Delawarean* considered the seven Republicans who had voted along with the Democrats for acquittal "as the ablest and best men in their party."[54]

Enfranchising the Negro was the principal issue in Delaware politics in the election of 1868. The Republican platform called for congressional control of the admission of the Southern states and endorsed Grant for the presidential nomination. A controversial third plank supported the congressional plan with its vital principle of "impartial suffrage" for the reorganization of the rebel states and urged the formulation of an amendment embodying the idea. By a vote of seventy-five to thirty-seven the resolution was approved, and by its ratification the *Delawarean* considered that its enemies had com-

[47] *Delawarean,* Jan. 17, 1868.
[48] *Ibid.,* Feb. 28, 1868.
[49] T. F. Bayard to J. A. Bayard, Feb. 23, 25, 1868, Bayard Papers, LC.
[50] *Daily Commercial,* March 13, 1868.
[51] *Delaware Republican,* March 21, 1868.
[52] *Smyrna Times,* Dec. 28, 1867.
[53] Smith, "Saulsbury," p. 64; Tansill, *Bayard,* p. 22.
[54] *Delawarean,* May 23, 1868; *Daily Commercial,* May 23, 1868.

mitted "political suicide."[55] In reply the Democrats at their convention opposed every form of Negro suffrage and requested all conservative and law-abiding men to join them.[56] The campaign was spiritless because the Republicans concluded that it was useless to battle in Kent and Sussex counties, so they sponsored few political rallies.[57] The Democratic majority in the state was over 3,000, and the Republicans lost, even in New Castle County. Negro suffrage was too much for Delawareans to swallow.[58]

The *American Annual Cyclopedia* characterized Delaware public affairs in 1869 as "quiet." Governor Saulsbury devoted his message to denouncing Congress, whose reconstruction measures he labeled "the most flagrant usurpation of powers that has ever been attempted in this country." Following his recommendation, the Delaware legislature rejected the Fifteenth Amendment, with resolutions explaining that the amendment would destroy states' rights, establish an equality between white and black not sanctioned by nature or God, and create difficult relations between citizens of different parts of the United States. Not until 1901 did the legislature ratify the Thirteenth, Fourteenth, and Fifteenth Amendments.[59]

In April, 1870, when the Fifteenth Amendment came into effect, the Democrats faced the problem of how they could check this flood of 4,500 Negro votes. Hostile sources told of a meeting of trembling, whipped Democratic leaders in the office of Senator Willard Saulsbury, in Dover. When they moaned that they would be snuffed out like a candle, the drunken Senator supposedly replied, "The Hell they will! Go home and yell White Man's Party!" Whether such a meeting ever took place is uncertain, but this was the policy pursued by the Democrats.[60] "White or Black" was the issue, asserted the Democratic *Gazette.* "Every voter is now brought face to face with horrid reality and must make his choice between a State government of white men,

[55] *Smyrna Times,* April 29, 1868; *Delawarean,* April 25, 1868.

[56] *Gazette,* Aug. 28, 1868; J. Townsend to Israel Townsend, Feb. 16, 1868, Townsend Papers, Morris Library, Univ. of Delaware. When John Townsend of the town of Townsend in New Castle County heard that his brother, a carpetbagger in Virginia, had been nominated for Congress by the "niggers" of his county, he wrote indignantly, "I would just as soon of heard that you had been arrested, for stealing a hurst [sic], for it would not be more of a disgrace to your family as to be one of the hell petts [sic] of niggerdom." Several days later his brother replied that he had been misinformed.

[57] *Smyrna Times,* Nov. 4, 1868.

[58] *Ibid.,* Nov. 11, 1868.

[59] *American Annual Cyclopedia,* 1869, p. 217, Hancock, "Politics, 1865–1913," in Reed, *Delaware,* 1:199.

[60] *Daily Commercial,* April 6, 1870.

for white men, by white men, or for a negro despotism, with its catalogue of misery, degradation, and infamous association."[61]

As early as May, a few Democrats met to organize a white man's party, but most of the prominent leaders stayed away.[62] At the Democratic convention in August, nine of the fifteen resolutions dealt with the Negro. The members voted to denounce the Fifteenth Amendment, to favor state support only for schools for white children, and to confine the benefits of state and federal government to white citizens only. James Ponder, brother-in-law of Senator Willard Saulsbury and a wealthy Sussex County landowner, secured the gubernatorial nomination, and the convention named Benjamin Biggs, a well-to-do peach grower in New Castle County, as the candidate for Congress.[63] When the Republicans met, they praised the recent amendments as "a final and just settlement of a vexed question," favored separate schools for newly enfranchised citizens, and condemned the extravagant and bad administration of Democrats in the state. The convention named Thomas B. Coursey of Kent County and Joshua T. Heald of Wilmington as candidates for the offices of governor and representative respectively.[64]

Early in October a group of prominent Kent County Democrats revolted against the domination of the Saulsbury family and nominated a separate ticket for county offices. Probably the principal reason was dislike of the domination by one family and a retinue of followers. Many of the insurrectionists were respectable men of good standing in the community. Former Representative Nicholson explained that the state was not run by the General Assembly, but that the whole power of the government was centered in one lawyer's office, and he pointed dramatically across Dover Green to the office of Governor Gove Saulsbury. Affairs had reached the point, he declared, that when the leaders took snuff the party sneezed.[65] Earlier in the campaign, the *Daily Commercial* had claimed that the domination of Democratic state conventions by the Saulsburys and their allies was so absolute that "the Ring says 'Up,' and they spring to their feet; 'Down,' and they crouch

[61] *Gazette*, April 26, 1870; J. P. Comegys to S. Townsend, April 16, 1870. Townsend Papers, Morris Library, Univ. of Delaware. This Democratic politician in Dover wrote to his Democratic friend in New Castle County that "the masses are for anything for relief from the dreadful future of Negro rule." Under certain hypothetical conditions he predicted that three-fourths of the Republicans would join with the Democrats in a new party. He concluded that "the body of the Republicans are as hostile to negro suffrage as you are."
[62] *Gazette*, May 6, 1870.
[63] *Ibid.*, Aug. 26, 1870.
[64] *Daily Commercial*, June 10, 1870.
[65] *Ibid.*, Oct. 7, 1870.

like spaniels; it cries 'Wiggle waggle,' and they are active as a basket of fresh caught crabs."[66] The *Smyrna Times* believed that the Bonapartes never ruled the people of France more despotically than the "Family Ring" governed the Democratic party and especially the affairs of Kent County. The "Ring" was accused of taking $35,000 from the Sussex County treasury and of profiting from having engineered the passage of a lottery bill.[67]

In spite of this uprising, Eli Saulsbury wrote Thomas Bayard that the Democrats would still carry the county by 500 votes.[68] Senator Willard Saulsbury told a political rally that the Democrats did not wish for the Negro vote under any circumstances and predicted that enough white men in the Republican party would abstain from voting or vote Democratic to return the Democrats to office.[69] At another meeting Governor Saulsbury declared that "the all absorbing question in this campaign is the fifteenth amendment and Negro suffrage."[70]

Election day was marred by disturbances, especially in Kent and Sussex counties. Each side accused the other of violence, fraud, and fighting. No federal troops were used, but deputy United States marshals were appointed to supervise the voting in several places. In Smyrna and Odessa deputy United States marshals were driven from polling places, Negroes were prevented from voting, and the ballot boxes were taken away. The United States District Attorney telegraphed President Grant on election day asking for marines from the Philadelphia Navy Yard (though they were not sent), because at those two places colored voters had been driven from the polls "by clubs, bludgeons, and revolvers." At one polling place in Wilmington shots were exchanged, and several persons were injured. As usual, the Democrats triumphed.[71]

In the legislative session of January, 1871, Governor Saulsbury, delivering his last message, condemned efforts of the federal government and the Chief Executive to control state elections. He denounced the Fifteenth Amendment, which "had been adopted by fraud and coercion and in opposition to the will of the white people of the country," and looked forward to its prompt repeal. In his inaugural

[66] *Ibid.,* Aug. 17, 1870.
[67] *Ibid.,* Oct. 1, 1870, quoting *Smyrna Times; Daily Commercial,* Nov. 3, 1870.
[68] Eli Saulsbury to T. F. Bayard, Sept. 29, 1870, Bayard Papers, LC.
[69] *Gazette,* May 3, 1870.
[70] *Daily Commercial,* Nov. 3, 1870.
[71] Amy McNulty Hiller, "The Disfranchisement of the Delaware Negroes in the Late Nineteenth Century," (M.A. thesis, Univ. of Del., 1963), pp. 9–10; A. Higgins to President Grant, Nov. 8, 1870, Attorney-General Papers, Letters Received, Delaware, NA; *Daily Commercial,* Nov. 10, 1870; *Gazette,* Nov. 11, 1870.

address Governor Ponder took a similar attitude toward Negro suffrage.[72]

The Republicans attempted to do something about the disfranchisement of Negroes in the previous election by bringing suits in New Castle County against all members of the Levy Court and several tax collectors for violation of the federal Enforcement Act. "At a low estimate" the United States District Attorney declared that 1,500 voters in the state had been disqualified by the illegal practices of such officials. A Grand Jury indicted all of these men, and, in a test case, Archibald Given, a tax collector in Wilmington, was found guilty of abridging the rights of five Negroes who had unsuccessfully tried to pay their taxes. He was fined $2,000 and court costs. Charges against the others were then dropped. This case seemed to demonstrate that the Democrats could not again use such practices to bar Negroes from voting, and the prospects for the Republicans winning the next election looked excellent.[73] Officials of the national Republican party did not take as much interest in the activities of the Republican party in Delaware in the 1870s and 1880s as might be expected. Perhaps they felt that the state was so overwhelmingly Democratic that it was a lost cause. In addition, the state had only three electoral votes. When chances became more equal, in the 1890s, they were more interested.

A Republican convention in May, 1872, endorsed Grant and praised his fine record, appealed for an improved system of public education, and asked for improvement in the handling of the state's finances. It also chose delegates to the national convention.[74] When the Democrats met, they condemned the Grant administration and claimed that the people of Delaware were not "morally bound" to abide by the recent amendments, all of which their legislature had rejected. Its delegates to the national convention were instructed to vote for Senator Bayard.[75]

At a ratification convention the Republicans expressed enthusiasm for Grant and nominated James R. Lofland of Milford for Congress.[76] The Democrats were unenthusiastic about Horace Greeley. Before the nomination ex-Governor William Ross had predicted that to name this eccentric editor as a candidate would be "political suicide for the party," and when word arrived of his selection, it fell "like a wet

[72] *Senate Journal*, 1871, pp. 10–25, 75–81.
[73] Hiller, "Disfranchisement," pp. 15–25; A. Higgins to Attorney-General George Williams, June 13, Oct. 21, 1872, Dept. of Justice Chronological Files—Delaware, NA; *Daily Commercial*, Jan. 9, 30, 1873.
[74] *Daily Commercial*, May 10, 1872.
[75] *Delawarean*, June 15, 1872; *Gazette*, June 12, 1872.
[76] *Delaware Journal*, Sept. 14, 1872.

blanket" on Delaware Democrats.[77]   The *Gazette* declared that "we
have no hesitation in saying that Mr. Greeley is not such a candidate
as we prefer or the Democratic party of the state would most delight to
rally under," but it also observed that no honorable choice was left
except to support the candidate duly nominated. In a letter to the
New Castle County ratification meeting, in July, Senator Thomas F.
Bayard expressed the same opinion. At the state convention, in August,
Benjamin Biggs was renominated for Congress.[78] Some Democrats so
opposed Greeley that they attempted to organize a "Straight Out
Democratic ticket," but they met with little success.[79] Greeley was too
much of an eccentric and not a sufficiently "dyed-in-the-wool" Democrat to win much support. Democratic apathy resulted in victories for
Republican electors and for Lofland, but the Democrats continued
to control the state legislature.[80]

When the legislature met, in 1873, determined Democrats sought a
way to circumvent the federal Enforcement Acts. Following the suggestion of Governor Ponder, they introduced separate bills to define
the duties of assessors and collectors of taxes in the counties. Returns
were submitted to the Levy Court in March and, at the discretion of
its members, names of delinquents were dropped. They could not be
returned to the list for another twelve months and reassessment came
the following February. By this device delinquent taxpayers might be
kept from voting for almost two years. Democratic assessors, collectors,
and members of the Levy Court usually saw that the names of Republicans were dropped and that the names of Democrats were retained
for redemption just before election.[81]

Judge Henry C. Conrad, who saw the law in operation in state
courts, commented many years later: "This Act was clearly designed
to make it difficult to get colored men qualified as voters, and those
who framed it builded even better than they knew, as by it the Democratic party was enabled to continue in almost uninterrupted control
in the state for twenty-five years after its passage." The Assessment
Law of 1873 became so notorious that the *North American Review*
sent a special investigator to the state in 1885. He reported that
through it "a very large part of the citizens of Delaware are as thoroughly disfranchised by legal chicanery, as any community of negroes

[77] William Ross to S. Townsend, June 10, 1872, Townsend Papers, Morris Library,
Univ. of Del.; *Delaware Republican*, July 15, 1872.
[78] *Gazette*, July 12, 1872.
[79] *Ibid.*, July 15, Oct. 19, 1872.
[80] *Delaware Republican*, Nov. 7, 1872; *Gazette*, Nov. 7, 1872.
[81] Hiller, "Disfranchisement," pp. 41–67; *House Journal*, 1873, p. 119; *Delaware
Laws*, 14:342–47.

in Mississippi were ever disfranchised by political intimidation." The *American Magazine,* in 1886, described Delaware as being in the "mediaeval period of American politics."[82]

In 1874 the Republicans nominated Dr. Isaac Jump of Dover and James R. Lofland for the offices of governor and congressman respectively. The platform attacked the new assessment law, favored representation in the General Assembly according to population, asked for a Constitutional Convention, and opposed mixed schools, but favored an improved educational system for all students.[83] The Democrats nominated John P. Cochran, a well-to-do peach grower of lower New Castle County, for governor, and James Williams, a Kent County farmer and legislator, for representative. The platform paid special attention to "the wild, cruel, and reckless measure called the Civil Rights Bill," and branded it "an undisguised attempt to enforce a social equality between negroes and white people, and to encourage, if not compel, an intermingling of those races whose essential differences have been marked and established by Almighty God."[84]

The campaign centered mainly on the Civil Rights Bill. At a meeting in Sussex County, Congressman Lofland was accused of wishing to have colored and white children sit on the same school bench, of favoring burial of the two races in a "common sepulchre," of ruining innkeepers by forcing them to provide bed and board for Negroes, and of degrading the jury system by compelling selection from the most ignorant class of the population. Senator Bayard told a political rally that the participation of Negroes in the past election had lowered the tone of state politics and that more fraudulent votes had been cast as a result than in the entire previous century.[85] By a substantial vote Williams and Cochran won the election.[86]

In January, 1875, the legislature enacted a law providing for the creation of a state board of education and for a state superintendent of public instruction. The statute required local school boards to levy minimum taxes of at least $100 in New Castle and Kent counties and of $60 in Sussex County. Negroes were now to be taxed at the rate of thirty cents per hundred dollars worth of property for the support of their own schools. Solons debated and defeated a bill to increase the representation of New Castle County, but read and passed for a second

[82] Henry C. Conrad, *History of the State of Delaware* (Wilmington, 1908), 1:227; Allen Thorndike Rice, "A Disfranchised People," *North American Review* 141 (Dec., 1885): 602; "The Politics of Delaware," *American* 13 (Nov., 1886): 56.
[83] *Gazette,* July 29, 1874; *Smyrna Times,* July 29, 1874.
[84] *Peninsular News and Advertiser,* Aug. 28, 1874; *Gazette,* Aug. 28, 1874.
[85] *Every Evening,* Oct. 1, 1874; *Gazette,* Oct. 3, 1874.
[86] *Every Evening,* Nov. 4, 1874; *Peninsular News,* Nov. 6, 1874.

time a bill providing for a general corporation law, thus making it an amendment to the constitution. Delaware took the first step toward becoming a haven for incorporation.[87]

By far the most important measure of the session entitled "An Act in Relation to Hotel Keepers and Others Pursuing a Public Occupation" authorized keepers of hotels, proprietors of places of amusement, and steamboat and railroad companies to provide separate accommodation for any class of persons who might be "obnoxious" to a majority of their patrons or passengers. Although the act contained no reference to Negroes by name, the authors designed it to offset the effects of the federal Civil Rights Bill in Delaware. So well did it succeed in this purpose that it remained on the statute books until 1963.[88]

In 1876 the Republicans instructed their delegates to the national convention to vote for James G. Blaine, though some Republicans favored Benjamin H. Bristow.[89] The Democratic delegates favored Senator Thomas F. Bayard for president, and he did receive thirty-one votes on the first ballot.[90] The Republican platform in September endorsed the nomination of Rutherford B. Hayes, favored an improved school system and equality of representation, and denounced the assessment law, which had cost the party 1,500 votes in the last election, as "the most infamous law upon any statute book." The convention nominated a Wilmington lawyer, Levi Bird, for Congress.[91] Also meeting in September, the Democratic convention supported the nomination of Tilden, condemned the corruption of Grant's administration, and protested against federal interference in state elections. A special resolution, introduced from the floor and passed, declared, "That we are now, as we always have been, in favor of the white men of the country controlling this government; and therefore, we appeal with confidence to the white voters *only*, for the success of the principles enunciated in the foregoing resolutions." James Williams secured renomination for Congress.[92]

The campaign was fought mainly on the issue of civil rights. The Republicans feared that many Negroes would be disfranchised by Democratic Levy Courts, and at the election for inspectors in October one Republican claimed that 4,000 voters had already been disquali-

[87] *American Annual Cyclopedia*, 1875, p. 231.
[88] *Delaware Laws*, 15:322; letter of Maurice A. Hartnett, III, Executive Director, Legislative Reference Bureau of Delaware, to writer, April 28, 1967.
[89] *Daily Commercial*, May 19, 1876; *Morning Herald*, May 19, 1876.
[90] *Delawarean*, June 17, July 1, 1876.
[91] *Daily Commercial*, Sept. 14, 1876.
[92] *Gazette*, Sept. 8, 1876.

fied. On election day disputes broke out in Wilmington between the special police appointed by the Democratic Mayor and the deputies of United States Marshal Dunn, a Republican. Both sides worked out elaborate arrangements governing the conduct of the deputy marshals and special police, and workers at the polls were so informed. Unfortunately this uneasy truce broke down later in the day, and rioting ensued. The newspapers reported cases of violence, fraud, and irregularities in the lower counties. As usual, voters returned a Democratic legislature and congressman.[93]

The Republican *Daily Commercial* announced Tilden's victory in a special edition on election night, but by Friday an editorial proclaimed "Hayes Beyond Doubt."[94] Other newspapers in Delaware were equally confused as to the victor. Delawareans followed the bitter dispute to determine the winner closely, especially as Senator Bayard was a member of the committee which decided the result. When the final result was known, the *Delawarean* asserted that "Fraud Triumphs" and that "in the annals of crime, no greater political wrong has scarcely ever been committed," while the *Every Evening* was more judicious and headed an article "Quiet Submission Only Sensible Course." Most Delawareans expressed relief at the peaceful settlement of the crisis.[95]

As an aftermath of the election difficulties in Wilmington, a grand jury indicted eleven persons for interfering with deputy marshals performing their duties, while two deputy marshals were charged with assault in the Delaware courts. The cases dragged on in court until 1879 when by agreement of the United States District Attorney and state officials charges in both sets of cases were dropped.[96]

The efforts of Republicans to win an election in Delaware continued unsuccessfully for another ten years before they gained a limited victory. In 1878 they were so discouraged that they made no nominations for state office, leaving the opposition to the Greenback-Labor party, whose candidates received less than 3,000 votes.[97] After the United States Circuit Court in January, 1880, authorized upon application the appointment of federal supervisors of elections to guard and scrutinize assessment lists, the Republicans re-entered the fray with

[93] *Every Evening*, Oct. 4, 1876; *Gazette*, Nov. 8, 1876; *Daily Commercial*, Nov. 7, 1876; W. C. Spruance to A. Taft, Jan. 16, 1877, and W. C. Spruance to C. Devens, April 24, 1877, Dept. of Justice, Chronological Files, Delaware, NA.

[94] *Daily Commercial*, Nov. 7, 8, 9, 10, 1876; *Every Evening*, Nov. 8, 1876.

[95] *Delawarean*, March 3, 1877; *Every Evening*, March 5, 1877.

[96] W. C. Spruance to C. Devens, April 12, 1879, Dept. of Justice, Chronological Files, Delaware, NA.

[97] Hancock, "Delaware," in Reed, *Delaware*, 1:188.

renewed energy. Prior to this time the Republicans in the state had expected to win through their own efforts, but now this hope seemed dead unless federal assistance corrected conditions.[98] The campaign was relatively quiet, and even though the Democratic Mayor of Wilmington appointed special police, and the United States District Attorney deputy marshals, on election day they were little needed.[99] Later when the United States District Attorney and his special assistant, Anthony Higgins, chosen for the purpose, tried to get convictions in cases involving several irregularities, they were unsuccessful, since juries voted their political convictions.[100] The Democrats won again in 1882 and 1884. In 1886 the discouraged Republicans again decided not to nominate state candidates, leaving only the Temperance Reform party in the field, whose nominees received fewer than 8,000 votes. An effort to hold a Constitutional Convention in 1887 was defeated by a close vote.[101]

In 1888 the first steps in a political revolution occurred when the Republicans "redeemed" the state after twenty-five years of effort. As a result of a Democratic fight between the followers and opponents of Eli Saulsbury for the office of senator, the Republicans at last gained control of the legislature, even though all other offices went to the Democrats. Unexpectedly John Edward Addicks, a wealthy stock promoter from Pennsylvania, appeared in Dover and announced his "availability" for the office of senator, but instead the prize went to Anthony Higgins. The Democrats won the next two elections, but in 1894 the Republicans elected the governor, congressman, and legislature. Addicks again appeared and began a fight to become senator, which lasted ten years, split the Republican party into two wings, and brought corruption on an unprecedented scale into Delaware politics. The legislature became deadlocked and elected no senator in 1895, 1899, 1901, 1903, and 1905, and from 1901 to 1905 the state was unrepresented in the United States Senate. Delaware became mainly Republican and remained so until the days of the Democratic victories under Franklin D. Roosevelt.[102]

The adoption of a new constitution in 1897 marks a convenient dividing line between the old and new in Delaware politics. The new constitution abolished the cumbersome methods of qualifying for

[98] *American Annual Cyclopedia*, 1880, p. 202; *Every Evening*, Jan. 24, 1880.

[99] *Morning News*, Nov. 3, 4, 1880; *Every Evening*, Nov. 3, 4, 1880.

[100] A. Higgins to B. H. Brewster, Jan. 5, 1882, and John Patterson to B. H. Brewster, Jan. 5, 1882, Dept. of Justice, Chronological Files, Delaware, NA.

[101] Hancock, "Delaware," in Reed, *Delaware*, 1:188.

[102] Harold Hancock, "The Political Career of John Edward Addicks in Delaware" (B.A., Wesleyan Univ., 1936), *passim*.

voting and modernized the system of government. New Castle County and Wilmington were given increased representation, although legislative control remained in Kent and Sussex counties. Before 1897 the Democrats were mainly successful in elections; after that time the Republicans dominated.[103] The Republican victory may be attributed to improved organization, more interest by the national party, and the rising influence of industry in New Castle County. "Jed" Addicks was a precipitating factor in paying the taxes of many voters in the lower counties and in instigating more intensive efforts. His opponents within the party fought back, and the party became revitalized and the winning of elections a matter of vital concern.

During these years, while the two parties quarreled over the position of the Negro in politics, legal, social, and occupational adjustments by the freedman were in process. A revised code of laws for free Negroes passed in 1863 forbade them to vote, hold office, or attend political meetings. Freedmen could not sit on juries, and they could testify in court only if white witnesses had not been present at the scene of the crime. They could not lawfully own a gun, pistol, sword, or warlike instrument. They could not hold religious meetings later than nine o'clock, and they must be home by ten o'clock every night in the week. Apprenticeship laws for freedmen did not include provisions for school attendance or for a gift of clothing at the expiration of the term of indenture, as did laws for white apprentices. If a free Negro left the state for more than five days, he was considered a nonresident and was not permitted to return. The state did not support any Negro schools, and members of that race were not permitted to attend white schools.[104]

Because of conflict between Delaware laws and the Civil Rights Act, the legislature in 1867 passed a statute providing the same penalties for Negroes and whites for the same offenses. When the case of the *State* v. *Rash,* involving assault and battery by a white man against a Negro, came before Chief Justice Gilpin in the state Supreme Court in 1867, the Judge was reminded of the Delaware statute forbidding testimony by a Negro when white persons were present at the scene of the crime. The Negro's attorney claimed that the Civil Rights laws overruled the action by the state. Gilpin ruled that the part of the Civil Rights Bill controlling evidence was "inoperative, unconstitu-

---

[103] Eckman, "Constitutional Development," in Reed, *Delaware,* 1:*passim.*

[104] *Delaware Laws,* 12:330–34; John A. Munroe, "The Negro in Delaware," *South Atlantic Quarterly* 56 (Autumn, 1957): 443–45. Dr. Munroe's article is a brief, interpretative and stimulating history of the Negro in the state.

tional and void," but admitted the testimony on the grounds of humanity and necessity.[105]

The Fifteenth Amendment extended the franchise to Negroes, but in Delaware the 1873 Assessment Law restricted their use of it. The Innkeeper's Law of 1875 restricted the use of facilities in hotels, restaurants, and theaters, as well as on railroads and steamboats. Only after the United States Supreme Court reversed the conviction of a Negro named Neal for rape, in 1880, because the names of no Negroes had been drawn for jury duty, were their names added, but none served until 1901.[106]

When a representative of the Freedmen's Bureau toured Delaware in the spring of 1867, he found considerable prejudice against Negro education, especially in Sussex County, but he believed that in the long run the attempt to establish schools would be successful. Wages, he thought, were "fair," being $1 per day for laborers and $2.50 for mechanics. Concerning the legal status of the Negro, he reported:

So far as the *reading* of the laws is concerned, the colored man in Delaware has fair justice secured to him; in the *workings* and *execution* of the laws the popular prejudice against the race, ever works to his disadvantage, and a Jury will have no hesitation in convicting a black man upon evidence that would be deemed insufficient for a white man's conviction. The general feeling of the whites towards the blacks is total indifference—their presence in the community being simply endured for their usefulness—and the colored people in Delaware must in a great measure—unless their political condition is improved—depend for elevation above their present condition upon their moral and educational improvement.[107]

The year after the war ended was a difficult time of adjustment for both races in lower Delaware. At Centerville in Sussex County in May, 1865, several white men complained to military authorities of an outrage committed at a colored Methodist meeting. A band of ruffians attacked the churchgoers with knives, clubs, slingshots, and pistols, cutting and slashing and knocking them down. They made the women "strip naked and then drug them all around the yard kicking and

[105] Helen T. Catterall, ed., *Judicial Cases Concerning American Slavery and the Negro* (Washington, 1936), 4:240; Hancock, "Delaware," in Reed, *Delaware,* 1:186.

[106] "William Neal vs. State of Delaware," Appellate Case File No. 9483, U.S. Supreme Court Cases, NA; *American Annual Cyclopedia,* 1880, p. 203. The pages of the case, which were damaged by water in a fire in 1895, had to be specially separated for examination in the National Archives in 1967.

[107] E. Knower to W. H. Wiegel, June 20, 1867, LR, Delaware and Maryland District, Records of the Bureau of Refugees, Freedmen and Abandoned Lands, RG 105, NA. I would like to acknowledge the assistance of Mrs. Sarah Jackson in research in the National Archives.

abusing them and made one of them get down upon her knees and lick the Blood that they had knocked out of them." When an Army captain investigated, he found the charges were true, and he took a number of depositions. He reported that the majority of the civil authorities were opposed to executing the laws of what they termed "the damned Abolition Government."[108] Rumors circulated in May that the slave trade continued in lower Delaware, and an Army colonel, who investigated the case of a Negro girl sold by her Maryland owner to a Delaware farmer near Centerville, reported that Negroes did not enjoy civil rights in the area and added: "I am convinced that the colored people of this District need the strong arm of the Federal Authority for their protection. The civil authorities of the lower part of Delaware and the Eastern Shore of Maryland accord them no rights; their churches are burned, their schools broken up, and their persons and property destroyed by vicious white men with impunity; and their appeals to the civil authorities are utterly disregarded."[109]

Later in the year at Dagsboro a Negro minister was forced to leave the country, and at Seaford three former Confederate soldiers led an attack upon a Negro congregation, broke several windows and searched several members for weapons. Kent and Sussex County authorities arrested several Negro veterans for possessing firearms contrary to state law, even though they had been obtained at the time of their discharge from the army. As late as October, 1865, Negroes in lower Delaware were sold into servitude for terms of up to seven years as part of court sentences, though in view of the impending Thirteenth Amendment, a Republican newspaper thought that such purchases were "ticklish investments."[110]

During 1866 few incidents of violence or mistreatment of Negroes were recorded, but on January 15, 1867, Special Order Number 15 from General Howard's office extended the operations of the Freedmen's Bureau into Delaware. It was part of the District of Maryland and Delaware until August 15, 1868, when the state was placed under the supervision of the District of Columbia, where it remained until

[108] Joseph Hall *et al.* to General Lew Wallace, May 8, 1865; Capt. W. H. Wenie to Lt. W. B. Norman, May 18, 1865, LR, SW, RG 107, NA.

[109] Col. J. M. Wilson to Lt. Col. Catlin, July 18, 1865, LR, Middle Dept., RG 108, NA.

[110] Hancock, *Civil War*, pp. 166–67; *Delaware Journal*, Oct. 31, 1865; Henry Draper to E. M. Stanton, Nov. 30, 1865, LR, SW, RG 107, NA; Richard B. Morris, "The Course of Peonage in a Slave State," *Political Science Quarterly* 65 (June, 1950): 238–63. Morris pointed out how the antebellum history of peonage in Delaware established the basis of a later system by which sheriffs farmed out prisoners.

the Bureau ceased to function in the state by the end of 1870. In Delaware most of the efforts of the Freedmen's Bureau concerned education, though the Bureau also assisted veterans seeking pensions and arrears of pay, and investigated instances of violence and brutality.[111]

The newly formed Delaware Association for the Improvement and Education of the Colored People co-operated with the Freedmen's Bureau. In 1866 only seven Negro schools under either Quaker or other philanthropic auspices were in operation in the state. In January, 1867, a group of Wilmington businessmen and philanthropists, many of whom were Quakers, organized the new society to aid the Negro, especially through education. They solicited support from organizations outside of the state, from England, and from private citizens. An agreement was worked out whereby the colored people provided land and erected the school building, the Freedmen's Bureau furnished lumber and some pecuniary assistance, and the Society selected, subsidized, and supervised the teachers. Each pupil, if he were able, was to pay ten cents per week, which sum was used for the room and board of the teacher.

In spite of several instances in 1867 and 1868 in which Negro teachers were driven away from schools and schoolhouses burned, the Society had decided success in spearheading the movement for Negro education. By 1875 there were twenty-eight schools outside of Wilmington, and the six in that city were controlled by the city Board of Education. The Association had agitated for state support, and in 1875 the General Assembly at last permitted Negroes to be taxed for educational purposes. The sum provided only about one-third of the funds necessary for the support of schools. In 1881 the legislature appropriated $2,400 for colored schools, and by 1891 it had increased the sum to $9,000. By 1890, 4,656 out of 5,542 Negro school-age students were enrolled for an average term of four and a half months. In 1891 Delaware State College for Negroes was established near Dover, with federal aid.[112]

[111] Maryland and Delaware 1867–1868, Freedmen's Bureau Records, *passim*, RG 105; E. M. Gregory to Col. U. P. Ketchum, April 11, 1867, LR, Assistant Adj.-Gen. Files.

[112] Lyman P. Powell, *The History of Education in Delaware* (Washington, 1893), pp. 168–71; Henry C. Conrad, *A Glimpse of the Colored Schools of Delaware* (Wilmington, 1883), pp. 1–10; Delaware Association for the Moral Improvement and Education of the Colored People of Delaware, Minutes, 1866–1890, *passim*, Historical Society of Delaware; Delaware Association for the Moral Improvement and Education of the Colored People of Delaware, *First, Second and Third Annual Reports* (Wilmington, 1868, 1869, 1870), *passim*; Scharf, *Delaware*, 1:460. In 1886 the *People's Witness* was a weekly newspaper being published in Wilmington for Negroes.

Economically the Negro remained at a disadvantage. A recent study of the Negro in Delaware began a discussion of his economic status with the statement, "The story of Negro economic progress in Delaware between 1865 and 1915 is quickly told: there was none." Minor exceptions were a slight increase in farm ownership and the beginnings of a middle class in Wilmington. Certainly it is true that the great majority of Negroes were engaged in manual work of some kind at the beginning and end of this period. As early as 1869 a colored conference to elect delegates to a national labor convention indicated the rise of a middle class in Wilmington. Thirty-six trades, including grocerymen, bricklayers, musicians, soap manufacturers, tanners, and hotel keepers sent delegates. The census of 1890 classified most colored males as agricultural laborers or general laborers, though it listed 809 as owners of farms or overseers. More than one hundred were grouped in each of the following categories: draymen and teamsters, iron and steel workmen, brickmakers, and livery stable keepers and hostlers. Over fifty were listed in each of these classifications: fishermen, clergymen, barbers, merchants, steam railroad employees, and leather curriers. Colored women worked mainly as servants. The list included only two physicians, one lawyer, and one government official. Tradition, discrimination and lack of education combined to keep Negroes confined to menial jobs.[113]

Beginning with 1870, the Negro began to take part in Republican conventions and to vote, but Democratic collectors and assessors disfranchised him. Democrats made no effort to gain the votes of Negroes in this period and frequently made the assertion that theirs was a white man's party in which the Negro was not welcome. Before 1900 no Negro was elected to any town, city, state, or federal office. A Negro became bailiff of a Wilmington court in 1893, and in 1901 one was elected to the Wilmington city council. In 1892 Negroes nominated a congressional candidate on the ticket of the Independent Colored Republican party, but he dropped out of the running before election time. A group of disgruntled colored Republicans in 1894 expressed dissatisfaction with the support given Negro schools and requested that a Negro be nominated for at least one office in each hundred and county, as well as for some state offices. The Negro was advised "to divide his vote with all parties, as does his more advanced brother in

---

[113] Harold C. Livesay, "Delaware Negroes, 1865–1915" (B.A., Univ. of Del., 1966), pp. 47–52; *Daily Commercial*, Nov. 25, 1869; "Report on the Population of the United States at the Eleventh Census," 1890, *The Miscellaneous Documents of the House of Representatives*, 52d Congress, 1891–92, part 8 (Washington, 1894), p. 542. In 1900, 44 per cent of Negro farmers owned their farms, 54 per cent were tenants, and less than 2 per cent were managers. See U.S. Census, *Agriculture*, 1910, p. 255.

every state in the Union." A subsequent conference of colored Republicans expressed confidence in the attitude of the Republican party toward the Negro.[114]

Thus the Negro took his first steps toward full citizenship in the postwar period, but he continued to face legal, social, occupational, and political discrimination. His position was better than in the states to the south, but he was less well-treated than in some Northern states.

During these postwar years Delaware also made economic adjustments to industrial America. Agriculturally Delaware, at the end of the nineteenth century, grew large quantities of wheat, corn, rye, and oats, as it did in 1860. The main difference was that the raising of fruit, especially of peaches, berries, and garden produce had greatly expanded, due to the extension of the railroad and the adoption of refrigerator cars. By 1900 census officials reported that Delaware, along with Maryland and New Jersey, supplied seven-tenths of the markets in New York and New Jersey with peaches, apples, and berries. Dairying was also profitable, but the production of broilers did not begin until the twentieth century. Efforts to attract Northern and European immigrants were mainly unsuccessful, the principal reason being probably that the West offered more opportunity to acquire land cheaply. Because of national overproduction of cereal crops and the spread of a disease called the "yellows" among the peaches, the income of Delaware farmers remained low, though they were satisfied enough not to be very active in the Populist movement. In 1892 a technicality in filing a petition kept the Populist party off the Delaware ballot.[115]

New Castle County contained the richest soil in the state, benefited from experiments by progressive farmers, and was located near large markets easily reached by good transportation. By 1870 the value of its agricultural products exceeded that of the other two counties combined, but it lost this superiority as it turned more to manufacturing and as other areas improved. By 1900 it still exceeded in value of agricultural products either of the other counties.[116]

[114] Livesay, "Delaware Negroes," pp. 13–28; *American Annual Cyclopedia*, 1892, p. 227; 1894, p. 238. In 1967, 70 to 80 per cent of the Negroes in the state were said by the state chairman of the Republican party to vote the Democrat ticket; *Evening Journal*, May 19, 1967.

[115] Hancock, "Agriculture in Delaware, 1789–1900," in Reed, *Delaware*, 1:383–89; *American Annual Cyclopedia*, 1892, p. 227; U.S. Census, *Manufacturers*, 1900, p. 105; U.S. Census, *Agriculture*, 1910, p. 266. Value of all farm property in 1900:

Kent	$18,668,000
New Castle	24,474,000
Sussex	20,036,000
Total	$63,178,000

[116] Hancock, "Agriculture," in Reed, *Delaware*, 1:386–89.

Although slower than New Castle County to accept change, Kent County surpassed Sussex County. By 1870 it claimed that it raised more peaches than any other area of similar size in the world, and the production of berries and garden produce had become popular. Basically it remained an area in which general farming predominated with emphasis upon the raising of cereal crops.[117]

Sussex County was the largest county in area, the most sparsely populated, and the most isolated. Sussex farmers only slowly accepted improvements, as is evidenced by the use of large numbers of oxen and the continued dependence upon the raising of cereal crops by traditional methods on worn-out soil. By the end of the century the suitability of its light soil for the raising of peaches, berries, and melons had been recognized, but like Kent County, it remained a section in which most farmers engaged in general farming.[118]

Throughout the nineteenth century manufacturing for other than local use was confined to Wilmington and its immediate vicinity, which possessed advantages of water power, transportation, capital, and proximity to nearby markets. In 1860 the following industries in New Castle County produced goods valued at more than $400,000 annually: car wheels, carriages, cotton goods, flour and meal, gunpowder, morocco leather, and ships. The Civil War greatly accelerated production, as the federal income taxes and assessments on manufactured goods show. By 1868 the city Board of Trade in its first annual report claimed that "Wilmington manufactures more iron vessels than all the rest of the United States combined, that we rate first in powder, second in carriages and second in leather, and the proportion of manufactures to each inhabitant is much greater than in Philadelphia, and excelled by very few, if any other cities in the Union." The Governor of Delaware in 1875 pointed out to the legislature that in capital, wages, and value of products, New Castle County exceeded ten times the returns in manufacturing of Kent and Sussex counties combined.[119]

In the postwar period, Wilmington businessmen created a thriving industrial city. A handful of employees became a hundred, one plant developed into a score of buildings, and stockholders and the corporation replaced family enterprises. "Our community had changed, like hundreds of others in the decades after the Civil War, from a market stand for the farm regions thereabouts to a center of manufacturing and trade," observed a descendant of one of the Quaker

---

[117] *Ibid.*
[118] *Ibid.*
[119] Hancock, "Delaware Manufactures, 1789–1900," in Reed, *Delaware*, 1:428–29.

business families. Many family enterprises passed into other hands in the nineties, and trusts acquired control of some of the largest firms.[120]

By 1900 manufacturing and mechanical industries employed more people than agriculture. New Castle County retained its dominance, with more capital invested, more employees, and more goods produced, than in the other two counties combined. Wilmington claimed to rank seventh in manufacturing among the smaller cities in the nation and to have greater diversity of industry than any other city. It was especially proud of its manufacture of gunpowder, ships, iron and steel, and leather.[121]

Culturally, just as economically, Philadelphia drew Wilmington ever closer, while, in turn, the small towns downstate came into closer contact with Delaware's only city.[122] Wilmington viewed with pride in the 1890s its paved streets, new water system, electric lights, streetcars, parks, library, theaters, churches, and public schools.[123] Two out of every five Delawareans lived in the metropolis in 1900, and its population of 76,000 more than equalled the combined total of Kent and Sussex. All other towns in the state, including Dover the capital, contained less than 4,000 inhabitants. Like an octopus, the city spread its tentacles in all directions. A "downstater" looking for medical treatment, private schools, the headquarters of religious and civic organizations, the latest fashions, or theatrical diversion usually visited Wilmington or Philadelphia.[124]

What culture there was in Wilmington was built upon business, which, as a resident of the 1880s and 1890s remembered, was "the nominal occupation and chief subject of thought in our community." Literature, music, painting, and the fine art of conversation, he believed, "suffered from an infantile paralysis" contracted under the

---

[120] *Ibid.*, 1:430; Henry S. Canby, *The Age of Confidence* (New York, 1934), p. 238.

[121] Hancock, "Manufacturers," in Reed, *Delaware*, 1:431; U.S. Census, *Manufacturers*, 1900, pp. 108–9.

Manufacturing Statistics in 1900:

	Value of Product	Capital	Number of Employees
Kent	$ 2,405,000	1,723,000	1,627
New Castle	40,900,000	38,139,000	18,692
Sussex	2,081,000	1,340,000	1,884

[122] Hancock, "Manufacturers," in Reed, *Delaware*, 1:426, 431.

[123] *Every Evening, History of Wilmington* (Wilmington, 1894), p. 50.

[124] U.S. Census, *Abstract of the Twelfth Census of the United States*, 1900 (Washington, 1902), p. 152.

Population in 1900:

Kent	32,762
New Castle	109,697
Sussex	42,276
	184,735

dominance of business. Hence this postwar generation read, but not too much, attended concerts, but not too often, supported ideas, but not too passionately, and concentrated on making money. Even the one real artist in Delaware at the time, Howard Pyle, who was nationally known for his illustrations in books and periodicals, was accepted more for his Quaker background, conservative Republican opinions, and substantial income than for aesthetic reasons. The philosophy of the period, then, was developed on the Protestant gospel of work accompanied by industry, thrift, obedience, and resistance to the pleasures of idleness, and little time was left for aesthetic indulgences.[125]

In the small towns and rural areas, cultural stimulus, such as it was, came mainly from Wilmington and Philadelphia, but also from travel, the reading of national magazines, and correspondence.[126] The intellectual climate improved as the schools expanded and raised their standards. By 1890 Delaware was spending more per pupil in attendance and more per capita than any Southern state, except for Maryland and the District of Columbia, though less than most New England or Middle Atlantic states.[127]

Thus the Reconstruction period brought change to Delaware. Unlike the South, Delaware was not occupied by federal troops, nor did she harbor carpetbaggers, scalawags, and the Ku-Klux Klan. Election irregularities increased, but the wholesale corruption and violence characteristic of political contests in some Southern states did not develop. Political control passed from the Democrats to the Republicans, who had close ties with the economic interests of Philadelphia and New York. The Negro took his first steps toward acquiring civil rights, but remained a second-class citizen. New opportunities appeared in agriculture, though most farmers clung to the old methods. Wilmington continued its industrial advance which the Civil War had stimulated, and the cleavage between it and the rest of the state became ever greater. Under the leadership of industrial Wilmington the state decided that its future lay with the North rather than with the South.

[125] Canby, *Age of Confidence*, pp. 226–45.
[126] De Valinger and Shaw, eds., *Ridgely Letters*, III:*passim*.
[127] U.S. Commissioner of Education, *Report*, 1890 (Washington, 1894), pp. 28, 31. Expenditure per pupil in attendance was $14.00, and $1.41 per capita was spent on education.

CHAPTER SEVEN

The Origins of Border State Liberal Republicanism
Jacqueline Balk and Ari Hoogenboom

Though Reconstruction historians have produced a vast literature,[1] they have tended to ignore the border states.[2] Emphasis on Radical Reconstruction in the South, economic development in the North, and geographical expansion in the West have overshadowed the murky, tangled developments in a complex area where predominantly Southern qualities mixed with Northern and Western influences.[3] Civil War turbulence and the demise of the traditional two-party system in the border states fostered confusion, factionalism, and unrealistic political combinations.[4] Suffering from abnormal war and post-

---

[1] For summaries of Reconstruction historiography, see David Donald, "Historical Synthesis," *Commentary* 44 (Sept., 1967): 94–98; Bernard A. Weisberger, "The Dark and Bloody Ground of Reconstruction Historiography," *Journal of Southern History* 25 (Nov., 1959): 427–47; John Hope Franklin, "Whither Reconstruction Historiography?" *Journal of Negro Education* 17 (Fall, 1948): 446–61; Francis B. Simkins, "New Viewpoints of Southern Reconstruction," *Journal of Southern History* 5 (Feb., 1939): 49–61.

[2] A small number of monographs varying in quality and content touch on postwar politics in individual border states. See, for example, Thomas B. Alexander, *Political Reconstruction in Tennessee* (Nashville, 1950); Thomas S. Barclay, *The Liberal Republican Movement in Missouri, 1865–1871* (Columbia, Mo., 1926); E. Merton Coulter, *The Civil War and Readjustment in Kentucky* (Chapel Hill, N.C., 1926); Richard Orr Curry, *A House Divided: A Study of Statehood Politics and the Copperhead Movement in West Virginia* (Pittsburgh, 1964); William Starr Myers, *The Self-Reconstruction of Maryland, 1864–1867* (Baltimore, 1909); William E. Parrish, *Missouri Under Radical Rule, 1865–1870* (Columbia, Mo., 1965); James Welch Patton, *Unionism and Reconstruction in Tennessee, 1860–1869* (Chapel Hill, N.C., 1934). We, in turn, have ignored Delaware in this essay because it played no significant role in the Liberal Republican movement. In the 1872 Democratic convention the Delaware delegation refused to vote for Greeley, and its leader Thomas Bayard bitterly opposed any alliance between Greeley and Democrats. Not bordering on any seceded state and in the firm military grasp of the Union, Delaware avoided the bitter factionalism that gave birth to Liberal Republicanism. For Bayard's opposition to the Liberal Republican platform and candidates, see *Official Proceedings of the National Democratic Convention* (Boston, 1872), pp. 42, 45–48.

[3] Several recent exceptions include Curry, *A House Divided*; Parrish, *Missouri Under Radical Rule*; and Alexander, *Political Reconstruction in Tennessee*.

[4] For the party chaos and the disintegration war brought, see W. H. Perrin, J. H. Battle, and G. C. Kniffen, *Kentucky: A History* . . . (Louisville, 1887), pp. 349–56, 360–61; Charles Lewis Wagandt, *The Mighty Revolution: Negro Emancipation in Maryland, 1862–1864* (Baltimore, 1964), p. 17; J. Reuben Sheeler, "The Development of Unionism in East Tennessee, 1860–1866," *Journal of Negro History* 29 (April, 1944): 185.

war conditions, the border states frequently anticipated national political trends and experienced them in an extreme form. Thus in the border states the Liberal Republican movement was rooted not in the months immediately preceding 1872 but in the political turmoil which began with the election of 1860. The interplay between geography, war, tradition, slavery, race, and personal ambition determined the tortuous course politics would take over the next decade.[5]

Perhaps at no time in our history were issues more important to politicians than during the era of the Civil War and Reconstruction. But even then the personal ambitions of most politicians overrode commitment to issues, and building coalitions in hopes of winning elections wreaked havoc with ideologies. Ideology was far from dead, but majority rule makes strange bedfellows. While protesting the course of national politics, border state Liberal Republicans were involved in a more basic quest. To those whom the vagaries of border state politics divorced from power, Liberal Republicanism offered hope. Though many spokesmen for the national Liberal Republican movement espoused civil service, tariff, and currency reform, the national movement, like that in the border states, was founded in large measure on personal ambition. The quest for office, however, did not make Liberal Republicans indifferent to reform, and a majority of border state Democrats favored their major rallying points of sectional reconciliation, administrative reform, reduction of state debts, and economic advancement. All politicians are a mixture of ideology and ambition, and the two do not necessarily clash. But when they do clash it becomes evident that the proportions of ideology and ambition vary from individual to individual and from time to time. Politicians sometimes do risk and wreck their political careers for principle, but they are also well aware that without compromise, political power may be lost and that without political power nothing

---

[5] For examples of border state turmoil during the secession crisis, see William T. McKinney, "The Defeat of the Secessionists in Kentucky in 1861," *Journal of Negro History* 1 (Oct., 1916): 377–91; Raymond D. Thomas, "A Study in Missouri Politics, 1840–1870: Missouri for the Union," *Missouri Historical Review* 21 (April, 1927): 438–54. As of 1860 the Negro population in the major border states was distributed as follows:

State	Slaves	Free Negroes	Total state population
Kentucky	225,483	10,684	1,155,684
Maryland	87,189	83,942	687,049
Missouri	114,931	3,572	1,182,012
Tennessee	275,919	7,300	1,109,801

U.S. Bureau of the Census, *Ninth Census, 1870* (Washington, 1872), 1: 31–32, 36, 43–45, 61–62.

can be accomplished. There is, however, the reverse side of the coin. A coalition can contain so many diverse ideologies and ambitions that it lacks cohesion and dies of the factionalism that gave it birth. The capstone, millstone, and headstone of this unstable and untenable Liberal Republican alliance was its nomination of Horace Greeley for President. Its first milestone in the border states was the campaign of 1860.

The possible consequences of a Republican presidential victory in 1860 thrust state and congressional elections into the background.[6] Though there was turmoil and uncertainty during the campaign, the border states reaffirmed their stable conservative stance in presidential contests by rejecting the extremism of both Southern Democrats and Northern Republicans.[7] Avoiding divisive issues and wishing to maintain the Constitution, the Union, and the laws, the Constitutional Union party led by John Bell carried Kentucky and Tennessee and narrowly missed taking Missouri and Maryland.[8]

[6] Roy F. Nichols, *The Disruption of American Democracy* (New York, 1962), pp. 332–47; Kenneth M. Stampp, *And the War Came: The North and the Secession Crisis, 1860–61* (Chicago, 1964), pp. 6–12.

[7]   Border State Voting Patterns, 1836–1860*

State	1836	1840	1844	1848	1852	1856	1860
Kentucky	W	W	W	W	W	D	CU
Maryland	W	W	W	W	D	A	SD
Missouri	D	D	D	D	D	D	ND
Tennessee	W	W	W	W	W	D	CU

* W–Whig, D–Democratic, A–American, CU–Constitutional Union, SD–Southern Democratic, ND–Northern Democratic.

When the Whig party disappeared from national politics after 1852, Kentucky and Tennessee rejected both Republican and American parties for the more conservative Democrats. In the crucial 1860 election, they sustained the Union by rejecting Republican and Southern Democratic extremes to vote for the Bell–Everett Constitutional Union ticket. Maryland deviates somewhat from the general pattern of political stability because of a powerful native American movement that altered its voting patterns in the 1850s. Like the other border states, it remained committed to Unionist principles, though in 1860 the Southern Democratic ticket carried Maryland by a narrow plurality. With four candidates in the field, John C. Breckinridge defeated the Constitutional Union candidate by only 722 votes. A traditionally Democratic state, Missouri embraced Stephen A. Douglas in 1860, rather than Breckinridge. W. Dean Burnham, *Presidential Ballots 1836–1892* (Baltimore, 1955), pp. 250, 252, 254.

[8]   Presidential Vote in the Border States in 1860*

State	D	R	SD	CU
Kentucky	25,641	1,365	53,146	66,068
Maryland	5,966	2,294	42,482	41,760
Missouri	58,502	17,020	31,427	58,362
Tennessee	11,410	—	64,406	68,768

* D–(Douglas) Democrat, R–Republican; SD–Southern Democrat, CU–Constitutional Union. Burnham, *Presidential Ballots*, pp. 250, 252, 254.

After the Republican victory in 1860, border state politicians unsuccessfully sought peace through compromise, and, when that failed, sought neutrality. On December 18, 1860, Kentucky's Senator John J. Crittenden proposed the first of several compromises designed to preserve the Union and restore harmony between the sections. The Crittenden Compromise and the subsequent Washington Peace Conference of February, 1861, won the support of leading border state politicians and Northern Democrats.[9] Opposition, however, from Republicans and Southern Democrats made compromise impossible. As compromise failed, practical alliances between supporters of Bell and supporters of Stephen A. Douglas in Kentucky and Missouri began to promote neutrality.[10] Political labels submerged and "fresh aggregates of power" rose to determine Maryland's course.[11] In Tennessee, the quarrelsome Whig element abjured both Southern secession and Northern coercion. Warning of Tennessee's inability to mediate between the North and South, Whigs urged the creation of a Border States' Confederation.[12] After hostilities began, with the fall of Fort Sumter in April, 1861, most border state politicians abandoned the sophistry of neutrality. The question became union or secession.

Before war smothered lingering hopes for compromise, border state Union men acted decisively. In early January, 1861, St. Louis Unionists caucused and appointed a "Committee of Public Safety" to insure "unalterable fidelity to the Union under all circumstances" and to stymie any move toward secession.[13] On January 8, Kentucky Unionists took similar action. A conservative amalgam of Douglas and Bell supporters formed the Union State Central Committee to stave off the hysteria that plunged wavering states into secession. With a small majority in the Senate and an almost evenly divided House, Unionists resisted Governor Beriah Magoffin's call for a state sovereignty con-

---

[9] Nichols, *Disruption of American Democracy*, pp. 444–52, 473–82; Stampp, *And the War Came*, pp. 123–78. For border state hopes during the Washington Peace Conference, see Robert Gray Gunderson, ed., "Letters from the Washington Peace Conference of 1861," *Journal of Southern History* 17 (August, 1951): 382–92.

[10] Robert M. McElroy, *Kentucky in the Nation's History* (New York, 1909), pp. 507–8; Perrin *et al.*, *Kentucky*, pp. 350–54; Walter B. Stevens, *Missouri: The Center State, 1821–1915* (2 vols.; Chicago, 1915), 1:244, 261–64; J. Thomas Scharf, *History of St. Louis City and County . . .* (2 vols.; Philadelphia, 1883), 1:391–94.

[11] Wagandt, *The Mighty Revolution*, p. 17.

[12] Sheeler, "Unionism in Tennessee," p. 181.

[13] Prominent Whigs, Free Soil Democrats, Douglas, Bell, and Lincoln supporters comprised the committee. Its chairman was O. D. Filley and members included James Broadhead, Samuel Glover, and Frank Blair, son of Francis Preston Blair and brother of Montgomery Blair, soon to be Lincoln's postmaster general. See Scharf, *St. Louis City and County*, 1:394; Stevens, *Missouri*, 1:244–45.

vention, lest Kentucky be carried into the Confederacy.[14] Maryland
occupied a particularly strategic and therefore precarious position. An
Ohio participant at the Washington Peace Conference predicted in
February that if Maryland attempted to secede "coercion will be used
to keep her in the Union, so as to have the Potomac for the boundary
—If she does not, the South will be placed comparatively in a state of
blockade, & ultimately, the constant irritation along the border will
involve the Country."[15] Despite pressure from Southern sympathizers,
Maryland's Thomas Hicks, an American party member and the only
non-Democratic Southern governor, refused to call the Democratic-
dominated legislature into special session to consider secession.[16]

Geography and socio-economic differences largely determined the
political division in Tennessee. Lowland slave-holding Democratic
and Whig plantation owners favored the Confederacy, while eastern
farmers, mountain men, and artisans supported the Union. On February 9, Tennessee by a majority of 8,833 refused to convene a sovereignty convention and remained in the Union until the fall of Fort
Sumter.[17] Despite strong resistance in some areas, by late autumn 1861
all of the border states except Tennessee declared for the Union.[18]
Yet political leaders who remained loyal had conflicting aspirations
that plagued the border states throughout the war and Reconstruction.

These conflicting aspirations varied. Although less important to
some than Lincoln's war aims, federal and state patronage determined
to a large extent political position within the broadly based Union
coalition. Slavery was an equally divisive issue since many prominent
slave owners had enlisted early in the Union ranks.[19] Jacksonian
Democrats and Clay Whigs who had indignantly shunned secession

[14] McElroy, *Kentucky*, pp. 510–12; Perrin, *Kentucky*, pp. 350–51.

[15] Gunderson, ed., "Letters from the Washington Peace Conference," p. 386.

[16] Nichols, *Disruption of American Democracy*, pp. 373, 447–48, 474. For an example of Maryland's loyalty to the Union, see resolutions adopted by the state
legislature and presented to Congress, January 2, 1862, in *The American Annual
Cyclopaedia and Register of Important Events of the Year 1862* . . . (New York: D.
Appleton and Company, 1863), 2:560.

[17] Exactly 68,282 voters opposed, while 59,449 favored a sovereignty convention.
Patton, *Reconstruction in Tennessee*, p. 12.

[18] Stanley F. Horn, ed., *Tennessee's War: 1861–1865, Described by Participants*
(Nashville, 1965); Ed Huddleston, *The Civil War in Middle Tennessee* (Nashville,
1965); Eric Russell Lacy, *Vanquished Volunteers: East Tennessee Sectionalism from
Statehood to Secession* (Johnson City, Tennessee, 1965); Marcus J. Wright, *Tennessee in the War, 1861–1865* . . . (New York, 1908); Patton, *Reconstruction in Tennessee*, pp. 3–74.

[19] For reactions in Maryland to the proposed emancipation of slaves in the District of Columbia, see *Annual Cyclopaedia* . . . *1862*, 2:560; for divisions in the
Union ranks over emancipation in Maryland, see *Annual Cyclopaedia* . . . *1863*,
3:616–18; for Missouri, see *Annual Cyclopaedia* . . . *1862*, 2:595.

were alarmed by presidential maneuvering and congressional radicalism as the war progressed. Republicans, too, found themselves at odds on these same issues. Alienated by Lincoln's caution and conservatism, the more radical among them gravitated toward their congressional counterparts for succor and spoils.

It was difficult to maintain loyal governments where secession was openly avowed and often abetted. The coalition Unionists were bound together only by what Lincoln called "the mystic chords of memory." When federal power menaced slavery, chords snapped, and both Union sentiment and alliances built upon it began to disintegrate. Conservative border state elements feared that Lincoln's promise not to disturb slavery would be broken. General John C. Frémont's unauthorized proclamation of August 30, 1861, emancipating the slaves of Missouri Rebels, substantiated this fear. In 1862 feuding broke out between the conservative "Claybanks," who supported gradual, compensated emancipation, and the radical "Charcoals," who favored immediate, uncompensated emancipation and would ask Lincoln in the summer of 1863 to extend the Emancipation Proclamation to Missouri.[20] In Maryland, Unionists also split over emancipation. To avoid alienating slaveholding Unionists, Conservatives entrenched in the State Central Committee and led by Governor Augustus Bradford and Thomas Swann, the former mayor of Baltimore, wished to postpone emancipation and related questions until after the war. On the other hand, the Unconditional Unionists or Union Leaguers, led by Henry Winter Davis, John A. J. Creswell, and Judge Hugh Lennox, supported immediate uncompensated emancipation.[21] While divided border state Unionists remained loyal, the obvious disregard of constitutional rights that seemed to characterize state and congressional Radicals, as well as the administration, alarmed conservative loyalists and caused the first break in Union ranks.[22]

[20] Harding, "Missouri Party Struggles in the Civil War Period," *Annual Report of the American Historical Association* (Washington, 1901), 1:97–100. Fremont's subsequent removal from his Missouri command angered the state's antislavery men but temporarily pacified the more conservative Unionists. *Annual Cyclopaedia . . . 1862*, 2:595.

[21] See Resolutions of State Central Committee Convention, June 23, 1863, in *Annual Cyclopaedia . . . 1863*, 3:616, and an address to the people of Maryland enunciating the dangers of immediate emancipation, *ibid.*, p. 617. For views of the Unconditional Union State Committee on immediate emancipation, see *ibid.*, pp. 617–18.

[22] Stevens, *Missouri*, 1:40; Charles Branch Clark, *Politics in Maryland during the Civil War* (Chestertown, Maryland, 1952), pp. 95–99; Wood Gray, *The Hidden Civil War: The Story of the Copperheads* (New York, 1942), p. 217; Sheeler, "Unionism in East Tennessee," pp. 191–200. For possible economic influences on emancipation, see Parrish, *Missouri Under Radical Rule*, p. 179; Barclay, *The Liberal Republican Movement in Missouri*, p. 5.

Border state Radicalism was more practical than ideological. The Republican (or Radical) minorities in Maryland, Missouri, Tennessee, and West Virginia initially sought political domination through alliances with Moderates.[23] But after secession was no longer a threat the expedient coalitions based on Unionist sentiment were, if challenged, almost certain to collapse.[24] Acutely aware both of the flimsiness of their alliances and of their minority status, Radicals used proscriptive legislation and state constitutional provisions to prevent the natural re-alliance of Conservative Unionists and Southern sympathizers. Though he spoke of Kentucky, Robert Breckinridge's observation that "the main source of political danger lies in the cooperation of disloyal elements in the state, with the proslavery element of the Union party" applied to all border states.[25]

Maryland's Constitutional Convention of 1864 disfranchised Rebels and Southern sympathizers and established precedents for Radicals of other border states. To proscribe more effectively and to insure loyal majorities, the legislature enacted an ironclad test oath and a state registration law.[26] By 1866, Missouri, West Virginia,[27] and reconstructed Tennessee (controlled by Unionists from the eastern sections of the state) restricted the franchise through new constitutions

[23] For an insight into the wartime political alliance of the anti-Democratic forces in Maryland, see George Patterson to Jeremiah Sullivan Black, Bethesda, Maryland, June 3, 1872, Black Papers, Library of Congress (LC).

[24] By 1863 this situation already existed in Missouri and Maryland. Clark, *Politics in Maryland*, pp. 95–101; Thomas, "Missouri for the Union," p. 454; Barclay, *The Liberal Republican Movement in Missouri*, p. 6.

[25] Robert J. Breckinridge to Reverdy Johnson, Danville, Kentucky, May 7, 1864, Reverdy Johnson Papers, LC. Charles Fulton made the same observation in a letter to Montgomery Blair: "I must again take the liberty of expressing to you my fears, amounting almost to conviction, that a portion of the Union men of Maryland are combining with the rebels of the counties first to defeat the call of the Convention, and failing in that to secure the election of delegates that are opposed to Emancipation, unless coupled with State compensation." Charles Fulton to Montgomery Blair, Baltimore, March 11, 1864, Blair Family Papers, LC.

[26] William Starr Myers, *The Maryland Constitution of 1864* (Baltimore, 1901), *passim.*

[27] Despite serious internal conflicts regarding its status, West Virginia entered the Union in 1863. After 1862 when the question of emancipation first arose, the Conservative fear that Radicalism might dominate state politics increased. Thus in the newest loyal state emancipation pierced the flimsy shield of Union, behind which discontended political elements had found temporary shelter. For an incisive study of the process and completion of West Virginia statehood, see Curry, *A House Divided.* Also see Milton Gerofsky, "Reconstruction in West Virginia," *West Virginia History* 6 (July, 1945): 295–309.

and laws.[28] But while they legitimized their minority control of the border states through loyalty oaths and registration laws, Radicals created and consolidated their enemies and ensured their own disintegration. United with Radicals under the Union banner, loyal Democrats were eager, after Appomattox, to regain their partisan individuality and to re-establish their political power. To recoup their political fortunes, the Democrats hoped to exploit issues such as the scope of federal power *versus* states rights, the course of tariff and fiscal legislation, and programs for internal improvements. These Unionists saw their ambitions thwarted by Radical insistence on and success in proscribing their potential supporters.

A Conservative mélange opposed to the course of national and state Republicanism strengthened the discontented. Republican propagandists, capitalizing upon war hysteria, branded as Copperheads conservative Northern Democrats hostile to the administration's conduct of the war. The vast majority of these conservative Democrats were loyal, but indiscriminate partisan use of the term Copperhead stigmatized them as disloyal. Varying from men actively opposing the war to strict constructionists, questioning the legality of Lincoln's policies, Democrats were all tarred with the same brush.[29] Whether they were disloyal or simply disturbed by growing federal civil and military power, they rallied in 1864 to the Democrat's conciliatory platform and their presidential nominee General George B. McClellan.[30] The Thirteenth Amendment (making emancipation uni-

[28] Gerofsky, "Reconstruction in West Virginia," pp. 309–20; James Morton Callahan, *History of West Virginia, Old and New* (3 vols.; Chicago, 1923), 1:402–3, 406; Parrish, *Missouri Under Radical Rule*, pp. 26–29; Barclay, *The Liberal Republican Movement in Missouri*, pp. 14–17, 28–29. For Tennessee's struggles with disfranchisement, see Alexander, *Political Reconstruction in Tennessee*, pp. 73–76; *Nation* 2, no. 47 (May 10, 1866): 593. The Kentucky legislature of 1865–66 repealed all wartime proscriptive legislation against Confederate soldiers and Southern sympathizers. Perrin, *Kentucky*, p. 478; Coulter, *Civil War and Readjustment in Kentucky*, pp. 287–95.

[29] For a review of Copperhead historiography, see Richard O. Curry, "The Union as it Was: A Critique of Recent Interpretations of the 'Copperheads,' " *Civil War History* 13 (March, 1967): 25–39.

[30] The 1864 Presidential Vote in the Border States*

State	Lincoln	McClellan
Kentucky	26,786	63,301
Maryland	37,353	32,418
Missouri	72,763	31,099
West Virginia	23,152	10,438

* Tennessee, having seceded, cast no votes in the 1864 election. Burnham, *Presidential Ballots*, pp. 251, 253, 255.

versal), the growing extremism of congressional policies, and the repressive actions of local Radicals further disenchanted many Unionists.

The Reconstruction policies of Andrew Johnson helped unite the politically dissatisfied. The new President rejected Radical plans for reconstructing the South. His "amnesty" address in December, 1865, and his veto of the Freedman's Bureau bill in February, 1866, encouraged Conservatives to unite against Radicals. By isolating many Moderate and Conservative Unionists from state power centers, Radicals forced them into a practical as well as an ideological bond with Johnson,[31] whose need for support grew as the rift between him and Congress widened.

The congressional elections of 1866 excited widespread interest in Missouri, Kentucky, Tennessee, Maryland, and West Virginia. Alienated Unionists of every stripe joined with Copperheads and Peace Democrats against Radicalism. Fearing political obscurity, they sought alliances which might lead to a restoration of position and power.[32] As early as October 26, 1865, Conservative Unionists, Copperheads, and other anti-Radicals met in St. Louis to support President Johnson's Reconstruction policies and to condemn Radicalism on both state and national levels. The "Verandah House" meeting marked the end in Missouri of formless opposition to Radicalism, although political victory would not come until 1870. Led by such undeniably loyal men as Frank Blair, James Rollins, and James Broadhead, and supported by the President and hopeful Northern Democrats, the politically dissatisfied consolidated their ranks for the congressional battle.[33] In Tennessee the Radicals under the quixotic editor turned governor, William Brownlow, controlled the government, but a growing number of Conservative Unionists thought the state's civil authority illegitimate. At a mass meeting on February 22, 1866, Conservatives supported the President's Recon-

---

[31] LaWanda and John H. Cox, *Politics, Principles, and Prejudice, 1865–1866* (New York, 1963), p. 51. For a discussion of Johnson's use of patronage in forging alliances, see *ibid.*, pp. 107–28; Ari Hoogenboom, *Outlawing the Spoils: A History of the Civil Service Reform Movement, 1865–1883* (Urbana, Ill., 1961), pp. 21, 23–24; Erick L. McKitrick, *Andrew Johnson and Reconstruction* (Chicago, 1960), pp. 377–94.

[32] McKitrick, *Andrew Johnson and Reconstruction*, pp. 397, 417–18.

[33] Prominent among the delegates to the Verandah House meeting were former Benton Democrats Frank Blair, Barton Able, and Samuel Glover, while James Rollins, William Switzler, and James Broadhead represented former Whigs. Southern sympathizers included Lewis Bogy and A. G. P. Garesche. Barclay, *The Liberal Republican Movement in Missouri*, pp. 67–69; Parrish, *Missouri Under Radical Rule*, pp. 57–58; Raymond D. Thomas, "A Study in Missouri Politics: Party Reorganization," *Missouri Historical Review* 21 (July, 1927): 579.

struction policies and sought to expose a Radical move to tighten the already repressive franchise law.[34] Ignoring public opinion, the legislature passed an even more rigorous voter qualification law. "Of course [summed the *Nation*] such a law provokes the bitterest hatred of a large majority of the population, and is pronounced infamous, tyrannical, and unconstitutional. Thus a thing which, as a matter of policy, Congress hesitates to do, which it does not attempt to do without a preparatory amendment to the Constitution, the Tennessee Legislature has done without scruple."[35] Radicals domination and repression not only thrust Conservative Unionists into opposition but also united them with former Confederates.[36] In West Virginia the politically proscribed and those of Conservative principles co-operated informally while in Maryland they forged an actual Conservative–Democratic alliance.[37]

Events of the summer and fall of 1866 disappointed those Unionists determined to oust Radicals from power. They shared the high hopes of Senator James R. Doolittle for the "grand success" of the move to "organize or rather reorganize the *National* Union party in contrast with the *present* treacherous intolerant sectional Disunion [Republican] party,"[38] but their hopes were dashed. The Philadelphia Convention of Johnson supporters in August, 1866, failed to organize an effective National Union party because anti-Radical Unionists would

---

[34] *Annual Cyclopaedia . . . 1866*, 6:729. For Brownlow's career, see E. Merton Coulter, *William G. Brownlow, Fighting Parson of the Southern Highlands* (Chapel Hill, N. C., 1937).

[35] *Nation* 2, no. 47 (May 10, 1866): 593. For provisions of the franchise law, see *Annual Cyclopaedia . . . 1866*, 6:728.

[36] Alexander, *Political Reconstruction in Tennessee*, pp. 102, 131.

[37] For the background of the division in the Unionist's ranks in Maryland, see Clark, *Politics in Maryland*, pp. 95–100. For this January, 1866, meeting of Independent (Conservative) Unionists in Baltimore and the division between "Unionists" and "Conservatives," see Matthew Page Andrews, *History of Maryland: Province and State* (New York, 1929), pp. 559–60, 563; Myers, *The Self-Reconstruction of Maryland*, pp. 50–52. On the aborted coalition of the Democrats with the Conservatives, see Coulter, *Civil War and Readjustment in Kentucky*, pp. 296, 300–5. For the reaction of West Virginia Conservatives to proscription and Radicalism in general, see Gerofsky, "Reconstruction in West Virginia," pp. 309–10.

[38] James R. Doolittle to Mary Doolittle, Washington, July 1, 1866, Doolittle Papers, State Historical Society of Wisconsin, Madison. Doolittle predicted support from the Democrats, "who with the real friends of the Union in our party will constitute a very large majority of the people of the United States. . . . We must rally upon principle and organize the country. The offices will come as incidents." *Ibid.* For a dissenting view of the goals of the National Union Convention, see *Nation* 3, no. 60 (August 23, 1866): 150. For preconvention arrangements to bring the "right kind of men" to the Philadelphia convention and keep those with "past political sins" from gaining ascendancy, see John A. Dix to James Doolittle, New York, July 10, 1866, Doolittle Papers.

not be dominated by the Democrats who had captured the move-ment.[39] To counter the Johnson convention, the "Southern Loyalists," or Radicals, met in early September in Philadelphia.[40] By branding Johnson's supporters as disunionists and his programs as dangerous and unlawful, Radicals hoped to secure the congressional support essential for their survival.[41] Although ostensibly agreeing on con-gressional Reconstruction, the convention hopelessly divided over Negro suffrage; this question would soon divide border state Radicals permanently.

While Radicals won a smashing national victory in the 1866 con-gressional elections, the outcome in the border states reflected intense internal dissension. In the North, Johnson's disastrous "swing around the circle," growing hostility toward Southern attitudes on Recon-struction and the Negro, and a powerful Radical press all contributed to the victory of Johnson's enemies.[42] Radicalism also triumphed in Tennessee, Missouri, and West Virginia, where proscriptive measures hindered opposition candidates. In Maryland, however, Governor Thomas Swann, though an original supporter of that state's registration laws, joined with other leading Conservative Unionists—such as Mont-gomery Blair and Charles E. Phelps—and opposed Radical candidates. Although Radicalism, with its "control of the South by a duplicitous

[39] *Proceedings of the National Union Convention* (Philadelphia, 1866); Samuel Hoard to Lyman Trumbull, Chicago, July 21, 1866, Trumbull Papers, Illinois State Historical Library, Springfield; Roy F. Nichols, "A Great Party Which Might Have Been Born in Philadelphia," *Pennsylvania Magazine of History and Biography* 57 (October, 1933): 359–74. For an incisive analysis of the National Union movement and those politically disaffected Unionists who sought and failed to find a place within its framework, see McKitrick, *Andrew Johnson and Reconstruction*, pp. 394–420.

[40] Among the prominent border state politicians attending the Loyalist convention were James Speed, president of the convention, and Robert J. Breckinridge from Kentucky; Governor William Brownlow, William Stokes, and Joseph Fowler from Tennessee; Charles Fulton and J. A. J. Creswell from Maryland; Governor Arthur Boreman and A. W. Campbell from West Virginia; Governor Thomas Fletcher, J. W. McClurg, and J. F. Benjamin from Missouri. Carl Schurz was one of the leading speakers. *Proceedings of the Southern Loyalist Convention* (Philadelphia, 1866); Joseph Schafer, ed., *Intimate Letters of Carl Schurz, 1841–1869* (Madison, Wis., 1928), pp. 366–70.

[41] The original call for a Loyalist convention on July 4, 1866, stressed that to re-store the Union, Radical control was essential. "Under the doctrine of 'State Sovereignty' with rebels in the foreground, controlling Southern legislatures, and embittered by disappointment in their schemes to destroy the Union, there will be no safety for the loyal element. . . . Our reliance for protection is now on Congress, and the great Union party that has stood and is standing by our nationality, by the constitutional rights of the citizens and by the beneficent principles of the govern-ment." Quoted in Edward McPherson, *The Political History of the United States of America during the Period of Reconstruction* (Washington, 1871), p. 124.

[42] McKitrick, *Andrew Johnson and Reconstruction*, pp. 421–47; Kenneth M. Stampp, *The Era of Reconstruction, 1865–1877* (New York, 1965), pp. 114–18.

combination of aliens, low-class native whites, and freshly enfranchised negroes," allegedly repelled Swann, his political enemies claimed that he abandoned the Radicals because he coveted a United States Senate seat.[43] With his eye on the main chance, Swann's basic conservatism and his thirst for political power led him from Radical extremism toward a more stable and conservative political alliance. By appointing election supervisors lax in administering requisite test oaths, Swann paved the road for a Conservative (or "Independent") Unionist and Democratic coalition victory.[44]

Coalition politics in Kentucky presented an unusual problem. Though alarmed by the potential power of returning Confederates and Southern sympathizers, Unionists divided into Radical and Conservative camps on basic questions of patronage, Reconstruction, and Negro suffrage. Working through the Democratic party in the 1865 congressional and state elections, Conservatives gained an edge over Radicals, and by December, 1865, repealed wartime proscriptive legislation.[45] In turn, they were challenged by the antebellum, pro-Southern Democratic leaders who demanded immediate reinstatement within the political hierarchy. Efforts by Conservative Unionists to rally their flagging supporters failed when Confederates damned them for timidly acquiescing to emancipation, federal military excesses committed in the name of "Union," and national policies in general. Successfully dominating the "Courier Convention" held at Louisville on May 1, 1866, former Confederates emerged triumphant.[46] Recognizing the futility of working within the Democratic party, or of unilateral action, and temporarily setting aside principles and policies, Conservatives allied with Radicals to defeat the Confederate-led Democrats. In the subsequent canvass for state offices, Democrats endorsed Johnsonian Reconstruction, condemned congressional extremism, and urged a return to constitutional government, while coalitionists challenged them on *ex post facto* issues of union or secession, loyalty or rebellion. The campaign made "a con-

[43] Andrews, *History of Maryland,* p. 560; *Nation* 3, no. 71 (Nov. 8, 1866): 361; *ibid.* 4, no. 83 (Jan. 31, 1867): 82; Myers, *The Self-Reconstruction of Maryland,* p. 64.

[44] For the Baltimore Police Commissioners' dispute, see *Nation* 3, no. 69 (Oct. 25, 1866): 321; *ibid.* 3, no. 71 (Nov. 8, 1866): 362; J. Thomas Scharf, *History of Baltimore City and County* . . . (Philadelphia, 1881), pp. 163–64; Myers, *The Self-Reconstruction of Maryland,* pp. 65–79.

[45] Kentucky sent five Conservatives and four Radicals to Congress. In the state senate the Conservatives won twenty seats to the Radicals' eighteen, while there were sixty Conservatives and forty Radicals elected to the state house. Perrin, *Kentucky,* p. 474. For the repeal of proscriptive legislation, see Coulter, *Civil War and Readjustment in Kentucky,* pp. 287–95.

[46] For the platform adopted at the convention, see *Annual Cyclopaedia . . . 1866,* 6:425.

sistently loyal man in Kentucky . . . of all men most miserable, persecuted under foot, hooted at by rampant rebels. And . . . disowned and cast off by the government he hazarded all to support."[47] Voters rejected this expedient alliance of mutually antagonistic factions running on an obsolete platform. Political leadership and control thus passed into the hands of unreconstructed Democrats.[48]

The 1866 elections unsettled the border states. Success of Radical candidates in West Virginia, Missouri, and Tennessee, based on limited suffrage secured by test oaths, hardened opposition forces and laid the groundwork for permanent party organizations. Hostility to vindictive Radical policies drove erstwhile enemies into each other's arms. Daniel Lamb, the West Virginia "Code Maker," wrote to Judge Gideon D. Camden, a prominent former Confederate, as the 1866 campaign began: "However we may differ on certain points, yet in many we concur. We want a real peace—So do you. We want good government—So do you. We want to put an end to prosecution and proscription & So do you; and we are going to do it. If we can find no better way, we propose, like Gen. Grant, to wear out the adversary 'by mere attrition.' "[49] Democratic victories in Maryland and Kentucky were also unsettling. The charge by the Radical minority in Maryland that the successful Conservative-Democratic coalition negated "republican government" prompted congressional Radicals to investigate. A watchful, hostile Congress coupled with a small but influential Republican cadre further disturbed Maryland's political environment.[50] The Democratic victory in Kentucky under antebellum leaders reordered but did not end political opposition. Ousted from the Democratic hierarchy, and with their Radical alliance a miserable failure, Conservative Unionists were isolated into a third force.[51] With Radicals, Conservative Unionists, and pro-Southern Democrats venomously opposing each other, Kentuckians faced political turmoil.

By the 1866 election the secession-created Union coalition had disintegrated. Radical and Conservative Unionists split over emancipation, congressional and executive intervention in the border states, and Reconstruction of the South. Too inflexible to co-ordinate their

[47] _____ [illegible] to Joseph Holt, Hardinsburg, Kentucky, Sept. 18, 1866, Joseph Holt Papers, LC.

[48] Coulter, *Civil War and Readjustment in Kentucky*, pp. 300–11.

[49] Quoted in Curry, *A House Divided*, p. 134.

[50] For the congressional investigation into Maryland's "form of government," see *Nation* 5, no. 120 (Oct. 17, 1867): 305. For denying Maryland's senator-elect his seat because of suspected Southern sympathies, see *ibid.* 6, no. 139 (Feb. 27, 1868): 162.

[51] For a resolution summing up the position of the Conservative Unionists, see *Annual Cyclopaedia . . . 1867*, 7:423.

partisan goals with popular sentiment, the Radicals lost any opportunity they had to establish a permanent power base. Confident of support from congressional Radicals, they lacked the foresight to seek pragmatic accommodations with partisan dissidents or political adversaries. Left with only a small minority of the white voters, they used every available means to sustain their control. Maryland Radicals even attempted to induce Congress to reconstruct their state.[52] Except in Kentucky, Conservatives joined with former Confederates to challenge the Radicals' political domination. Desperately needing a popular power base, Radicals espoused Negro suffrage. But most Radicals, as well as Conservative Unionists and secessionists, feared the Negro. As early as 1863 the old Jacksonian and stanch Unionist Francis Preston Blair expressed this fear when he conjectured to his son Frank (soon to enter the Thirty-eighth Congress as a Representative from Missouri) "that the Negro is to be made the foundation of a northern aristocracy as heretofore of a Southern Oligarchy . . . by Capitalists as hirelings and gifted with equal rights among our poor citizens. . . . It strikes me as possible that the whole struggle of parties growing out of slavery will work down to the point of negro citizenship and equality as the means of destroying our Democratic Institution."[53] In their uncompromising determination to grant Negroes the right to vote, Radical leaders disintegrated what was left of their moderate-white following. The Republican party became known as the "Nigger's Party" and was an anathema to white border state voters.

Anathema or not, border state Republicans moved to enfranchise the Negro. Though slavery was once as entrenched in these states as in the Confederacy, it was gone, and the establishment of the Freedmen's Bureau and the Union League Clubs and agitation for what became the Fourteenth Amendment seemed to forecast Negro suffrage.[54] Early in September, 1866, the *Nation* urged border state

[52] For congressional reaction, see *Congressional Globe*, 40th Cong., 1st sess., 415–19. For Democratic minority opinion against such investigations, see *ibid.*, 40th Cong., 2d sess., 230–31.

[53] Francis Preston Blair, Sr., to Francis Preston Blair, Jr., Silver Spring, Maryland, Dec. 23, 1863, Blair Family Papers, LC.

[54] Coulter, *Civil War and Readjustment in Kentucky*, pp. 278–80, 285–86; Perrin, *Kentucky*, pp. 475–77; Weymouth T. Jordan, "The Freedmen's Bureau in Tennessee," *East Tennessee Historical Society Publications* 11 (1939): 47–61. "I see by your remarks," a constituent wrote his senator, "that you wish the freedman's bureau to have jurisdiction over Maryland because some of the freedmen have been badly treated by returned rebel soldiers. . . . I can assure you that there is the very best feelings between the whites and blacks in this as well as the adjacent counties & certainly there must be some mistake on the part of your informant relative to the bad treatment you referred to. Certainly our state government can & will no doubt protect the negroes in their rights of persons and property without the aid of the so called freedman's bureau." R. V. Page to John A. J. Creswell, Callington, Maryland, Jan. 23, 1866, Creswell Papers, LC.

Unionists to enfranchise the Negro: "The Union men of the Border States, such as Tennessee . . . must have the aid of negroes as voters, or these States will be ruled by people who are still rebels in wish and will. . . . A demand for negro suffrage made by these men would have great weight with the country, and no doubt, the Union majority will feel considerably strengthened in its present position."[55] Some Radical Unionists, however, favored immediate suffrage for the freedman, while maintaining proscriptive measures against the formerly "disloyal." Others supported universal manhood suffrage, enabling both the proscribed and the Negro to vote. Still others favored the removal of political disabilities from the white population, coupled with the gradual extension of Negro suffrage.

After the 1866 elections, Negro suffrage did indeed become the focal point of border state party disputes. Though in power since 1865, Tennessee's Governor William Brownlow and Radical cohorts had avoided the question of Negro suffrage. When it became apparent in early January, 1867, that without Negro support Radical control would be upset, Brownlow urged the Tennessee legislature to enfranchise freedmen immediately.[56] The legislature granted the Negro the vote, but denied him the basic rights to hold office or serve on a jury.[57] Obviously, newly enfranchised voters would support Radicalism, and it was equally clear that the Radicals widened the suffrage, not from ideological commitment but simply to stay in office. Negro suffrage was a weapon, not a cause. Attempts by the Conservative Union party, an amalgam of moderate and conservative former Whigs, Democrats, and dissatisfied Radicals, to attract the Negro voter during the canvass of 1867 failed. Radicals reaped nine-tenths of the Negro vote by giving the Negro the essence, though denying him the substance, of democracy.[58]

Similar conditions existed in Missouri. Although Democrats had little influence within the state, their apparent willingness to join with those Republicans opposed to proscription presented a future threat to Radicalism. Challenged by Democrats without and dissension within, Radical leaders there also embraced Negro suffrage. Radical refusal to conciliate the disaffected white majorities made broadening their constituents to include both Negro and white

[55] *Nation* 3, no. 62 (Sept. 6, 1866): 182.
[56] Alexander, *Political Reconstruction in Tennessee*, p. 130; Patton, *Unionism and Reconstruction in Tennessee*, pp. 124–43.
[57] Alexander, *Political Reconstruction in Tennessee*, pp. 130–31.
[58] "Southern Politics," *Nation* 5, no. 110 (Aug. 8, 1867): 110. Negro Conservatives did meet in convention at Nashville on April 5 and adopted resolutions supporting the "Union Conservatives." *Annual Cyclopaedia . . . 1867*, 7:707.

citizens impossible. By uncompromisingly demanding that Negro suffrage stand alone and not be contingent upon removing the voting disabilities of whites, the Radicals further alienated moderate factions within their organization.[59] As atttudes hardened, intra-party factions struggled for control of the Radical political machinery. Differing over plans for political reconciliation and social economic progress, dissidents fought Radical leaders for power and patronage. Failing to gain control of their party, some of these anti-Radical Unionists allied themselves with the Democratic party, but most waited within the party for the opportunity to regain power.

In West Virginia, however, Radicals shied away from Negro suffrage and nothing was accomplished until the nation adopted the Fifteenth Amendment. With widespread "Negrophobia" in Republican as well as Democratic ranks, Radical leaders feared white backlash would more than offset the 3,600 potential Republican Negro voters. Furthermore, those potential voters were politically insignificant when compared to almost 20,000 disfranchised former Confederates. Indeed, as a leading West Virginia Republican explained to Charles Sumner:

we must relax the rigor of our policy towards our ex-rebels in order to maintain ourselves as a party in the State. Our present laws not only exclude them from the ballot but do not permit them to pursue the vocations of law and teaching, nor to sue in the courts, act as jurors or hold any official position however unimportant. . . . Unless we inaugurate measures for repeal promptly, my conviction is that they will carry the State over our heads long before 1872. Our only hope of perpetuating Republican ascendancy in the State is by a magnanimous policy which shall bring a portion of the ex-rebels into cooperation with us when they become voters. A very large number of them were old line whigs before the war. They do not like the Democracy and they would come to us if we gave them the ballot. But if we wait for the Democrats to enfranchise them, they will, of course fall into that party.[60]

Factionalism was also rampant in the states under Democratic control. Although Kentucky had been "redeemed" by 1866, its politics remained chaotic. While the Union party fragmented, Confederate Democrats overwhelmed Union Democrats and controlled the Kentucky Democracy. "There was," Henry Watterson exclaimed, "a party of reaction in Kentucky, claiming to be Democratic, playing

[59] For dissatisfaction among Republicans with Radical determination to continue proscription, see Parrish, *Missouri under Radical Rule*, pp. 268–73, 278–86.

[60] Granville D. Hall to Charles Sumner, Sept. 14, 1869, copy in Granville Davisson Hall Papers, West Virginia Collection, West Virginia University Library, Morgantown. We are indebted to Richard Orr Curry for this quotation.

to the lead of the party of repression at the North. It refused to admit that the head of the South was in the lion's mouth and that the first essential was to get it out.[61] By March, 1867, Kentucky boasted three distinct political organizations: Democratic, Radical, and Conservative Union Democratic. The awkward Radical–Conservative coalition of 1866 disintegrated immediately after its disastrous rout at the polls and an uneasy truce resulted between the successful Southern Democrats and their Union Democratic opponents, whom they had so unceremoniously jettisoned. Rumor that former Confederates would monopolize nominations at the February 22, 1867, Frankfort convention provoked speculation that Union Democrats would form a third party. When rumor turned to reality, the Unionists, led by Lieutenant Governor Richard Jacob, bolted the convention and called for a new political organization. "[Y]ou have forsaken the Democratic party," cried a "Rebel." "Yes I have," responded a bolter, "because my party are all Rebels . . . and you would bring on a war now had you the power."[62] Four days later optimistic Radicals[63] convened at the Capitol and adopted nominees and a platform designed to capture Conservative support.[64] But their plan failed. Democratic dissidents found more congenial company among prominent conservatives of Whig antecedents, and on March 6 the Conservative Union party was born. Denouncing both congressional Radicalism and Southern partisanship, it claimed to be in sentiment and policy the national Democratic party's true representative in Kentucky. In the special May congressional election, however, Southern sympathizers overwhelmed their opponents. With a plurality of 48,649 votes over the Radicals and 71,377 over the Conservative candidates, the Democrats captured all nine congressional seats.[65] The August state elections additionally and emphatically proved that Southern Democrats dominated Kentucky politics. Though refused concessions, Conservatives recognized their hopeless position and crawled back to the

[61] Henry Watterson. *"Marse Henry": An Autobiography* (2 vols.; New York, 1919), 1: 173.

[62] Coulter, *Civil War and Readjustment in Kentucky*, pp. 320–21; C. C. Green to Joseph Holt, Louisville, March 1, 1867, Holt Papers, LC.

[63] "If the Democrats are controlled by the rebel element on the 22nd, as I believe they will be, we can beat them. The quiet pluck & determination of the Radicals has amazed the Rebels and confounded the Conservatives. It begins to look like we would promptly recover from the confusion of last summer." James Speed to Robert J. Breckinridge, Louisville, Feb. 20, 1867, Breckinridge Family Papers, LC.

[64] Written by James Speed, the platform supported neither executive nor congressional policies. It declared for the restoration of the Southern states to their proper place in the Union, but reaffirmed opposition to "the rebel Democracy" in Kentucky. Coulter, *Civil War and Readjustment in Kentucky*, pp. 322–23.

[65] *Annual Cyclopaedia . . . 1867*, 7:423.

Democratic party.[66] The *Nation* darkly foresaw that "time, or Mr. Sumner's bill for national impartial suffrage" were the only weapons available to combat reactionary forces in Kentucky.[67]

Desperate to oust the Democrats, a few Kentucky Radicals urged Congress to reconstruct the state, but others preferred Democratic domination to federal occupation and interference with political and social institutions. Although some Radical Republicans in Congress moved to exclude seven of the newly elected Democratic delegation, the House refused to seat only two of the nine Democratic congressmen-elect.[68] With the Democratic congressional delegation relatively intact, the scheme to reconstruct Kentucky collapsed.

With the adoption of the Fifteenth Amendment, Radicals attempted to increase their power base by an alliance with freedmen. They engineered a Negro Republican convention at Frankfort in February, 1870, which roundly endorsed their colleagues' policies, as well as belief in God and the restriction of Chinese Labor.[69] The Democrats shrewdly did not attack Negro suffrage openly. To offset nearly 100,000 potential Negro votes they counted on their own solid organization and the defection of Radicals infuriated by the Fifteenth Amendment. Yet Democrats did not rely completely on organization and white backlash. Threats to Negroes about future employment, insistence on receipts at the polls for taxes that freedmen were not required to pay, and inadequate polling facilities limited the Negro vote.[70] Another and larger Democratic victory in the August, 1870, elections ended meaningful Radical opposition in Kentucky. The clash, however, between those anxious to forget the war and to formulate current economic and social policies and the Democratic leaders whose antebellum policies made them anxious to remember the war, fostered intra-party factionalism and, ultimately, open rebellion.

Almost immediately after coming to power in January, 1867, Maryland's Democratic–Conservative coalition attempted to destroy the props of Radical power, such as test oaths, registration laws, and constitutional disfranchisement. To restore "constitutional" order the coalition majority repealed prohibitory qualifying legislation and

[66] The results of the overwhelming Democratic victory over Conservatives is discussed, *ibid.*, pp. 323, 411–12.

[67] *Nation* 5, no. 110 (Aug. 8, 1867): 101.

[68] For Radical reaction to the return to power of the Southern Democracy and plans to prevent the newly elected Democratic congressional delegation from being seated, see Coulter, *Civil War and Readjustment in Kentucky*, pp. 329–38.

[69] *Proceedings of the First Republican Convention of the Colored Citizens of the State of Kentucky* (Frankfort, Ky., 1870).

[70] Coulter, *Civil War and Readjustment in Kentucky*, pp. 425–33.

called a constitutional convention to obliterate traces of Radical
control. Bent on utilizing potential Negro voters, Republicans demanded that the new constitution include an impartial suffrage
amendment. But the coalition leadership rejected this suggestion, and
it received little consideration from the convention delegates. Indeed,
not all Maryland Republicans favored Negro suffrage. Some abandoned the Republican party when the state committee espoused
Negro suffrage, while others, equally opposed, remained within the
party biding their time.[71] Despite opposition within and overwhelming opposition outside the party, Maryland Republicans continued
to call for Negro suffrage and with the passage of the Fifteenth
Amendment realized the much sought alliance with Negroes. In the
1870 congressional elections, Republicans reduced Democratic majorities but failed to significantly challenge Democratic supremacy.[72]

Democratic losses indicated both growing Republican strength and
growing Democrat discontent.[73] As in Kentucky, many Maryland
Democrats rejected the reactionary policies of their leaders and
struggled with them for party control. Underscoring this struggle was
the battle between the Pennsylvania and the Baltimore and Ohio
railroads for a rail monopoly from Baltimore to Washington. This
issue was so disruptive that political careers and the general welfare
of the state often depended on the desires of the railroad lobbyists at
Annapolis. Incessant demands by these two major railroad companies upon the successful and overconfident Democrats encouraged
party disagreement over the railroads' influence on state politics.[74]
This disagreement further widened differences within the party
structure and enlarged the split in the organization.

Around 1870, certain patterns became apparent in the tangled
skein of border state politics. Radicals emerged from the war with
much ambition but little popular support. As Andrew Johnson's
lenient policies toward the South and the Democratic party became
an obvious threat, Republicans, for political as well as social and

[71] Myers, *The Self-Reconstruction of Maryland*, pp. 30, 83–112.

[72] In the 1869 state elections Democrats gained complete control of the Maryland
legislature and their candidate for comptroller of the treasury received a majority
of 29,342 votes. *Annual Cyclopaedia . . . 1869*, 9:410. In the 1870 congressional elections, the Democratic majority was reduced to 19,015. *Annual Cyclopaedia . . .
1870*, 10:468.

[73] Democratic majorities had been on the decline since the 1868 presidential election. The Democratic majority in the 1868 contest was 31,919; the 1870 congressional elections gave Democrats a majority of 18,778. The gubernatorial election
of 1871 gave Democrats a majority of 15,135. *Annual Cyclopaedia . . . 1871*, 11:486.

[74] Railroad influences in postwar Maryland are discussed in Frank R. Kent, *The
Story of Maryland Politics* (Baltimore, 1911), pp. 24–25, 30–32.

economic reasons, sought aid from congressional Radicals. Federal support breathed life into Radicalism and made this curiosity within a traditionally conservative society a force with which to contend. Where Radicalism held sway, however, division among its advocates ultimately destroyed or rendered it powerless. Radicals differed less upon political ideology than upon practical solutions to partisan problems. Their debilitating disagreements over proscribing former Confederates, enfranchising Negroes, and abandoning partisan inflexibility were rooted as much in differing concepts of political strategy as in ideological commitments.

The dominant Democratic party in Maryland and Kentucky suffered the same dissension, fragmentation, and division as its Radical counterpart in Missouri, Tennessee, and West Virginia. Its leaders primarily wished to re-establish the antebellum status-quo society. On the other hand, a Democratic minority wanted to repudiate secession, accept the verdict of war, follow the national party and thus make the "new departure," regain political respectability, and develop responsible positions on current problems. But above all policy differences, leaders of dissident Democrats wished to wrest party control and power from the ruling clique. Whether Democratic leaders fought for a new socio-economic order or the antebellum status quo, for Hamilton or Jefferson, or a combination of both, self-interest and expediency helped determine their choice of policy, just as it did the Radicals'.

In Missouri, Tennessee, and West Virginia, the moderate or "liberal" wing of the Radical party ultimately helped defeat extreme Radicalism. When Carl Schurz won a United States Senate seat in 1869, Moderates struck a mortal blow at Missouri Radicalism.[75] Schurz conceived of Radicalism as "narrowly despotic"[76] and rhapsodized that his victory signaled "the disappearance of the dour party zealotry . . . and its replacement by a liberal policy. It is the substitution of a friendly, forgiving policy for the bitter feeling of hatred which originated in the war and has characterized the spirit of the party struggle up to this point."[77] Perhaps more important, Schurz's victory gave him and the Moderates power within the Republican ranks to activate a political chain of events that in 1871 destroyed

[75] Barclay, *The Liberal Republican Movement in Missouri*, pp. 150–62; Parrish, *Missouri Under Radical Rule*, pp. 259–67; Carl Schurz, *The Reminiscences of Carl Schurz* (3 vols.. New York, 1907–8), 3:293–301; Schafer, *Intimate Letters of Carl Schurz*, pp. 458–68.

[76] Carl Schurz to Margaretha Meyer Schurz, Jefferson City, Mo., Jan. 10, 1869, Schurz Papers, State Historical Society of Wisconsin.

[77] Carl Schurz to Margaretha Meyer Schurz, St. Louis, Jan. [no day], 1869, *ibid.*

Radicalism. The party thus disorganized was left defenseless against the increasing partisan aggressiveness of the Democrats now standing ready to capitalize upon the disintegration within the Republican organization. Dissident strife among Radicals climaxed in late August and early September, 1870, at their state convention. When that convention—dominated by extreme radicals—failed to endorse three constitutional amendments designed to end white proscription, dissidents bolted. These bolters, or Liberal Republicans, nominated former Senator Benjamin Gratz Brown for governor and with transitory Democratic aid defeated the Radicals. Following the defeat of Radicalism and the Democracy's legislative gains in the 1870 elections, Democrats abandoned their bipartisan stance and by 1872 controlled Missouri completely.[78]

The Missouri Liberal Republican bolt had national overtones. President Ulysses S. Grant, already attacked as incompetent and inept by congressional antagonists, believed it the opening gun of the 1872 campaign and used his power to defeat the bolters.[79] With such articulate spokesmen as James Rollins and William Grosvenor in Missouri and the national publicity given the schism by Carl Schurz, Charles Sumner, and Jacob Dolson Cox, the Liberal Republican movement seemed rooted in Missouri soil. By January, 1872, Grosvenor, Brown, and other Missouri Liberals called for a Cincinnati convention to unite the disenchanted.[80] Liberal Republicanism had broadened into a national movement.

Less publicized events charged the political atmospheres in other border states. As in Missouri, the overt provocation for liberal dissent from Radical rule in Tennessee and West Virginia lay in political proscription and Negro suffrage. And, as in Missouri, the opportunity to seize the party and the spoils of office did not escape the party recalcitrants.

[78] Parrish, *Missouri Under Radical Rule*, pp. 291–98, 309–19, 323–24. *Annual Cyclopaedia . . . 1870*, 10:516–22. For an analysis of Missouri voting in the senatorial election of 1869, the gubernatorial election of 1870, and the presidential election of 1872, see Michael Burlingame, "Liberal Republicanism in Missouri, 1869–1872" (seminar paper, Johns Hopkins University, May, 1966).
[79] Earle Dudley Ross, *The Liberal Republican Movement* (New York, 1919), pp. 31–32; Thomas A. Bailey, "A History of Party Irregularity in the Senate of the United States, 1869–1901" (Ph.D. diss., Stanford University, 1927), p. 63; *Nation* 11, no. 275 (Oct. 6, 1870): 214–15; "Things Plain to Be Seen," *ibid.* no. 276 (Oct. 13, 1870): 232; *ibid.* no. 281 (Nov. 17, 1870): 322; Patrick W. Riddleberger, "The Break in the Radical Ranks: Liberals vs. Stalwarts in the Election of 1872," *Journal of Negro History* 44 (April, 1959): 153.
[80] *Annual Cyclopaedia . . . 1872*, 12:552; Ross, *The Liberal Republican Movement*, pp. 51–52.

Attacked both by a reorganized Democracy and the Ku-Klux Klan and racked by internal dissension, Tennessee Radicalism weakened. The extremist policies of Governor Brownlow hopelessly divided Moderate and Radical Republicans.[81] By 1869 a fierce and inconclusive convention battle for the gubernatorial nomination split the party, and two Republican candidates ran for office. Moderate Republicans nominated DeWitt Senter, a Brownlow supporter who wished to end proscription. By supporting Senter, Democrats brought success to the Liberal element of the Republican party.[82] More important, however, Democrats gained a strategic foothold in the Radical-dominated political structure. The Tennessee Republican split enabled the Democrats to regain their traditional political control of the state, while it simultaneously condemned Moderate and Liberal Republicans to a futile search for political sanctuary. Noting only the Liberal Republican success and not realizing its long-run implications for all Republicans, the *Nation* urged "that some of the other Border States—notably Missouri . . . follow the new example Tennessee sets them."[83]

With a governor opposed to continued proscription and a state supreme court decision in May, 1869, rendering "unconstitutional the acts of the Legislature authorizing the Executive to set aside registrations of voters in cases of fraud and irregularities," Tennessee's voter registration law became inoperative. In the fall Democrats won the legislature. Disturbed by their defeat, Radical Republican leaders wanted Congress to reconstruct the state.[84] Disappointed by Grant and angered by the Radical suggestion of congressional interference, moderate Republicans (including some former Whigs)

[81] Alexander, *Political Reconstruction in Tennessee*, pp. 199–204.

[82] Brownlow resigned as governor on Feb. 12, 1869, to take a United States Senate seat on March 4. DeWitt Senter, speaker of the Tennessee senate, was inaugurated as governor on Feb. 25. At the Republican nominating convention in Nashville, May 20, Senter's gubernatorial nomination for a full term was challenged by William B. Stokes. Although opposed to continuing proscription, Stokes urged gradualism while Senter wanted an immediate end to electoral disabilities. Despite his earlier extremist stance, Brownlow supported Senter throughout the campaign. *Goodspeed's History of Tennessee* (Chicago, 1887), pp. 786–87; *Nation* 8, no. 205 (June 3, 1869) ; 425; *ibid.* 8, no. 207 (June 17, 1869) ; 465–66. For Senter's views on the franchise, see *Annual Cyclopaedia . . . 1869*, 9:663.

[83] *Nation* 8, no. 205 (June 3, 1869): 425. The Missouri bolt did not take place until early September.

[84] *Annual Cyclopaedia . . . 1869*, 9:663–64; Alexander, *Political Reconstruction in Tennessee*, pp. 234–37; *Goodspeed's History of Tennessee*, p. 788. The Democratic majority in the Senate was fifteen and in the House forty-nine. *Annual Cyclopaedia . . . 1869*, 9:664. For the attempt at Reconstruction and Governor Senter's testimony before the Congressional Reconstruction Committee at Washington, see *Annual Cyclopaedia . . . 1870*, 10:706–7.

drifted even further from the party. Hoping to attract former Union Conservatives from the Democracy, they wished to challenge both major organizations with a third party based on Whig principles. Having anticipated the Missouri Liberal bolt, Tennessee dissidents easily supported the call for the Cincinnati Convention of Liberal Republicans.[85]

By 1869 Radical control had exasperated West Virginia. Radical refusal to relieve the proscribed had alienated the more liberal and moderate elements within the Republican party. A three-way race among Republican, Liberal Republican, and Democratic candidates developed in the October, 1869, legislative elections. Many Conservative Republicans, adverse to an alliance with increasingly "belligerent" Democrats, hurried to the Liberal camp, and even some Democrats deserted their party's candidates for Liberal nominees. The election made it clear that a majority favored eliminating political disabilities. The ensuing legislative struggle among Republicans, over a constitutional amendment making Negro suffrage and the removal of disqualifications contingent upon one another, further widened the gulf between the factions. By 1870 the lack of unified party action, the backlash protest over Negro suffrage, the increasing strength of the Democratic party, and the lax enforcement of registration laws brought Republican defeat in the gubernatorial and general state elections.[86]

As in Missouri and Tennessee, dissident West Virginia Moderate Republicans had been stymied. Their own party leaders rejected attempts to broaden party appeal through liberal concessions to the disfranchised. The practical plan to widen the Republicans' power base was lost in the murky struggle for party control. The Republican defeat in 1870 loosened the remaining ties between the party factions. Many liberal dissenters left the party organization to the "bitter-enders" and sought elsewhere alliances which would prove salutary to their ambitions. When Missouri Liberals called for the Cincinnati Convention, West Virginia dissidents enthusiastically responded.[87]

In border states where Radicalism held away, Republican malcontents—frustrated for practical as well as ideological reasons—were guilty of political naïveté. To traditional Democratic constituencies,

[85] Alexander, *Political Reconstruction in Tennessee*, pp. 237–38.

[86] Curry, *A House Divided*, p. 135; Callahan, *History of West Virginia*, 1: 406–7; Gerofsky, "Reconstruction in West Virginia," pp. 330, 352–54.

[87] On April 18, 1872, Liberal Republicans and Liberal Democrats met at Parkersburg, West Virginia, and endorsed the Cincinnati call, urged the nomination of Salmon P. Chase, and adopted a liberal platform similar to the Missouri platform. *Annual Cyclopaedia . . . 1872*, 12:800.

alienated from and hostile to Radicalism, these dissidents issued a call for co-operation and coalition against an artificial power structure. The Democrats recognized that such unified action was practical. Co-operation with Liberal and Moderate Republicans offered them an opportunity to rid their states of Radical domination and to regain political control. Liberal and moderate Republicans, however, gained nothing but the transitory success of seeing Radicalism defeated within their states. Indifferent to or optimistically contented with Democratic assurances of unity and reconciliation, Republican dissidents helped destroy their party as an effective political force in the border states and found themselves faced with immediate political extinction. Unable to gain a hearing for their views from the national leadership, a third force marshaling both national and state discontent was their only hope of survival.

In Maryland and Kentucky, the struggle between Unionists and former Confederates had created dissension within the Democratic party. Though reactionaries "proposed to win in politics what had been lost in battle,"[88] they provoked opposition within their party. Missouri's call for a national reform convention was answered in Maryland by dissident Democrats as well as dissident Republicans, who, like former war governor Augustus Bradford, were angered and dismayed by national policies and state politics.[89] In Kentucky, the ambitious and able editor of the Louisville *Courier–Journal*, Henry Watterson, moved to oust the yeoman-dominated legislature and the planter-centered leaders of the Democratic party. He "proposed to lead and reform it, not to follow and fall in behind the selfish and short-sighted time servers who thought the people had learned nothing and forgot nothing."[90] The "new departure" Democrats also attacked the "reactionary" economic policies of Democratic leaders that failed to attract railroad, mining, and industrial enterprises to Kentucky.[91]

The internal clash over goals weakened the party despite continued success at the polls. Temporarily abandoning their "bloody shirt" candidates and platforms in the gubernatorial contest of 1871, Republicans nominated the highly respected Conservative John M. Harlan on a platform of social and economic reform. Though the lackluster Democratic candidate Preston H. Leslie became governor by utilizing

---

[88] Watterson, *"Marse Henry,"* 1:240. Although Watterson blames reactionary policies on the Union wing of the Kentucky Democratic party, the Confederates dominated both the party and Kentucky after 1866.

[89] *Annual Cyclopaedia . . . 1872*, 12:497.

[90] Watterson, *"Marse Henry,"* 1:177; Thomas D. Clark, *A History of Kentucky* (New York, 1937), pp. 584–87; Coulter, *Civil War and Readjustment in Kentucky*, pp. 435–37.

[91] Clark, *A History of Kentucky*, pp. 585–87; Coulter, *Civil War and Readjustment in Kentucky*, pp. 436–37.

the old formula of Northern extremism and Southern "rights," the party's stance disturbed moderate Democrats.[92] Without power base or patronage, they could not topple those in power, but the discontented had found in Watterson a leader whom they would follow in 1872.

Whether Radical or Democratic, border state ruling elites found themselves under increasing pressure by 1869. Intra-party schisms accompanied by increasing social and economic unrest demanded new leaders and new policies. Obtuse to the demands of a growing society, old leaders—whether restrictive Radicals or reactionary Democrats—pursued a rigid course designed to retain their personal political power. The thwarted political ambitions of challengers, coupled with readily available issues, produced formidable opposition within the dominant Radical and Democratic parties. Rebuffed on questions of policy, dissatisfied with economic progress, and divorced from the centers of power, frustrated dissidents declared their political independence. Parallel circumstances on the national level among former wielders of power and dictators of policy whom Grant had recently excluded from the decision-making process made an alliance probable.

Discontented Republicans forged a national alliance at the May, 1872, Cincinnati Convention.[93] The obvious opportunism of many present and the ludicrous nomination of Horace Greeley published to the world the cross-purposes of Liberal Republicans. Called to achieve tariff and administrative reform, the convention opposed Grant with a man who personified protection and had vilified civil service reform. Postwar state political factionalism was too weak a foundation for a permanent Liberal Republican structure. The shifting alliances and conflicting aspirations that characterized border state politics in the late 1860s and culminated in the Liberal Republican movement anticipated and magnified its fundamental weaknesses. Political oranges and apples were as impossible to add on the national as on the state level. Ironically, Democratic support enabled Greeley to carry the border states of Maryland, Kentucky, Tennessee, and Missouri, in addition to Georgia and Texas, but Ulysses S. Grant swept all the other states for the Republican party. Created from discontent, nourished by repression, and victimized by reality, the Liberal Republican movement was preordained for defeat.

[92] Clark, *A History of Kentucky*, pp. 585–86; Coulter, *Civil War and Readjustment in Kentucky*, p. 436.

[93] For the most recent insight into the Cincinnati convention, see Matthew T. Downey, "Horace Greeley and the Politicians: The Liberal Republican Convention in 1872," *Journal of American History* 53 (March, 1967): 727–50. For a broader view of the political factionalism that culminated in the Liberal Republican movement in 1872, see Riddleberger, "The Break in the Radical Ranks," pp. 136–57.

CHAPTER EIGHT

The Freedmen's Bureau in the Border States
W. A. Low

Introduction

The "dark and bloody ground" of Reconstruction reveals the Freedmen's Bureau as something of an anomaly, an anachronistic creation of its time, an unprecedented and controversial arm of the government during a period of turmoil in the nation's history. Within the border states and the South, the Freedmen's Bureau was an ill-fated innovation, an agency charged with the new and difficult task of implementing freedom and equality for nearly four million ex-slaves.

The Bureau was neither consciously nor carefully planned to serve the purposes of a social agency of government, either for postwar rehabilitation or for long-range experimentation. Its work, however, anticipated the philosophical and practical necessity of replacing the old slave régime with a viable program for extending the nation's ideals of freedom and equality to an oppressed and displaced people.

When regarded in this light, it may be seen that the Bureau, even with its scant resources, attempted to bridge the educational and cultural chasm between the freed Negro and the white American middle class. Bridging the chasm was not only complicated by the problems of readjustment caused by war but by the racist attitudes of an overwhelming majority of white Americans. Confronted by political opposition and overt violence, the Bureau's task was not an enviable one. Its very existence was regarded by many as an affront and a threat to white supremacy. Even if racial antagonism had not existed, however, the Bureau would still have been embroiled in controversy. It was, after all, an agency of the federal government which had no precedent in the nation's history.

The Role of the Bureau in the Border States

Generally, the aims and objectives of the Bureau were essentially the same in the border states as in the Deep South. Its work fell into four clearly defined categories, namely, *relief:* by providing food, clothing, shelter, and medical care for freedmen and refugees; *the administration of justice:* by protecting the political and civil rights

245

of black men; *protection:* by defending freedmen from physical violence or fraud, by military arms if necessary; and *education:* by cooperating with agencies, individuals, and local officials in providing schools and teachers for freedmen. In the border states, however, the Bureau's most significant work was performed in the field of education. Indeed, the Bureau was responsible for much of the formal education provided for freedmen.[1] Unlike the Deep South, however, the border slaveholding states had not seceded from the Union. Thus, the borderland was not affected by congressional Reconstruction. In this area Bureau activities were rarely supported by federal troops, and, in most instances, had to endure the indifference and hostility of state officials.

Maryland

Paul S. Peirce, who wrote the first comprehensive history of the Bureau, summarized its role in education quite accurately when he wrote:

It inaugurated a system of instruction, though it did not perfect that system nor assure its continuance. It gave central organization, encouragement, protection, and financial support to the efforts of philanthropists, freedmen, and states. By affording protection and encouragement, it induced more teachers to engage in the education of Negroes. By extending government supervision and sanction, it inspired philanthropists with increased confidence in the work of the benevolent and religious societies.[2]

---

[1] There is no adequate general history of Negro education and the few in existence give only scant recognition to Bureau efforts. Horace Mann Bond, *The Education of the Negro in the American Social Order* (New York, 1934; rev., 1965), however inadequate as a history, has been a standard reference for many years. D. O. W. Holmes, *The Evolution of the Negro College* (New York, 1934), is neither profound nor penetrating. Henry A. Bullock, *A History of Negro Education in the South: From 1619 to the Present* (Cambridge, Mass., 1967), surveys the field more widely but with hardly more success, depth, or bibliographic excellence; his sources are limited and he adds little to the scholarship of the field.

[2] Paul S. Peirce, *The Freedmen's Bureau; A Chapter in the History of Reconstruction* (Iowa City, Iowa, 1904), p. 83.

A separate assistant commissioner for Maryland was appointed in March, 1866. The command included all of the state except the counties of Montgomery, Prince Georges, Charles, Calvert, and St. Marys which remained under the jurisdiction of the District of Columbia. In June, 1866, six counties of Virginia and two of West Virginia were added to the Maryland command and called the Shenandoah Division, which itself was transferred to the Virginia command the following September. On Jan. 16, 1867, by Special Order Number Seven, Delaware was added to the Maryland command, then under the command of General Edgar M. Gregory. (*Note:* This section on Maryland is adapted from the author's article, "The Freedmen's Bureau and Education in Maryland," *Maryland Historical Magazine* [March, 1952], with permission of the Director of the Maryland Historical Society.)

Peirce's analysis, which is concerned primarily with the activities of the Bureau in the Deep South, also applies to Maryland. While this state was not one of the "military districts" established to administer the "insurrectionary" or "rebel" states, the Bureau was quite active in Maryland. Unlike the states of the Deep South, however, the Bureau's work in Maryland did not extend to medical and food services or to the care and disposition of "abandoned" Confederate property. With the exception of settling veterans' bounty claims, the Bureau in this state was concerned largely with the closely related problems of education and the administration of justice.

In attempting to provide education for Negro youths in Maryland, the Bureau was faced with the problem of protecting school-age children from a system of illegal apprenticeship. This system carried the stamp of its slave origins, binding many young Negroes to their former masters for indefinite periods of time. The apprenticeship system was adopted by pro-slave interests when it became apparent that there would be no compensation for former slaveholders and that Negroes could readily be apprenticed in some areas of the state, with the consent of local authorities. The federal government, acting through the Bureau, could not always enforce its program of emancipation and civil rights. Making allowance for the number of cases that were not reported and the prevalence of the system on the Eastern Shore and in Southern Maryland, approximately ten thousand young Negroes were bound out as apprentices between 1864–67. A universal complaint made by former masters against the establishment of schools for Negroes was that children would be taken away from the fields.[3] Thus, in its fight against the apprenticeship system, the Bureau gave indirect encouragement to Negro education.

The Bureau's attack upon the apprenticeship system was so successful that the Orphans Court in most counties soon abandoned the practice. General Edgar M. Gregory, Freedmen's Bureau Commissioner for Maryland, stated in 1867 that "reports from the counties show that the system has begun to yield to the continual pressure brought through this office and the legal solicitors of the State."[4] It was expressly forbidden by the Maryland Constitution of 1867, and by the summer of 1868 the apprenticeship system had virtually been destroyed.[5]

[3] Record Group 105, Maryland, report by George J. Stannard to O. O. Howard, June 30, 1866.

[4] Record Group 105, Maryland, report by Edward Ketchem, April 11, 1867.

[5] Record Group 105, Maryland, report by Horace M. Brooks to O. O. Howard, May 29, 1868; letter from Brooks to Howard, July 29, 1868.

The Freedmen's Bureau also provided direct aid in establishing the first school system for Negroes in Maryland. The Bureau furnished materials, equipment, and money for the construction, rental, or repair of school houses. In addition, protection and transportation were provided for teachers hired by civic and religious groups. The Bureau's educational activities began at a time when state support for public schools was nonexistent for Negroes and in its infancy for whites. The traditionally negative attitude of Marylanders toward public education, combined with a scarcity of state funds, prevented the establishment of a satisfactory public school system—even for whites. These factors, combined with racism, resulted in an almost complete neglect of the needs of freedmen.

The first annual report of the Reverend Libertus Van Bokkelen, Maryland's first superintendent of public instruction, recommended that the state provide separate schools for Negroes in "every district where 30 or more pupils will regularly attend."[6] But Van Bokkelen, a former president of St. John's College, Annapolis, frankly admitted that nothing "has been done for this class in the State." In fact, the state provided practically no material support for Negro education during the first five years after the war—and this, despite the fact that the Maryland constitutions of 1864 and 1867 expressly stipulated that a uniform system of education be established to serve *all* school-age children. According to the annual reports of the State Board of Education, the amount of money spent by the state of Maryland (excluding Baltimore) on Negro education amounted to only $4,580.31 in 1870.[7] In other words, the allocation by the legislature in 1870 amounted to only one-fifth as much as the Bureau spent annually from 1867 onward.

As in other states, private and religious philanthropic organizations also made important contributions to Negro education. Prominent among these groups were the Baltimore Association, the American Missionary Association, and the Freedmen's Union Association. All, with the exception of the Baltimore Association, were national groups established to provide relief for freedmen. Many of the first Negro schools in the state were founded by these organizations.

The work of the Baltimore Association was by far the most impressive. In fact, the Association's co-operation with the Freedmen's Bureau was instrumental in the establishment of the first state-wide system of Negro schools. The Association was a nonsectarian civic group founded in December, 1864. It obtained its support primarily from local

---

[6] Maryland State Board of Education, *Annual Report* (1866), p. 64.
[7] *Ibid.* (1870), p. 6.

sources, but by 1867 financial difficulties forced it to seek funds elsewhere. Its search did not meet with overwhelming success, and by 1869 its treasury was depleted. As a result the Association was forced to stop sending its representatives throughout the state for purposes of examining and supervising Negro education.[8] In 1867–68, however, the Association requested and received $12,000 from the Freedmen's Bureau to aid in the establishment of a "Colored Normal School" in Baltimore.[9] Several years later the school began to receive some financial support from the state. In 1911 the school was moved to Bowie, becoming the Maryland Normal and Industrial School, later the Maryland State Teachers College at Bowie.

Despite several notable successes engineered by the Bureau, the Baltimore Association, and other groups, public hostility to Negro education sometimes erupted into violence. J. W. Alvord, the Bureau's national superintendent of education, reported in 1866 that:

The educational work in Maryland has had much opposition, such as "stoning children and teachers at Easton," "rough-handling and blackening the teachers at Cambridge," "indignation-meeting in Dorchester county, with resolutions passed to drive out the teacher," and the "burning of a church and school-house in Annapolis"; etc. Colored churches have been burned in Cecil, Queen Anne [sic], and Somerset counties, to prevent schools being opened in them, all-showing that negro hate is not by any means confined to the low[er] South.[10]

Reaction was strongest in the old slave belt areas, principally the Eastern Shore and Southern Maryland on the western shore. There were some rumors that the Klan would be organized in the state, but these did not materialize. Despite evidence of occasional violence within the state,[11] resentment never burst into the full-blown conflict that characterized some aspects of Reconstruction in Kentucky and

[8] Record Group 105, Maryland, report by Charles McDougall to Edward C. Knower, March 5, 1867.

[9] In one of his earliest printed reports (1866), the Bureau's national superintendent of education, John W. Alvord, made a brief statement that thirty-four schoolhouses were to be built in Maryland from government lumber. See John W. Alvord, *Semi-Annual Report on Schools for Bureau of Refugees, Freedmen, and Abandoned Lands* (Washington, D.C., 1866), p. 19. John Watson Alvord was a central figure in the history of the Bureau. He studied at Lane Theological Seminary and Oberlin College. While attending the former, he taught in a Negro school in Cincinnati, and some of his former students later became important leaders in freedmen's activities in the South. He also served as a minister of Congregational churches in Connecticut and Massachusetts. For a brief biographical sketch, see Henry L. Swint, *The Northern Teacher in the South* (Nashville, Tenn., 1941), pp. 143–44.

[10] Alvord, *Semi-Annual Report* (1866), p. 13.

[11] See, for example, Record Group 105, Maryland, report by Thomas H. Gardner, Oct., 1866.

some areas of the Deep South. Hostility directed against the Bureau, the Negro, and Negro schools began to subside even before the Bureau closed its headquarters in Baltimore. As the years passed, much of the bitter opposition to Negro education disappeared.

Kentucky

The activities of the Freedmen's Bureau in Kentucky were supervised by authorities in Tennessee in 1866. As a result, the Bureau's effective period of operation in the bluegrass state was limited to only two years. In Kentucky, as elsewhere in the border states, the Bureau's work was confined largely to educational endeavors.[12] Considering the size of Kentucky's Negro population and its need for protection, this was unfortunate. Such agencies and facilities as freedmen's courts, labor farms, and labor colonies, which were characteristic features of Bureau activities in the Deep South, did not exist in Kentucky. Consolidated reports for the last quarter of 1867 when Bureau operations reached their peak reveal that its involvement in noneducational matters was extremely limited.[13] A statistical breakdown compiled from these reports reads as follows:

	October	November	December
Number of labor contracts	7	6	11
Abandoned minors or apprentices	9	6	0
Fines	0	0	0
Forfeitures	0	0	0
Outrages and cruelties against freedmen by whites	15	7	3
Arrests (for same)	4	0	0
Rations issued	0	480	496
Clothing issued	0	0	0
Number of suits adjudicated	9	9	12
Number of marriage certificates issued	2	0	2
Soldier claims forwarded	9	10	10

[12] Kentucky was divided into five districts: Northwest, Southwest, Louisville, Central, and Lexington. Lexington, the hub of the bluegrass country, was not only the center of the old slave belt but it was the most important district from the standpoint of the operational importance of the Bureau (and also for the relative volume of extant manuscript material in Record Group 105). One of the first reports from the Lexington District in June, 1866 (other districts were not sending in reports at this time) lists only two teachers for two schools being maintained by the Bureau. See Record Group 105, Kentucky, School Report, June, 1866.

[13] Record Group 105, Kentucky, Reports on Operations, Lexington District, Oct., Nov., Dec., 1867.

Equally important, protection for the Bureau's operations in Kentucky was conspicuous by its absence. Violence in general and organized violence in particular made life extremely hazardous for Bureau officials and Negroes alike. In addition, violence was so widespread that freedmen's aid societies tended to avoid operations in this state. The fact that Kentucky had not seceded from the Union clearly compounded the Bureau's problems and it received very little support from either state or national authorities.

Nevertheless, in the fall of 1867, the Bureau maintained a staff of nearly sixty persons in the important Lexington district.[14] In this district alone, the Bureau maintained thirty-four schools, with only forty-six Bureau schools existing in the entire state. In addition to Lexington, there were schools in such well known places as Frankfort (2) and Versailles (1); and in such lesser known places as Africa (1) and Tiger (1).[15]

The small emphasis placed upon nonschool activity is shown in the Bureau's handling of labor contracts and apprentices. Inadequately staffed, the Bureau's refugee and labor activities were conducted mainly at Camp Nelson and Paducah, former "contraband" stations. Perhaps no more than six hundred labor contracts altogether were supervised by the Bureau. This number represents a bare trickle when compared with South Carolina, an example of a Deep South state, when in the summer of 1866 alone the Bureau approved 8,000 contracts effecting 130,000 workers; or more significantly it approved 300,000 contracts during its lifetime, according to Martin Abbott, *The Freedmen's Bureau in South Carolina, 1865–1872* (Chapel Hill, N.C., 1967), pp. 73, 131. The first labor contract for Kentucky, however, is preserved in Record Group 105 and clearly numbered as such. It was made at Camp Nelson between Jesse Graddy and Robert Hicks, a farmhand, for one hundred dollars for one year's service. Graddy signed and Hicks made "his mark" on Jan. 1, 1867 before J. W. Read, an agent of the Bureau, who was salaried at seventy five dollars per month. Needless to say, such contracts in Kentucky were hardly enforceable by the Bureau, which simply lacked the necessary enforcement machinery.

Akin to the contracts for adults were the apprenticeships of youths. This system seems to have been considerably less widespread in Kentucky than in Maryland. At least this may be concluded from the evidence found in the Bureau's records on Kentucky. Certainly, there is no evidence of the Bureau's successful attack against this "great injustice," as Howard called it, in Kentucky as compared with Maryland. For the Bureau's valiant attack against the system in Maryland, see W. A. Low, "The Freedmen's Bureau and Civil Rights in Maryland," *Journal of Negro History* 37 (July, 1952): Vol. 37, pp. 221–47. There is a need for further study of the Bureau in regard to the apprenticeship system in Kentucky. It is not clear, for example, whether the Bureau was acting unwittingly or unwillingly as a party to the indenture of Negro youths in the state.

[14] Record Group 105, Kentucky School Reports, Consolidated report by R. E. Johnston, Oct., 1867. Johnston served during the war with the 8th Pennsylvania Reserves and the 43rd U.S. Infantry. He was brevetted for gallantry and meritorious service at Gaines Mill and Fredericksburg.

[15] Record Group 105, Kentucky, Consolidated School Report, March, 1868.

Legally the Bureau provided support for these schools through its generally established policy of making rent payments amounting to fifteen dollars per room each month. It was empowered to pay the transportation of teachers but not their salaries. It did, however, pay the salaries of its civilian agents who served in capacities such as co-ordinators and supervisors, and in fact, if not in theory, rent payments by the Bureau were usually regarded as salary payments to teachers.

Most Bureau schools consisted of one room and one teacher. However, there were exceptions. Howard School in Lexington was by far the largest in the Bluegrass country, having an enrollment of 448 pupils out of a total enrollment of 2,834 in the entire district.[16] It was named for H. C. Howard who was appointed chief agent of the Lexington district on July 1, 1867, at a salary of $150 per month. The school had first opened a year earlier under the sponsorship of the American Missionary Association and the freedmen themselves. In addition to the Howard School there were four other schools in Lexington which were supported by the Bureau and by tuition paid by Freedmen.[17]

Berea was another important school in the Bluegrass district that received financial support and moral encouragement from the Bureau. It was the only integrated school in existence in Kentucky during the antebellum period, and one of the very few in the entire nation. Under pressure brought to bear in the wake of John Brown's raid, Berea was forced to close its doors to Negroes. With the coming of emancipation, and financial aid and encouragement from the Bureau, Berea readmitted Negroes.[18] J. A. R. Rogers, its principal, reported in February, 1868, that the school received $100 a month from the Bureau, in addi-

[16] Record Group 105, Kentucky, School Report for March, 1868. The Bureau required and usually received a monthly report from each school; reports were likewise consolidated for the entire district on a monthly basis. A great number of these reports for the numerous individual schools, as well as the consolidated reports, provide a rich source for students interested in the early institutional history of Negro education.

[17] Record Group 105, Kentucky, School Reports, Oct., 1867; March, 1868. There is also a brief reference to the Howard School in William Newton Hartshorn, ed., *An Era of Progress and Promise, 1863–1910* (Boston, 1910), p. 165, a valuable and highly illustrated work dealing with the early history of Negro educational institutions.

[18] Berea was forced again to close its doors to Negroes after its unsuccessful challenge against Kentucky's segregation laws; its appeal to the U.S. Supreme Court was denied in 1908 in *Berea College* v. *Kentucky*. In the face of this setback, however, Berea opened the segregated Lincoln Institute the following year (1909) at Lincoln, Kentucky. Lincoln was operating as a vocational high school when it was acquired by the state in 1947, according to C. H. Parrish, "The Education of Negroes in Kentucky," *Journal of Negro Education* (Summer, 1957), p. 359.

tion to a sizable grant to aid in the construction of four buildings. According to Rogers only 45 of the 155 students were white.[19] Thus, in keeping with the Bureau's national policy of aiding or establishing at least one institution of higher learning in each state where it operated, Berea benefited materially in a time of great need.

The Bureau encouraged several noteworthy attempts to establish schools in other areas. For example, in 1867 it contributed $17,000 for purchasing land and constructing a normal school in Louisville. The school was named the Ely Normal School and O. H. Robbins, a graduate of Oberlin College, was its first principal. The Runkle High School in Lebanon and the Runkle Institute in Paducah also received substantial aid from the Bureau. Both were named in honor of the Bureau's assistant commissioner, General Benjamin Piatt Runkle of Ohio.[20]

Other than the Freedmen's Bureau, the greatest financial support for schools in Kentucky came from freedmen themselves, and their support seems to have been more common in Kentucky than it was either in Maryland or Missouri. Only two well-established freedmen's aid societies operated in the state—the American Missionary Association and the Western Freedmen's Aid Commission—and their contributions were extremely limited. Many freedmen, at great personal sacrifice, became their own patrons. In many cases each pupil was required by the Bureau to pay a monthly tuition fee to supplement the grant by the Bureau (usually fifteen dollars a month per school). There was practically no support at the local governmental level. Quite unlike Missouri, county support for Negro schools in Kentucky came much later—long after Reconstruction ended. As in the Deep South, public education for the Negro in Kentucky was virtually non-existent until after the turn of the century.[21] As a result, the schools that the Bureau built or aided had a precarious existence. When the Bureau went out of existence many Negro schools closed their doors.

[19] Record Group 105, Kentucky, School Reports, 1868–70, Berea School Report for Feb., 1868.

[20] Runkle began his war service as a Captain in the 13th Ohio Infantry and was brevetted a Major General on Nov. 9, 1865. He was cited for gallantry and meritorious service on March 2, 1867, for action in the Battle of Shiloh. After a court martial in 1873, he was cashiered out of the service for misappropriation of monies connected with the Bureau. However, Runkle eventually took his appeal to the U.S. Supreme Court which on May 27, 1887, ruled that he was never legally cashiered on the charge of misappropriation of monies, and was thus entitled to his claim for longevity pay. See *United States Supreme Court Reports* (Rochester, N.Y., 1887), nos. 118–122, Book 30, p. 1172.

[21] W. A. Low, "The Education of Negroes Viewed Historically," in Virgil A. Clift, ed., *Negro Education in America*, Sixteenth Yearbook of the John Dewey Society (New York, 1962), p. 43.

Some survived, however, benefiting from financial support provided by religious or civic groups.

In the states of the borderland, Kentucky had the dubious distinction of being in the forefront in its violent opposition to the activities of the Freedmen's Bureau. Bureau officials, contemporary observers, and historians, whether traditional or revisionist in orientation, at least agree on this aspect of the Bureau's history in Kentucky. A "carnival of crime" swept through the state during Reconstruction. Bands of lawless terrorists known as "Regulators," "Skagg's Men," and "Rowzee's Band," threatened, bullied, and lynched throughout the state.[22] But the Bluegrass district, the region of the greatest Bureau activity, witnessed more violence than any other section.

General Howard took cognizance of violence in his official report of 1867. Since October of the preceding year, he stated, freedmen were victims of 20 murders, 18 shootings, 11 rapes, and 270 other cases of maltreatment.[23] T. K. Noble, the Bureau's able superintendent of schools for Kentucky, not only reported threats on the life of a teacher in 1868 but the murder of one of her pupils. He further declared: "The Ku-Klux were out parading through the streets . . . numbered over 100, all mounted and armed, and disguised in the usual manner."[24] Another report stated that an "armed band of about 50 men" burned down a freedmen's school.[25] Indeed, the burning of freedmen's schools was not uncommon; ten were burned and another blown up in a period of two years. One Bureau official commented that violence was a nightly occurrence in the state.

One group of Negroes from Frankfort courageously petitioned Congress for protection.[26] It claimed that the Klan was "riding nightly" over the countryside "going from county to county . . . spreading terror wherever they go, by robbing, whipping, ravishing and killing our people without provocation." The committee enumerated

---

[22] E. Merton Coulter, *The Civil War and Readjustment in Kentucky* (Chapel Hill, N.C., 1926), p. 359.

[23] O. O. Howard, *Report*, 1867, p. 72. There is no reason to downgrade these figures. On the contrary, there is reason to upgrade them. Under the prevailing atmosphere of terror or potential terror, when protection was practically nonexistent, friends or relatives of the victims, themselves fearing reprisals, often remained silent. Sometimes freedmen dissappeared under "unknown" circumstances, attacked by "unknown" persons. In either case, there was not much likelihood that identity would be revealed to the authorities. Indeed, it is quite probable that local authorities were actually in cahoots with the attackers in some instances.

[24] Alvord, *Semi-Annual Report* (Jan., 1869), p. 44. Though a former governor was accused of being a member, officials of the state persistently denied that the Klan operated in Kentucky.

[25] *Ibid.*

[26] U.S. Senate, 42d Cong., 1st sess.

a chronicle of terror, listing sixty-four attacks in the two year period from November, 1867, to December, 1869. The first ten items on the list were as follows:

1. A mob visited Harrodsburg in Mercer County to take from jail a man named Robertson, No. 14, 1867.
2. Smith attacked and whipped by Regulators in Zelun County, Nov., 1867.
3. Colored school house burned by incendiaries in Breckenridge, Dec. 24, 1867.
4. A Negro Jim Macklin taken from jail in Frankfort and hung by mob, Jan. 28, 1868.
5. Sam Davis hung by mob in Harrodsburg, May 28, 1868.
6. Wm. Pierce hung by a mob in Christian, July 12, 1868.
7. Geo. Roger hung by a mob in Bradsfordsville, Martin County, July 11, 1868.
8. Colored school exhibition at Midway attacked by a mob, July 31, 1868.
9. Seven persons ordered to leave their homes at Standford, Aug. 7, 1868.
10. Silas Woodford, age sixty, badly beaten by disguised mob. Mary Smith Curtis and Margaret Mosby also badly beaten, near Keene, Jessemine County, Aug., 1868.

Clearly, Kentucky lived up to its old Indian name, "Dark and Bloody Ground." In fact, violence and obstruction were so widespread that some Freedmen's Bureau officials believed that it was useless to continue operations in Kentucky. Equally important, as mentioned earlier, violence and terrorism discouraged civic and religious freedmen's aid societies from sending agents and teachers into Kentucky. By contrast, in neighboring Tennessee, where there was a much stronger military presence, aid societies operated more freely, spending ten times as much money as in Kentucky.[27]

In the face of violence, many freedmen wondered if they were not better off under slavery—at least more secure, relatively speaking, from the standpoint of life and limb. As a result, the Reconstruction period witnessed the first great migration of Negroes to the North. The movement from Kentucky was by far the most spectacular of that in any ex-slave state, and its geographical position as a border state does not account entirely for the migration. Missouri, for example, which was favorably situated to Kansas, Iowa, and Illinois, lost only half as many

[27] Alvord, *Semi-Annual Report* (Jan., 1868), p. 43.

Negroes (proportionately) as did Kentucky. In Kentucky, violence was clearly a prime contributing cause. No natural decrease in births led to a decline of 14,000 (or 6 per cent) in Kentucky's Negro population in the decade between 1860–70). If the usual natural increase of about 6 per cent is added to this figure, at least 30,000 freedmen left the state. To what cities did the emigrants flee? Relatively more went to Indianapolis and St. Louis than to Cincinnati. Some also settled in Columbus, Cleveland, and Chicago.[28]

For all practical purposes, the fall of 1868 marks the beginning of the end of Bureau activities in Kentucky. Despite the severity of the opposition, however, the Bureau left a legacy that was missionary and symbolic. During its brief existence it pioneered in the field of Negro education by providing at least *some* type of instruction (usually the three R's) for thousands of freedmen. Moreover, freedmen themselves contributed, at great financial sacrifice, to the Bureau's program of education. Undoubtedly the Bureau could have accomplished more had greater protection by federal troops been available. Even so, the idea of Negro education, though never overcoming entrenched opposition, began to gain limited acceptance as the Reconstruction period waned. Many schools collapsed with the demise of the Bureau, but others received support from civic or religious groups, which partially filled the vacuum until the Kentucky legislature finally began to provide state aid. The Bureau had demonstrated in Kentucky, despite overwhelming odds, that Negroes were willing and able to function as responsible citizens in a "free" society.

Delaware, West Virginia, and the Middle West

In these states the Negro population was small and Bureau operations were minimal. However, Negroes did receive some tangible financial aid from the Bureau for education. In Delaware, for example, the Bureau was instrumental in constructing eleven Negro schools. In addition, some aid was given to schools set up by benevolent, civic organizations, the chief of which was the Delaware Association for the Moral Improvement and Education of the Colored Race.

Of interest also was a trip made by General O. O. Howard to Wilmington, Delaware, in 1868, where he appeared before the city council in support of Negro education. Howard promised Bureau support of $5,000 to a project which eventually materialized in the building of a

[28] St. Louis, Richmond, and Louisville, in this order, showed spectacular increases in their "colored" population during the period of 1860–70; St. Louis increased approximately 13 times, Richmond 9, Louisville 7, Washington 4, and Baltimore 1.5.

school named for him.[29] Beyond this, however, the Bureau made little impact in Delaware.

West Virginia was a special case. Problems of transportation made it difficult for itinerant agents to reach the Negro population in some areas of the state. However, the Bureau was able to establish nine schools and co-operated primarily with freedmen themselves.[30] The Bureau also extended substantial financial aid, amounting to $6,000, to the newly established Storer College in Harpers Ferry, a Negro institution founded by the Home Mission Society of the Free Will Baptist Church.

Some Bureau activity also took place in Kansas. One school in Leavenworth and one in Kansas City received support from the Bureau, and some aid appears to have been given to the "Freedmen's University" at Quindaro.[31]

The Freedmen's Bureau also lent a sympathetic ear to the plight of the Negro in Ohio, Illinois, and Indiana, states where little was being done either to provide public education for freedmen or to protect their civil rights. Prejudice and discrimination clearly existed on a massive scale north as well as south of the Ohio River. Despite the fact that this region lay outside the Bureau's jurisdiction, Bureau officials provided aid to Wilberforce University, a school established by Negro Methodists in 1856. It also supported a Free Will Baptist school in Cairo, Illinois, established in 1865 by the Reverend J. S. Manning. Unfortunately, the Manning school was burned by racial bigots in December, 1868. Hearing of this lawless act, General Howard dispatched the Bureau's Superintendent of Schools in Missouri to Cairo to make an investigation. His official report stated: "I found Cairo by far worse off as respects the education of freedmen than any town in this State [Missouri], or of my acquaintance. One quarter of the population are negroes, the mass of them living in abject poverty, and no provision made for their education by public law. . . . I recommend a liberal appropriation towards a new building on the lot

---

[29] Record Group 105, Maryland, Report by William H. Wiegel, Dec. 31, 1866; Alvord, Semi-Annual Report (Jan., 1869), p. 11. Margaret L. Kane, "The Development of Secondary Education in Delaware," (Ph.D. diss., University of Pennsylvania, 1947), p. 272, makes a lone reference to early Negro education in citing a request for the expansion of this school in 1879.

[30] Alvord, Semi-Annual Report (Jan., 1868), p. 19.

[31] For a reference to the school in Leavenworth, see Record Group 105, Missouri, letter from R. Brown to F. A. Seeley, Oct. 22, 1867. Kansas was operated from the Bureau's headquarters in Missouri. For a reference to the school in Quindaro, see Record Group 105, Missouri, letter from Eben Blachly to F. A. Seeley, Aug. 4, 1868. The school in Quindaro was taken over by the African Methodist Episcopal Church in 1880 and given the name of Western University.

owned by the mission." Howard approved the recommendation even though the Bureau was cutting back its operations at this time and was turning its buildings over to benevolent societies. The Bureau contributed $3,000 for rebuilding this school so "recently burned by rebels."[32] Such actions by the Bureau were more symbolic than lasting, but, as in so many of its actions, the Bureau held out the hope that the nation's old Revolutionary promise might indeed apply to all men—even former slaves.

Missouri

Of all the states in which the Freedmen's Bureau operated, the situation in Missouri was unique. First, racial prejudice and hostility toward Negro education prevailed, but there was less violence in Missouri than elsewhere—especially in comparison to Kentucky. Second, the political domination of the state by the Radicals (1865–70) created a friendlier atmosphere for Bureau operations than that which existed in any other state. Third, Bureau activities received encouragement and support from a large segment of the foreign-born German population.[33] Even so, the operations of the Bureau in Missouri were similar to its activities elsewhere in the borderland, and its greatest contribution lay in the field of Negro education. Unlike other border states, however, several schools for Negroes were already in existence, or were in the process of being established by secular and religious freedmen's aid societies, when the Bureau opened its offices in St. Louis. For example, the American Missionary Society established a school for freedmen at Warrensburg in 1864, and the Western Freedmen's Aid Commission (WFAC) co-operated with military authorities in providing public instruction at Benton Barracks. The WFAC also helped to establish an orphans' home for Negro children in St. Louis. In fact, there were approximately thirty-eight Negro schools in operation when the Bureau's first and only superintendent, Frederick A. Seeley, arrived in Missouri in 1867. A dozen or more schools were in operation in the St. Louis area alone. Ira Divoll, the city's able superintendent of schools, was of the opinion that these "colored schools" were being supported largely by the tuition fees of "1,000 or 1,500

[32] Record Group 105, Missouri, letter from F. A. Seeley to O. O. Howard, March 22, 1869.
[33] Record Group 105, Missouri, letter from Llewellyn Davis to F. A. Seeley, Sept. 5, 1867. Davis, the assistant superintendent for public schools in Missouri, wrote that "the Germans among whites have contributed as liberally as they could" toward Negro education.

children."[34] Some state aid was available, but at this time it was extremely limited. Indeed, tuition fees paid by Negro parents at great personal sacrifice constituted the primary source of support for Negro schools in the interim between emancipation and the development of a state-wide educational system for Negroes.

Considering the fact that the foundation for a system of Negro schools in Missouri had already been laid when the Bureau arrived, Bureau officials were not primarily interested in establishing additional schools in this state. Instead, Superintendent Seeley believed in giving support and encouragement to local groups interested in establishing Negro schools. In fact Seeley devoted much of his time attempting to persuade local governments to absorb most of the cost involved in expanding and maintaining an educational system for Negroes. In time, such efforts paid off, as state aid for Negro education was provided in Missouri much earlier than it was in other border states.

Nevertheless, the Bureau did erect schools, wholly or in part, in Warrensburg, Kansas City, Westport, Carondolet, and St. Louis. Warrensburg was a special case that first came to the attention of the Bureau through the efforts of Mrs. C. A. R. Briggs, a war widow and a woman of indomitable character whose bustling energy and courage belie the stereotype of the timid Victorian "school marm." In 1864 she was sent by the American Missionary Association to Warrensburg from her home in St. Anthony, Minnesota. She arrived shortly after a violent raid by Confederate General Sterling Price, whose army swept through most of the Missouri River Valley region—which was called "Little Dixie"—before their defeat at Westport. At Warrensburg Mrs. Briggs came face to face with the meaning of the "Southern attitude" toward Negroes, encountering "all manner of opposition and trouble," including threats on her life. Undaunted, she pleaded with the Governor—perhaps "demanded" would be a better word—for protection "at the point of bayonets" for herself and her school. Despite Mrs. Briggs's entreaties, the school was burned, and the "connivance of

[34] Record Group 105, Missouri, letter from Ira Divoll to F. A. Seeley, April 23, 1867. Of course, reliable and up to date information on the state of Negro schools was not available to Divoll or anyone else at the time this letter was written. One great purpose that the Bureau served was that of a centralized, co-ordinating office, or clearing house, for information on the status of Negro education. It is not surprising, therefore, that one of Seeley's first official acts as the Bureau superintendent was to ascertain the status of Negro education in the state. Accordingly, he wrote to various superintendents of public schools with this in mind. Divoll's reply came in response to one of his queries. Thus, this letter and other Bureau records shed light on the few early years in the state before local governments entered the field and provided regular reports.

Copperheads" and the hostile attitude of the former "rebel" owner of the property prevented conscientious Negroes from rebuilding it. As a result, Mrs. Briggs left Warrensburg and accepted a position at the newly opened Lincoln Institute (later Lincoln University) at Jefferson City.[35]

When Mrs. Briggs arrived, R. B. Foster, the first principal at Lincoln, was desperately in need of funds and was trying valiantly to keep the school open. The history of Lincoln University has already been written. Thus, it suffices here to point out that Foster's correspondence, like that of Mrs. Briggs and so many others who sought Bureau funds, provides invaluable new light on the origins of Lincoln University and the early education of Negroes in Missouri.[36] Foster's letter to Seeley deserves quotation in full.[37]

Jefferson City, Mo.
April 16, 1867

Maj. F. A. Seeley
Dis. Off. Bureau R.F. & A.L.
St. Louis, Mo.

Sir,

I have the honor to acknowledge the receipt of your communication of the 9th inst. in which you inform me of your appointment as superintendent of Freedmen's schools for this state and request "such information as I may be able to give on this subject" etc. I forwarded by the same mail that takes this, the last annual report of the superintendent of common schools for the state. I enclose a circular containing the articles of incorporation of Lincoln Institute and the following summary statement regarding that school.

It originated in the spontaneous movements in the 62nd U.S. Colored Infantry in January 1866, the regiment then being stationed in Texas. The officers gave $1,000, and the enlisted men $4,000 for the purpose of establishing "an educational institution in Missouri which should be opened to the Colored people."

I was an officer in that regiment but did not originate the movement excepting that I consented to take charge of the school.

The committee of officers to whom the enterprize [sic] was entrusted imposed upon themselves the obligation that if the sum of $20,000 were not

---

[35] Record Group 105, Missouri, letter from C. A. R. Briggs to F. A. Seeley, March 17, 1868.

[36] W. Sherman Savage, for many years a professor of history at the school which by then was known as Lincoln University, does not mention her name in his pioneering, *A History of Lincoln University* (Jefferson City, Mo., 1939). This is quite understandable in the face of the woeful scarcity of materials in the first years of the school's history.

[37] BRF & AL was an abbreviation, frequently used in correspondence referring to the full title of the Bureau: Bureau of Refugees, Freedmen and Abandoned Lands. Seeley, appointed to the rank of lieutenant colonel, effective March 13, 1865, and assigned to the Bureau two years later, had the official title of superintendent and chief disbursing officer.

raised for the school by July 1, 1867, the contributions of the colored soldiers should be refunded. This condition was not required by the donors but was in a manner forced upon us by the commanding officer of the regiment. I regretted it at the time, and have never ceased to do [so] since.

Our receipts since that time have been as follows:

From the enlisted men of the 65th U.S. Col'd Infty, $1,360 (same condition as to the $20,000).

From the R.F. & A.L., Washington, Dec. 19, 1866 (for school house) $2,000.

From miscellaneous sources $255.92. Total a little over $8,600. The exact total of receipts according to my books is $8,619.20. Our Treasurer, James E. Yeatman Esq.[38] may have receipts that I do not know off [sic].

I made a trip to the East last summer, but found the ground so entirely occupied by organized societies that I, an obscure individual, could not hope to make a successful appeal to the public. I returned with the conviction that my best course was to establish the school and make it at least deserve to live.

I commenced the school in September in a very indifferent house, containing two rooms each 22 feet square. In that house I have taught since [,] having two different teachers, Mr. Festus Reed and Mrs. C. A. R. Briggs.

We have thus given instruction to 235 different pupils with an average attendance of 70.

My expectations and hopes are somewhat as follows. I expect to continue the school until the close of the school year about the first of July. During the summer vacation, if not sooner, I hope to see a new school house pushed rapidly forward, perhaps completed. It is at present doubtful whether we shall be able to raise the $20,000 by July 1, 1867. Our next hope then will be that few if any of the colored soldiers will recall their contributions if they see that the proposed object is likely to be secured. And finally there seems to be a very good prospect that the legislature will give us 30,000 acres of the Agricultural College land grant to this state.[39]

Judge Krekel,[40] one of our trustees and a man of great influence, delivered a lecture by invitation before that body during the session in which he claimed this as a right, and so far as could be judged by conversation the proposition met with great favor. The subject will come up again at the adjourned session in January next.

Of the two assistants whom I named, Mrs. Briggs was commissioned by the N.W.F.A. Com.[41] which only gave her five dollars per month besides her board; and Mr. Reed has given his services gratuitously, boarding in my

---

[38] Yeatman served with the Western Sanitary Commission; see W. R. Hodges, *The Western Sanitary Commission and What It Did for the Sick and Wounded of the Union Armies from 1861 to 1865, with Mention of the Services of Companion James E. Yeatman* (n.p., 106). He was a director of the Merchants Bank in St. Louis. For a biographical reference, see J. Thomas Scharf, *History of St. Louis and County* (Philadelphia, 1883), 1:552–53.

[39] Foster is referring to the Morrill Act of 1862; however, grants for the school did not materialize until after the passage of the second Morrill Act of 1890. See W. A. Low, "The Education of Negroes Viewed Historically," pp. 46–47.

[40] Arnold Krekel, born in Prussia but then a resident of St. Charles, was judge of the United States District Court. The school later named a building in his honor.

[41] Northwestern Freedmen's Aid Commission.

family. I have received $100 per month salary since June 9, 1866. I should be quite willing if possible to labor gratuitously until the school was established on a firm basis but the necessities of a large family labor this impossible. But I will not stand an hour in the way of the prosperity of the school. If any other man will do my work better, or for less, as well I am ready to step out of the way.

I deem that the school has been very successful and that the best good of the State demands that it should be maintained.

I should have mentioned before that I made an application some weeks since to the trustees of the Peabody grant but have heard nothing from it. I respectively request you, if you have occasion in your official capacity, to make recommendations either to that or other benevolent societies as to how contributions should be applied to give favorable mention to Lincoln Institute.

Could I be assured of $10,000 by the first of June from any source, I would undertake that the other $1,400 should not be asking.

Hoping to see you soon I remain—

Your Obt Servant
R. B. FOSTER
Principal, Lincoln Institute

In addition to providing aid to Lincoln Institute,[42] the Bureau also gave notable attention to the St. Louis area. On at least two noteworthy occasions direct grants were made to freedmen for educational purposes. The first grant, amounting to $800, was made to a group of Negroes for the purpose of erecting a school at Jefferson and Cinde streets in south St. Louis. The second grant, amounting to $1,300, was given to a group of local Negro Methodists in Carondelet to aid in the construction of a building to be used both for religious and educational purposes. The second group turned to the Bureau after being refused a grant by local school authorities and after having failed to raise enough funds by subscription. A moving letter was sent to the Bureau by the pastor, Moses Dickson, who also enclosed a printed circular that the group had used in their many rallies to raise money.[43]

[42] Lincoln Institute became Lincoln Unversity in 1921. A boy's dormitory, named for Foster in later years, still preserves his memory.

[43] Record Group 105, Missouri, letter from Moses Dickson to F. A. Seeley, Aug. 18, 1868. Dickson stated that a plot of land for the building was donated by Henry T. Blow who "has always been our friend." (Blow was the unsung hero behind Dred Scott.) The lot was located on the corner of Market and Third streets and the building became known as Quinn Chapel, an African Methodist Episcopal denomination. One of the earliest Negro schools in Missouri was set up by this denomination in its church, St. Paul, in St. Louis in 1854. The pastor, and teacher as well, was Hiram R. Revels who later became much better known as the first Negro to be elected to the United States Senate.

Though violence never reached the magnitude that it did in Kentucky, it did frequently occur in some parts of the state. One of the most striking cases took place in Roanoke, located in Howard County in "Little Dixie." Maggie Mary Powers, the teacher of the Negro school in Roanoke, fearfully wrote to Seeley in the utmost confidence on March 5, 1868, about one attack on the Negro community. Fearing another "season of bushwhacking," she conveyed something of the feeling of terror that left her "sick of heart." She related that John Finney, a prominent member of the Negro community and a trustee of the school was shot and his home burned. She further stated that

men on horseback, one of them carrying a gun on his shoulder . . . passed the little settlement of colored people, conversed with each other, and passed out of immediate sight. Fifteen minutes [later] the stable and smoke house was in a blaze. The building and contents were entirely consumed. . . . [A change of wind] and the mercy of God preserved the settlement. . . . [John Finney] is entirely ruined. . . . [He] leaves with his family today . . . others will follow. . . . There is just a desire among them [Negroes] to leave this County.[44]

Certainly, many Negroes fled from the state, a large number emigrating into nearby Kansas. During the decade, 1860–70, Kansas's Negro population increased from 627 to at least 17,108. Quite possibly, the number was even greater inasmuch as early census figures were not altogether reliable.

In addition to its educational activities, the Bureau also concerned itself with a few other problems. For example, in St. Louis it established a branch of the ill-fated Freedmen's Savings Bank, and it processed hundreds of veterans' claims throughout the state. Nevertheless, Negro education was its primary concern. Despite its limited financial resources, the Bureau led the way and helped to hasten the day when state aid for Negro education became a reality.

Epilogue

That the Freedmen's Bureau did not accomplish its major goals is hardly surprising. Alone, it could not resolve the stupendous problems involved in securing justice, civil rights, and equality for freedmen. Yet, as we have emphasized, it left a creditable legacy in education. It became in effect, if not in intent, a national office of education. It created, supervised and partially maintained schools throughout

[44] Record Group 105, Missouri, letter from M. M. Powers to F. A. Seeley, March 5, 1868.

half of the nation, including the borderland and fringe areas in Kansas, Ohio, Illinois, and Indiana. More important, however, was the symbolism implied in the Bureau's existence: its firm devotion to the idea that freedmen should be educated as free men; its hope and promise that *all* Americans should be treated with human dignity and justice. The central tragedy of Reconstruction was the subversion of these ideals. The Bureau's struggle to create and sustain equality in the face of violence and racial bigotry was one of the few hopeful developments during one of the most turbulent periods of the nation's history.

Looking back upon a remarkable career, General O. O. Howard reflected in later years that the Bureau achieved greater results than the war itself. "My glory," Howard said, "if ever I have any, consists in results attained; and the results in any case of the Freedmen's Bureau are, for me, more marked than those of the war. . . . It is a pleasure to know that Institutions of learning like Howard University, Hampton Institute, Atlanta University and others in whose incipiency I bore a part, are now increasing in power and influence, and will continue their work long after I am gone."[45] Howard might also have included other schools—Bowie in Maryland, Storer in West Virginia, Lincoln in Missouri, as well as scores of lesser known schools that were eventually aborbed into the public school systems.

---

[45] John A. Carpenter, *Sword and Olive Branch* (Pittsburgh, 1964), p. 168, has written a biography of Howard, making use of the extensive Howard Papers at Bowdoin College, Howard's alma mater. Howard himself has chapters on the Bureau in his *Autobiography of Oliver Otis Howard: Major General United States Army* (New York, 1907).

CHAPTER NINE

Anatomy of a Failure:
Federal Enforcement of the Right to Vote in the Border States during Reconstruction
William Gillette

When the Fifteenth Amendment was ratified in March of 1870, eligible Negroes in all the border states could vote for the first time.[1] How Negroes would be able to use their newly won right was anxiously awaited. Negroes could now protect and advance their own interests and help order their new freedom, thus enabling the borderland to break out of its war psychosis and attract new blood, new lines of thought, and two-party politics.

The prospective Negro voter often evoked daydreams in the minds of Republican candidates. The promise of Negro enfranchisement had earlier spurred unstable and unpopular Republican régimes in West Virginia and especially in Missouri to push through ratification of the Fifteenth Amendment, in the face of the deep resentment of most whites, in the desperate hope that Negro voting would keep them in power. Loyalty to the national party and the lure of federal patronage also generated support. Yet Republicans were not united for ratification. Those in control approached ratification with extreme caution, while a few deserted their posts on the day of battle. Some Republicans out of power, notably in Maryland and Delaware, felt that they had nothing to lose and much to gain by boldly and openly championing Negro suffrage. But others were wary of common cause with the Negro: they could not identify themselves with him or stand alongside him on election day—the pull of prejudice was too strong. Moreover,

---

[1] Research was supported in part by grants from the Penrose Fund of the American Philosophical Society and from the Graduate Studies Division of The City University of New York.

All Negroes, free or slave, were explicitly disenfranchised in Delaware in 1792, Kentucky in 1799, Maryland in 1810, Missouri in 1821, Tennessee in 1834, and West Virginia in 1863. Under a radical régime in Tennessee, Negro suffrage was reintroduced in 1867. Charles H. Wesley, "Negro Suffrage in the Period of Constitution-Making, 1787–1865," *Journal of Negro History* 32 (April, 1947): 143–68.

U.S. *Constitution*, Admt. 15. The first section provides: "The right of citizens of the United States to vote shall not be denied or abridged by the United States or by any State on account of race, color, or previous condition of servitude." The second section provides: "The Congress shall have the power to enforce this article by appropriate legislation."

it was not altogether clear whether the Negro voter would prove to be an element of weakness or a source of strength.

Democrats, for their part, performed party ritual and exploited sectional mores by rejecting not only ratification but the real need for a postwar political settlement as well. In their one-party fiefs in Delaware, Maryland, Kentucky, and Tennessee, the border Democrats, without federal occupation and with relative freedom of action, sounded more Southern than those in the Deep South and thus became addicts of Southern ideology. On the other hand, the Fifteenth Amendment presented grave problems, for it could upset that delicate balance which kept Negroes in their places—politically impotent, socially subordinate, and economically exploited. In particular, Democratic control was jeopardized in Delaware and Maryland, while in West Virginia and Missouri Democratic resurgence might be checked, and in Kentucky and Tennessee the Republican party might, in turn, be kept intact. Politicians, then, in both camps knew that much was at stake. Brave words often cloaked great evasions, for many politicians were alarmed. It remained to be seen whether a fresh breeze would blow away not only the cobwebs but the spiders.[2]

In any case, the Fifteenth Amendment would amount to little or nothing south of the Mason Dixon line unless the right was secure and

---

[2] See for a treatment of ratification in the border states, William Gillette, *The Right to Vote: Politics and the Passage of the Fifteenth Amendment* (Baltimore: The Johns Hopkins Press, 1965), pp. 105–12.

The Border States and the Potential Negro Vote

State	Negroes percent in population[a]	Number of Negroes[b]	Potential Negro vote[c]	Democratic presidential majority 1868[d]	Seats in House of Representatives, 1872[e]
Maryland	22.5	175,391	35,078	31,919	6
Delaware	18.2	22,794	4,559	3,257	1
Kentucky	16.8	222,210	44,442	76,313	10
Missouri	6.9	118,071	23,614	25,883 Rep.	13
Tennessee	25.6	322,331	64,466	30,499 Rep.	9
West Va.	4.1	17,980	3,596	8,719 Rep.	3

[a] U.S. Bureau of the Census, *Negro Population, 1790–1915.*

[b] U.S. Bureau of the Census, *Ninth Census,* 1, 5.

[c] The potential Negro vote is estimated at one-fifth of the Negro population. During the ratification fight newspapers used that figure. ([Cumberland, Md.] *Civilian and Telegraph,* Feb. 10, 1870; Galveston *News,* April 1, 1870; the Patterson *Daily Press,* March 31, 1870.)

[d] *Tribune Almanac* for 1869, pp. 67, 68, 83, 85; *Tribune Almanac* for 1870, p. 63.

[e] *Tribune Almanac* for 1872, p. 56.

its exercise guaranteed. In this vital matter of enforcing the right of the Negro to vote, the new federal role would prove decisive. The incumbent Republican administration of Ulysses Grant praised final ratification of the amendment in March, 1870, as the dawn of a new era. More significantly, President Grant made sweeping declarations of federal protection and support to insure that Negroes could freely register, vote, and have their ballots counted in fair elections. Obviously, such affirmations of equal opportunity in voting sparked vast expectations in the minds and hearts of Negroes. Congress acted as well when five enforcement acts were passed which spelled out in detail the federal enforcement role. The first Enforcement Act of May 31, 1870, banned the use of force, bribery, or intimidation which interfered with the the right to vote because of race. This prohibition significantly applied to all elections and thus affected local and state election officials. Prosecution under the law would be conducted in federal courts in order to circumvent unco-operative state courts. Execution of the law included both the use of local posse and federal forces. The second Enforcement Act of July 14, 1870, provided enforcement machinery in congressional elections in cities of 20,000 persons, affecting eight border cities. Specifically, special deputy marshals were created to police elections and empowered to make arrests without warrants. Since local and state elections were often held at the same time as congressional elections, the practical effect was to extend federal influence still further. The third Enforcement Act of February 28, 1871, amplified the earlier law by defining the duties of enforcement officers and the crimes in more detail, while also requiring written ballots in congressional elections. This act specifically provided that in large cities with 20,000 population a federal judge of the circuit court, upon request, could appoint two election supervisors in each election district. Such supervisors were to stand guard at the ballot box, challenge doubtful voters, and count all ballots. To oversee the entire enforcement operation in each judicial district in the circuit, a United States commissioner could be appointed to serve as chief supervisor. The fourth Enforcement Act of April 20, 1871, or Ku-Klux Klan Act, outlawed in effect the Klan and similar groups which conspired to deprive citizens of their civil and political rights by interfering with trials or voting. Stiff punishment was provided. The fifth Enforcement Act of June 10, 1872, which was inserted into the Sundry Civil Appropriations Act, enlarged election supervision to cover rural areas, but disarmed supervisors by not allowing them the power of arrest or interference, thus reducing them to powerless poll watchers, quite unlike their counterparts in large cities. Congress also prescribed that congressional elections be held on the same day in November. Armed with such purpose, authorized by unprecedented statutory powers during peacetime, supported by federal troops, attorneys, marshals, and supervisors, the Attorney General of the United States undertook election enforcement.[3] No one knew how enforcement would work. The only way to find out was to try. In the process, the will and skill of the government of President Grant was to be tested. This study will assess the direction, administration, and results of that effort in the six border states.

Mob violence toward voters was certainly among the most pressing problems of federal enforcement, threatening to paralyze not only the foundation of federal authority and the integrity of the democratic process but the order of society itself. The Ku-Klux Klan and similar organizations conducted guerrilla warfare against political opponents and often against constituted authority. Intending to undermine Radical power by disenfranchising Negroes and enfranchising former Confederates, such bands of masked men, usually drunk on Saturday nights, rode off into the woods to whip some and murder other Negroes who might vote the wrong ticket. To be sure, violence was not handed out to Negroes alone but to white Republicans as well. Such mass lawlessness mounted where pothouse politicians spoke irresponsibly, when passions ran high, where frontier violence was an old local habit, and when young firebrands were in ample supply. Violence, of course, was not unusual in the borderland, or southward, in fact it simmered below the surface in most societies. But a secret, organized, deliberate campaign of political terror against another race was new. The activities of the Klan and similar organizations varied, of course. Motives and methods changed with different conditions and different men. Tennessee was a good example—torn between the thrust of the Deep South into West Tennessee and the Appalachian influence in East Tennessee, the state became, in effect, a variation on divergent political themes. On the one hand, Tennessee was the only border state to join the Confederacy and to undergo military occupation

[3] The 20,000 population provision affected key voting in Wilmington, Delaware; Baltimore, Maryland; Covington and Louisville, Kentucky; Nashville and Memphis, Tennessee; St. Louis and Kansas City, Missouri.

Richardson, *A Compilation of the Messages and Papers of the Presidents* 7 (March 30, 1870): 55–56 (March 23, 1871): 127–28 (May 3, 1871): 134–35 (Dec. 4, 1871): 150–51 (April 19, 1872): 163–64 (Dec. 2, 1872): 199–200; *Statutes at Large of the United States*, 16 (1871): 140–46, 254, 433–40; 17 (1873): 13–15, 348–49; U.S., Bureau of the Census, *Ninth Census*: 1870, 1:642–54; Robert A. Horn, "National Control of Congressional Elections" (Ph.D. diss., Princeton University, 1942), pp. 137–79.

during the war as the price of her folly. On the other hand, Tennessee was fortunate in being the only Confederate state to escape congressional reconstruction after the war, thanks to the resourceful Radical leadership of East Tennessee rather than to the absence of Rebel reaction, for Klanism began in fact in Tennessee.

The Tennessee Klan was first organized in Middle Tennessee, at Pulaski, as a social club of ex-Confederates, in December, 1865, during the first year of Radical rule, but it did not become a major political force until 1867, when Radical rule became firmly entrenched by proscribing former Confederates and by enfranchising Negroes so as to align them with East Tennessee Republican whites. The inevitable Radical Republican victory in August, 1867, brought enactment of civil rights legislation in January, 1868. This was the last provocation to white Conservatives, who not only were scandalized by former slaves serving on juries or holding public office but were disappointed as well by the failure of Conservative candidates to woo the Negro voter. Conservative reaction set in, exploited by the Klan and pressed to its limits. With the increase in Klan membership and mounting disorder during 1867 and 1868, lawlessness expanded from Middle to West Tennessee, where more Negroes lived. The result was clear: many Negro voters were scared away from the polls during the federal elections of 1868. The Negro vote dropped off in West Tennessee and was cut in half in Middle Tennessee. Although the decline was particularly sharp in areas where the Klan was most active, such as the Fourth Congressional District in Middle Tennessee, what Republican votes were lost through Negro absentees were counted in turn by a Republican Congress, which proceeded to unseat two Conservative winners from the state. When Klan violence continued during 1869, the Radical régime in the state ostensibly cracked down, but without real success, for the régime was powerless. A new and more conservative governor, originally a Radical, paved the way for the overthrow of Radicalism by disbanding the state militia, lifting martial law, re-enfranchising Conservatives, and introducing the poll tax to reduce the Negro vote still further. Then, with the inauguration of a Democratic governor, John C. Brown, himself once a Klan member, and with Democratic control of the legislature assured by 1870, Radical reconstruction was ended. The Klan had helped to accomplish it in its own way. Then after 1870, Klan violence began to decline, but it did not disappear.[4]

---

[4] Thomas B. Alexander, "Ku Kluxism in Tennessee, 1865–1869," *Tennessee Historical Quarterly* 8 (Sept., 1949): 195–219; Alexander, *Political Reconstruction in Tennessee* (Nashville: Vanderbilt University Press, 1950); Edgar Needham to Benjamin H. Bristow, Nov. 15, 1870, Benjamin H. Bristow MSS, Library of Congress (LC); *New York Times*, June 29, 1871, July 18, Nov. 1, 1872.

All, however, was not to go smoothly for the Democrats in Tennessee. Without real competition from the Republicans, they reverted to various factions, squabbling with one another. Short years later, weakened by the 1872 presidential candidacy of Horace Greeley and ravaged by factional fighting, the Democrats lost badly: six Republicans were elected to Congress, and, significantly, the first Negro was sent to the Statehouse (Sampson Keeble from Memphis, West Tennessee). Republicans had reassembled to become a serious political force, thanks in part to the Negro voter. Now, with independents, Republicans seized control of the state legislature and repealed the poll tax requirement for voting. With potentially a still larger Negro vote, the state and federal elections in 1874 would decide the matter of Republican resurgence. The contest for power became the most heated and most bloody since secession.

Faced with imminent danger, Democrats needed political ammunition, which Republicans in Washington supplied to the last full measure. With the civil rights bill pending in Congress, integrating public and private accommodations, and which Tennessee Democrats declared would force social equality, most whites "were lashed into a frenzy." An incendiary press arousing prejudice, spreading fear, and retailing rumor was just the beginning. Organized violence was also resumed for a brief but brutal campaign: threatening and shouting, whipping and shooting, became almost daily occurrences. It was all a change for the worse, observed a federal marshal: "I had been quite hopeful that a better state of feeling was growing and that we had done with Ku-Klux murders. Unfortunately I have been disappointed." The upshot of the Democratic barrage was to put state Republicans on the defensive, for most East Tennessee whites were more anti-Negro than pro-Republican when the question was civil rights for the Negro. Straight Republicans and strong Unionists appeared on the verge of bolting, while Negroes throughout the state defended themselves against attack and from abuse.[5]

[5] Marshal L. B. Eaton to Attorney General, Aug. 12, 1874; Marshal W. Spence to Attorney General, Sept. 3, 1874, Source–Chronological File for Tennessee, Record Group 60, Department of Justice Records, National Archives (NA). Since all unpublished official communications cited in this essay are from the files of the Department of Justice in Record Group 60 in the National Archives, subsequent references to them will be dispensed with. Such records can be identified easily, for all source–chronological files, containing communications from federal officials and other interested persons in each state, as well as Justice Department instruction books, letter books, and opinion books containing orders and advice from officials in the department in Washington are from the same source, Record Group 60. *New York Times*, June 6, Aug. 8, Oct. 15, 1874.

Violence was worst in Gibson County, West Tennessee. Describing that county's election, held on August 6, 1874, the United States Marshal reported: "there was a mob at every poll and created a perfect reign of terror. Intimidation, violence . . . preventing of the colored citizen from voting, was the order of the day." He estimated that in a fair vote the Republicans should have carried the county by roughly two thousand votes, but instead Democrats won by double that figure. Even more ominous for the fall elections were the unofficial returns. While some Democrats, obviously not satisfied with voting out Republican officials, proceeded to murder them, most attention was given to hapless Negroes. One night in August, following the local election, a group of Negroes fired back when fired upon by a band of masked men, thereby breaking off the engagement. The next day, however, state authorities arrested local Negroes, including two preachers who were taken bodily from their churches. Sixteen Negroes were thrown in jail and many were forced to make confessions. Then, on the night of August 26, a band of about 100 armed, disguised, and mounted men surrounded the jail at Trenton, forced the sheriff to give them the prisoners, and took the Negroes to a nearby riverbank, where, unarmed, their bodies were riddled with bullets. Five men died, and the rest were severely wounded. The uproar which followed the murders forced the Democratic governor's hand: he offered a reward of $500, but his high-sounding message meant little in fact when state authorities dragged their feet about prosecution, and the Governor himself protested to President Grant against any federal interference.[6]

In the face of local paralysis, federal prosecution started. Despite state and local harassment, federal arrests were made, indictments returned, and a trial held involving fifty-three defendants. No one, however, was convicted. Failure stemmed in part from difficulty in securing proof. Reluctant Negro witnesses were understandably afraid to tell the court what they had seen, for fear of becoming the next victims. Reporting to Washington, the Federal Attorney stated the problem of Negro witnesses subjected to rigid cross examination: "They are ignorant and afraid and easily become confused, and in this case were confronted not only by the very men who had attempted to murder them, but the sheriff of Gibson County or his deputy [who] came into open court and demanded of the court in their presence these witnesses to be taken to that county and tried for a trumped up charge of felony now pending there against them and these witnesses thereupon became so terrified that some of them in tears and piteous

[6] *New York Times*, Aug. 30, Sept. 2, 10, 19, Oct. 13, 1874.

tones besought the court to allow them to be excused from testifying."
Some culprits were not prosecuted because there were not enough
funds to hire detectives to investigate and break their alibis. It was all
to become a familiar story: no convictions, accompanied by Democratic landslides.[7]

Violence was also epidemic in Kentucky. Seizing control of the
Democratic party, former Confederates, largely from the bluegrass
region, gained state-wide power on a platform of unrepentant reaction
by 1868. Such a course of events led one Yankee newspaper to remon-
strate: "It will take either a constitutional amendment, an act of
Congress, or a thousand years to make Kentucky a civilized state."
Preferring not to wait for the millennium, state Republicans badgered
Washington to expedite ratification of the Fifteenth Amendment and
to enforce it effectively. They counted on the Negro voter possibly to
overthrow the Bourbon establishment.[8]

With the Negro either as an issue or as a voter in Kentucky politics,
there was bound to be trouble. Indeed, differences between the races
were transmuted into differences between the parties, and a speaker
told the Kentucky Democratic convention of 1871 that he wanted "no
nigger votes, and that is the principle on which" he wanted Democrats
to stand. Of course, he declared, if he were "a nigger," he would be a
Radical, but since he was a white man, he was a Democrat.[9] The
political war was about to become a race war.

Immediately, guerrilla bands sprang into action. One newspaper
gave 115 instances of shootings, hangings, and whippings between 1867
and 1871. A virtual reign of terror prevailed in many counties, particularly in the area surrounding the state capital at Frankfort, in the
bluegrass country. After several outrages in the region, a Ku-Klux
outfit had the audacity, in February 1871, to free a white man from the

---

[7] Marshal W. W. Murray to Attorney General, Sept. 5, Oct. 2, 1874, April 26,
1875; *New York Times*, Sept. 12, 15, 18, 1874. The 1874 elections were the supreme
disaster for Tennessee Republicans: only one Republican out of six returned to
Washington, while the stronghold of Republicanism in East Tennessee could not
even carry the Republican candidate for governor. *Ibid.*, Nov. 3, 13, 1874. *Tribune
Almanac* for 1875, pp. 84–85. Compare the brief three-page account of the Tennessee Klan in Everette Swinney, "Suppressing the Ku Klux Klan: The Enforcement
of the Reconstruction Amendments, 1870–1874" (Ph.D. diss., University of Texas,
1966).

[8] Bangor *Daily Whig and Courier*, March 18, 1869; Rumsey Wing to Charles
Sumner, Feb. 16, 1870, Charles Sumner MSS, Houghton Library, Harvard University; W. C. Goodloe to Sumner, March 6, 1870, *ibid.*

[9] Louisville *Courier Journal*, May 10, 1871, quoted in Hambleton Tapp, "Three
Decades of Kentucky Politics, 1870–1900" (Ph.D. diss., University of Kentucky,
1950), p. 55; James Speed to Lewis Ashmead, Dec. 9, 1871, Simon Gratz MSS, Historical Society of Pennsylvania, Philadelphia.

Frankfort jail who had been charged with murdering a Negro. Although this episode took place while the legislature was in session, the legislators refused to take action to suppress the Klan. During that same bloody month a witness who had testified against the Klan was murdered after leaving the courtroom. In the crucial state elections the following August—the first since Negro voting began—riots occurred. And again the state capital was the scene of an offense when two Negroes were lynched by a mob on election eve. The time for federal patience and restraint necessarily came to an end.[10]

Now federal officials became energetically involved. The launching of a federal investigation sent a wave of shock, surprise, and fear through the community. The Klan, however, was powerful and appeared to have not only the support of many state officials but a large, popular following as well. In order to counteract Klan violence, the Republican candidate for governor, John M. Harlan, who had just been defeated in the August election, during which he had openly attacked the Klan, made an interesting proposal. Observing the "universal dread amongst Republicans, white and black," who feared for their lives and property if they testified against the Klan, and noting as well that state authorities were doing nothing to suppress the Klan out of fear or preference, Harlan suggested that the federal court ought to have a grand jury called into continuous session to find out who the members of the Klan were. He followed up his proposal by speaking to President Grant, urging him to hire detectives "who lived in the neighborhood of the [K.K.K.] operations—in other words, the information must be bought from some of the gang or some of their sympathizers." Yet although Grant was interested enough to authorize the hiring of some detectives,[11] it was all to no avail.

Despite the fact that the Federal Attorney worked hard on the Frankfort case and even advanced some of his own money to pay for the cost of investigation, he reported that at the trial "lies and silence prevail," and worried about intimidated Negro witnesses who might be lying in behalf of the defense. His fears were justified, for one of the accused was a son of the most prominent political family in Kentucky, the Crittendens. As a result, the trial was postponed until

---

[10] Frankfort *Weekly Commonwealth,* March 31, 1871, cited in E. Merton Coulter, *The Civil War and Readjustment in Kentucky* (Chapel Hill: University of North Carolina Press, 1926), pp. 358–65; *New York Times,* March 25, Aug. 25, Nov. 6, 1871; Tapp, "Three Decades of Kentucky Politics," pp. 315–28; M. B. Belknap to Solicitor General Benjamin H. Bristow, Feb. 25, 1871, Bristow MSS, LC.

[11] Bristow to Attorney General, Aug. 8, 1871, U.S. Attorney G. C. Wharton to Bristow, Oct. 1, 1871, Source–Chronological File for Kentucky; Harlan to Bristow, Sept. 10, 27, 1871, Bristow MSS, LC.

January, 1872. Meanwhile, alluding to a bill legalizing Negro trial testimony, a correspondent of the Solicitor General foresaw that state legislators would "move heaven and earth if possible to have such a law enacted." He concluded: "When you strike a Crittenden you strike the State of Kentucky and his friends will never consent to have justice meted out to him." This prediction was borne out when, on January 29, the Kentucky legislature passed a law giving Negroes the right to testify in court for the first time and, significantly, made the law applicable to cases now pending. With Negroes providing an alibi for Crittenden, apparently the case was then dropped.[12]

The pattern of terror in the border states was either identical or closely parallel. Its source was not to be found in the mountain country of Appalachia—the antebellum nonslaveholding areas, wartime Unionist strongholds and postwar Republican safe districts, as was the case in some states of the South[13]—but rather in counties with a middle or high range of Negro concentration, in which elections would be decided by Negro voters, and in which the Confederate loyalties of whites were deeply rooted. Violence, then, coincided with crucial elections and often appeared politically motivated. Terrorist activity was concentrated in the Kentucky bluegrass, middle and west Tennessee, southeastern Missouri, southeastern West Virginia, downstate Delaware, and tidewater Maryland, although there were many ugly incidents, particularly in big cities along the Delaware, Patapsco, Kanawha, and Missouri rivers.[14] Such places covered most, but not all, of the dark and bloody ground of the borderland, and political terror

[12] Wharton to Bristow, Sept. 30, 1871, U.S. District Court Clerk W. A. Meriwether to Bristow, Nov. 8, Dec. 5, 1871, Source–Chronological File for Kentucky; Wharton to Bristow, Oct. 1, 1871, Bristow MSS, LC; *New York Times,* March 15, 1871, Jan. 23, 1872; Louisville *Courier Journal,* Jan. 26, 27, 1872. The case of *United States* v. *Crittenden* et al., which was argued in United States Circuit Court at Louisville, Kentucky on Jan. 25, 1872, went unreported in the local newspaper and published court records. Subsequently, on Feb. 22, 1872, Judge Bland Ballard, in charging the grand jury in the United States District Court, announced that the jurisdiction of that court in all cases arising under the "civil rights act" ceased when the Kentucky legislature authorized Negro testimony in January. Lewis Collins, *History of Kentucky* (2 vols.; Covington: Collins, 1878), I, p. 224. Many old court records were destroyed in the Louisville flood of 1936. United States District Court Clerk Martin Glenn to author, Nov. 1, 1967.

[13] Compare the opposite conclusion that terrorist activity was strongest in "eastern Kentucky and Tennessee" on p. 217, in Everette Swinney, "Enforcing the Fifteenth Amendment, 1870–1877," *Journal of Southern History* 27 (May, 1962): 202–18.

[14] Often terrorists seemed to alternate between attacking Negroes and making moonshine. For Missouri, see: *New York Times,* Aug. 4, 6, 1872; Marshal W. W. Leffingwell to Attorney General, Feb. 5. 1878, Source–Chronological File for Missouri. For West Virginia: John R. Sheeler, "The Negro in West Virginia Before 1900" (Ph.D. diss., West Virginia University, 1954), pp. 193–213.

did not disappear when the Klan organization folded or when national reconstruction came to an end.[15] Perhaps the Klan was dead, but Klanism was very much alive.

Since, on numerous occasions, physical violence was more a threat than an occurrence, it was doubly difficult to prosecute in a court of law. How could discriminatory intent be proved? How could one bring justice to men who fired scattered shots in the night, who shouted behind one's back, who wrote anonymous notes? Pervasive fear was rampant in the countryside, yet only hard facts mattered in the courtroom. What Negroes left unsaid, the indignities they endured, the intimidation they suffered—all were left quietly undisturbed on the steps outside the federal courthouse.

The bitter experience of Negro citizens and enforcement officials alike called into question the credibility of the Grant administration, which had promised much in securing life and liberty and in enforcing effectively federal laws in every part of the country, but had delivered little. Pathetic was the plea of Negroes from Trousdale County, in Middle Tennessee, who wrote a letter to their President during that bloody month of August, 1874. Describing the murder

[15] Violence only subsided but did not disappear after Republicanism was routed. Such was the case at Pyburn's Bluff, Hardin county, West Tennessee, during Sept., 1878. R. K. Baird to Attorney General, Sept. 18, 1878, Source–Chronological File for Tennessee. For clear-eyed observations of the incidence of violence see Alrutheus A. Taylor, *The Negro in Tennessee, 1865–1880* (Washington, D.C.: Associated Publishers, 1941), pp. 102–5. The outburst of racism in Tennessee elections is evident in the campaigns of 1874, 1876, 1890, and 1898. Verton M. Queener, "The Republican Party in East Tennessee, 1865–1900 (Ph.D. diss., Indiana University, 1940), pp. 221–30. Compare the estimate of lessened violence because of enforcement in Tennessee, Swinney, "Enforcing the Fifteenth Amendment."

Similarly, political violence did not fade away in Kentucky. An epidemic of disturbances spread through Owen county between 1873–75. Deputy Marshal Willis Russell to Marshal E. H. Murray, Sept. 1, 1874, Source–Chronological File for Kentucky, was one graphic account; *New York Times*, Nov. 5, 8, 1872, April 26, Aug. 23, 1873. Republicans in their platform of May, 1875, attacked the dilatory efforts of the state government to suppress such violence. Murders by gunshot and fire occurred near Frankfort, Ky., in 1879. In the gubernatorial election of 1887, Democratic intimidation was so great (as well as before and after), that white Republican ex-Union officers openly carried Colt revolvers while leading long lines of Negroes to the polls. Tapp, "Three Decades of Kentucky Politics," pp. 126, 182, 311–12, 407–8. For reference to prevailing level of violence in general in the redeemed South and borderland, see C. Vann Woodward, *Origins of the New South, 1877–1913* (Baton Rouge: Louisiana State University Press, 1951), pp. 158–60, and for the political violence, pp. 57–58. Negro lynchings, although less than in the Southern states (except for Tennessee) were as follows between 1882–1936: Tennessee, 200; Kentucky, 141; Missouri, 70; West Virginia, 28; Maryland, 27; Delaware, 1. George Snowden, "The Political Status of Negroes in the United States with Particular Reference to the Border States" (Ph.D. diss., Indiana University, 1943), p. 68.

of a local teacher and detailing intimidation of Negroes by night riders, these Tennesseans begged President Grant for help: "We want the promise of U.S. protection, Mr. President—not only the promise but we want the aid, and if you will not help us, send us arms and say you will help us; be as good as your word."[16] Looking around the countryside there seemed good reason to doubt his word. Too often the suffrage for Negroes had become less of a boon and more of a danger; enforcement had become less of a protection and more of a curse.

The officials on the firing line were not in much better shape. Federal marshals and attorneys were whipsawed between awesome presidential commitments, inadequate federal support, local governmental sabotage, and individual apathy. One federal marshal in Kentucky put the matter squarely: "If it is the policy of the administration to act I beg that such action will be taken as will be swift and certain." But there was usually little or no swift and certain action from Washington. The United States Attorney for Kentucky, when asked about the security of Negroes, replied to his superiors that great progress was being made in breaking up the Klan and in suppressing violence. Like other subordinates, he knew that his chances for promotion might depend on how much progress he reported. But he also implied that the federal effort was modest at best—or, as he understated the situation: "although this is true I cannot say that there is as much protection . . . as to be desired." He went on to say that no new laws were needed, but then quickly added that if "these outrages should continue and Congress should conclude to legislate further on this subject I think the Courts of the United States should be increased to three times their present number." Reading between the lines of his letter, he was telling Washington that if it really meant business, federal attorneys must have the tools to do the job: more detectives, more money, more troops, more and better paid officials, as well as better laws, better and more co-operative judges, and additional judicial districts. The same refrain was to be heard from scores of other enforcement officials, but the inadequate means remained inadequate.[17]

[16] Mrs. M. C. Manson to President Ulysses S. Grant, Aug. 23, 1874, Source–Chronological File for Tennessee.

[17] Marshal Eli Murray to Attorney G. C. Wharton, Sept. 10, 1873; Wharton to Attorney General, March 27, 1872, Source–Chronological File for Kentucky; John Marshall Harlan to Benjamin Bristow, Sept. 27, 1871, Bristow MSS, LC. Compare the defeatist attitude of Marshal W. W. Murray in Murray to Attorney General, Oct. 2, 1874, Oct. 5, 1878, Source–Chronological File for Tennessee.

Negro voters and federal marshals were, in effect, like soldiers going into battle only to find out that their comrades on the battle-field had vanished. Thus both Negroes and officials were fair game for white terrorists. United States troops were, of course, another matter, but only a handful of them remained in the borderland. In Tennessee, for example, only 185 continued on in the eventful year of 1874, half the original 1870 complement, while only fifty soldiers were to be assigned after 1876. In Kentucky, too, there was a steady and drastic reduction. Although troops were doubled during 1871, the troop level was slashed from 1,324 in 1871 to a mere 178 by 1873. More troops were, in fact, requested during 1873, but there were few to go around, between standing guard in the occupied South and controlling Indians on the frontier. And although a permanent garrison of army regulars would have proved helpful in trouble spots had they been available, all enforcement problems would not have been solved thereby. One Federal Marshal frankly told Washington that soldiers were not very useful in making arrests or securing convictions; rather, in most cases, they could be a definite disadvantage. By duplicating congressional reconstruction in the South, an obnoxious occupying force would only arouse counter-productive pressures. When the Democratic press tended to play-down terrorist incidents and explain them away as ghosts conjured up by Republicans "to hide Radical rottenness behind a cloud of Ku Klux," it was difficult to justify the sending of federal troops, which would have been regarded as arbitrary and unnecessary by border men.[18] Sending just enough troops to create ugly incidents and arouse a sense of common grievance, yet not stationing enough troops to stamp out disorder, meant playing right into the hands of the rabble-rousers. It was a dilemma that remained unresolved.

The real root of the problem, however, was that Washington failed to follow through with enforcement. Whenever elections came up, a clarion call for mobilization would come forth from Washington. But once the elections were held, the Justice Department would order deactivation. For example, Attorney General George Williams instructed federal attorneys and marshals in Kentucky and Tennessee on September 3, 1874, to "proceed with all possible energy and dispatch to detect, expose, arrest, and punish the perpetrators of these

[18] William Brown to Benjamin Bristow, Jan. 31, 1872, Bristow MSS, LC; Swinney, "Enforcing the Fifteenth Amendment," p. 190; G. C. Wharton to Attorney General, Sept. 15, 1873, Aug. 25, 1874; A. W. Spence to Attorney General, Sept. 3, 1874; Source–Chronological File for Kentucky; Nashville *Union and American*, Nov. 4, 6, 1874; Memphis *Daily Appeal*, Nov. 9, 1876.

crimes; and, to that end, you are to spare no effort or necessary expense . . . [so that there will be] protection to all classes of citizens, white and colored in the free exercise of the elective franchise." He added that the mobilization order was "issued by the authority of the President and with the concurrence of the Secretary of War." After the elections Attorney General Williams, on November 30, 1874, in a brisk communication to federal marshals in Kentucky, Tennessee, and Missouri, stressed that there should be "proper care and economy," and added: "I am constrained once more to invite your attention to the matter with the request that you will consult with the other officers of the courts and endeavor by every means in your power to have the expenses of your district materially lessened." Subsequently, in response to a plea for assistance to cope with an outbreak of violence in Kentucky in February, 1875, the Attorney General responded: "I do not feel at liberty to incur any extra expense in these cases as appropriations are very small." On the other hand, while the trickle of appropriations was bad enough, the situation was even more disastrous when Washington deferred first to state authority and then gave up enforcement altogether.[19] In other words, Washington did not curb shot-gun politics.

Another problem in enforcing the right to vote in the border states—even more pervasive than the overt intimidation of electors—was the covert dishonesty in elections. Not only was bribery as endemic as whiskey but cheating was positively ingenious. Ballot boxes were stuffed, votes were repeated, counts were manipulated. The Baltimore *American* described the south Baltimore election of 1878: "There was, however, much quiet work done by the judges and clerks at the polls, where Democratic majorities were manufactured with amazing rapidity." In one race in the Fifth Congressional District of Maryland the Democratic ballot was headed with a lithograph of President Grant to lure unsuspecting Negro voters. Democrats apparently concluded that if Negroes could not be scared away from the polls or wooed or fooled into voting Democratic, then the only options left were to buy their votes or bury the returns. Bribery became common, especially relied upon by Maryland Democrats, who paid Negroes to stay at home in the gubernatorial elections of 1871 and 1875. Taking the opposite

[19] Attorney General George Williams to Marshals and Attorneys, Kentucky, Tennessee, Sept. 3, 1874, Instruction Book; Williams to Marshals, Kentucky, Tennessee, Missouri, Nov. 30, 1874, Letter Book; Williams to G. C. Wharton, Feb. 25, 1875, Instruction Book; W. W. Murray to Williams, April 25, 1875, Source–Chronological File for Tennessee.

tack, West Virginia Democrats used the purported bribery of Negro voters as an excuse to deprive a Republican of the governorship in 1890. Indeed, the uses of fraud were many and nonpartisan: Tennessee Democrats fired Negroes from their jobs for voting Republican, while Kentucky Republicans recruited Negro voters by getting them drunk.[20]

In West Virginia, however, the main problem was not bribery but erroneous enforcement. During 1870 a conservative federal district judge, John J. Jackson, interpreted the federal legislation to require voter registration of every adult male. He thus, in effect, overturned a state test oath by allowing former Confederates, who had been proscribed, to vote. Such conservative harassment of local election officials by federal commissioners appointed by Jackson caused no end of trouble for loyal Republicans in state and federal office, until the whole business was thrown out of court during 1871. In the meantime, however, such tactics worked by opening up the voting lists to thousands of disenfranchised Democrats, even before local amnesty went into effect.

Sailing under false colors, playing tricks in the law, trading in white Conservative voters to offset Radical voters, the Democrats won the election of 1870 and overthrew the old régime. With the tables turned, Republicans were first caught and then paralyzed in a web of their own making. However, in Missouri, where state voter qualification and federal enforcement machinery still remained in friendly but trembling hands, disqualification of Democrats deliberately stopped while federal enforcement never really started. But Radical appeasement in the Missouri election of 1870 merely guaranteed the same result wrought by Conservative subversion in West Virginia. Despite dissimilar superintendence, it appeared clear that the administration of federal law was tailored to local needs, serving their own political ends rather than following federal policy harnessed to national objectives. Indeed federal enforcement was so loose, so decentralized, so diverse as to suggest that Washington often lacked effective control.[21]

[20] *Baltimore American*, Nov. 6, 1878; Nov. 5, 1872; Frank R. Kent, *Story of Maryland Politics* (Baltimore, 1911), pp. 22, 47–52; W. A. Merriwether to Benjamin H. Bristow, Nov. 11, 1870, Bristow MSS, LC's Richard Burke to Attorney General Alphonso Taft, Oct. 16, 1878, Source–Chronological File for West Virginia; *New York Times*, Nov. 8, Aug. 8, 1874.

[21] A. I. Boreman to E. D. Morgan, June 14, 1872, William E. Chandler MSS, LC; *ex Parte McIlwee*, 16 Fed. Case 147; Gerald W. Smith, "Nathan Goff, Jr.: A Biography" (Ph.D. diss., W. Va. University, 1954), pp. 87–89. See also, on enforcement in West Virginia, the essay in this volume by Richard O. Curry, "Crisis Politics in West Virginia," especially notes 37–41. See also, William E. Parrish, *Missouri Under Radical Rule, 1865–1870* (Columbia: University of Missouri Press, 1965), pp. 306–7.

White opposition to Negro voting in Kentucky often took the form of distracting and delaying tactics. The cities of Paris and Nicholasville, for example, prevented Negro voting by eliminating Negro neighborhoods from the city, while the city of Danville tried to offset Negro participation by including white voters from the county, who bought four-inch lots on the day before the election. In August, 1870, city authorities in Frankfort let Negroes wait at the polls all day, until they left at dusk without voting. Gerrymandering of judicial, legislative, and congressional districts was also employed to neutralize black voting, exemplified in the West Virginia constitution of 1872. The repressive will of a Bourbon spawned reckless and resourceful ways.[22]

In Delaware the ingenuity of the Democrats matched their desperation. Since the struggle for power in that state depended largely upon the new Negro voter, the stake was immense and the consequences were more flagrantly widespread than in any other border state. If eligible Negroes voted in full force, Republicans would carry their federal and state-wide tickets. The first showdown came in November, 1870: Democrats tried to prevent Negroes from voting by practicing registration fraud, by bragging about "the white man's party," and by using naked force. They succeeded.

To begin with, Democratic officials refused to qualify Negroes by not collecting their poll taxes. Without payment of this tax or a property tax one could not qualify to vote. Thus many Negroes were listed as either dead or departed. Qualifying became extremely difficult, while challenging at the polls was always a last resort on election day. When Negroes were slated to vote for the first time under the Fifteenth Amendment, Democrats made fresh appeals to arouse prejudice. Angry, snarling, quarreling Democratic rowdies, fortified with whiskey, spoiled for a fight. Unable any longer to keep their prejudices down, they rushed to the polls crying "down with the nigger" or "clean 'em out." When riots erupted in Wilmington's sixth ward on election eve and day, as bricks were thrown and pistol shots were fired, Republican municipal police and the federal marshal tried to calm both whites and Negroes. Downstate at Broad Creek, in Sussex County, a drunken mob prevented Negroes from voting, while at Smyrna, in Kent County, a crowd shoved Negroes away from the Republican window. Most significant was a riot in Odessa, the polling place for St. George's Hundred, in nominally Republican New Castle County. There, a crowd cursed, knocked down, and so badly beat Negro voters that

[22] Coulter, *Civil War and Readjustment in Kentucky*, pp. 423–24; J. R. Hubbard to William E. Chandler, Aug. 28, 1872, Chandler MSS.

they were driven away from the polls. In the latter two places deputy United States marshals also were driven away from the polls, causing the Federal Attorney in Delaware to telegraph President Grant to send the marines in, but nothing came of it.[23]

When the smoke of battle cleared away, the Republican defeat in Delaware was complete. Two Republicans left in the legislature were ousted in New Castle County, while the state and congressional ticket also failed. Democratic terrorism and trickery paid off handsomely when the Democrats captured the New Castle County levy court, which functioned in effect as the voting registrar. There was no doubt about what had happened in Republican New Castle. The Delaware *Republican* attributed the county defeat to the Odessa riot. The influential Wilmington *Commercial* agreed: "Republicans have lost New Castle county and the Democrats secure control of the Levy Court, solely on account of the intimidation used against the colored people in St. George's Hundred." The promise of the Negro vote was not realized. Republicans had optimistically counted on 4,500 Negro voters throughout the state, but estimated that less than half that number actually were allowed to vote on election day. Robbing Republicans of victory, Democrats inaugurated an era of bad feeling.[24]

Infuriated Republicans plotted revenge and sought federal help in enforcing the Negro's right to the franchise. Their motives happily combined impartial justice and partisan expediency. At stake, at a low estimate, was "from one thousand to fifteen hundred colored citizens," reported the Federal Attorney in Delaware. Not being bashful, he added that "partisan interest felt in the case was intense." He

[23] Wilmington, *Daily Commercial*, Nov. 9, 10, 1870; Amy M. Hiller, "The Disenfranchisement of the Delaware Negroes in the late Nineteenth Century" (M.A. thesis, University of Delaware, 1965), p. 9.

[24] Hiller, *ibid.*; Wilmington *Delaware Republican*, Nov. 10, 1870; Wilmington *Daily Commercial*, Nov. 10, 11, 14, 1870. Although losing, Republicans still had grounds for hope. The Democratic majority in key New Castle county declined from 713 in 1868 to 57 in 1870, while there was an absolute Republican gain of 656 votes "under the influence of the colored vote," as the *Commercial* put it. White conservative Republican defection could be offset if the Negro voters were all allowed to vote. If about 1,000 more Negro males would vote, the Democratic majority of 57 could be easily overcome in New Castle County, while the eligible Negroes throughout the state, about 2,000 to 2,600, might overturn the state Democratic majority of about 2,300. As it was, the Republican candidate for Congress carried the county by thirteen votes but lost the election downstate. Suggestive of the close call was the aggressive tone of the inaugural address of Governor James Ponder, who accurately observed that it was a "source of gratification to me that I owe my election exclusively to the voters of the white citizens of the State." He lashed out at Negro voting as "unwise in policy, unsound in principle," detrimental in practice, and motivated exclusively by the Republican quest for power. Wilmington *Daily Commercial*, Jan. 18, 1871.

got what he asked for. Washington provided additional money for extra expenses and personnel, since the Attorney General believed that the case was one "in which the United States is interested."[25]

Federal prosecution commenced in 1872 and concentrated upon New Castle County. The tax collector for the western district of Wilmington, Archibald Given, was tried in federal court under the second section of the Act of May 31, 1870, which required officials to qualify any voter impartially. Federal counsel showed that tax collector Given had gone out of his way to prevent five Negroes from qualifying to vote—by being absent from his office, by refusing payment of the tax on the street, by failing to provide tax bills, by entering the names of the five Negroes in his "can't find" list but then changing them to his "left the State" list, and by avoiding inspection of his records by Republican officials. Given made matters worse by being indiscreet. He was found guilty of submitting false returns and was fined roughly $2,000, barely escaping imprisonment. Judge Edward Bradford, former member of the National Republican Executive Committee, subsequently ruled that the tax collector was, in effect, an election official and not merely a revenue officer; further, he was subject not only to state authority but to federal authority. The Federal Attorney reported the decision to his superior: "No event has happened in the history of the State, which will go so far to secure to its citizens pure and free elections." He predicted that Negro voting now would be protected to the last full measure. The object lesson "will be salutary beyond expression," he concluded confidently.[26]

But it was the timing of the federal enforcement effort that made the difference. The initial decision against the Democratic registrars was made in October, 1872, just before the election. The significance was not lost upon Delaware Democrats when Senator Eli Saulsbury wrote to Senator Thomas Bayard that Republicans were now insisting that "any person not on the assessment rolls offering to pay to a collector a tax thereby becomes entitled to vote if otherwise qualified. And that the election officers are bound to receive and count the vote of such person offering to vote under such circumstances." Saulsbury

[25] Anthony Higgins to Attorney General, Jan. 29, June 13, Oct. 21, 1872, Source–Chronological File for Delaware; Attorney General George Williams to Higgins, July 2, 1872, Instruction Book, quoted in Hiller, "Disenfranchisement of Delaware Negroes," pp. 15–25; John Cameron to William E. Chandler, June 24, 1872, and H. F. Pickels to Chandler, Sept. 17, 1872, Chandler MSS.

[26] Wilmington *Daily Commercial*, June 10, 14, 1872, Jan. 30, 1873; *United States* v. *Given*, 25 Fed. Cas. 1324, 1328; Higgins to Williams, Feb. 15, 1873, Oct. 21, 1872, Source–Chronological File for Deleware; Thomas F. Bayard to Thomas Holcomb, March 7, 1875, Bayard MSS, LC, and Bayard to Archibald Given, March 1, 1875.

concluded that the practical effect was "to intimidate some from opposing the right of such persons to vote and will possibly induce Inspectors and Judges of elections to receive the votes of the negroes not on the Assessment lists."

Grounds for pessimism were reinforced by the 1872 election returns. Republicans did so well in New Castle County that they won the state for their presidential and congressional candidates and gained eight seats in the legislature, where before they had none. While Democratic defections from Horace Greeley's candidacy and platform were important, an increase in the Negro electorate proved decisive, especially when federal election supervisors were stationed at the polls. The Republican *Commercial* regarded the election as a vindication of Republican principles and a "rebuke to political trickery." The editor predicted that "with a full assessment and full vote," Republicans had forged a new majority party in Delaware.[27]

But actually victory at the polls and in the courtroom was a delusion; what it amounted to was a successful skirmish in a larger campaign that was lost. Reacting to the sting of defeat, Democrats gambled on a bold stroke, and the gamble succeeded. Capitalizing on their solid control of the state government and exploiting the widespread feeling that the Negro was not ready for self-government and was in fact a mere slave and party tool of Republican leaders, Democrats were determined to change the law to keep Negroes away from the polls. At the request of the Governor, and on a strictly partisan vote, Democrats, in April, 1873, rammed through the legislature a new scheme in the form of the delinquent tax law. The 1873 statute continued county taxation as a prerequisite for voting. However, it provided that persons who were not taxed for property, mostly Negroes, must pay their individual tax or poll tax to the collector each year. If they failed to do so, the collector had the option to return them as delinquents to the county commissioners (levy courts), who were required to drop the names of such persons from the tax assessment list. Once off the list, it took monumental endurance and almost two

[27] Saulsbury to Bayard, Oct. 29, 1872, Bayard MSS, LC. Wilmington *Daily Commercial*, Nov. 6–9, 1872; Wilmington *Delaware Republican*, Nov. 7, 1872; Wilmington *Delaware Gazette*, Nov. 28, 1872; *New York Times*, Nov. 7, 18, 1872. The Democratic *Gazette* observed in particular that Delaware Negroes "held the balance of power and threw it in the Radical scale. . . . in this state without the whole negro vote the Radicals would have been several thousand in the minority. Even in this county [New Castle] they would have been beaten over a thousand and in this city [Wilmington] several hundred votes. In fact without the negro's aid the Radicals could not have expected to have elected anything." Republican papers were more discreet; there was a point beyond which the obviousness of a connection would yield diminishing returns.

years to get back on. The law, by dropping the requirement that tax collectors list all citizens who were to pay their poll tax, thus relieved officials from the fate of Archibald Given. Most important was the way in which the law was administered, for Republicans were hurt and Democrats were helped: that is, Democratic officials would drop Negro delinquents just before election day but would carry Democratic delinquents for as long as they dared. Democrats, too, slipped in the back door of city hall and were easily qualified, while Negroes stood in long lines in front of city hall and had a rough time qualifying inside. When Negroes appeared before them, Democratic qualifying officials performed their duties in a state of perpetual absent-mindedness about proper form, along with consistent misspelling of their names, omitting an initial, or entering the wrong number of an address. Often such officials played hide-and-seek with prospective Negro voters; indeed, at one point Negroes had to follow their tax collector to Philadelphia, where they forced their taxes on him at gunpoint after having knocked down his hotel room door. But while strictness was the rule for Negroes, who were required to comply fully and exactly with the letter of the law, Democratic officials supplied the proscriptive spirit. In short, Negroes found out that their assessors failed to assess and that their tax collectors failed to collect; therefore Negroes failed to vote. By relieving qualifying officials of their legal responsibilities but not their real power, Democrats had smooth sailing as long as the county crew continued to be Democrats.[28]

A second prong in the Democratic attack was directed toward federal enforcement officers. Such officials, notably the marshal and election supervisors, were harassed and attacked by local police, arrested on trumped-up charges of assault and battery, shoved away from the polls, and denounced by local and state officials, including the Democratic governors. In the presidential election, for example, on November 7, 1876, there were several instances of conflict of authority between federal marshals and local police which resulted

[28] Wilmington *Daily Commercial,* Jan. 7–8, 1873, Sept. 3, 1873, Oct. 6, 1874, Nov. 2–5, 1874; Wilmington, *Daily Gazette,* Nov. 7, 1873; Hiller, "Disenfranchisement of Delaware Negroes," pp. 41–67; Harold C. Livesay, "Delaware Negroes, 1865–1915" (B.A. thesis, University of Delaware, 1966), pp. 13–28; New York *Age,* Feb. 11, 1887. The problem arose when the Republicans captured control of the qualifying machinery in two counties in 1890. But Democrats got around this by the legislature repealing the delinquent law in the two affected counties only. Thus they avoided the bitter taste of their own medicine. When Democrats returned to power in both counties in 1892 they promptly reintroduced the delinquent law. But by 1897 political revolution and Republican resurgence swept out the delinquent law and tax requirement forever. Speech of Senator Anthony Higgins on Jan. 29, 1894, U.S., *Congressional Record,* 53d Cong., 2d sess. (1894), 1588.

in the rescue of prisoners from the custody of the marshals. These cases promised to become head-on collisions between state and federal authority, for Delaware threatened to nullify the enforcement acts and try two federal deputy marshals in her courts. But federal prosecution was not pressed once the subsequent election of 1878 turned out to be quiet. Yet it should have been, for there was no Republican candidate to contest the Democratic governorship in the first place. With the face-saving device of each side dropping its case at the same time, by gentleman's agreement, the federal attorney wrote to Washington that it was a good time to quietly and finally dispose of the case: "This action can now be taken without attracting attention, or comment from any quarter, and would, I am sure, be wise and judicious." Certainly the damage had long been done, but further damage would result by ducking a fight and by further eroding federal authority. The sad state of enforcement activity was suggested during 1880 when Washington merely wished good luck to the federal attorney in Delaware but furnished no aid. Washington was avoiding confrontation.[29]

The pattern of fraud in Maryland tended to parallel but not to duplicate developments in Delaware. Maryland Democrats were less discreet about maintaining the semblance of law, particularly in local and state elections, at which federal inspectors were not present. Some Negroes discovered quickly that it was better to stay at home than to try to vote in such elections, while others were paid to stay at home. During federal elections, however, the Democrats tended to be better behaved; indeed, fraud was not so open or widespread with the federal presence. Still, restriction of Negro voters was achieved by the covert ways of registration, while direct harassment was more often confined to federal election inspectors. Because the Maryland Negro population was proportionately and actually greater than in Delaware, and the caliber of some federal officials was higher and Republican strength

---

[29] Wilmington *Daily Commercial*, Nov. 7, 1876; William C. Spruance to Attorney General, Nov. 29, 1876, Jan. 16, 1877, April 12, 1879, Source–Chronological File for Delaware; Attorney General Charles Devens to Spruance, April 18, 1879, Devens to U.S. Marshal H. H. McMullen, Nov. 1, 1880, Instruction Book; *Delaware* v. *Emerson*, 8 Fed. Cas. 411 (1881). Subsequent federal efforts after 1880 proved also unsuccessful. See Harold Hancock, "Reconstruction in Delaware," in this book, specifically notes 98–100. Suggestive of the mediocrity of enforcement officials by 1880 was the tart reply of the Attorney General to the request of the federal attorney in Delaware for a standard form for election law indictments: "You are presumed to know the facts, and I need hardly add that the indictment in each case, must be drawn so as to meet the facts, which you expect to prove. Indictments framed upon only a general knowledge of the cases would very likely turn out to be bad." Charles Devens to John C. Patterson, April 5, 1880, Instruction Book. There were instances as well of lack of local federal co-ordination between marshals, supervisors, and attorneys.

stronger and more aggressive, Democrats were less successful in disenfranchising the Negro than in Delaware.[30]

By 1875 the federal enforcement record in the border states was at
best a mixed bag. There was minor success but also major reversal in
eliminating coercion and cheating. However, another test was yet to
come, the first case to reach the Supreme Court in which the justices
would be required to spell out the meaning of the Fifteenth Amendment and decide the constitutionality of the enforcement acts. This
crucial case, bearing directly on the right to vote, was to arrive from
Kentucky in *United States* v. *Reese,* and was to be decided six years
after the Fifteenth Amendment was adopted and enforcement undertaken.

The Reese case originated in the city of Lexington, Kentucky—an
appropriate battleground, since the Negro population outnumbered
whites and therefore threatened incumbent Democrats in city hall.
Before the Fifteenth Amendment was ratified, in March of 1870, the
Kentucky legislature allowed the city to hold a municipal election in
February, just before Negroes could vote. When the Fifteenth Amendment went into effect, these officeholders tried to delay city council
elections by lengthening their term of office, but they failed. The
feared election took place in September, 1871. Not eager to welcome
Negroes at the polls, the mayor, city clerk, and police chief, among
others, turned their guns on Negro voters and thus won the election.
The next time elections came around, on January 30, 1873, United
States troops and election supervisors were on hand. Changing tactics,
the officials introduced the poll tax as a prerequisite for voting and
thereby left two-thirds of the city's Negroes disenfranchised, thus
insuring re-election once again.[31]

It was this time that state and federal authority collided in the
Third Ward. Several Negroes who had appeared at the polls were not
allowed to vote by state election judges, who contended that they had

---

[30] *Baltimore American,* Nov. 6, 1872, Nov. 8, 1876; New York *Age,* May 26, 1888;
Special Assistant U.S. Attorney W. W. Danenhower to Attorney General, Feb. 11,
1874; A. Sterling to Attorney General, Nov. 10, 1873; Chief Supervisor G. Morris
Bond to Attorney General, Nov. 17, Dec. 1, 1876, Dec. 13, 1878; Sterling to Attorney
General, Jan. 31, 1879, Sept. 8, 1879, Source–Chronological File for Maryland. The
Supreme Court in *Ex Parte Siebold* (100 U.S. 371, 1880) ruled that a state election
official could not stuff a ballot box, but significantly on grounds other than the
Fifteenth Amendment and then solely in regard to a congressional election.

[31] *New York Times,* Nov. 6, 1871, Jan. 31, 1873; Louisville *Courier Journal,* Jan.
31, Feb. 1, 1873; Tapp, "Three Decades of Kentucky Politics," p. 91; Coulter, *Civil
War and Readjustment in Kentucky,* p. 423.

not paid their poll tax. As a result, the state election officials were indicted in federal circuit court at Louisville on February 17, 1873, for violating the first Enforcement Act. The cases were argued during November before District Judge Bland Ballard and Circuit Judge Halmor Edmunds, who differed on points of law. Judge Ballard, an avowed enemy of the enforcement acts, found several counts of the indictment insufficient, because, he contended, the act covered not all obstructions to Negro voting but only a clear-cut case of racial discrimination. Upon a certificate of division the case went to the Supreme Court for decision.[32]

The pivotal case was argued before the Supreme Court during January and October of 1875. Counsel for the state election judges maintained that the right to vote in a municipal election under state law was not a right within the authority of Congress to enforce and regulate but was instead a state matter falling under state control and protection. The attorney argued that the indictments were faulty in not specifying and proving racial discrimination, and that the Fifteenth Amendment did not reach beyond discriminatory state law. He thus concluded that the enforcement act was unconstitutional and that the third and fourth sections, which substituted federal for state election procedures when racial discrimination occurred, were therefore inoperative. In reply, federal counsel—the Attorney General and Solicitor General—breezily dismissed the argument of the defense, asserting that Congress could ban and rectify any racial discrimination in any election—local, state, or federal—by the force of the Fifteenth Amendment alone. In so doing, they failed to grapple with the key questions on which the case would turn.[33]

The Supreme Court, in making its decision, drastically narrowed the claim of the Attorney General and made future enforcement vastly more difficult, if not, in some cases, clearly impossible. Speaking for the majority, Chief Justice Morrison Waite observed, in the first place, that the federal government had merely the negative or latent power to prevent racial discrimination in voting, not the positive or overt power to confer suffrage outright and regulate it accordingly. Thus he noted that the Fifteenth Amendment did not confer the right to vote on anyone. Instead, the amendment only gave the right not to be discriminated against as Negroes. It was a fine legal point,

[32] Benjamin Bristow to Attorney General, Oct. 19, 1873; G. C. Wharton to Attorney General, Nov. 10, 1873; John M. Harlan to Attorney General, July 15, Nov. 18, 1874, Source–Chronological File for Kentucky; Louisville *Courier Journal*, Nov. 5, 6, 1873.

[33] *United States* v. *Reese*, 92 U.S. 214 (1876); *New York Times*, March 28, 1876; C. Peter Magrath, *Morrison R. Waite* (New York: Macmillan Co., 1963), pp. 122–29.

with immense constitutional significance and fraught with political consequences, for it meant that Congress could only legislate upon the subject of "exemption from discrimination in the exercise of the elective franchise on account of race," and not exercise plenary authority to pass direct and primary legislation. In other words, he was saying that regulation of elections remained a state responsibility primarily and that Congress had better stay within bounds by minding its proper business. Since Congress had limited powers in the matter, it had better confine its statutes to those powers. In the second place, Waite argued, the Fifteenth Amendment authorized federal penalties, not for every refusal to receive the vote of a qualified voter at a state election, but "only when the wrongful refusal at such an election is because of race." Thus it was not all actions of interference but interference because of race alone that mattered. The assault had just begun.

The question then turned on where and how one draws the line between federal and state power. Scrutinizing the indictments under the third and fourth sections of the act,[34] the Chief Justice observed that the general language of the sections and the act as a whole was broad enough to cover every conceivable instance in which Negroes, for whatever the reason, were denied the franchise. In fact, the act's grasp might be greater than the amendment's reach. The act, he reasoned, was like a huge net which embraced all instances of Negro nonvoting, with the result that the Justices of the Supreme Court were required to choose which fish were to be kept and which were to be thrown back into the sea. But Waite quickly added that the Court was not about to become a fisherman or to masquerade as Congress by making new law in the guise of interpreting old law, and Congress, as well, ought not to play court by tampering with the Constitution. Such tampering was clear if there was an undermining of state control over suffrage regulation by Congress, prescribing ground rules not provided by the states, if racial discrimination was assumed merely because the victim was Negro, and if, in fact, the section of the law and case in question did not allege and prove racial discrimination at all. Moreover, the practical operation of the statute, which substituted

---

[34] The third section of the Act of May 31, 1870, provided that if a Negro citizen gave proof that he was prevented from qualifying to vote because of his race, he then could actually vote on election day. Election officials were required by this law to receive and count the Negro's vote upon his showing an affidavit that he had intended to qualify, could indeed qualify, had been prevented from qualifying, and thus must be considered as having qualified automatically to vote by law. Officials who refused to comply with the act were subject to stiff penalties, while any individual under the fourth section who used force, bribery, or threats in obstructing a Negro's right to vote would be similarly punished.

"performance wrongfully prevented for performance itself," was indeed a radical legal point of departure, since the applicant's affidavit was supposed to be conclusive evidence of racial discrimination. Besides, if offenses were not spelled out clearly, there was bound to be trouble in potential abuse and future uncertainty. To be specific, an election officer would be held responsible for refusing a Negro the ballot when it was not at all clear that the refusal was because of color, while a Negro had the right of action which might or might not result from racial discrimination. On narrow legalistic grounds, broader constitutional grounds, and still wider political grounds, Waite found, in effect, that the two sections of the Enforcement Act of May 31, 1870, were null and void.[35]

From the viewpoint of the nineteenth century, Waite saved electoral federalism at the high price of undercutting federal enforcement, by restricting rather than protecting Negro voting rights. In effect, Waite had distinguished between the privilege of suffrage and its exercise, by confining the federal role in guaranteeing exercise. But the opportunity had been provided largely by Congress in drafting the law and by the Justice Department in arguing the case. Most significant of all, the country was downright relieved and delighted with the Supreme Court decision, and that told something about popular support for enforcement by March, 1876. The New York *Times,* in an editorial, argued that the source of the blunders of the enforcement acts was the belief that the United States had either the power or the obligation "to do police duty in the States," which the *Times* editor still capitalized. The editorial went on to note that the decision in the Reese case was a "respectful but vigorous warning to Congress against the passage of hasty and loosely-worded laws."[36]

The Reese case marked the beginning of the end of electoral enforcement, and sounded the retreat from Reconstruction. Repeal of various voting sections of the law came under Democratic control in February, 1894. Then, in *James* v. *Bowman* in 1903, the Supreme Court ruled that the fifth section of the Act of May 31, 1870, was unconstitutional because it might apply to state elections, not merely congressional elections, while the indictment itself was directed solely against private persons, not against the actions of public officials.

[35] The effect of Waite's decision was the same in *United States* v. *Cruikshank,* 92 U.S. 542 (1876), which invalidated the sixth section of the same enforcement act, but the questions bore more on civil rights than voting rights and therefore came more under the protection of the Fourteenth Amendment than the Fifteenth.

[36] *New York Times,* March 28, 29, 1876. For other press reaction see Charles Warren, *The Supreme Court in United States History* (3 vols.; Boston: Little, Brown, 1922), 3:326–30; Magrath, *Morrison R. Waite,* pp. 129–34.

Further, the bribery was not alleged to have been done because of race. It is suggestive that the two most important cases directly affecting voting rights under the Fifteenth Amendment originated not in the South or in the North but in the border state of Kentucky.[37]

If there were substantial weaknesses in the enforcement effort, there were also strengths that nourished and sustained Negro suffrage, and thereby helped the enforcement effort for a time. The clear interest of state and local Republican politicians and federal officials within the border states to insure Negro voting was vital. If there had been no need of Negro voters—that is, if Negro voters at the polls had not meant Republican votes in the ballot box—it is doubtful whether the enforcement effort would have been undertaken in the first place in the South and the borderland. To be sure, Washington stressed that enforcement was to be strictly impartial—that there would be no double standard in punishing violators of the law. But, of course, violation generally occurred in Democratic strongholds, and there was often an excess of partisan zeal in coping with it. Moreover, the enforcement effort, despite its ploy for fair play, did not mean nonpartisan employment of enforcement officials. On the contrary, Democratic attorneys were not to be hired as special counsel; Republican lawyers were preferred. One Federal Attorney General summed it up when he wrote that Republican employees "are more likely to have their hearts in the work."[38]

Although federal intervention appeared justified on several counts, it was striking as well that interest in enforcement mainly involved members of other federal agencies and of state Republican organizations at the grass roots. Moreover, the timing of their letters coincided with forthcoming elections, and the substance of the messages was the same: help us "as friends of the Government and the men loyal to the Government." In other words, party interest was synonymous with national interest. As former Senator and Republican chairman E. D. Morgan wrote to Senator John Sherman: "It [the "Elections or En-

[37] *James v. Bowman*, 190 U.S. 127 (1903), concerned bribery in the Fifth Congressional District of Kentucky on Nov. 8, 1898. Note the different line of reasoning with doctrinal consequence concerning federal powers in congressional elections but rooted in the original Constitution and not precisely under the reach of the Fifteenth Amendment, in *Ex Parte Siebold* cited above and *Ex Parte Yarbrough*, 110 U.S. 651 (1884).

[38] Attorney General Amos T. Akerman, quoted in Homer Cummings and Carl McFarland, *Federal Justice and the Federal Executive* (New York: Macmillan, 1937), p. 234.

forcement Bill"] is of great importance to the party and to all who want justice at the ballot box." Clearly, the ideal served self-interest, and it is instructive to note whose, for Morgan, came first. In short, border politicians read politics, talked politics, smoked politics, and drank politics the year round, in and out of office, and the Negro voter was on their minds a good deal of that time. Therefore, so was federal enforcement.[39]

The career of Nathan Goff in West Virginia illustrates the close relationship between public service, professional politics, and the Negro voter. Radical Goff, a former Union officer, supported until 1870 complete disenfranchisement of West Virginia whites, once Confederate, then Democratic, while endorsing comprehensive enfranchisement of state Negroes, all Republican. When appointed United States attorney for the state, he served from 1868 to 1882. As was the custom, he found time during his tenure not only to perform duty but also to campaign for Republican presidential candidates. He ran unsuccessfully for Congress in 1870 and 1874, and for governor in 1876, while dispensing federal patronage for the state. He deftly accommodated to border state realities by turning a bit more conservative in accepting universal white suffrage after 1870 and in opposing a federal civil rights bill in 1874–75. Yet he still championed a free ballot for all. By making calculated appeals to both white and Negro voters, he finally won election to Congress in 1882, and only then terminated federal employment. While representing the First District for three terms, he introduced a resolution banning racial segregation on railroads in 1884, and condemned attempts to disenfranchise southern Negroes in 1886. The upshot of his stands was solid Negro support. Thus a Negro newspaper, The New York *Age,* observed that Goff was "a good friend of the Negro." Nominated for governor, Republican candidate Goff received the endorsement of Negro groups. He won election by 110 votes, while the Negro vote was estimated at 11,000. But a Democratic legislature in 1890, after a purported investigation, rejected the election returns because they charged that thousands of Negroes had been bribed and brought into

[39] A reading of Justice Department correspondence underscores the political consideration. Federal Marshal and Republican state executive committee chairman L. B. Eaton to Attorney General, Aug. 12, 1874, Source–Chronological File for Tennessee; Annapolis Postmaster W. O. Bigelow to Attorney General, Aug. 11, 1873; Baltimore Custom House employee H. R. Torbert to Attorney General, Oct. 19, 1874, Source–Chronological File for Maryland; Greenbrier County Republican central committee president J. F. Caldwell to Attorney General, Dec. 24, 1872, Source–Chronological File for West Virginia; E. D. Morgan to John Sherman, Feb. 21, 1871, John Sherman MSS, LC.

the state on election day to vote for Goff. Goff thus lost the governorship, if not the election. Appointed a federal circuit judge in the 1890s, he tried to end proscription of South Carolina Negro voters. Inside or outside federal office, Goff remained both a professional politician and an effective supporter of Negro voting rights. Doubtless principle played a role, although not always including civil rights, but a West Virginia Republican could scarcely do otherwise on both scores. Goff knew who his reliable supporters were and West Virginia Negroes knew who their good friend was.[40]

Of course, Republican action generated Democratic reaction. With political victories under their belts, border Conservatives felt free enough and secure enough to blaze a trail backward. In doing so, they were to show the way for Southerners to follow. Thus Tennessee gave the Klan to the nation in 1865 and introduced the poll tax in 1870. Tennessee and West Virginia pioneered in creating racial segregation laws, the latter on separate but equal guidelines. Delaware perfected sophisticated means to keep Negroes at home on election day, while Kentucky and Maryland, among others, made bribery into a fine art. Missouri, along with West Virginia, initiated liberal Republicanism in confusing reform with restoration by endorsing universal amnesty and general re-enfranchisement. In other words, in the aftermath of civil war and reconstruction, in the wake of fighting their own civil wars, border men moved away from the political middle-ground which they had occupied for so long, and veered abruptly to the right of center. But the mood was not to last. Because the border states were the first to embrace reactionary redemption, they escaped earlier from its grip than did the southern states. Despite violence and fraud, border men did exercise some restraint. Of the border states, only Tennessee adopted the poll tax as a requirement for voting, as Delaware did with its county tax, while only Tennessee in 1901 and Kentucky in 1903 adopted the white primary. But the border states, to their credit, went no further, while the southern states flagrantly used as weapons property, ownership, education, ancestry, character, and understanding tests. West Virginians, for example, thus rejected

[40] Smith, "Nathan Goff, Jr.," pp. 71–89, 113–50, 168–70, 181–84, 317, 344–51; New York *Age*, Sept. 22, 1888. Similarly, John M. Harlan, a Republican gubernatorial candidate, state party leader, and special prosecutor against the Klan, reflected in his Supreme Court decisions a political bent toward Negro rights which had been forged in Kentucky. See the perceptive observations of Alan F. Westin, "John Marshall Harlan and the Constitutional Rights of Negroes: The Transformation of a Southerner," *Yale Law Journal* 61 (April, 1957): 637–710, and of Stanley Hirshson, *Farewell to the Bloody Shirt* (Bloomington: Indiana University Press, 1962), pp. 251–55.

Negro proscription in 1872 and 1908; Missourians did the same in 1875; Kentuckians, in 1891; Marylanders, between 1903 and 1911; while Delawareans rejected their county tax altogether in 1897. Border moderation was re-emerging and was confirmed by Republican resurgence and Negro advance during the 1890s, precisely when the southern Negro was in deepest trouble. In the long run, existential forces and partisan organization propelled the border Negro forward politically.[41]

Negro gains came slowly and painfully, and ironically occurred in the states where federal enforcement had proved to be an outstanding failure. The greatest and earliest gains were made in Tennessee, where both political violence and fraud were flagrant. Yet Tennessee Negroes formed the largest Negro group in the border states, both numerically and proportionately. They asserted themselves accordingly, since they represented a large share of the state Republican vote. Negro Tennesseans elected their first state legislator in 1872, after the state radical régime was overthrown, and they sent ten more Negroes to the statehouse until 1897. Significantly, seven of the eleven legislators came from urban counties and probably reflected the three-fold increase in the Negro urban population, as well as the relative ease and safety of Negro political organization and mobilization in urban rather than rural areas. Suggestive as well was the election of Negro aldermen in Chattanooga and Knoxville, and other officials in Memphis and Nashville. Negro political progress tapered off about 1890 when, interestingly, for the first time the percentage of Negroes in the state population declined sharply. The political weather vane pointed to stormy days ahead, and the forecast was borne out when no Negro was sent to the Republican national convention in 1896, and the last Negro state legislator was unseated without objection in 1897. Only in 1964 did a Negro Tennessean return to the legislature. Tennessee then, during the 1890s, appeared to parallel the Southern pattern rather than the border trend.[42]

Dissimilar West Virginia, with the lowest proportion of Negroes in the borderland, also represented Negro political advance in the border states. There the reviving power of the Republican party meshed with the growing strength of the Negro voter. It was noteworthy that Negro West Virginians helped elect the first black state

[41] Gilbert T. Stephenson, *Race Distinction in American Law* (New York: D. Appleton, 1910), pp. 324–37. *New York Times,* Feb. 22, 1870.
[42] U.S., Bureau of the Census, *Negro Population, 1790–1915,* p. 51; Robert E. Corlew, "The Negro in Tennessee, 1870–1900" (Ph.D. diss., University of Alabama, 1954), pp. 134–65; and Taylor, *Negro in Tennessee.*

legislator, outside of Tennessee, in 1896. Significantly, the Negro share of the state population continued to rise in West Virginia between 1870 and 1910—the only border state in which this occurred. Freer voting also enabled Negroes to advance in Missouri, particularly in the cities. The pattern was similar elsewhere. But it required farming the precincts for border Republicans and Negro politicians to reap the rich harvest of the Negro vote. In Baltimore, the first Negro was elected to the city council in 1890; others followed. In Wilmington, a Negro was elected to the city council for the first time in 1901. But election of Negroes for the first time to state legislatures was an agonizingly slow process: Tennessee, 1872–97; West Virginia, 1896; Missouri, 1919; Kentucky, 1935; Delaware, 1940s; Maryland, 1954; Tennessee, 1964.[43]

The border Negro electorate influenced Presidential elections but did not affect the outcome in a border state until 1896, except in 1872. In the short run, great Republican gains were registered in 1872 and were in part attributed to Negroes voting for the first time. In a comparison between the 1868 and 1872 presidential vote, there was a marked increase in the Republican percentage of the two-party vote: an increase from 41 per cent to 52 per cent for Delaware; 25 per cent to 46 per cent in Kentucky; 32 per cent to 49 per cent for Maryland. Political scientist Dean Burnham concludes that the shift "seems to be largely a result of Negro enfranchisement." The two, border, Republican presidential victories in 1872 were achieved by indispensable Negro support. Delaware produced a Republican majority of 921 votes, with roughly 2,000 Negro voters in the state. Similarly, in West Virginia there was a Republican majority of 2,864, with a Negro electorate between 2,000 to 3,000. Elsewhere in 1872, except in Missouri, Democratic victories were narrow indeed. Between 1880 and 1892 Democratic presidential victories usually were kept marginal. The new departure started in 1896, when border states went Republican for the first time since 1872. The Negro electorate now vitally mattered once again. William McKinley in 1896 had a Republican presidential majority of 4,000, while the Delaware Negro vote was estimated at 6,000; he had the Maryland majority of 34,000, while the Negro voters numbered about 45,000; he had the Kentucky majority of 34,000, while the Negro vote was roughly 58,000. In brief, either in achieving Republican victories or in reducing drastically Democratic

[43] *Negro Population,* p. 51; Sheeler, "Negro in West Virginia," pp. 193–213; New York *Age,* Nov. 17, 1888.

pluralities, the Negro electorate was hardly irrelevant in presidential contests.[44]

The more significant Republican gubernatorial resurgence came about first in Delaware in 1894 when Joshua Marvel won by a margin of 1,225 (51 per cent), with an estimated 6,000 Negro electorate. The Republican reign in Dover began in earnest in 1900 with the victory of John Hunn by a margin of 3,613 (54 per cent), with at least 6,000 Negro voters. In Maryland, the Democratic monopoly of the governor's mansion was broken in 1895 when Lloyd Lowndes won by 18,767 votes (52 per cent), with an estimated Negro vote between 45,000 and 48,000. In Kentucky, William Bradley was elected in 1895 by 8,912 votes (48 per cent). The Negro electorate there was between 34,000 and 58,000. In West Virginia, the first post-Reconstruction Republican governor was George Atkinson, in 1896, and he carried the state by a plurality of 12,070 (52 per cent), with that margin supplied by Negroes. In Missouri, Republicans defeated the Democratic establishment when in 1908 Herbert Hadley became governor. He won by 15,339 votes and the Negro electorate numbered at least 33,000. In Tennessee, the most Southern-oriented of the border states, Republican Ben Hooper was elected in 1910 by a margin of 12,325 votes, with at least 64,000 to 80,000 Negro voters in the state. In every border state, then, the Negro vote was larger than the Republican gubernatorial plurality. Negroes proved indispensable in capturing border governorships and in mounting the Republican comeback.[45]

[44] In particular, Burnham notes the differences in the county returns between 1868 and 1872 for Sussex County, Delaware; Calvert and Prince George's counties, Maryland; Franklin and Woodford counties, Kentucky. W. Dean Burnham, *Presidential Ballots, 1836–1892* (Baltimore: The Johns Hopkins Press, 1955), p. 114. See also, for an estimate of the effect of Negro voting in Kentucky counties, John Fenton, *Politics in the Border States* (New Orleans: Hauser, 1957), p. 61. Democratic victories in 1872 were kept marginal in Maryland (50 per cent), Kentucky and Tennessee (52 per cent). Between 1880 and 1892 Democratic victories were usually marginal in the four presidential contests as follows: in Delaware twice (51 per cent in 1880 and 49 per cent in 1892); in Maryland every time (54 per cent in 1880, 52 per cent in 1884, 50 per cent in 1888, 53 per cent in 1892); in Missouri every time (52 per cent in 1880, 53 per cent in 1884, 50 per cent in 1888, 49 per cent in 1892); in Tennessee every time (53 per cent in 1880, 51 per cent in 1884, 52 per cent in 1888, 51 per cent in 1892); in West Virginia every time (50 per cent in 1880, and in 1884, 49 per cent in 1888 and in 1892). Svend Petersen, *A Statistical History of the American Presidential Elections* (New York: Ungar, 1963), pp. 43–61. See E. A. Johnson, *Negro Almanac and Statistics* (Raleigh: Capital, 1903), p. 73. Eligible Negro males of voting age about 1880 were estimated as follows: Delaware: 6,396; Maryland: 48,584; West Virginia: 6,384; Kentucky: 58,642; Tennessee: 80,250; Missouri: 33,042. Speech of Senator Henry Cabot Lodge on Jan. 24, 1894. U.S., *Congressional Record*, 53d Cong., 2d sess. (1894).

[45] *Tribune Almanac for 1895*, p. 280; *for 1896*, pp. 238, 240; *for 1898*, p. 296; *for 1901*, p. 320; *for 1909*, p. 338; *for 1911*, p. 701.

Congressional voting, as reported in the *Tribune Almanacs* and census reports, is also suggestive. The total Republican congressional vote in the six border states increased from 220,928 in 1868 to 262,202 in the off-year congressional elections of 1870. The increase of 41,374 votes was due to Negroes voting for the first time. But the Negro turnout was quite small, given a potential Negro electorate of 87,000 to 233,000. Force and fraud encouraged many Negroes to stay away from the polls. The Republican increase, moreover, was offset by a much larger Democratic gain, because with the end of proscription whites in Tennessee, West Virginia, and Missouri were now able to vote for the first time since the war. The Democratic increase, 79,118, doubled the Republican. As a result, Republicans in 1870 lost seven congressional seats in Missouri, six in Tennessee, and one in West Virginia. Except for Missouri, the Republican defeat would have been worse had it not been for the Negro electorate. For example, in East Tennessee in the First and Second Congressional Districts the Republican pluralities were 605 and 532 respectively, while a mere 10 per cent of the Negro population in each district was double the margins of victory (1,374 and 1,597). Similarly, in the Second District of West Virginia, the Republican margin (913) was less than the estimated Negro electorate (947).

With more Negroes voting by 1872, the results were impressive. Republican pluralities were smaller than the Negro electorate (figured conservatively at 10 per cent of the Negro population within the district) as follows: in Delaware at large, 362 and 2,279; in Maryland in the Fifth District, 1,105 and 4,756, and in the Sixth District, 1,713 and 1,901; in Missouri in the First District, 142 and 477; in Tennessee in the Third District, 1,081 and 1,786, in the Fifth District, 1,902 and 4,790, in the Eighth District, 1,613 and 4,370, in the Ninth District, 3,243 and 6,737, and at large, 15,637 and 32,000. The situation repeated itself in 1874 in the Ninth District of Kentucky and in 1876 in the First District of Tennessee. Indeed, in congressional districts in which Republican congressmen displaced Democrats between 1870 and 1874, in ten out of eleven cases the Negro voter made the difference. Subsequently there were twenty-nine instances of Republicans defeating Democrats between 1876 and 1892.

To sum up, the growth of Negro politics in the borderland was organic, not mechanistic. It was not to be a hothouse affair. It took time and patience, cultivation and education, organization and mobilization for Negro voter power and patronage to develop. It thus appears illusory to note that the congressional score was not improved immediately for Republicans eight months after ratification of the

Fifteenth Amendment, when in fact many Negroes who were entitled to vote were prevented from doing so in 1870, while whites formerly forbidden at the polls voted in that election. It is also curious to dismiss the results in 1872 as merely an unusual presidential election, when in fact it was the Negro voter who provided the margin of victory in almost every instance, despite another increase in the Democratic congressional vote over that of 1870, because the Republican gain was much greater. Clearly the statement that "Any hope that may have been entertained of gaining substantial strength [for Republicanism] in the loyal border states was lacking in realism," appears a trifle hasty in the long run or in the short run in 1872. To write off black political power in the borderland was something border politicians could not and did not glibly do, then or today.[46] But the fruits of Negro suffrage ought not to be confused with the record of federal enforcement.

An editorial in the New York *Times* scarcely exaggerated when it declared that just as the border states "were the main campaigning grounds in war, so in peace, the political cauldron has in them seethed with greatest fury."[47] Under the federal enforcement program in the border states, indictments were many but convictions were few. Despite indications of some political violence and electoral fraud against Negroes in West Virginia and Missouri, there was not a single conviction in the decade between 1870 and 1880. The record was much worse in Tennessee, where there were a great number of such cases, in fact more than in the rest of the border states combined. Yet with three federal judicial districts, the conviction record average was 3 per cent. Kentucky could boast a better caliber of officials, but it was cursed with endemic violence and with crowded court dockets handling the second highest number of cases in the borderland: its record was 13 per cent. Although federal attorneys in Delaware appeared to do somewhat better, with 17 per cent, the state law of 1873 proved more significant. Maryland achieved the best comparative record of 22 per cent, with almost the highest number of actual convictions, but bribery continued to prevail. When one considers that today a state prosecuting attorney regards an average of 70 per cent as a competent conviction rate, and when one further finds that there were only 66 convictions and 1,076 cases lost during a decade of

---

[46] Compare LaWanda and John H. Cox, "Negro Suffrage and Republican Politics: the Problem of Motivation in Reconstruction Historiography," *Journal of Southern History* 33 (August, 1967): 303–30, especially 327. On subsequent Southern developments, see C. Vann Woodward, *The Strange Career of Jim Crow*, 2nd rev. ed. (Oxford University Press, 1966), pp. 83–86.

[47] *New York Times*, Jan. 11, 1870.

Cases Terminated under Enforcement Acts in Border States: 1870–80 [a]

States with [1] Number of cases with convictions, [2] % of convictions, [3] Number acquitted or dismissed

Year ending:	Tennessee			Kentucky			Maryland			Delaware			West Virginia			Missouri		
	[1]	[2]	[3]	[1]	[2]	[3]	[1]	[2]	[3]	[1]	[2]	[3]	[1]	[2]	[3]	[1]	[2]	[3]
(calendar)																		
Dec. 31, 1870	11	73%	4	15	63%	9	0		0	0		0						
Dec. 31, 1871	9	10%	80	0		6	1	17%	5	0		0	0		24			
Dec. 31, 1872	0		455	2	17%	10	0		5	1	11%	8						
(fiscal)																		
June 30, 1873	0		256	0		0	1	9%	10	1	9%	10						
June 30, 1874	2	17%	9	0		44	0		1	0		0						
June 30, 1875	0		10	0		0	0		29	0		0						
June 30, 1876	0		11	0		0	2	50%	2	0		3						
June 30, 1877	0		0	0		42	17	63%	10	4	100%	0				0		2
June 30, 1878	0		0	0		0	0		2	0		0						
June 30, 1879	0		2	0		0	0		10	0		9						
June 30, 1880	0		0	0		0	0		12	0		0						
	22	3%	836	17	13%	111	21	22%	76	6	17%	30	0		24	0		2

Average per cent of border convictions: 6%

Total number of cases terminated and rank by border state:	858 first	128 second	97 third	36 fourth	24 fifth	2 sixth
Rank by state of highest number of convictions:	first	third	second	fourth	none	none
Rank by state by per cent of convictions:	fourth	third	first	second	none	none

[a] U.S., Congress, House of Representatives, Annual Report of the Attorney General, House Exec. Docs., 41 Cong., 3 sess., No. 90; U.S., Congress, Senate, Senate Exec. Docs., 42 Cong., 3 sess., No. 32; House Exec. Docs., 43 Cong., 1 sess., No. 6; ibid., 43 Cong., 2 sess., No. 7; ibid., 44 Cong., 1 sess., No. 14; ibid., 44 Cong., 2 sess., No. 20; ibid., 45 Cong., 2 sess., No. 7; ibid., 45 Cong., 3 sess., No. 7; ibid., 46 Cong., 2 sess., No. 8; ibid., 46 Cong., 3 sess., No. 9.

federal prosecution in the border states, such tabulations suggest comprehensive failure. Doubtless the resistant locale must be reckoned with, but the border sectional pattern was even worse than that in the South. It also must be taken into account that office-holding and civil rights cases were not election cases, while duplication between civil and criminal actions along with some erroneous cases inflate the total number of cases. Still, the original impression remains. Of course, the effect upon deterrence must be reckoned as well, but since convictions were few and escapes from the law were many, its value must not be overstressed. To be sure, where federal troops were garrisoned and where urban election supervisors kept a sharp eye, there was less chance for cheating. But noting as well the shortage of troops and officials while force and fraud prevailed in many areas of the border states between 1870 and 1890, the picture was not bright. Indeed, the over-all ineffectiveness of enforcement was so great as to raise the fundamental question of the priority of federal effort. The North often mattered more than either the South or the borderland.[48] But if border enforcement was empty of positive result, it was full of political consequence.

[48] The computation of criminal cases alone, by year and by region from 1870–95, is conveniently provided by Horn "Congressional Control of Elections," pp. 186–87, 363–64. But Horn includes in his border classification only four border states: Delaware, Maryland, Kentucky, and Missouri, thus excluding significant Tennessee and insignificant West Virginia.

Everette Swinney maintains that the over-all federal record was not so bad until after 1874, and notes that the government won 74 per cent of its enforcement cases in the best year, 1870. But this statistic is less than impressive when one notes that half of the convictions secured during 1870 were obtained in the North. Suggestive of the relative effectiveness in the North was the abrupt drop in voting in the first eight wards of New York City following the imposition of federal election enforcement. Between the state election for chief justice in May, 1870, and the congressional election in November, 1870, the vote in the eight wards dropped by almost half, noted Senator Henry Cabot Lodge in his speech cited above, because of federal enforcement which eliminated fraudulent voting.

It has been customary to focus on the Deep South in respect to the enforcement acts. But, as a matter of fact, Robert Horn in his dissertation makes a compelling case that one primary preoccupation of federal enforcement legislation was outside the Deep South in the big northern cities and, to a much lesser extent, the border states. Certainly this was the case in the principal supervision Act of February 28, 1871. Horn buttresses his persuasive thesis by specific findings. In the first place, real power under the enforcement acts was only granted to election supervisors in cities with 20,000 population and not to supervisors in rural areas. That was the great difference between the Act of February 28, 1871, and the Act of June 10, 1872. Since practically all of the cities of 20,000 were in the North, except for five cities in the South and eight in the borderland, the practical intent and effect were clear. In the second place, the great bulk of enforcement expenditures were not in the South but in the North. Horn notes that half of the disbursements for

With such a record—with enforcement often amounting to pious platitudes and administrative pennypinching; being governed by episodic expedients and often administered by mediocrities; lacking central control and local co-ordination; being plagued by delay, timidity, and even premature pardoning; being beset by an unwieldy and inefficient court system; with the scope of the enforcement problem being greater than the scope of the federal remedy; with unenforceable law being abandoned because border mores prevailed; and with state statutes legalizing noncompliance and federal courts often rationalizing practice—one may only conclude that the law of enforcement was no law at all. Where power ends, responsibility ends.

Blame for such a performance, we have been told, was to be found at the battered door of the Grant government, which did not govern, or on the heads of unfriendly judges, who did. But such a judgment, which virtually ignores the congressmen who initiated the policy and drafted the law, cannot be said to be entirely fair. Certainly too little was achieved because too little money was appropriated. But equally important are the grounds of policy and law. One wonders whether the legislators, in framing the law, appreciated the immensity of the racial problem or properly assessed the strength of disaffection. One wonders, too, whether congressmen carefully tailored ends to means or matched their purpose to federal power. It is also questionable whether members of Congress drafted legislation to assure Negro voting without circumscribing state autonomy, given the prevailing values of the nineteenth century. And finally, it is debatable whether the law itself was sound, whether its broad and vague statutory language left too much up to the courts or simply left crucial matters up in the air. Without subscribing to Dunningesque notions of subtle racism or state rightism, without agreeing with William Davis that the enforcement acts stood for oppression and iniquity, one may suggest that provisions of the enforcement acts did not satisfy fully the requirements for proper law: good law must be clear and definite;

---

deputy marshals were in New York City alone. Other large expenditures also originated in the politically important states of Illinois, California, Maryland, New Jersey, Pennsylvania, and Massachusetts. In the third place, Horn finds that there were a higher number of convictions in the North than in the South after 1874, and also discovers a much higher ratio of convictions to acquittals in the North. Horn, pp. 142–55, 183–200, 231–34, 363–64. The thrust of the Horn argument is to redress the balance of interest from exclusive concern with the South, which both William Davis and Everette Swinney stress. In contrast to his article published in 1962, Swinney in his doctoral dissertation, completed in 1966, takes some note of Northern developments. Compare William W. Davis, "The Federal Enforcement Acts," in *Studies in Southern History and Politics* (New York: Columbia University, 1914), pp. 205–28; Swinney, "Enforcing the Fifteenth Amendment," *Journal of Southern History*, pp. 205–18; Swinney dissertation, pp. 103–18.

sound law must be reasonably enforceable; law is sounder still if it is not only just in objective but also impartial in execution. Clearly, the enforcement acts suffered from both statutory indigestion and administrative malnutrition.

What seemed forgotten sometimes in the enactment of the enforcement acts was the immediate past. After all, the Fifteenth Amendment had been but a modest step forward, even if bold method and great effort had gone into achieving it. Surprise, speed, and luck had helped, but caution, care, and indirection had countered for more in the face of white prejudice. Prudence, then, had dictated strategy; sound expediency had governed tactics. Nevertheless, the amendment had barely survived the ordeal of congressional fire. Its ratification had provoked immense opposition and required extraordinary means to clear the hurdles of many statehouses. But the risk had to be run to get the northern Negro voter, while time was running out in controlling Congress by a two-thirds margin. Although the legislative history was rather inconclusive in conveying the meaning of the enforcement section of the Fifteenth Amendment, it was clear by what was voted down by Congress that the framers had intended to deal not with the whole problem of election regulation but only with the worst of it, and there was greater concern about the North than the South. The amendment was not intended to do away with electoral injustice and inequality all at once. Few had invited a future Congress under the reach of the amendment to set or upset voter qualifications or to massively assault the foundation of electoral federalism. Instead, the limited nature of the reform to ban racial tests in voting but not all tests—such as the poll tax and literacy requirement—underscored caution and emphasized the North; moreover, the close call of congressional passage and the hard fight of ratification sounded a clear warning. When subsequently Congress enacted five enforcement acts which seemed to ignore recent experience, there was bound to be trouble.[49]

Why, then, did Congress pass the enforcement acts as framed in the first place, and move beyond the shadow of the Fifteenth Amendment? Why, in short, was the enforcement effort often planned so badly, executed so inadequately, and supported so feebly? Perhaps, as good American lawmakers, congressmen fell victims to their hopes

[49] See, for legislative history of the Fifteenth Amendment, Gillette, *The Right to Vote*, pp. 46–78; for the postwar years prior to passage of the amendment, *ibid.*, pp. 21–45; for summary and significance of the amendment, *ibid.*, pp. 159–65. See also articles by LaWanda and John H. Cox, "Negro Suffrage and Republican Politics," and C. Vann Woodward, "Seeds of Failure in Radical Race Policy," in Harold M. Hyman, ed., *New Frontiers of the American Reconstruction* (Urbana: University of Illinois Press, 1966), pp. 125–47.

by quickly passing a law and expecting too much of it, while imagining that the law would somehow enforce itself. The very magnitude of the problem also demanded immediate attention and decisive action. Yet ends were invited without marshaling sufficient means. Too much was clearly intended; thus too much was left at loose ends. In addition, such legislation was not sufficiently tested. Republicans no longer had a two-thirds majority in March, 1869;[50] but more importantly, they no longer needed it once the Fifteenth Amendment had been sent to the states. Without the need to amend the Constitution and without the further need of overriding a presidential veto, Republicans in Congress required only a simple majority to pass bills as the enforcement acts. The care and consensus in effecting a broad compromise was no longer necessary. Perhaps most significantly, the enforcement legislation was spurred by sheer desperation. After all, Republican radicalism had been waning after the impeachment fiasco in 1868; reaction set in amidst widening corruption, conservative resurgence, and growing public apathy. Congressmen plainly saw that something had to be done; their last chance to do themselves and their party some good was to reverse the course of events. Certainly only a bloody-shirt appeal—the Klan issue—would keep the Republican party together, retain Reconstruction intact, and hold key voters. Ohio Governor Rutherford Hayes thus wrote to Senator John Sherman: "I thank you for your speech on the Ku Klux outrages. It will do us great good. You hear but the wail on the hearer. Nothing can harmonize the Republican Party like the conviction that Democratic victories strengthen the reactionary and brutal tendencies of the late rebel states. It is altogether the most effective thing that has lately been done." Of course, certain members of Congress wanted, in an election year, to make a Radical record in a hurry so as to dispel in advance any charge of going Conservative or of giving slack to the rebels. Thus many in Congress would follow the lead of men like John Sherman, for they dreaded every vote that seemed to be opposing any measure punishing the Klan. Such political posturing, under the covering fire of refighting the war and advancing impartial suffrage, might possibly explain why the most radical reconstruction legislation of a national character came about precisely when Radicalism was weakest.[51] Certainly not all features of the acts were sound,

[50] *New York Times*, March 2, 1869; Gillette, *The Right to Vote*, p. 45. See also the forthcoming study of the Radicals by Professor Hans Trefousse of Brooklyn College and "Negro Suffrage and Republican Politics," by La Wanda and John H. Cox, p. 318.

[51] Professor David Donald of Johns Hopkins University raised the interesting question of the curious irony of late Reconstruction legislation during a history department seminar at Princeton University, April 12, 1961.

but there seemed political mileage in every statute. Beneath the rhetoric and the posturing, however, there were politicians who were
jockeying for immediate partisan advantage from the practical effect
of various provisions to be inserted into the enforcement acts. How
else can one explain the extraordinary, indeed spectacular, circumstances of the birth and death of these acts, which Congress dealt
with over a quarter of a century? They were adopted in all-night
sessions, which were kept going by policemen rounding up congressmen for quorums; often they were adopted in the last days of lame-
duck sessions by a strict party vote on final roll call; and the fifth
enforcement act became law as a rider to an appropriation act.
Republicans wanted to pass an enforcement bill—any bill—and they
grabbed what they could get, providing that the North was taken
care of first. Democrats, in contrast, mustered all their forces and
tricks to prevent passage of the so-called force bills, through filibus-
ters and crippling amendments, and if such bills were enacted, they
tried to sabotage them by miserly appropriations, obstructive investigations, and inactive administration. Democrats with some Republican support also fought off attempts by other Republicans to enlarge
the scope of enforcement in 1875, 1876, and 1890, and with complete
control, Democrats finally achieved wholesale repeal of enforcement
law in 1894. Clearly, enforcement stirred politicians because it cut a
nerve. Power, not philanthropy, was the object; necessity was the
tack. But conflicts of interest between national Republicans, and
between national and state Republicans, caused deep trouble for
enforcement.[52]

Ironically, the very efforts to save, or at least salvage, Reconstruction had the opposite and unintended effect of accelerating the retreat
from Reconstruction. By ignoring the fact that the protection of the
Negro had become unpopular in the North, by further taxing public
tolerance by talking about racial integration in white schools,
theaters, or hotels through a federal civil rights bill, and by exploring
the outer boundaries of the nineteenth-century Constitution, Republican nationalism, radical equalitarianism, and congressional central-
ism had gone a bit too far. The backlash of reaction and racism
brought about the disastrous election returns of 1874 which enabled

[52] Rutherford B. Hayes to John Sherman, April 1, 1871, John Sherman MSS, LC;
Congressman James A. Garfield to L. W. Hall, April 22, 1871, to J. H. Rhodes,
April 21, 1871, James A. Garfield MSS, LC; Senator Blanche K. Bruce to Roscoe
Conkling, Sept. 21, 1879, Roscoe Conkling Papers, LC. See also Horn "Control of
Congressional Elections." Conservative congressional coalitions nibbled away at en-
forcement statutes before 1894. Congress prohibited the use of the army as posse
in 1878 and as police in any election, in 1880. See Edward McPherson's *Handbook
of Politics: 1876*, p. 185; *Handbook of Politics: 1878*, pp. 180–81.

Democrats to seize control of the House of Representatives for the first time since 1859. The Republican Baltimore *American* observed that the Republican party throughout the border region and the nation had committed "unmistakable and persistent suicide," because the election was a "harvest of bad management [now] fully reaped." The courts, too, were to follow the election returns in their own way. As a result, enforcement was now to go downhill all the way, outside the North; Reconstruction had about run its course.[53]

It might, however, be argued that the enforcement legislation was not, in fact, radical in nature—that the so-called drastic legislation was not drastic at all, that it was too tame, too conservative, too naïve without massive administrative apparatus to make informed decisions and insure decisive action, without military methods of control to suppress violence at the grassroots, without federal voting registrars to stop registration fraud at the source. Moreover, the constitutional propriety of the legislation would probably not be questioned today, and, in fact several sections of the laws have been upheld or re-enacted in some fashion. By this line of reasoning, then, the moderation even of the Radicals was not radical enough in a time of revolution. But it takes an illusion for disillusion—that is, expecting the impossible to be possible; believing that the present was the past, and ignoring the real, but difficult choices open at the time. The limits of Reconstruction enforcement in the border states all too clearly reflected the borderlines of government and the inhibitions of the people. Enforcement generated in turn the highest hopes, the deepest hates, and the bitterest disappointments.

[53] *Baltimore American*, Nov. 4, 1874. Various historians have explored the implications of race prejudice upon national politics: John Hope Franklin has done so in his *Reconstruction: After the Civil War* (Chicago: University of Chicago Press, 1961), *From Slavery to Freedom: A History of Negro Americans* (New York: Alfred A. Knopf, 1967), and his paper on the Civil Rights Act of 1875 presented to the American Historical Association meeting on Dec. 29, 1964; the numerous works of C. Vann Woodward, in this connection particularly, *The Burden of Southern History* (New York: Vintage Books, 1961), pp. 69–107.

For the earlier period of Reconstruction, there are the studies by LaWanda Cox and John Cox, *Politics, Principles, and Prejudice, 1865–1866* (Glencoe: Free Press, 1963), Eric L. McKitrick, *Andrew Johnson and Reconstruction* (Chicago: University of Chicago Press, 1960), David Donald, *The Politics of Reconstruction* (Baton Rouge: Louisiana State University Press, 1965), W. R. Brock, *An American Crisis* (New York: St. Martin's Press, 1963), and Richard Current, *Old Thad Stevens* (Madison: University of Wisconsin Press, 1942). Dissection of the points where law and politics intersect is accomplished in, Alexander M. Bickel, "The Original Understanding and the Segregation Decision," *Harvard Law Review* (Nov., 1955), pp. 1–65; Alan Westin, "John Marshall Harlan"; Peter Magrath, *Morrison R. Waite*. The author is preparing a work on the retreat from Reconstruction.

Bibliographical Essay

MISSOURI

The standard work dealing with the rise of the Radicals in Missouri is William E. Parrish, *Turbulent Partnership: Missouri and the Union, 1861–1865* (Columbia, Mo., 1963). A comprehensive study of political, economic, and social developments in Missouri during the Reconstruction period is William E. Parrish, *Missouri Under Radical Rule, 1865–1870* (Columbia, Mo., 1965). Thomas S. Barclay, *The Liberal Republican Movement in Missouri* (Columbia, Mo., 1926), and Ida M. Nowells, "A Study of the Radical Party in Missouri, 1860–1870" (M.A. thesis, University of Missouri, 1939), are also useful.

Relatively few significant studies on specific topics within the larger framework exist. The test oath controversy as it affected the clergy is covered in Thomas S. Barclay, "The Test Oath for Clergy in Missouri," *Missouri Historical Review* 18 (April, 1924). A thorough résumé of the Cummings case is found in Harold C. Bradley, "In Defense of John Cummings," *ibid.* 57 (October, 1962). Unfortunately no similar treatment has been given to the plight of Missouri's lawyers. Maynard G. Redfield's "Some Social and Intellectual Influences in the Development of Public Education in Missouri, 1865 to 1900" (Ph.D. dissertation, Washington University, 1956), contains a masterful survey of Republican contributions to the public school movement. Kurt F. Leidecker's *Yankee Teacher: The Life of William Torrey Harris* (New York, 1946) provides excellent insights into the St. Louis public school system. Robert I. Brigham, "The Education of the Negro in Missouri" (Ph.D. dissertation, University of Missouri, 1946), and Henry S. Williams, "The Development of the Negro Public School System in Missouri," *Journal of Negro History* 5 (April, 1920), are useful, but not comprehensive, studies of Negro education.

The history of Missouri's railroads is covered in John W. Million, *State Aid to Railways in Missouri* (Chicago, 1896), an old but still valuable work; Edwin L. Lopata, *Local Aid to Railroads in Missouri* (New York, 1937); Wyatt W. Belcher, *The Economic Rivalry between St. Louis and Chicago, 1850–1880* (New York, 1947); A. Theodore Brown, *Frontier Community: Kansas City to 1870* (Columbia, Mo., 1964); and Charles N. Glaab's *Kansas City and the Railroads: Community Policy in the Growth of a Regional Metropolis* (Madison, Wis., 1962).

The promotion of immigration is well covered in Norman L. Crockett, "A Study of Confusion: Missouri's Immigration Program, 1865–1916," *Missouri Historical Review* 57 (April, 1963). The growth of veteran's organizations and their political overtones is well treated in James N. Primm, "The G.A.R. in Missouri, 1866–1870," *Journal of Southern History* 20 (August 1954).

Biographies of leading politicians are scarce. David D. March, "The Life and Times of Charles Daniel Drake" (Ph.D. dissertation, University of Missouri, 1949) contains a penetrating analysis of Missouri's leading Radical. Key portions of this study are summarized in March's "Charles D. Drake and the Constitutional Convention of 1865," *Missouri Historical Review* 47 (January, 1953), and "The Campaign for the Ratification of the Constitution of 1865," *ibid.* 47 (April, 1953). One of the leading opponents of ratification is discussed in W. E. Parrish's "Moses Lewis Linton, 'Doctor of Epigrams'," *ibid.* 59 (April, 1965). The standard biography of Carl Schurz is Claude M. Fuess's *Carl Schurz, Reformer, 1829–1906* (New York, 1923). Norma L. Peterson's *Freedom and Franchise: the Political Career of B. Gratz Brown* (Columbia, Mo., 1965) is a good, recent treatment of a key figure. The Conservatives' leading figure, Frank Blair, is treated adequately in William E. Smith's *The Francis Preston Blair Family in Politics* (2 vols.; New York, 1933).

The journal of the Missouri State Convention of 1865 was printed by authorization of the convention itself. For the daily proceedings, however, one must rely on the *Missouri Democrat* and the *Missouri Republican*. The political bent of each of these newspapers is directly opposite to what their names imply. Isidore Loeb's "Constitutions and Constitutional Conventions in Missouri," *Missouri Historical Review* 16 (January, 1922) provides a good analysis of the final document.

The most important of the outstate newspapers were the Columbia *Missouri Statesman,* with its strong conservative bent; the Jefferson City *Missouri State Times,* the unofficial organ of the Fletcher administration; and the Springfield *Missouri Weekly Patriot,* which reflected the ardent Radicalism of the southwest.

The file of the St. Louis *Industrial Advocate* in the State Historical Society of Missouri (August, 1866–February, 1867) provides revealing insights into the Missouri labor movement during this brief period. The St. Louis *Journal of Education* does the same for the public school movement.

The manuscript collections of Missouri Radicals are virtually nonexistent. The William M. Grosvenor Papers which Barclay used in his work have disappeared. Most valuable, however, is the manuscript "Autobiography" by Charles D. Drake in the State Historical Society of Missouri at Columbia. Written in 1886, near the close of his life, it is based on extensive notes and correspondence. Unfortunately, the narrative ends with Drake's election to the United States Senate in 1867. The Carl Schurz Papers in the Library of Congress are important for understanding the later Radical period and the Liberal Republican bolt. Joseph Schafer's collection, *The Intimate Letters of Carl Schurz* (Madison, Wis., 1928) contains revealing correspondence on Schurz's political career, especially his successful campaign for election to the United States Senate in 1868–69. The William K. Patrick Papers in the Missouri Historical Society at St. Louis cover the 1867–68 period and provide valuable insights into the personalities of leading Radical politicians, patronage matters, the manipulation of veterans' organizations, and the 1868 campaign. Patrick was an ardent Drake Radical and a member of the St. Louis city committee.

The Andrew Johnson Papers in the Library of Congress portray the early hopes of Missouri's Radical leaders that the President would champion their cause. The Johnson Papers also contain pertinent correspondence from Missouri Conservatives relating to patronage and the election of 1866. The Gist Blair Papers in the Library of Congress are equally important for insights into Conservative (later Democratic) strategy and the role played by Frank Blair during this period. The two most important surviving collections of the papers of Missouri Conservatives are the James O. Broadhead Papers in the Missouri Historical Society and the James S. Rollins Papers in the State Historical Society of Missouri. Unfortunately, the Rollins Papers are closed to researchers at the present time.

TENNESSEE

Several secondary treatments cover the process of political Reconstruction in Tennessee in considerable detail. In addition to Thomas B. Alexander, *Political Reconstruction in Tennessee* (Nashville, Tenn., 1950), of which this essay essentially is an abridgement as far as facts and evidence are concerned, the following are of major value: James W. Patton, *Unionism and Reconstruction in Tennessee, 1860–1869* (Chapel Hill, N.C., 1934); Alrutheus Ambush Taylor, *The Negro in Tennessee, 1865–1880* (Washington, D.C., 1941); E. Merton Coulter, *William G. Brownlow: Fighting Parson of the Southern Highlands* (Chapel Hill, N.C., 1937); Clifton R. Hall, *Andrew Johnson, Military Governor of Tennessee* (Princeton, N.J., 1916); and Stanley J. Folmsbee, "The Radicals and the Railroads," in Phillip M. Hamer (ed.), *Tennessee: A History, 1673–1932* (4 vols.; New York, 1933), 2, 659–73.

Several newspapers are major primary sources. The Knoxville *Whig* is invaluable, and the Library of Congress holds the editor's personal file upon which William G. Brownlow's son, John Bell Brownlow, wrote many marginal notations and occasionally inserted extensive comments. Other Knoxville papers were the *Commercial, Free Press, Herald, Press and Herald,* and *Press and Messenger.* Several Nashville papers are valuable, including the *Union,* the *Union and American,* and the *Union and Dispatch.* Memphis papers of value are the *Avalanche,* the *Commercial,* and the *Post.*

The Tennessee legislative *Journals* and the *Acts* of Tennessee for the period are basic sources.

Manuscript collections of outstanding value are: William G. Brownlow Papers and DeWitt C. Senter Papers (both in the Tennessee State Library and Archives, Nashville); David Campbell Papers, incorporating the William

B. Campbell correspondence (Duke University Library, Durham); Joseph Smith Fowler Papers and Andrew Johnson Papers (both in the Library of Congress); Leonidas Campbell Houk Papers, Thomas A. R. Nelson Papers, and the Maryville Union League Minutes Book (all in the McClung Collection, Lawson McGhee Library, Knoxville); Oliver P. Temple Papers (University of Tennessee Library, Knoxville); and the Records of the Bureau of Refugees, Freedmen and Abandoned Lands (National Archives, Washington, D.C.).

WEST VIRGINIA

The complexities of statehood politics in West Virginia must be understood before developments during Reconstruction can be comprehended. See especially: Richard O. Curry, *A House Divided: A Study of Statehood Politics and the Copperhead Movement in West Virginia* (Pittsburgh, Pa., 1964); Curry, "A Reappraisal of Statehood Politics in West Virginia," *The Journal of Southern History* 28 (November, 1962); Curry, "The Union As It Was: A Critique of Recent Interpretations of the 'Copperheads,'" *Civil War History* 13 (March, 1967); and F. Gerald Ham (ed.), "The Mind of a Copperhead: Letters of John J. Davis on the Secession Crisis and Statehood Politics in Western Virginia, 1860–1862," *West Virginia History* 24 (January, 1963). Charles H. Ambler, *Francis H. Pierpont, Union War Governor of Virginia and Father of West Virginia* (Chapel Hill, N.C., 1937); Edward Conrad Smith, *The Borderland in the Civil War* (New York, 1927); and George E. Moore, *A Banner in the Hills* (New York, 1963), are also useful. The relationship of guerrilla warfare to both Civil War and Reconstruction politics is explored in Richard O. Curry and F. Gerald Ham (eds.), "The Bushwackers' War: Insurgency and Counter-Insurgency in West Virginia," *Civil War History* 10 (December, 1964). A comprehensive bibliography on statehood politics is contained in Curry's *A House Divided*.

Relatively little significant work, published or unpublished, has been done on the Reconstruction era in the mountain state. Two older narratives by James M. Callahan, *Semi-Centennial History of West Virginia* (Charleston, W. Va., 1913), and *A History of West Virginia, Old and New* (3 vols.; New York, 1923) contain much useful information. The same holds true for Charles H. Ambler, "Disfranchisement in West Virginia," *Yale Review* 14 (May, 1905); Milton Gerofsky, "Reconstruction in West Virginia," *West Virginia History* 6 (July and October, 1945); Maud F. Callahan, *The Evolution of the Constitution of West Virginia* (Morgantown, W. Va., 1909); Charles M. Pepper, *The Life and Times of Henry Gassaway Davis* (New York, 1920); Harvey M. Rice, *The Life of Jonathan M. Bennett* (Chapel Hill, N.C., 1943); Wayne G. Smith, *Nathan Goff, Jr.: A Biography* (Charleston, W. Va., 1959); and Festus P. Summers, *Johnson Newlon Camden: A Study in Individualism* (New York, 1937).

The following M.A. theses, West Virginia University, if used with discrimination, also provide useful material: Robert W. Bayless, "The Attitude of

West Virginia Senators and Congressmen toward Reconstruction, 1863–1871"
(1949); Louis D. Corson, "The Legislative Career of Waitman T. Willey"
(1942); Mary G. Tourney, "Arthur I. Boreman and His Times" (1939);
Harvey M. Rice, "The Conservative Re-Action in West Virginia" (1933);
Everet F. Whitener, "Peter Godwin Van Winkle" (1946); and Lawrence
C. White, "West Virginia and her United States Senators in the Impeachment
Trial of Andrew Johnson," George Peabody College for Teachers (1928).

The county histories listed in Curry's *A House Divided* can occasionally
be used with profit. Biographical sketches of prominent West Virginians of
this period are found in George W. Atkinson and Alvaro F. Gibbens,
Prominent Men of West Virginia (Wheeling, W. Va., 1890). Other useful
special aids are W. Dean Burnham, *Presidential Ballots, 1836–1892*
(Baltimore, 1955), and the *Biographical Directory of the American Congress,
1774–1949* (Washington, D.C., 1950).

Studies of the Negro in West Virginia are badly needed. The subject can
be approached in Kate J. Anthony, *Storer College, Harper's Ferry, West
Virginia* (Boston, 1891); Charles H. Ambler, *History of Education in West
Virginia* (Huntington, W. Va., 1950); Thomas E. Posey, *The Negro Citizen
of West Virginia* (Institute, W. Va., 1934); Byrd Prillaman, *The Growth of
Colored Schools in West Virginia* (Charleston, W. Va., 1907); Reuben J.
Sheeler, "The Negro in West Virginia Before 1900" (Ph.D. dissertation,
West Virginia University, 1954); and Booker T. Washington, *Up From
Slavery* (New York, 1901). See also: Mary V. Brown, "A History of Negroes in
Monongalia County" (M.A. thesis, West Virginia University, 1930); Earl C.
Clay, "The Negro in Greenbrier County" (M.A. thesis, Virginia State College,
1946); and John R. Drain, "A History of West Virginia State College" (M.A.
thesis, West Virginia University, 1950).

The essay in this book is based almost entirely upon primary source
materials, most of which have not been utilized in depth by previous writers.
Among the most important newspapers are: *Wheeling Intelligencer, Point
Pleasant Weekly Register, Ritchie County Star, Ravenwood News, Morgan-
town Post, Martinsburg–Berkeley Union, Kanawha Journal, Fairmount West
Virginian, Parkersburg State Journal,* and *Parkersburg Times.* Significant
Democratic papers include: *Clarksburg Conservative, Wheeling Register,
Charleston Courier, Lewisburg Journal, Kanawha Republican, Greenbrier
Independent, Virginia Free Press,* and *Shepherdstown Register.* The files of
most of these newspapers are located at the West Virginia University Library,
Morgantown.

The following manuscript collections are of outstanding value: Francis
H. Pierpont Papers (Virginia State Library, Richmond); the Executive
Papers of John J. Jacob, Arthur I. Boreman, Francis H. Pierpont, and
William E. Stevenson (all in the West Virginia State Department of Archives
and History, Charleston); the W. H. H. Flick and Charles J. Faulkner
Papers (both in the Alderman Library, University of Virginia); Isaac H.
Strickler Papers (owned by Mrs. Arthur H. Dayton, Lewisburg, West

Virginia); Charles J. Faulkner Papers (owned by T. T. Perry, Charles Town, W. Va.) ; Nathan Goff, Sr., and Nathan Goff, Jr. Papers (both in the Goff Mansion, Clarksburg, W. Va.); the Papers of Waitman T. Willey, Francis H. Pierpont, Arthur I. Boreman, Granville D. Hall, the Hubbard Family, Judge Gideon D. Camden, John J. Jacob, Nathan Goff, Jr., Colonel David Goff, Maxwell-Bonnifield Families, Samuel Woods and Spencer Dayton (all in the West Virginia Collection, West Virginia University Library, Morgantown). Some useful items were found in the Papers of George R. Latham, A. B. Fleming, Johnson N. Camden, Archibald W. Campbell, Jonathan M. Bennett, Louis Bennett, Henry Gassaway Davis, and William E. Price (all in the West Virginia Collection, West Virginia University Library). A few items of interest were also found in the Garrett Papers (B & O Employees' Library, Baltimore) ; Garrett Papers (Library of Congress) ; and W. H. H. Flick Papers (Duke University Library).

In addition to manuscripts and newspapers, an extremely rich source of primary material was discovered in county court house records. Unfortunately, time and circumstances permitted the exploration of local materials in only three key counties, Greenbrier, Monroe, and Randolph. Especially useful were the Journal of the Board of Supervisors, 1866–1872; Order Books, Law, 1865–1872; Order Books, Chancery, 1865–1872 (all located in the Monroe County Court House, Union, W. Va.) ; Journal of the Board of Supervisors, 1865–1872; Order Books, Law, 1865–1872; Order Books, Chancery, 1865–1872 (all located in the Greenbrier County Court House, Lewisburg, W. Va.); and the Minutes of the Board of Registration, 1866–1871 (in the Randolph County Court House, Elkins, West Virginia).

Indispensable printed source materials include the *Journals* of the West Virginia Senate and House of Representatives (1863–1872); *Acts* of the West Virginia Legislature (1863–1872) ; and West Virginia *Public Documents.* The public documents include the annual reports of the State Treasurer, Auditor, Adjutant General, Quartermaster General, Superintendent of Free Schools, and the Commissioner of Immigration. Finally, the *West Virginia Reports,* vols. 1–7, contain dozens of opinions of the West Virginia Supreme Court of Appeals pertaining to Reconstruction issues.

KENTUCKY

Any bibliography of Kentucky history in the postwar years must include E. Merton Coulter's *Civil War and Readjustment in Kentucky* (Chapel Hill, N.C., 1926). This is a detailed study of the political, economic, and social aspects of the Civil War and Reconstruction period in the Bluegrass State to 1872. Professor Coulter displays strong pro-Confederate leanings, but the volume is invaluable as a reference work. W. E. Connelley and E. M. Coulter (under the editorship of Judge Charles Kerr) prepared a most useful *History of Kentucky* (5 vols.; Chicago, 1902). The first two volumes cover the history of the state, while the remaining volumes provide biographies of latter-nineteenth-century Kentuckians. Thomas D. Clark's *History of Kentucky* (Lexington, Ky., 1960) is the best single volume work, even though it is not footnoted. It contains, however, a well-annotated bibliography. Thomas Speed's *The Union Cause in Kentucky, 1860–1865* (New York, 1907) and N. S. Shaler's *Kentucky: A Pioneer Commonwealth* (Boston, 1884) are highly pro-Union in outlook, but provide valuable insights. Several county histories were consulted. The most valuable were those by W. H. Perrin, J. H. Battle, and G. C. Kniffen (W. H. Perrin, *A History of Bourbon, Scott, Harrison and Nicholas Counties, Kentucky* [Chicago, 1882]; and *History of Fayette County, Kentucky* [Chicago, 1882]. J. H. Battle and W. H. Perrin, *Counties of Todd and Christian, Kentucky* [Chicago and Louisville, 1884]. W. H. Perrin, J. H. Battle, and G. C. Kniffen, *History of Kentucky* [Louisville, Ky., 1886].) Any researcher in this period must make use of Lewis and Richard H. Collin's two volume *History of Kentucky*. Volume I contains "Annals of Kentucky, or Important Events in the History of Kentucky, 1539–1874." It was reprinted by the Kentucky Historical Society in 1966. *The American Annual Cyclopedia and Register of Important Events, 1860–1899* (New York, 1861–1900) is also an excellent source book of annual data. To understand the intellectual outlook of Kentuckians requires the reading of Arthur K. Moore's *The Frontier Mind* (Lexington, Ky., 1957). *The War of the Rebellion: A Compilation of the Official Records of the Union and Confederate Armies* (129 vols.; Washington, D.C., 1900), and Walter L. Fleming (ed.), *Documentary History of Reconstruction* (2 vols.; Cleveland, Ohio, 1906–07) provide some materials pertinent to Kentucky. Alvin F. Lewis's *History of Higher Education in Kentucky* (Washington, D.C., 1899) is one of the better sources on Kentucky education. The best study on the railroad controversy is E. M. Coulter's *The Cincinnati Southern Railroad and the Struggle for Southern Commerce, 1861–1872* (Chicago, 1922). No adequate history exists on the history of the Louisville and Nashville Railroad. Arthur Krick's *The Editorials of Henry Watterson* (New York, 1923) provides an insight into Watterson's political philosophy.

The best sources dealing with the complex political history of Kentucky are to be found in newspapers. The Frankfort *Commonwealth* (A. G. Hodges, editor) and the Louisville *Commercial* (R. M. Kelley, editor) present the Republican position while the Louisville *Journal* (George A. Prentice, editor), the Louisville *Courier* (Walter N. Haldeman, editor), the Louisville *Courier–Journal*, 1868–76 (Prentice, Haldeman, and Watterson, editors), and the Frankfort *Daily Kentucky Yeoman* (S. I. M. Major and J. Stoddard Johnston, editors) provide the Democratic philosophy. Two Cincinnati papers are also valuable for their reviews of Kentucky affairs: the Cincinnati *Commercial* (Murat Halstead, editor), and the Cincinnati *Gazette* (E. B. Mansfield and Richard Smith, editors). The *Congressional Globe* (1861–73) contains congressional debates on Kentucky during this period. Numerous congressional documents are valuable. See especially, "Freedmen's Affairs in Kentucky and Tennessee, 1867, 1868," House *Exec. Doc.* no. 329, 40th Cong.,

2d sess., and "Report of the Commission of the Freedmen's Saving and Trust Company," House *Misc. Doc.* No. 16, 43d Cong., 2d sess.

State publications of real importance include *Acts of Kentucky, 1860–1876,* and *Journal of the Senate of Kentucky, 1860–1876.* The General Records of the Department of Justice (Record Group 60) and the Treasury Department (Record Group 56) were consulted at the National Archives. The manuscript collections at the Filson club in Louisville, the library of the Kentucky Historical Society in Frankfort, and the Margaret I. King Library of the University of Kentucky, in Lexington, contain indispensable materials. Of particular interest were the John Marshall Harlan Papers at the Law Library of the University of Louisville.

MARYLAND

Necessary background information on Civil War politics in Maryland is contained in Charles L. Wagandt's *The Mighty Revolution: Negro Emancipation in Maryland, 1862–1864* (Baltimore, Md., 1964). Useful secondary works, published and unpublished, which treat various aspects of Reconstruction history, include Jeffrey R. Brackett, *Notes on the Progress of the Colored People of Maryland Since the War* (Baltimore, Md., 1890); Heinrich E. Buchholz, *Governors of Maryland* (Baltimore, Md., 1890); Margaret Law Calcott, *The Negro in Maryland Politics, 1870–1912* (Baltimore, 1969); Richard P. Fuke, "The Break-up of the Maryland Union Party, 1866" (M.A. thesis, University of Maryland, 1965); Grace H. Jacobs, "The Negro in Baltimore, 1860–1900" (M.A. thesis, Howard University, 1945); Frank R. Kent, *The Story of Maryland Politics* (Baltimore, Md., 1911); John R. Lambert, *Arthur Pue Gorman* (Baton Rouge, La., 1953); William S. Myers, *The Maryland Constitution of 1864* (Baltimore, Md., 1901); Myers, *The Self-Reconstruction of Maryland, 1864–1867* (Baltimore, Md., 1909); S. B. Nelson (publisher) *History of Baltimore, Maryland from Its Founding as a Town to the Current Year 1729–1898* (n.p., 1898); Galbraith B. Perry, *Twelve Years Among the Colored People* (New York, 1884); Morris L. Radoff (ed.), *The Old Line State: A History of Maryland* (Baltimore, Md., 1956); Elihu S. Riley, *A History of the General Assembly of Maryland: 1635–1904* (Baltimore, Md., 1905); William A. Russ, Jr., "Disfranchisement in Maryland (1861–1867)," *Maryland Historical Magazine* 28 (1933); John T. Scharf, *History of Maryland from the Earliest Period to the Present Day* (3 vols.; Baltimore, 1879); Helen W. Smith, "Montgomery Blair and the Negro" (M.A. thesis, University of Maryland, 1967); Bernard C. Steiner, *Citizenship and Suffrage in Maryland* (Baltimore, 1895); and William E. Smith, *The Francis Preston Blair Family in Politics* (2 vols.; New York, 1933).

The following published documents, speeches, and official records are indispensable: *Address of the Unconditional Union State Central Committee to the People of Maryland, September 16, 1863* (Baltimore, 1863); *Agriculture of the United States in 1860; Compiled from the Original Returns of the Eighth Census* (Washington, 1864); Roy P. Basler (ed.), *The Collected*

Works of Abraham Lincoln (9 vols.; New Brunswick, N.J., 1953); *Communication from Major Gen'l Lew Wallace, in Relation to the Freedmen's Bureau, to the General Assembly of Maryland* (Annapolis, 1865); *A Compendium of the Ninth Census* (June 1, 1870) (Washington, 1872); *Speeches and Addresses Delivered in the Congress of the United States, and on Several Public Occasions,* by Henry Winter Davis (New York, 1867); *Journals* of the Senate and House of Delegates of the State of Maryland (1865–1876); Maryland House and Senate *Documents* (1862–1870); P. B. Perlman (comp.), *Debates of the Maryland Constitutional Convention of 1867* (Baltimore, 1923); *Manufactures of the United States in 1860; Compiled from the Original Returns of the Eighth Census* (Washington, D.C., 1865); *Population of the United States in 1860; Compiled from the Original Returns of the Eighth Census* (Washington, D.C., 1864); *Proceedings of the State Convention, of Maryland, to Frame a New Constitution, Commenced at Annapolis, May 8, 1867* (Annapolis, 1867); M. L. Radoff (comp.), *Maryland Manual 1965–1966* (Annapolis, 1966); and *Report of the Constitutional Convention Commission* (Annapolis, 1967); *The Statistics of the Population of the United States Embracing the Tables of Race, Nationality, Sex, Selected Ages, and Occupations* (Ninth Census, vol. 1, Washington, 1872); U.S. Department of the Interior, *Official Register of the United States, Containing a List of Officers and Employees in the Civil, Military, and Naval Service. . . .* (Washington, 1859–1877); and *The Statistics of Wealth and Industry of the United States* (Ninth Census, vol. 3, Washington, D.C., 1872).

The most important Maryland newspapers of the period are: *Baltimore American, Baltimore Clipper, Baltimore Republican,* Baltimore *Sun, Cecil Whig* (Cecil County), *Civilian and Telegraph* (Allegany County), *Easton Gazette* (Talbot County), *Easton Star* (Talbot County), Frederick *Examiner, Montgomery County Sentinel,* and *Port Tobacco Times* (Charles County).

The following manuscripts were invaluable: Blair Family Papers, Salmon P. Chase Papers, John A. J. Creswell Papers, Garrett Family Papers, Ulysses S. Grant Papers, Andrew Johnson Papers, Reverdy Johnson Papers, Robert Todd Lincoln Collection of the Papers of Abraham Lincoln, Edward B. McPherson Papers, Benjamin F. Wade Papers, and the Gideon Welles Papers (all in the Library of Congress); the Blair-Lee Papers (Princeton University); the Hugh L. Bond Papers, Augustus W. Bradford Papers, Anna Ella Carroll Papers, George Gale Papers, Graves Papers, Diaries of Mrs. Benjamin G. Harris, Journal of Dr. Samuel A. Harrison, Norris Family Papers, Alexander Randall Papers, Charles T. Simpers Letters, and the John L. Thomas Papers (all in the Maryland Historical Society); Correspondence of the British Consul in Baltimore (Foreign Office Papers, Public Record Office, London, England); Samuel Francis Du Pont Papers (Eleutherian Mills Historical Library, Wilmington, Delaware); Governors' Letterbook and the Maryland Executive Papers (both in the Hall of Records, Annapolis); Maryland Investigation, Papers of the House of Representatives (Record Group 233, National Archives); Middle Department, U.S. Army Commands (Record

Group 98, National Archives) ; Charles Sumner Papers (Harvard College Library); and the Notebooks of Thomas Swann (privately owned by Mrs. Sherlock Swann, Baltimore).

DELAWARE

Delaware historians have neglected the Reconstruction period. No special account has ever been written. Only in the last five years have students at the University of Delaware studied certain aspects of the period. Harold B. Hancock's *Delaware in the Civil War: A Political History* (Wilmington, Del., 1961) provides background. The most detailed political account of Reconstruction is in J. Thomas Scharf's *History of Delaware* (Philadelphia, 1888), and it is taken primarily from the *American Annual Cyclopedia.* Judge Henry C. Conrad's *History of Delaware* (Wilmington, Del., 1908) updates Scharf's account. H. Clay Reed asked many historians for contributions to *Delaware: A History of the First State* (New York, 1947), and Harold Hancock wrote the chapter on politics after the Civil War. Charles Tansill's *Congressional Career of Thomas F. Bayard* (Washington, D.C., 1946) is revealing concerning that statesman's attitudes on national questions. Wayne S. Smith's "The Senatorial Career of Willard Saulsbury, 1859–1871" (M.A. thesis, University of Delaware, 1966) is also useful.

Wilmington newspapers may be examined at the Historical Society of Delaware and the Wilmington Free Institute Library. The *Republican* and the Democratic *Gazette* present opposing points of view. The *Daily Commercial* is an excellent and lively newspaper. The Democratic *Every Evening* begins in 1871. The *Smyrna Times* has been microfilmed by the Delaware State Archives, and the *Delawarean,* published at Dover, is in the Morris Library at the University of Delaware (with the exception of the Civil War years, which are at the Historical Society of Delaware in Wilmington).

Two interesting magazine articles on politics are Allen Thorndike Rice's "A Disfranchised People," in the *North American Review* (December, 1885), and "The Politics of Delaware," in the *American Magazine* (November, 1886).

The testimony of seven Delaware Republicans, before a committee of the House of Representatives, as to whether the state had a republican form of government is in the legislative branch of the National Archives. Department of Justice files in the same depository contain correspondence between national officials and the state's United States Attorney. Included in the Thomas F. Bayard papers at the Library of Congress are many letters from local politicians. Letters to Andrew Johnson in the same library reveal that Delaware Democrats strongly endorsed his policies.

On the Negro, John A. Munroe's essay in the *South Atlantic Quarterly* (1957) on "The Negro in Delaware" is a good starting point for research. A stimulating article by Richard B. Morris, "The Course of Peonage in a Slave State," appeared in the *Political Science Quarterly* (1950). Harold Livesay's paper on "Delaware Negroes, 1865–1915" is an outstanding undergraduate essay (University of Delaware, 1966), in *Delaware History* 13 (Oct., 1968): 87–123. Amy McNulty Hiller's "The Disfranchisement of Delaware Negroes in the Late Nineteenth Century" in *ibid.,* pp. 124–53 (M.A. thesis, University of Delaware, 1963), is an outstanding study. Harold B. Hancock published an article on "The Status of the Negro in Delaware after the Civil War, 1865–1875," *ibid.* Good accounts of Negro education appear in Lyman P. Powell, *The History of Education in Delaware* (Washington, D.C., 1893), and Henry C. Conrad, *A Glimpse of the Colored Schools of Delaware* (Wilmington, Del., 1883). Delaware was combined with Maryland and then with the District of Columbia in the operations of the Freedmen's Bureau, and the records on Delaware in the National Archives deal mainly with the establishment of Negro schools. Hancock is preparing an article on the work of the Bureau in the state. The illuminating minutes of the Delaware Association for the Moral Improvement of Colored People are in the Historical Society of Delaware, Wilmington.

A suggestive treatment of agricultural developments in nineteenth-century Delaware is found in Hancock's chapter in Reed (ed.), *Delaware*. New studies of nineteenth-century agriculture and industry are greatly needed. Hancock is currently preparing a study of income and manufacturing taxes, 1863–1873, based on material in the National Archives. The Eleutherian Mills Historical Library in Wilmington is collecting material on the economic history of the Delaware Valley and has already acquired industrial records of many Wilmington firms. Hancock is also preparing a study of the Brandywine workman during the nineteenth century, based primarily on manuscripts in this library.

THE FREEDMEN'S BUREAU IN THE BORDER STATES

The primary focus of previous scholarship on the Freedmen's Bureau has centered in the Deep South. Paul S. Peirce, *The Freedmen's Bureau* (Iowa City, Iowa 1904) and George R. Bentley, *A History of the Freedmen's Bureau* (Philadelphia, Pa., 1955), who have written the only full-length studies of Bureau activities, virtually ignore developments in the borderland. Only a few historians have studied the area at all. E. Merton Coulter's chapter, "The Negro, The Freedmen's Bureau, and Organized Violence," in *The Civil War and Readjustment in Kentucky* (Chapel Hill, N.C., 1926) concerns itself almost exclusively with opposition to the Bureau's activities. William E. Parrish's chapter, "The Negro in Post War Missouri," in his excellent study *Missouri Under Radical Rule, 1865–1870* (Columbia, Mo., 1965) does not deal specifically with the Bureau's work but acknowledges its influence. W. A. Low has written two articles on Maryland: "The Freedmen's Bureau and Education in Maryland," *Maryland Historical Magazine* 47 (March, 1952), and "The Freedmen's Bureau and Civil Rights in Maryland," *Journal of Negro History* 37 (July, 1952). There are several studies on Tennessee: Henry L. Swint (ed.), "Reports from Educational Agents of the Freedmen's Bureau in Tennessee, 1865–1870," *Tennessee Historical Quarterly* 1 (March,

1942) ; Weymouth T. Jordan, "The Freedmen's Bureau in Tennessee," *East Tennessee Historical Publications* (no. 11, 1939); and Paul D. Phillips, "White Reaction to the Freedmen's Bureau in Tennessee," *Tennessee Historical Quarterly* 24 (March, 1966). Delaware and West Virginia remain unstudied, although Harold B. Hancock is currently investigating the Bureau's activities in Delaware. The essay in this book is the first attempt to treat the Bureau's activities in the borderland as a whole.

The major primary sources used in this study were the Records of the Freedmen's Bureau, which are classified as Record Group 105 in the National Archives. Elizabeth Bethel, Sara Dunlap, and Lucille Pendell, members of the staff of the War Records Office of the National Archives, have compiled a useful checklist for this material—"Preliminary Checklist of the Records of the Bureau of Refugees, Freedmen and Abandoned Lands." There are more than five hundred general entries in this guide. An idea of the voluminous material contained in the entire Record Group is revealed by the fact that Kentucky alone requires nearly twenty-one feet of shelf space— far too much to be evaluated for the scope of this essay—but enough was utilized, nevertheless, to extend kind thanks to the assistants at the National Archives.

THE ORIGINS OF BORDER STATE LIBERAL REPUBLICANISM

In addition to numerous primary and secondary sources previously cited, the Breckenridge Family Papers, the Jeremiah Sullivan Black Papers, the Joseph Holt Papers and the John Stevenson Papers (all in the Library of Congress) were extremely helpful. Moreover, the James R. Doolittle Papers and the Carl Schurz Papers at the State Historical Society of Wisconsin, in Madison, proved valuable.

FEDERAL ENFORCEMENT OF THE RIGHT TO VOTE IN THE BORDER STATES

Indispensable primary sources for this essay were the Source–Chronological Files of the Justice Department at the National Archives, certain border newspapers at the Library of Congress and elsewhere, and the published annual reports of the Attorney General.

Although the Archives files were significant and useful, evaluations were lacking for several states. Official records, of course, have their limitations, for one needs to exercise care in accepting versions at face value.

The plunge into newspapers was both refreshing and helpful, especially in grasping the political dimension; and reports of the prevailing level of political murder and fraud were suggestive in assessing federal response and prosecution. But newspapers must be used with considerable care, for the Republican papers in the border states played up incidents while the Democratic papers dismissed them entirely or toned them down. Moreover, the quality of border newspapers was not up to the standards of the rest of the country. The *New York Times* was extremely useful for both news and opinion, as was to a lesser extent the Negro newspaper, the New York *Age*.

While the reports of the Attorney General were fundamental, the classifications often do not fit the needs of historians. As for the published census reports, in certain instances they helped to underscore political developments.

The limitations of state and local history in general and Negro history in particular in bearing upon federal election enforcement were painfully clear. Histories of Maryland, Kentucky, and Missouri Negroes are sorely needed, while the Negro's political relationship to state, local, regional, and national history merits further study as well for every border state. An example of what can be profitably done for all of the border states is Amy Hiller's "The Disfranchisement of Delaware Negroes in the Late Nineteenth Century" (M.A. thesis, University of Delaware, 1966).

Index

319

THE JOHNS HOPKINS PRESS

Designed by James C. Wageman

Composed in Baskerville text with Stymie Extra Bold display
by Baltimore Type and Composition Corporation

Printed on Perkins and Squier R
by Universal Lithographers, Inc.

Bound in Columbia Riverside Chambray RVC-3771
by L. H. Jenkins Company, Inc.